Dr Caroline Campbell is Director of the National Gallery of Ireland. She was previously Director of Collections and Research at the National Gallery in London, a curator at the Ashmolean Museum, Curator of Paintings at the Courtauld Gallery and the Jacob Rothschild Head of the Curatorial Department at the National Gallery. Caroline was educated at University College, Oxford and the Courtauld Institute of Art, and is a former fellow of the Center for Curatorial Leadership in New York. She cares deeply about widening public engagement with art and has spoken to audiences around the world on numerous subjects from art history.

THE
POWER
OF ART

A World History in Fifteen Cities

Caroline Campbell

The
Bridge
Street
Press

THE BRIDGE STREET PRESS

First published in Great Britain in 2023 by The Bridge Street Press
This paperback edition published in 2024 by The Bridge Street Press

1 3 5 7 9 10 8 6 4 2

Copyright © Caroline Campbell 2023

The moral right of the author has been asserted.

All rights reserved.
No part of this publication may be reproduced, stored in a
retrieval system, or transmitted, in any form or by any means, without
the prior permission in writing of the publisher, nor be otherwise circulated
in any form of binding or cover other than that in which it is published
and without a similar condition including this condition being
imposed on the subsequent purchaser.

A CIP catalogue record for this book is available from the British Library.

ISBN: 978-0-349-12849-8

Typeset in Classica by M Rules
Printed and bound in Great Britain by Clays Ltd, Elcograf S.p.A.

Papers used by The Bridge Street Press are from well-managed forests and
other responsible sources.

The Bridge Street Press
An imprint of
Little, Brown Book Group
Carmelite House
50 Victoria Embankment
London EC4Y 0DZ

An Hachette UK Company
www.hachette.co.uk

www.littlebrown.co.uk

For John, Isobel and Edward

CONTENTS

INTRODUCTION

In the spring of 1518 the Renaissance artist Michelangelo Buonarotti visited Pietrasanta in Tuscany, north of Lucca, in the midst of a stormy argument with Pope Leo X. Michelangelo had come to this remote coastal town to source marble for a major commission for the pope, the façade of the Florentine church of San Lorenzo. The two men, born less than a year apart, had known each other since boyhood. San Lorenzo was Leo's family's parish church, and the pope was extremely invested in the project. But Pietrasanta was not where Michelangelo wanted to be. He declared to his brother: 'Trying to tame these mountains and instilling skills here is akin to resurrecting the dead.' He thought the most suitable stone for his task was a short distance up the coast. The pope disagreed, and in spite of several violent quarrels, Michelangelo was forced to follow his patron's instructions. It was one of many such incidents in the artist's long career, and in retrospect we know that he might have spared himself the effort of rage. That's because the scheme never came to fruition; five hundred years on San Lorenzo is still missing its façade.

Michelangelo's anger, however, did encourage him to produce another work of art, not that he would necessarily have regarded it as such. On the back of a letter dated 15 March 1518 is a shopping list written in a neat and readable hand. It is accompanied by a remarkable series of sketches, gradually getting bigger in size, of the objects it lists. Presumably Michelangelo's servant was not able to read perfectly so the drawings made clear what he had to buy. What is preserved, therefore, is the artist's vision of a simple series of meals for himself and a number of guests. It was Lent, and so meat was off the menu, but Michelangelo's fish and vegetable dishes promised to be delicious. He wanted to eat tortelli (a stuffed pasta that remains a speciality of the area), anchovies (then just in season) and herring, presumably pickled or smoked, and imported from northern Europe, accompanied by a salad, spinach, fennel and bread rolls, washed down with jugs of wine. The artist was, unsurprisingly, concerned about how the food was to be served. The salad is in a wide, shallow bowl with a slim base, the anchovies' tails are arranged over the edge of the serving vessel, and the herring is elegantly plated on a large dish.

Even geniuses – and if you subscribe to the concept then Michelangelo undoubtedly was one – had to eat. For all his success, he still had to occupy himself with banal and sometimes tedious detail, and he cared about it very deeply. The artist who enables us to soar and fall with his imagination, from the creation of mankind on the Sistine Chapel ceiling to the imprisoned souls of his marble slaves, spent a lot of his life arguing over money, how he would support his extended family, complaining about colleagues, fighting with his employers and dealing with his shopping. Artists, like everyone, have to live with circumstances that aren't of their choosing or making, and events out of their control (although many endured far worse than not being able to have their first choice of marble).

To read most histories of art, the reader might be forgiven for supposing that great artists weren't human, or weren't bound by the same constraints that limit all of us – money, people and external events. Instead, these histories imply that artists' exceptional talent gave them the opportunity to follow their own single-minded trajectory and mission, as if they were gods rather than mere mortals. Also, that loosely connected by influences, training or style, artists' careers follow in neat relationship to each other as part of an overarching and progressive narrative defined by period labels – such as Medieval and Baroque – and filled with 'isms' – Mannerism, Impressionism, Cubism, Modernism, Post-Modernism. Of course, these period divisions and terms are helpful, as they enable us to set artists in historical context and to categorise them, or see that a number of individuals shared a purpose and motivation. They can show that artistic expression has tended to follow particular patterns and fashions at different moments in time. Yet their usefulness should not blind us to the problems they bring.

One of the most persistent is the idea that you need to know these words and concepts to understand art. You don't actually need anything but your eyes or your mind to start thinking about a work of art. Art isn't a novelty, but something that has existed for as long as there have been humans. It's part of the fabric of our lives, including the buildings we live and work in, the streets we walk along, the objects we use from morning to night. We are all highly trained in looking at art and analysing its meanings. The terminology of art is further limited, moreover, because it tends to apply to art made in the Western world, and to objects that were made as art for its own sake, including paintings or sculpture, rather than with a functional purpose like eating or drinking, as is the case for many ceramics and furniture, or for wider cultural, social or religious purposes.

Looking at artistic style in isolation can also be problematic as it suggests that artists didn't think about what they were representing in their image, object or building, nor about its function. Context – what things mean and what things are for – is as important as how things look. Take Édouard Manet's painting *Olympia*, first exhibited publicly at the Salon in Paris in 1865. One analysis of this work would emphasise Manet's expressive brushstrokes, his liking for lively, sketchy pictorial surfaces, and his interest in the work of earlier gestural painters like Velázquez and Titian, whose paintings he admired and studied, particularly those of beautiful women. All this is true. But it's the subject Manet tackled that made *Olympia* infamous in his own time, more than the way he painted it. At the Salon it was hung high up the wall so that critical visitors wouldn't damage it. By convention, art was for ideals, not reality, and some were disgusted that Manet had depicted a real woman, Victorine Meurent, in the persona of a goddess, with the accoutrements of a prostitute. The white artificial light made her face look sour and her skin old. She and the picture were ugly, not alluring. If Victorine was meant to represent a modern Venus, goddess of love, this suggested the corruption and lack of sensibilities of contemporary society.

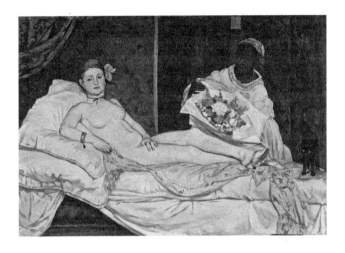

In this book I've wanted to bring style, meaning and context together, to write a history that has the material world at its heart. Some historians remain unconvinced that buildings, objects and images provide useful evidence for the past. They worry about their subjectivity, in comparison to the written or spoken word. But there's no such thing as an objective source, and documents are no less partisan or subjective than any other artefact made by humans. Art gains its power from its ability to fuel and drive our emotions. Because it is able to appeal to our inner beings, it can give solace and connection, linking us to people and experiences far removed from us by time or distance. Just as emotively, it can foment difference and dissent, intensifying our sense of dislocation, rage or violence.

Growing up in Northern Ireland during the Troubles has particularly sensitised me to this issue. Art is dangerous, and it can influence us in eloquent and sometimes uncontrollable ways. But it is also uniquely able to connect us to the peoples and worlds of the past. Handling a ceramic bowl, looking at a painting or standing in a building makes us physically aware of those who have done the same before us, and of our similarities as much as our differences.

Art, like life, is about the interaction of people and society, and artists have always had to interact with the world at large. The wider conditions in which they've found themselves – including their difficulties and frustrations – have provided the stimulus for their artistic production. And although art has been made everywhere, it's been particularly connected to cities. Today, over half the world's population live in large urban centres, and by 2050 – if present trends continue – more than two-thirds of us will be city dwellers. Life in cities is not always civilised, but since the eighth millennia BCE they've been beacons for creativity and artistic dynamism. Cities bring people together from many places and backgrounds; they engender a spirit of competition; and the wealth concentrated within them gives people the opportunity to make and patronise art. Nowhere do we find more stimulation or interaction. Whether we love cities or loathe them, we can all identify with them.

This book brings together the stories of fifteen cities at moments in their history that coincided with intense creative activity, with fifteen of the qualities and emotions that make us human. It aims to explain what these cities were like and the forces that shaped them. In each chapter I have chosen a few objects that exemplify the artistic achievements of the particular place and time. My motivation has been to write a history of art centred on humans, the makers and users of art, but which also explains the social, cultural, political and economic contexts within which artists have worked. I want to tell the story of people as well as art. It's true that art can convey the viewpoint of the elite, but it's also been a powerful means of expressing counter-cultural views, division and dissent. I write this as a European, and that perspective inevitably shapes this narrative, but I have also deliberately set out to look beyond Europe and North America. For much of human history these continents weren't the centre of the world but relative backwaters, responding after a time-lapse to what was going on elsewhere. Yet this wider artistic world is still barely known in the West.

If I have one hope for this book, it is that it inspires readers to think hard about the art that we see around us, the role it plays in our world, and in each of our lives – and the positive difference it can make to us all.

Stele with the Code of Hammurabi

1

BABYLON: RESILIENCE

1800–323 BCE

My first encounter with Babylon was within the pages of a children's Bible. I was entranced by a picture of a towered metropolis, its turrets reaching high into the sky, populated by people scurrying like busy ants. The city rises like a mountain from the plain, as if it were built not by man but by nature. Hordes of tiny figures are busily constructing it, and it's still covered in scaffolding. Boats arrive at the harbour crammed with building materials, including stone, wood and bricks. Men make mortar, lift huge blocks of stone onto a pulley, and carve more from the rock on which the city is founded. Others carefully transport equipment to a building site above the clouds. Tiny figures clamber precariously up dizzyingly high scaffolding.

This is the Tower of Babel, described in the Book of Genesis as the centre of the city of Babylon, built from mud bricks on the Plain of Shinar in what is now central Iraq. Genesis recounts that the Babylonians wanted to build a city and a tower that would reach to the heavens, making a name for themselves and gathering the nations together. The Hebrew

God, rarely cowed by anything, was terrified by their ambition. Understanding that if these people continue to speak one tongue they will be capable of anything, even overthrowing God, he confounds them by introducing a variety of languages. For the first time, the people of the world can't understand each other. They hear meaningless babble – hence Babel – making it impossible to continue with the building of the city. Just to be sure, God scatters the people over the face of the earth.

The picture my image was based on is by the sixteenth-century Flemish artist Pieter Bruegel. It is one of the most influential and copied depictions of a story familiar to many. The story of Babel's Tower, and the hubris of human achievement, was a stalwart of the Western European artistic imagination. The biblical text gives enough descriptive details to enable a talented artist like Bruegel to make a compelling and individual version of this tale. Babylon was also sufficiently distant, and so unfamiliar to Europeans in Bruegel's day, that there was no concern about depicting it accurately. Its setting in green countryside, next to a river and with distant hills, recalls the topography of Antwerp itself, on the Schelde Estuary.

My story is very typical of how many Westerners encounter Babylon. We know it primarily from its appearance in the Old and the New Testaments: the city which exemplified pride and arrogance, a place of exile for the Jews, and – equally evocatively – the summation of all human evil. In the Book of Revelation, that crazed and beautiful vision of the end of the world, St John sets up Babylon as the polar opposite of the 'New Jerusalem', embodying human evil. He envisions the city as a gorgeous but monstrous woman, dressed in purple and scarlet, sitting upon a scarlet beast, with seven heads and ten horns. John goes on to relate the cataclysmic destruction of Babylon by fire from heaven, encapsulating the end of the world: 'The fruit that your soul longed for has gone from you, and all the things which are rich and splendid have gone from you, and you will find them no more at all.' The Christian and Jewish mythology of this metropolis is fascinating. But Babylon's real story is one of the most thrilling of human civilisation. Both in physical and imaginative form, it is among the most resilient of cities.

Cradle of civilisation

During the third and fourth millenniums BCE, a number of urban centres developed in settled river valleys across the northern hemisphere. We will probably never know which of the many contenders, including Jericho, Mohenjo-daro and Çatalhöyük, was first. These cities housed tens of thousands of people, living in dwellings separated by regular streets, with irrigation, basic sanitation systems and fortifications. They were supported by a stable agricultural network, meaning that the inhabitants of these cities bought most of their food, rather than growing or gathering it themselves. These were prosperous places, where the comfortably off were able to fulfil more than their basic human needs, and able to devote themselves to activities and tasks which in other places might be considered luxuries. It was possible to build and to make art on a far larger scale than had previously been possible.

In comparison to these cities, Babylon was a relatively late bloomer. It was founded during the third millennium BCE in the Fertile Crescent. This is the land mass between Europe, Africa and Asia which stretches from the eastern end of the Mediterranean to the Persian Gulf, bounded to the north by the Taurus and Zagros Mountains. The very first permanent human settlements, some twelve thousand years ago, were

nestled in the north of this region, in the hills of northern Iraq
and Syria. Some, including Mosul and Aleppo, are still inhabited today. Babylon is further south, at the top of Mesopotamia,
the floodplain that reaches down to the Persian Gulf.

Each spring for thousands of years, until the construction of
large barrages and reservoirs, rich alluvial deposits of mud and
sediments would fertilise Mesopotamia (in ancient Greek the
land 'between the rivers') as the influx of snowmelt from the
mountains made the Tigris, Diyala and Euphrates rivers burst
their banks. A network of canals, dykes and dams developed
so that this valuable resource could be managed, and they
spread across the cultivated land. As a result barley, wheat,
millet, sesame and date palms could be grown successfully,
in spite of the limited rainfall, enough to feed the population
of large cities and to provide a surplus for offering to the gods
and for trading. According to the Greek historian Herodotus
in the fifth century BCE, no other country – not even Egypt,
the breadbasket of the subsequent Roman Empire – was so
fruitful in grain. The rivers were a perfect conduit for the
movement of goods in and out of the region, including the fine
woollen cloth from the sheep herds of the upper Euphrates
and Tigris, and the metals and semi-precious stones from Iran,
Afghanistan and India which came down the Diyala from the
Zagros Mountains.

The Mesopotamian miracle depended on the development of two further human skills: mathematics and writing.
It would have been impossible to irrigate the land without a
sophisticated numerical system. This came into being in order
to reconcile the lunar and the solar calendars. Calculated
in units of sixty, it is still how we tell the time and measure
angles. It is hard to imagine how we could live our lives without it. The same could be said of writing. A set of symbols and

logograms first used as an accounting system in the southern Mesopotamian city of Uruk developed into cuneiform script. It was flexible enough to record speech in a number of different languages over many centuries. Writing itself was done by impressing symbols into wet clay tablets and cylinders with a reed stylus – both materials easy to come by in an area subdivided by many rivers and streams. They provide most of the evidence we have about Babylon. Clay, when dried or fired, is remarkably durable, particularly in a climate with little rain. It was the essential element for the enduring creation of knowledge and architecture in this great city.

From the time of its foundation Babylon was one of the most important cities in the region. It was also the most resilient, changing and evolving after every invasion or change of regime: from the Hittites to the Kassites, Assyrians, Neo-Babylonians, Persians and Greeks. Babylon's name means 'Gate of the God', and the city was consistent in its veneration of Marduk, the tallest and mightiest god in the pantheon. According to one tale, Marduk created the earth by heaping mud on a raft floating on the sea. Then he made the cities of Eridu and Babylon and the Esagila temple. Humans, animals, the Tigris and Euphrates rivers, the marshes, vegetation and domestic beasts were the next to be created. Woods and palm groves soon followed, and other cities. Serving Marduk and the other gods, bringing food and drink to their temples, and caring for their property, would be key to Babylon's identity. Not for nothing was the Esagila the heart of the city. Symbolically, Marduk – or rather his influential priests – chose Babylon's king. They were the power behind the throne. Every year, as part of the New Year Festival, the king would ritually humiliate himself before Marduk. Without the great god, the king and the city were nothing and would fall.

The materials of Babylon

Without clay, neither Marduk's temples nor the city of Babylon would have existed, nor would we know about them. Clay was formed into bricks to build the city, its fortifications and its irrigation system, and into the tablets and cylinders which recorded the life of the city, from state administration and religious affairs to private matters. The city's rulers ordered hundreds of clay inscriptions celebrating their achievements – usually the building or reconstruction of a palace, temple, wall or gate – to be buried deep in the foundations of these structures. The intention – as indeed happened, thanks to the enterprising Nabonidus, the last king of Babylon, and modern archaeologists – was that these would be discovered and praised by posterity.

This was even the case for those foreigners who seized control of this rich and cultured city state. Cyrus the Great, in his own words 'King of the Universe', placed one in the foundations of Esagila. This was to commemorate his speedy conquest of the city in 539 BCE, and his reconstruction of the great city wall and moat. Cyrus had seen similar inscriptions by other monarchs in Babylon, including one by the great Assyrian king Ashurbarnipal, which inspired him to do the same. The Cyrus Cylinder is the first surviving manifesto of what a ruler should do. He sees his role as saving Babylon from evil, and giving it peace, by maintaining the defences of the city and reverence for the gods. Cyrus records how he 'sought the welfare ... of Babylon and all its sacred centres', relieving the people's weariness and 'settling all the lands in peaceful abodes'.

Less important tablets give us all sorts of information about the city's life. For instance, we know that the Jewish exiles from Jerusalem in the early sixth century BCE were well fed, on cereals, dates and sesame oil, because of a cache of clay documents abandoned in the basement of the Southern Palace. We also know a lot about the lives of the city's elite, particularly those who took responsibility for the temples, because they continued writing in cuneiform on clay tablets long after the civil service had moved on to papyrus and leather. Because these new materials were less robust, we know very little about the day-to-day work of Babylonian state officials.

Lengthy inscriptions, on mountain cliffs or crafted hard stones, are an invaluable source for how the Babylonian rulers saw themselves and how they wanted their subjects to behave. The most remarkable is a tall monument – termed a stele – of a black rock called diorite, dating to the eighteenth century BCE. Its inscription written in Akkadian, the language of the Babylonian court, it reveals the legal and moral code of King Hammurabi. His military and diplomatic success transformed Babylon into the political centre of Mesopotamia, and shaped the sophisticated artistic, literary and religious culture that endured until the Roman Empire.

The thin, curved stone, standing over two metres tall, shows Hammurabi with Shamash, god of the sun and of justice, who is sitting on a throne. Flames shoot from Shamash's shoulders, a sign of his divinity, and he is handing the king the sceptre and ring of his royal office. Hammurabi, standing, is the same height as the sitting god, and is presumably also of divine status. Beneath the image is a great body of text in cuneiform script. It enumerates Hammurabi's many titles, and three hundred laws, evidently divinely sanctioned. Diorite, imported from far-away Oman on the Arabian Peninsula, is hard, uncompromising, and difficult to carve. It resembles a meteor, something which has fallen from the sky, reflecting the king's belief that his law and rule was divinely ordained. The stone's unforgiving nature reflects the rigour with which the law should be applied.

Hammurabi's code is the underpinning of Babylonian civilisation. It has been praised for its clarity, and its even-handedness. But it is also cruel. Here, a thousand years before the Bible, are the origins of the expressions 'an eye for an eye' and 'a tooth for a tooth'. Essentially, the law code is deter-mined to preserve the rights to property, both human (slaves and wives) and material (food, crops, houses, irrigation and land). To us, many of the laws seem hateful: a woman's body is not hers to use as she wishes; slaves do not control their own destiny; a nobleman is punished less than others. And the punishments, of which at least a third involve bodily mutila-tion or death, seem shockingly harsh. But by the standards of their day, and many others since, Hammurabi's laws were fair. Importantly, they established rules which bound members of the elite as much as the ordinary people. Hammurabi's stated intention, as king, was to bring about 'the well-being of the oppressed', to 'enlighten the land, to further the well-being of mankind' and to maintain the state.

Only in the early twentieth century was it possible to glean some understanding of the urban environment in which Babylonians lived in accordance with the codes of Hammurabi and his successors. Generations of travellers, excited by the myth of Babylon and the hubris of its conquest, as prophesied in the Bible and told by Herodotus, were drawn to the site from at least the twelfth century. In 1899, the German artist, archi-tect and archaeologist Robert Koldewey began the first serious archaeological investigation of Babylon. Until then, unsystem-atic digging had unearthed individual treasures but there had been little sense of the city's sophisticated structure and order. Two years earlier, Koldewey's eureka moment had come when he had uncovered strikingly bright turquoise-blue bricks. He was convinced that these were only the smallest elements of the city's famed walls, as described by Herodotus and others. And he was right. The bricks had survived because they had been fired in a wood-fired kiln, a rare luxury in a dry land with little rainfall and limited wood, and a sign of their significance. Koldewey was able to demonstrate that they dated from the city in its heyday during the sixth century BCE, under the rule of King Nebuchadnezzar II, a figure of exhausting vigour and energy. They were part of the Ishtar Gate, on the Processional Way that led to the centre of Babylon.

Koldewey's excavations were halted by the arrival of British troops in 1917. He was unable to return to Babylon before his death. But his legacy was a fuller understanding of this multi-layered city than was ever possible before, as slow as it was meticulous. From 1927, hundreds of crates containing fragments of bricks were carefully unpacked by a team in Berlin. They were desalinated, and coated in liquid paraffin to intensify their coloured glazes. Carefully, the fragments were sorted into groups of the same colours and shapes. It was an intricate jigsaw puzzle which would last months rather than hours. It took two years to piece the remains of seventy-two animal reliefs together. Modern bricks were then used to complete the reconstruction, which then became whole in the kiln. The result – the reconstructed Ishtar Gate and Sacred Way in the Pergamon Museum Berlin – is stunning. Most modern archaeologists would decry this fusion of archaeological evidence with modern materials, but it undeniably gives a real sense of ancient Babylon, its innovation and modernity. The dry documentary record is translated with a bang into the firework hues of a living city, created more than 2,500 years ago.

Nebuchadnezzar II

Nebuchadnezzar's Babylon, as recreated in twentieth-century
Berlin, was a place of brilliant colour, built in brick of many
hues – turquoise, blue, red, white, black and yellow. It appears
not once but twice in the Greek poet Antipater of Sidon's list
of the Seven Wonders of the Ancient World in around 140
BCE: first for its walls and second for the Hanging Gardens.
Sadly there's no firm evidence that these celebrated gardens,
allegedly built on a series of terraces to assuage the home-
sickness of a Persian princess for her native mountains, ever
existed, although the idea has been extremely resilient. It had
a particular hold on the nineteenth-century Romantic imagination – John Martin, the extraordinary Northumbrian painter
of apocalypse, depicted women running in panic from gardens
that reach into the heavens as they flee Cyrus' soldiers.

Even if the great gardens did not exist, the reality of Babylon
is fabulous enough. This extraordinary city, largely as we see it
today the work of Nebuchadnezzar, contained many wonders.
In his own words, recorded on several clay cylinders, he had
'no opponent from horizon to sky'. Born the son of a successful king, Nebuchadnezzar was resolved to surpass his father's
achievements. He rebuilt Babylon as a great imperial capital,
with a grand temple to Marduk – the Esagila with its accompanying tower, Etemenanki – three royal palaces, and two lines of
walls. The rectangular structure of the inner walls, punctuated
with eight gates, housed approximately 180,000 people. The
Euphrates ran through the middle of the city, roughly from
north to south, bounded by a brick quay, and a great bridge
connected its eastern and western sides.

The monarch was particularly proud of his new 'strong
wall that cannot be shaken' encircling the entire city, which

'no previous king had done'. Constructed with bitumen and baked bricks, Nebuchadnezzar 'laid its foundation on the breast of the netherworld', and 'built its top as high as a mountain'. Herodotus tells us that the wall was so wide a four-horse chariot could pass (and turn) on top of it, and although his stories are often inaccurate, archaeological evidence confirms the immensity of the structure. This wall, protected the gardens and date plantations which were Babylon's major source of food.

Its very bricks were stamped with the king's name and his principal titles – 'Nebuchadnezzar, king of Babylon, provider for Esagila and Ezida, eldest son of Nabopolassar, king of Babylon'. Nebuchadnezzar's priorities were twofold: adding to the territorial might and power of Babylon so that it could support the city, its king and its gods; as well as beautifying and improving the city itself. In this, the requirements of Marduk and the king, his servant on earth, were of paramount importance. There were, cuneiform tablets tell us, about four hundred temples in the city, together with approximately a thousand shrines. Nothing was as important as Marduk's temples. Every luxury was lavished on them, and on the members of the city's elite who served the god in his dwelling places on earth.

The most important temple complex was the Esagila, the heart of the city. Its significance was underlined by its separation from the rest of Babylon. Visitors had to pass through the Pure Gate and cross a huge courtyard, the Sublime Court, which gave access to temple, as well as a number of shrines to lesser gods, including Marduk's father Ea, his wife Zarpanitu and his son Nabu. The area is now a bleak ruin, but we can partially reconstruct the temple from the stories of travellers and cuneiform tablets, one of which even gives measurements for the space. The temple was enormous in size and height, with doorways nine metres tall. Its walls were adorned with lapis lazuli, a semi-precious blue stone mined in distant Afghanistan, and alabaster. The internal furnishings were made from a variety of precious woods, metals and stones. Nebuchadnezzar notes that the interior was covered completely in gold.

Golden statues of Marduk and Zarpanitu were the principal features of the temple. She was accompanied by her hairdressers, Marduk by a butler and baker, and other attendants, including a door keeper, and dogs. Winged gods called kurubs guarded the entrance. During the rituals of each day, the gods were groomed, dressed in valuable textiles and jewellery, fed and entertained by the temple's priests. A well-stocked library gave answers to any theological questions that might arise. The priests and Marduk's servants were extremely proud of the inherited positions they held, which granted exemption from public work and from taxation.

To the north of the temple, the traveller came to Etemenanki, 'the link between Heaven and Earth', on the east side of the Euphrates. It was under Nebuchadnezzar's personal authority that this structure, the inspiration for the biblical Tower of Babel, was brought to completion. At sunrise, its shadow stretched across to the opposite bank of the river. It could be seen for many miles around. Etemenanki stood within a large square enclosure, surrounded by chambers for servants of the god. The tower was a huge mountain of clay bricks, tiles and wood, topped by a temple to Marduk. It was torn down by the Assyrian invader Sennacherib in 689 BCE. Nothing remains of Etemenanki today but a vast pond in a strange geometric shape, like a tall chimney attached to a rectangle, an image of the tower in negative form.

According to the cuneiform E-Sangil Tablet, it was a square building, 180 cubits (about 90 metres) wide and 180 cubits tall. From Nebuchadnezzar's own words, we know he began this work as an act of filial piety, to finish the structure that Nabopolassar 'had made pure through the craft of exorcism, the skill of Ea and Marduk'. If his father had fixed the tower's foundations 'on the breast of the underworld', it was his son who finished it 'so that it vied with the heavens', setting the people of his empire from 'the upper sea to the lower sea, the distant nations, teeming people of the world, kings of remote mountains and far-flung islands' to build Marduk's tower.

Majestic gates, each furnished with pure cedar door leaves, guarded the entrance to the complex. At the centre was the tower, rising upwards on a terrace of baked clay. Sturdy cedars from Mount Lebanon and special 'musukkannu' wood from the Indian subcontinent were coated with bronze and laid on top of this base as the foundation of a holy sanctum for Marduk, 'a chamber of repose as in bygone times'. In a charming detail, Herodotus tells us there was a resting point with some little seats about halfway up, so that people could catch their breath before ascending to the summit. Marduk's high sanctuary at the top of the tower may have been a two-storey structure. From this, it would have been possible to look over the flat plains of southern Iraq. At night it would have functioned as a marvellous observatory for the astrologers who were part of the temple's religious staff.

For all the evidence, there remains no consensus about some important elements of the design, from the number of levels – were there six or seven? – to the correct order of the staircases that led from the courtyard to the upper levels. But what is clear from the disparate sources is that the top and bottom levels were considerably broader than the others. The external walls of the middle levels were probably made up of alternating buttresses and recesses, meaning that in the strong

Mesopotamia sunlight the flat surfaces of the façade were broken up by the play of light and shade. This is very typical of Babylonian architecture.

In the northern section of the city, just inside the inner wall, stood the confusingly named Southern Palace. This was an administrative and military centre as well as a dwelling place. On a stone tablet discovered in the ruins of Babylon, and now in the British Museum, Nebuchadnezzar described this enormous structure as the 'house of the people's wonder'. It was reputed to have two hundred and fifty rooms, with a throne room at its heart, and was built around a series of five courtyards. These moved from the most public to the most private spaces, those reserved for the queen, her retinue and the rest of the king's women, including those sent to him as tribute. Unfortunately, as we know from Nebuchadnezzar's inscriptions, he considered the palace too small for comfort. It was also exceptionally damp. Almost immediately he began building the Northern Palace outside the city walls. Raised on an earth mound eight metres high, it seems perhaps a superfluous construction funded by cities and religious institutions from across the empire as a symbol of the king's authority.

The Southern Palace was situated between the river and the Processional Way that led to the Ishtar Gate. Royal triumphs were celebrated here, and Nebuchadnezzar spared no expense on the construction of the gate and the avenue. He notes with pleasure his outlay on the road, paved with stone slabs, on top of a layer of bricks each inscribed with his titles and respect for Marduk. This was the ceremonial route that Marduk himself took on the occasions the god was processed through the city by his priests. The Ishtar Gate was dedicated to the chief goddess of the Babylonian pantheon, and was a structure of which Nebuchadnezzar was exceptionally proud:

I laid the foundation of the gates down to the ground water level and had them built out of pure blue stone. I covered their roofs by laying majestic cedars lengthwise over them. I hung doors of cedar adorned with bronze at all the gate openings. I placed wild bulls and ferocious dragons in the gateways and thus adorned them with luxurious splendour that people might gaze on them in wonder.

Part of the gate, including this building inscription, survives in the reconstruction erected by Koldewey's team in Berlin. In spite of the king's words, the dazzling blue front is not stone but brick, fired with a cobalt glaze that came from ground-up blue glass, and further decorated with baked clay reliefs in brilliant yellow and orange. As Nebuchadnezzar states, these depict serpent dragons and aurochs, symbols of Marduk and Adad, the god of weather. Each beast is as tall as an average person, intended to impress and terrify. Marduk's sinuous dragon, the mušḫuššu, is both attractive and frightening. It has the head of a snake, the body and forelimbs of a lion with reptilian scales, and long talons on its back legs, like those of an eagle. These beasts stalk purposefully across the gate, tails as long and as erect as their necks. Adad's animal form is simpler and somewhat less malevolent, though the auroch was notoriously vicious. It was an ancestor of domesticated cattle, with horns, a strong body and sturdy legs. These are not animals – or gods – to be trifled with.

The Ishtar Gate was important for the annual celebration of the Babylonian New Year, at the moment of the spring equinox, the first day of the month of Nisan. As part of this festival, the city's creation myths were re-enacted, and several of the gods taken to the river in a funeral procession that represented their journey to the underworld. On the twelfth day of the New Year, they were triumphantly returned to the city in the House of the New Year's Festival, through the Ishtar Gate and along the Processional Way. The cycle of birth and rebirth was complete, and the seasons could begin again.

North of the gateway, the sides of the road were lined with more aurochs and serpent dragons, as well as life-size lions with open, roaring mouths. The lion was a symbol of Ishtar, beautiful yet bellicose. Their presence served to protect the street, the ceremonial way connecting the city with the New Year festival. They are emblematic of the power of Babylon, and how it channelled artistic expression to convey its spirit, beauty and buoyancy.

In 1979, Saddam Hussein came to power in Iraq. As his rule lengthened and deepened, he came to believe that he was following in the footsteps of Nebuchadnezzar and other Babylonian heroes of the early world civilisations. He made explicit connections between the country's antiquities, 'the dearest relics that the Iraqi people have', and the potential of modern Iraq. In 1981, it was at Babylon that Saddam celebrated the first anniversary of the war with Iran, using the slogan 'Nebuchadnezzar yesterday, Saddam Hussein today'. A 1980s mural shows Saddam and Nebuchadnezzar together, separated by Hammurabi's Law Code, and a recreation of a ceremony on the Processional Way at the Ishtar Gate.

In the midst of the Iran–Iraq war, Babylon's walls were recreated, and raised to a height unsupported by the archae-ological evidence. The Ishtar Gate and Southern Palace were reconstructed on their surviving foundations. This 'restoration' went far beyond internationally established norms, and was denounced by heritage conservators. Like Nebuchadnezzar, Saddam had bricks stamped with his name, with inscriptions in Arabic praising his own work. He also built a new stadium, and a palace for himself on the outskirts of the ancient city. From the balcony of his bedroom, he overlooked the ditches and broken walls of ancient Babylon, and the new walls he had built in the Babylonian style.

Further destruction occurred after the fall of Saddam Hussein's regime in 2003 and the invasion of Iraq, when American and Polish troops turned part of the site into a military base. Soldiers filled sandbags with archaeological evidence; tanks crushed the remains of the sixth-century bricks of the Processional Way; there were reports of looters removing parts of the remaining beasts on the Ishtar Gate. As the leading archaeologist Dr John Curtis has commented, this was 'tantamount to establishing a military camp around the Great Pyramid in Egypt or Stonehenge in Britain'. It is hard to understand why an encampment was required on an archaeological site, save as a provocation.

The omens are not promising, but Babylon has a history of resilience. Not for nothing is the Processional Way named 'the enemy shall not prevail'. The recent recuperation of the Lion of Babylon gives some cautious grounds for hope: this 2,600-year-old basalt sculpture, representing a lion trampling a man, symbolising the power of the goddess Ishtar, was made by the Hittite peoples from Anatolia in modern Turkey and Syria, who conquered Babylon in 1595 BCE, although it is unclear if it was carved in Anatolia or in Babylon itself. The Lion is first mentioned by Western travellers in the late eighteenth century, and in 1852 it was the first statue to be excavated, somewhere in the northern section of the city rebuilt by Nebuchadnezzar. Unfortunately, because of the paucity of the documentary record, we will never know exactly where, but it has been exhibited near that site since that date.

A photograph album compiled by a British army doctor during the First World War shows the Lion standing (rather precariously) on a mound of rubble. A scarcely credible story from 1917 alleges that local people damaged its face, searching for coins which a magician had apparently conjured from its mouth. More recently it has been placed on the Processional Way, near the site of the Northern Palace. For Iraqis the statue is a celebrated symbol of their country, appearing on bank notes, stamps, restaurant menus and napkins. But enthusiastic admirers had been damaging the Lion, climbing on its back, where a statue of Ishtar would originally have sat, and in 2016 it was placed on a list of antiquities at risk. Following work by the Iraqi State Board of Antiquities and Heritage and the World Monuments Fund to repair the statue's base and to protect it from visitors, the sculpture can once more admired in a manner that respects and preserves its antiquity and its historic value. The Lion, like Babylon itself, survives to endure.

An aerial view of the Temple Mount in east Jerusalem, looking north

2

JERUSALEM: FAITH

Tenth Century BCE

O Jerusalem the Holy City!

Isaiah, 51:1

Perhaps the most unlikely sporting anthem in the world is the song that the English bellow before their national rugby union team goes into action. As fans wait for a display of skill and brawn, they launch into some of the most impassioned and idealistic verses in the English language, written by the visionary artist and poet William Blake. Those who sing 'Jerusalem', set to Hubert Parry's inspiring tune, are promising that they 'will not cease from mental fight ... / Till we have built Jerusalem, / In England's green and pleasant land'. Why this improbable ambition and why such effort? The answer, of course, is bound up with the reputation and associations of this city.

Jerusalem is one of the holiest places for three of the world's great monotheistic faiths, collectively known as the People of the Book. For Jews, it is home to the only, and lost, Temple, on the site of Abraham's sacrifice of Isaac. For Christians, it is the earthly gateway to Paradise, where the Passion of Jesus took place, while for most Muslims it is the place from where Muhammad ascended a ladder to Heaven, and where the Last Judgement will take place. In each and every regard it has inspired people who wish to remake the world in different images of the divine. As a result, this indomitable city has been built, destroyed and rebuilt – both in reality and in the imagination – for centuries.

The whole story of the Heavenly City on earth is exemplified in the life and afterlife of one remarkable building within it: King Solomon's Temple on Mount Moriah, between the Mount of Olives and Mount Zion. First built in the tenth century BCE and twice destroyed, perhaps no other building in history has been so intensively missed, so fulsomely reimagined or regularly and widely copied. In the lost proportions and forms of this one structure have been seen the paradigms of wisdom and spirituality, beauty and paradise, divine order and perfect proportion. No wonder it has so obsessed subsequent generations.

The spiritual power of the original Temple has echoed around the world in the form of other sacred buildings that have been claimed to be built in its image. Reconstructing the Temple has enabled Jewish, Christian and Muslim architects and their powerful patrons to evoke the Heavenly City, in structures that reflect their times and their religions. The Temple has been a powerful blueprint for other architectural wonders, particularly in the two cities that have fought hardest for the title of the new Jerusalem – Rome and Constantinople. In these cities, at different moments, and in the service of different faiths, the authorities used the architectural structures and ideas associated with Jerusalem's Temple to bolster and legitimise their religious and political authority.

The Jewish Temple

The Temple as first constructed is evocatively described in the Old Testament Book of Kings. This account was written after its destruction, by a Jewish exile in Babylon, but it constitutes the foundation for our understanding of this building. The text explains that Solomon's father, David – poet, musician, soldier, adulterer and murderer – had united the two kingdoms of Judah and Israel, and brought the Ark of the Covenant back to Jerusalem. It was necessary, therefore, to build a temple to house this holy object. This would be the only place where the faithful could hope to experience the actual presence of God. Every Jew was required to come in person to Jerusalem three times a year for the major religious festivals, and to pay the temple tax.

Yahweh, 'I am that I am', by this account, was a deity of stern and forthright character. He countenanced no moral failings, no other competing deities, nor even any images of himself. And he decreed that David, because he was a man of war, could not build the Temple, so the work was passed to his son. Construction began in the fourth year of Solomon's reign, in around 960 BCE. Because Yahweh considered iron an instrument of war, no iron tools, including the hammer and the chisel, were used on the building site. The walls were made of carefully worked stone imported to the site. Even heavy items such as window frames, doors and the altar itself were only shipped to the temple once they had been completed.

There are many complications to reconstructing the Temple as described in the Book of Kings, though many people have tried. All the dimensions of the building, for example, are given in cubits. These measurements, like all the numbers in the description, are probably symbolic rather than strictly accurate, to show the divinely inspired order of the holy structure. Added to which, we still do not know exactly what a biblical cubit was. Yet, paradoxically, in such ambiguities and in what the account fails to tell us, the description has even greater power for those who wish to use it as the basis for visualising this lost building.

The Temple was enclosed within a walled court that stood within a yet greater court that also enclosed Solomon's palace. It was a rectangular building sixty cubits long, twenty wide, and thirty high, and made from the finest stone, quarried by a hundred thousand workers, and prized woods (sweet-smelling cedar, cypress, white broom and olive). The building comprised three internal elements: a porch, a chamber for worship and the sanctuary. This last, the home of the Ark of the Covenant, was entered through a set of olivewood doors, carved with cherubs, palms and flowers, and covered with gold. Its interior was lined entirely with cedarwood clad in beaten gold.

Two enormous golden angels, measuring ten cubits wing to wing and carved from olivewood, were the only moveable objects in the room, save the Ark itself. This contained the most precious items in the Jewish faith, the tablets on which Moses had received the Ten Commandments from Yahweh. Chains of beaten gold blocked off the altar from the Holy of Holies, where the Ark was placed under the sheltering wings of the angels, so that it and the poles it was carried on were invisible. We should imagine – although there is no evidence from the Jewish sources – that the sanctuary was built directly onto the rock of the Temple Mount. Perhaps this detail was too sacred to be put into words.

The Temple contained an astonishing range of opulent portable goods. This included numerous objects made from gold: ten lampstands; one hundred bowls for sprinkling lustrations;

pots, shovels and meat forks for animal sacrifices; carved flowers, lamps and tongs; wick-trimmers for candles; as well as other miscellanea 'and all related articles'. Solomon additionally commissioned numerous fixtures and fittings from the skilled bronze worker Hiram of Tyre.

These included two bronze pillars that framed the main temple portico, each eighteen cubits high and twelve cubits in circumference, and were named Boaz ('Strength') and Jachin ('He Establishes'). They were crowned with capitals in the shape of the pure and sweet-smelling lily, surrounded by bronze chains and two hundred pomegranates, a fruit associated with fecundity and plenty. Hiram also created a vast fountain, the so-called Molten Sea. This was a brass basin, standing on a base supported by ten bronze bulls and with a rim as thin as 'a lily blossom' circled by hundreds of gourds. The basin was used for ritual ablutions and held enough water for three thousand baths.

After seven years of work, in the month of Bul, in the eleventh year of Solomon's reign, the building was complete. The priests withdrew from the Holy Place, and, standing on the east side of the altar, musicians of the house of Levi, singing and playing cymbals, lyres and harps, joined with 120 trumpeters to give praise and thanks to the Lord. Kneeling in prayer before the altar, Solomon dedicated the temple to the service of God. He asked God to remember the covenant that he had agreed with the Israelites, and to 'come to your resting place, you and the ark of your might ... Lord God, do not reject your anointed one. / Remember the great love promised to David your servant.'

Fire immediately consumed the sacrifices, and the Temple was filled with the Cloud or presence of God. In the dead of the night, the Lord returned to Solomon, warning 'I have chosen and consecrated this temple so that my Name may be there forever. My eyes and my heart will always be there.' If Solomon and his people ever rejected the name of the Lord and worship other gods, he would abandon them: 'I will uproot Israel from my land … and will reject this temple … This temple will become a heap of rubble. All who pass by will be appalled …'

Solomon's Temple, planned for eternity, probably lasted less than five hundred years. In 587 BCE, the armies of King Nebuchadnezzar sacked Jerusalem and razed it to the ground. The exiled Jews went, in the words of Psalm 137, to the 'rivers of Babylon' and 'wept when we remembered Zion'. According to the Book of Ezra, the Jews were invited to return to Jerusalem and rebuild the Temple at the behest of King Cyrus of Persia in 539 BCE.

It was to the second Temple that Jesus was brought for his circumcision as a baby, for instruction as a teenager, and for disputation and torment by the Pharisees as an adult. It was also here that, in fury, he overturned the traders' tables and expelled the money lenders. Soon after his crucifixion in about 29 CE – the exact date is uncertain – the Temple was enhanced by Herod Agrippa, associate of the Roman emperors.

In 70 CE the Jews rebelled against the Romans and Jerusalem was besieged by the future emperor, Titus. During the sack of the city that followed, the building was destroyed. According to the Jewish historian Josephus, who witnessed the destruction, every stone, every floor, every foundation of the Temple was pulled down and its rich contents were carried in triumph to Rome. Following a second Jewish revolt in 132–135 CE, the city at large was re-founded by the Emperor Hadrian as a Roman colony and a new temple to Capitoline Jupiter was raised on Mount Moriah. Jewish access was forbidden and Jerusalem was renamed Aelia Capitolina. In 324 Emperor

Constantine restored the original name, reinventing Jerusalem as a Christian city.

Mourning the lost Temple and their Holy City would be the fate of the Jewish people for centuries, and came to be symbolically recalled in the actions of ordinary life. An item of a meal would be omitted, or a woman would fail to put on all her finery, in remembrance of Jerusalem. The Jews who had spread out all over the world looked towards Jerusalem in their prayers, and the Seder service on the Eve of Passover ends with the hope, 'Next year in Jerusalem.' The aura and spiritual power of the Temple Mount, meanwhile, remained palpable to others beside the Jews.

The Muslim Temple

When the Prophet Muhammad began to share his revelations in the early seventh century CE, he recounted a vision in which he rode on the lightning steed Buraq from the Kaaba in Mecca, the holiest place in Islam, to the 'furthest mosque'. This is identified in the hadiths, which record his sayings and actions, as the 'Aqsā Mosque in the Holy House of Aelia', at the southern end of the Temple Mount. There, in the company of the prophets Abraham, Moses and Jesus, Muhammad was tested by the Archangel Jibril (Gabriel to Jews and Christians) with the offer of a bowl of wine or of milk. He chose the latter, which Jibril said was the 'natural instinct', and was transported on a golden ladder – reminiscent of Jacob's Ladder in the Book of Genesis – to Heaven.

At each of the seven levels of paradise, Muhammad spoke to the earlier prophets, including Abraham, Moses, John the Baptist and Jesus, and at the summit, God instructed him that

Muslims should pray five times a day. This narrative includes
two key elements of Islamic faith, abstinence from alcohol and
regular prayer. Recognising both Abraham (Ibrahim) – who
attempted to sacrifice his son Isaac on the site of the Temple –
and Solomon (Suleiman) as prophets sent to guide humanity, it
was appropriate that the Temple Mount, which became known
as the Haram al-Sharīf or Noble Sanctuary, was the first direction, or qibla, that Muhammad instructed his followers to face
in their prayers.

From Muhammad's journey derives a vast body of literature that places Jerusalem at the centre of Islamic beliefs
concerning life after death. According to tradition, at the Last
Judgement the saved and the damned will be sorted on the
Haram al-Sharif and a rope as thin as a hair will stretch from it
to the Mount of Olives, where the Garden of Eden will appear.
Beneath the rope will open the pits of Hell. Those who trust
their faith and cross this perilously narrow tightrope will enjoy
Paradise; those who slip will fall to eternal doom and those too
fearful to make the attempt will be saved, if they repent. The
Haram al-Sharīf, therefore, is a place of peace that promises
paradise, for those who are prepared to make the leap of faith.

Muhammad died in 632 and within six years Jerusalem,
like most of the Near and Middle East, was under the rule
of his followers. Caliph Umar, Muhammad's father-in-law, is
said to have built a wooden mosque on the Haram al-Sharīf,
and the Islamic authorities lavished money and care upon it.
It was not until the late 680s, however, that the present stone
structure, called the Dome of the Rock, was built on the site of
Solomon's Temple by the fifth caliph, Abd al-Malik, who ruled
from Damascus. He gave seven years of his Egyptian revenues
to enable construction of a building to cover and venerate the
exposed rock face that had witnessed the faith of Abraham,

Solomon and Muhammad himself. At that point the caliph did not control the Kaaba in Mecca, and was fighting a civil war, so the Mount was the holiest site in Islam under his direct rule.

Since Abd al-Malik also aspired to rule those territories of the Byzantine Empire that he and his co-religionists had not already overrun in their triumphant march to the Mediterranean from the Arabian Peninsula, it is perhaps not surprising that this building, full of light and mystery, recalls Byzantine architecture, in particular the spirit of the Hagia Sophia in Constantinople. It is also indebted to Jerusalem's Holy Sepulchre, the domed church built on the site of Christ's tomb, first constructed on the orders of Constantine the Great in 326 CE, and the fifth-century octagonal church of the Kathisma, now a ruin, but made to cover the rock where Mary was said to have rested on her way to Bethlehem.

The building's octagonal plan is consciously halfway between the man-made perfection of the square and the God-given purity of the circle, a line without end, befitting a shrine that commemorates Muhammad's transition between the earth and heaven. Two rows of columns create walkways, or ambulatories, around the building, between the outer walls and the first columns, and the second close to the rock itself. This was always intended as a site for pilgrimage. The Dome of the Rock (in Arabic, *Qubbat al-Sakhra*) is an egalitarian space for Muslims and women can enter as freely as men. Although the rock itself is protected by a screen, anyone can descend to the shrine beneath it.

Beautifully patterned grey and white marble, cut in sheets, clads the lower section of the interior. From the first row of columns, abundantly carved with acanthus leaf capitals, spring a series of arches. Brightly coloured mosaics, in gold, blue and green, with glints of white and red, show geometric and vegetal forms, interspersed with winged crowns. Many of these recall the mosaics found in Byzantine churches; the winged crowns were a symbol of the Sassanian emperors, whom the Arab Muslims had finally defeated in 651. This is a holy place, and a regal one too. It exudes its spirituality through joy, promise and confidence. The light which breaks in through the four open doors, the windows in the upper level of the octagonal base and the drum underneath the dome, makes the mosaics sparkle, and casts shafts of light on the variegated marble.

And if you raise your eyes upwards, you can see inscriptions running along the outer and inner arcades. This is one of the earliest examples of the architectural calligraphy that is such a key part of Islamic art. Starting from the qibla, the outer inscription proclaims the ineffable nature of God. In an unusually direct swipe at Christianity, and the figure of Jesus, the God made Flesh, it is written: 'God is one; God is central – birthing no child, nor birthed in turn – nothing and no one is comparable'. In the inner arcade, this message continues, urging the reader to see Jesus as a messenger of God, but never as God: 'Lord Almighty! That God would beget a child! Either in the heavens or on earth?'

Fourteen hundred years of repair and adaptation have done nothing to diminish the impact of this extraordinary building, though they have changed it. The striking blue tiles which cover the upper external walls of the octagonal base and the drum of the dome, for example, were not installed until the sixteenth century, under the patronage of the Ottoman sultan Suleiman the Magnificent, and most of those still in place were heavily restored in the 1920s, and again in the 1960s. Both the external and internal faces of the building were originally covered in gold and green mosaic (a feature unparalleled in any other ancient or medieval structure); however, the gleaming dome is the result of repairs during the 1960s and 1990s.

There is nothing quite like the Dome of the Rock. It commands by virtue of its location, impresses by the clarity of its conception and dazzles by the beauty and quality of its construction. As early as the tenth century CE the Jerusalem-born traveller Muqadisi wrote, 'At the dawn, when the light of the sun first strikes the cupola, and the drum catches the rays; then this edifice is a marvellous sight to behold, and one such that in all Islam I have never seen its equal; neither have I heard tell of aught built in pagan times that should rival in grace this Dome of the Rock.' More prosaically, but quite as affectingly, the fifteenth-century historian of Jerusalem and Hebron, Mujir al-Din, remarked that happiness was 'eating a banana in the shade of the Dome of the Rock'.

The 'New Jerusalem': Solomon's Temple in Turkey

For Christians, the Temple in Jerusalem – though it was a point of biblical reference and highly significant as a divinely ordained and proportioned building – was perhaps less important as a place than as an idea. If the New Testament superseded the Old Testament, should there not be a new Temple? In this regard it was helpful that in the Old Testament Book of Ezekiel, the Hebrew prophet recounts a vision that took place in 573 BCE, fourteen years after the first destruction of Jerusalem. He describes being transported to the top of a high mountain where he was presented with an apparition of a future Temple by a man, seemingly made of bronze, with a measuring rod. Perhaps, this vision described the Temple of the New Testament and authorised its construction.

In 324 Constantine the Great, the first Roman emperor to convert to Christianity, created a new capital on the site of a long-established Greek city, Byzantion, on the geographical border of Europe and Asia. Rome still retained some value, but his new creation emphasised a decisive shift in the centre of political and economic gravity from the 'old world' of Western Europe to Greece and the Eastern Mediterranean. He named the new city after himself – Constantinople – and tried to recreate within it the topography of Rome. The character of the city as a second Rome was never wholly lost, but from at least the fifth century it also began to be identified as a new Jerusalem.

This idea found particular expression in the city's principal church of 'Holy Wisdom' or Hagia Sophia, situated beside the Royal Palace on the acropolis, looking down to the Bosphorus and the Sea of Marmara. The current church is the third on the site, built when Constantinople, and the Byzantine Empire, was at its zenith. Like Solomon's Temple, it was a prodigy building which brought God to the heart of the city. The structure we see today was built by Justininan, emperor from 527 to 565, whose energy was boundless and who reportedly never slept. Justinian wanted his new centrally planned church covered with a great dome to be a new Temple and in 537, when it was consecrated after only five years of construction, he was reported to have remarked pointedly, 'Solomon I have surpassed thee!'

Although the emperor liked to take sole credit for the church, it was really the work of two mathematically minded architects, Anthemius of Tralles and Isidore of Miletus. They seem to have had some understanding of Heron of Alexandria's mathematical theories of how to span large spaces with vaults, written five hundred years earlier. Thus there was a connection to, and possibly some architectural knowledge of, the great domed and circular buildings of Imperial Rome. Hagia Sophia's structure was daring to the point of foolhardiness. Its shallow foundations, vast scale and speed of construction made it particularly vulnerable to the earthquakes to which the Bosphorus region is prone. That it survives is nothing short of a miracle.

Despite many changes of use, from church to mosque to museum and now to mosque again, it retains its sixth-century form and character to a remarkable degree. Here we find a new Christian architecture at the heart of a Christian empire in which the church and state are one. In two related mosaics above the south-west doors, Constantine offers the city to God and the Virgin, and Justinian gives them the church itself. The emperor, of course, was also the head of the church and appointed the patriarch of the city. In this sense the building unites heaven and earth to create a spiritual heart of the empire.

The building combines a centrally planned space, based on a circle, with another on a longitudinal axis. Its central dome is enormous, at more than 180 feet high. Unlike earlier monumental domes, such as that over the Pantheon in Rome, which sat on circular buildings, this sits on a square one. To support the dome, therefore, the angles of the square plan are infilled with triangular segments termed pendentives. Forty windows pierce the dome, and their light moves across the interior during the course of the day in a manner that is at once magical and gentle.

Overall, it is clear that the architects were more interested in architectural form and the challenge of constructing a huge dome than creating a strictly functional space. Consequently, many spaces were designed as part of the monumental structure without knowing what they would be used for. It's not clear, for example, if the north galleries ever had a defined function, although those in the south became the private quarters of the emperor and patriarch. An enormous silver screen protected the sanctuary and only the patriarch, the emperor and their attendants were allowed behind it. A vast body of clergy served the building, and from the eleventh century an elaborate daily liturgy was celebrated. Pilgrims also came from around the Christian world to venerate the relics that were gathered and displayed here.

The dedication of the church was to an idea – Holy Wisdom – and in the first phase of decoration a decision was made largely to avoid human or figurative imagery. Instead, the interior was decorated with marble quarried on the nearby Marmara Islands. Slabs were split and laid edge to edge with veins and patterns in mirror image so as to create abstract, or allusive, patterns and symbols. All the clear glass was originally coloured red and blue, and the floor consists of sheets of marble, worn by the passage of so many feet that it seems as if waves of water have shaped it.

There is also extensive architectural sculpture in the capitals and cornices. Amid the stylised acanthus leaves are the monograms of Justinian and his empress, Theodora. Opus sectile, a form of picture-making with marble, mother-of-pearl, glass and semi-precious stones, was used to decorate the gallery level. It includes birds and plants in white marble set against a dark background; the impression everywhere in Hagia Sophia is of a strong contrast between light and dark. The embassy of Vladimir, Prince of Kyiv, recording their impressions in the eleventh century, were profoundly struck by the unplaceable beauty of the place: 'God dwells there among men ... We knew not whether we were in heaven or earth.'

Justinian's creation, in turn, exerted a powerful influence

on later Muslim architecture in the city. In 1453, when Sultan Mehmed captured Constantinople, he converted Hagia Sophia into a congregational mosque with a marble mihrab (prayer niche) and minbar (raised pulpit), both oriented towards Mecca, together with a minaret to call the faithful to prayer. As adapted, the building became a source of inspiration for Ottoman architects, particularly the great Sinan, architect to Suleiman the Magnificent, in whose reign during the sixteenth century the Ottoman Empire stretched from Central Europe to the Persian Gulf, encompassing both Jerusalem and Mecca.

We know that Sinan studied Hagia Sophia closely – he called it 'unequalled in the world' – and we are well informed besides about his thoughts on architecture because he dictated several autobiographical essays to his friend Mustafa Saʿi. In his view, while everything ultimately derived from God, a man could nevertheless build solid foundations, create adequate support and make his buildings look as 'agreeable' as possible. In this last regard he thought it his achievement to have refined the style of Hagia Sophia, a view exemplified in one of his greatest works, the mosque he created for Suleiman the Magnificent from the spoils of war in Belgrade, Malta and Rhodes.

The Süleymaniye Mosque, on a hilltop site above the Golden Horn, takes the shape of Hagia Sophia and, with its great central dome, is a direct challenge to the earlier building, about half an hour's walk away across the city's tightly packed streets. It formed part of a complex that also included several Islamic colleges or *madrasas*, a hospital, a hospice, a kitchen, a bath-house, shops, a caravanserai and mausolea for the sultan and his principal wife. It was endowed by the sultan for the practice of religion and the study of the religious sciences, to 'strengthen the mechanisms of worldly sovereignty, and to reach happiness in the afterworld'. The *waqfiyya* or legal document establishing the charity calls Suleiman 'the Solomon of the age'; again we sense the long shadow of the Temple in Jerusalem.

Incorporated into the mosque are materials from all over the empire, including four colossal red granite columns, cut from single pieces of stone, that are said to have come from Baalbek and Alexandria. Baalbek was believed to be the site of the palace that Solomon built for the Queen of Sheba, while the Ottoman Sultans believed themselves to be sovereigns in the line of Alexander the Great. This assemblage of building materials from venerated locations recalls the gathering of precious materials from Mount Lebanon used in the original Temple in Jerusalem.

The light and airy structure is quite unlike most Islamic architecture of the preceding half century. There's a sense, like in Hagia Sophia, of being in a divine space, one where the order and unity of Heaven and earth is expressed. The light is physical, but it expresses the divine and filters down from hundreds of small arched windows with pierced stone grilles. The effect, combined with the huge circular mosque lamps lit with oil in hundreds of glass vessels, suspended from the ceiling with ostrich eggs and reflective balls of mirror, must have been spellbinding, like the sky on a very clear night. The atmosphere is ethereal. Like the original Temple, this is a home for God on earth.

The Temple in Rome and Solomon's Columns from Jerusalem

While Constantine was building his new capital on the Bosphorus, he was also involved in erecting a new church on the banks of the Tiber in Rome. This dignified the site of the tomb of St Peter, Jesus' close companion, on the Vatican Hill. As first conceived this building had nothing to do with the Temple in Jerusalem, but many centuries later and by the most curious sequence of events, it came to represent it.

Peter, the first pope, leader of the disciples and founder of the Roman Catholic Church, had died in ignominy in the first century CE. Tradition holds that he was crucified and buried in Rome. His modest grave, initially marked by a small monument, has grown organically over centuries into what is today an extraordinary architectural presence, and the most easily recognised symbol of the Roman Catholic Church. Since the late sixteenth century its massive egg-shaped dome, designed by Michelangelo Buonarotti, has dominated the Roman skyline, while the encircling arms of its piazza, by Gianlorenzo Bernini, reach out to draw visitors into the building.

For all that St Peter's has changed and grown, it still embodies the essentials of Constantine's vision. The church was to be a sanctuary that enclosed the saint's original burial site, in a building that was large enough to enable Christian worship and the development of the cult of St Peter. The solution – as in many early churches designed on a large scale – was to design a large rectangular building on the model of the ancient Roman basilica, a public building which contained meeting rooms and law courts.

St Peter's tomb remains the focus of the Basilica, as it was in Constantine's day, although its appearance has changed dramatically over time. In the fourth century, it was a primitive shrine, encased in marble and given architectural focus by the canopy that stood over it. This was held up by four of the six twisted columns that Constantine had brought from Greece to adorn the tomb. Two more supported the small curved structure, or apse, at the head of the interior behind the shrine.

Alterations in the sixth century made the six columns even more prominent. They were made into a screen in front of the tomb, rendering it invisible. For most visitors to the Basilica, the six swirling columns *were* St Peter's tomb.

The columns are extraordinary objects, elaborately fluted like a corkscrew or a piece of barley sugar. The sense of movement they embody is both wonderful and unsettling, because we expect columns to act as firm supports. This sense of dynamism is enhanced by their decoration with a combination of abstract and figurative forms. Parts of the columns are carved with sinuous lines moving upwards in a gentle spiral, tricking our eyes into believing they are animate. Alternate zones are populated with vines, with growing shoots, spreading leaves and bunches of luscious grapes. Little winged cupids fly in and out of the stalks, greedily grabbing the sweet fruit.

These cupids are acolytes of Dionysus, the ancient Greek god of wine, festivity and ecstasy. Constantine's use of such obviously pagan imagery for an important Christian shrine might seem strange, but his evident intention was to honour St Peter with innovative and striking pieces of architectural sculpture. And because of the role that wine plays in the Eucharist, the ceremonial re-enactment of the Last Supper when it becomes the Blood of Christ, they were appropriate in a Christian context.

The screen of columns (augmented by six more added by Pope Gregory III in the eighth century) became a defining feature of St Peter's Basilica, and was mentioned in the increasing number of guidebooks written for real or armchair pilgrims to the Holy City. Admiration and familiarity extended by degrees to imitation, and copies began to appear in churches across northern Europe, for example as far afield as the eighth-century royal burial crypt of St Wystan's Church in Repton, Derbyshire.

By the late fourteenth century, when the popes returned permanently to Rome after a seventy-year period of exile in France, the columns were no longer just beautiful things.

Somehow, these twisted columns had assumed the character of relics from Solomon's Temple, brought 'triumphantly' to Rome by Titus after his sack of Jerusalem in 70 CE, and stored in the Temple of Peace in the Forum. One of Gregory III's additions was even accorded the special status of being the 'Holy Column' on which the teenage Christ had leaned when disputing with the doctors in the Temple. It was attributed miraculous powers. Collectively, these originally pagan objects were henceforth known as the Solomonic Columns.

How and why all this happened is not really clear. Reliable record-keeping had certainly suffered when the popes and their efficient civil servants left the city for France. More generally, throughout fourteenth-century Europe, elaborate provenances were often created for old and revered sacred objects. In the case of Constantine's – or now Solomon's – columns, a combination of specific factors was at play. Because they were very old, beautiful and part of St Peter's tomb, they were particularly worthy of veneration. Perhaps most importantly, they could be connected – although they were not made of bronze – with Hiram's marvellous columns that are so evocatively described in the Book of Kings.

It took two great artists and two ambitious popes to cement the special status of the Solomonic columns and to make these objects critical to how Solomon's Temple was rebuilt in Rome. By 1515 Raffaello Sanzio, better known as Raphael, operated the most successful artistic workshop in Rome; he was the sworn foe of the equally talented (but less urbane) Michelangelo. Their rivalry was to produce some of the greatest works in the canon of Western art. Raphael had recently completed the redecoration of the pope's private apartments, known simply as the Rooms, or Stanze, with paintings celebrating the intellectual, spiritual and military power of the papacy. The project had been begun by one pope, Julius II, and finished by the next, Leo X, who succeeded him in 1513.

It was under Leo's papacy that the Protestant storm which had been brewing for almost a century finally broke. In 1517, Martin Luther nailed his ninety-five theses, identifying what he considered wrong in the Catholic Church, to a church door at Wittenburg in Germany. This was the beginning of a long, painful and multi-faceted upheaval within the Western Church, known as the Reformation, which transformed the political and theological face of Europe. In the face of this crisis, Leo concentrated on things he could actually achieve: securing the rule of his family, the Medici, in Florence, and transforming the Vatican and St Peter's Basilica into a complex befitting its status as the premier church in Christendom, the headquarters of the papacy and the spiritual home of a pope who was convinced he was following in King Solomon's footsteps.

Rebuilding the ancient church was never going to be quick – it took more than a century – although Raphael was eager to continue the process that had already been begun by his friend Donato Bramante. So Leo and Raphael came up with an ingenious, quicker and more impactful beginning to the lengthy process of re-creating Solomon's Temple. This was interior decoration, although of a very expensive and prestigious kind: a series of tapestries depicting the miracles described in the Acts of the Apostles, as performed by Saints Peter and Paul after Jesus' ascent into Heaven. These lavish hangings, designed by Raphael using huge drawings, known as cartoons, woven with silk, gold and silver thread, were destined for the

Sistine Chapel, the spiritual heart of the papal court and the site of papal elections.

Although the subjects were hardly surprising, Raphael's way of representing them was remarkable and closely connected to Leo's manifesto for his papacy. The pope seems to have believed that he had been elected to cure evil and erase differences, like Solomon himself. It's for this reason that Raphael made significant edits to the scene of St Peter's Healing of the Lame Man. This was the first miracle performed by St Peter in Jerusalem, and crucial for establishing his spiritual leadership of Jesus' followers, the community that would become the early Christian Church. The Acts narrate that Peter told a man, disabled since birth, to rise up and walk. Strength returned to the man's feet and ankle bones, and he followed Peter into the Temple. Raphael moved the location for this miracle from its biblical setting beside the 'beautiful gate' at the entrance to Jerusalem's temple complex to the portico of the building itself, where the great columns Boaz and Jachin are said to have stood.

Raphael's scene of Peter curing the man in Solomon's Temple, moreover, is framed by columns so large and dominant that they are almost protagonists in their own right. Their distinctive twists and curves, carved with panels of vines and cherubs, interspersed with sculpted lines, make it clear that Raphael is depicting the very objects that in his day still formed the screen protecting St Peter's shrine. Neither Raphael nor Leo doubted that these columns came from Solomon's Temple, and were the objects described in the Old Testament. Raphael crams his scene with spiralling Solomonic columns to give it greater veracity, and to explicitly connect St Peter's to Jerusalem, Leo to Solomon, and the lost temple to its reinvention in Renaissance Rome.

It took two more centuries for the Solomonic Columns of St Peter's to become an indivisible element of the fabric of the mother church of orthodox Catholicism. When the façade and dome of the Basilica were finally complete, the seventeenth-century pope Urban VIII turned his attention to the decoration of the vast interior. He largely entrusted it to his close associate and friend the sculptor, architect and painter Gianlorenzo Bernini. His biographer Filippo Baldinucci described his intensity, carving for perhaps seven hours a day, seeming to pour his life into hard marble and cast metal. It's impossible to look at his works in a cold, collected way – they were made to elicit visceral responses.

Bernini created a spectacular centrepiece in the form of an enormous bronze tent that covers the saint's tomb. It is experienced today as part of the building as a whole. Entering St Peter's is a deliberately daunting experience. The visitor feels insignificant, dwarfed by the scale and magnificence, from the marble columns that reach up to the golden roof and the floor of polished hard stones, to the vast sculptures that flank the columns of the nave. Commanding the interior, however, is Bernini's bronze baldacchino, which grows in scale as you approach the altar.

The structure is a permanent re-creation of the ephemeral constructions that were used in the open air to protect dignitaries or sacred objects from the people, as well from as the elements. Four curving bronze columns, sixty-six feet tall, twist majestically upwards to a framing cornice. Set on the top of each is an angel holding a garland that disappears under the cornice, giving the illusion that the angels themselves are holding the overarching crown of the structure. It's not clear if Bernini was aware that Constantine had covered Peter's tomb with a canopy borne by four spiral columns, but he certainly knew that Constantine had brought spiral columns from the Temple in Jerusalem.

Bernini's massive bronzes comprise three rather than the four sections found on Constantine's columns. The lower level consists of the abstract curved lines so familiar from the originals; the two carved upper sections are quite different. Although the (not so little) cupids are still present, the vines of the originals have been replaced with laurel leaves, and there's a further addition of buzzing bees. Pope Urban's family, the Barberini, used three bees on their coat of arms, interspersed with laurel leaves – which were also sacred to the sun god Apollo, considered by Christians of Raphael's and Bernini's days to be a pagan forerunner of Christ. Powerfully, and word-lessly, Bernini is imprinting his patron's identity all over an object designed to honour the Christian God.

The original Solomonic Columns were not forgotten in all this majesty. The piers that hold up the dome were hollowed out by Bernini, somewhat terrifyingly given what they support, to create galleries. From these the Basilica's most important relics – St Longinus' spear, St Veronica's veil, St Andrew's head and the largest fragment of the True Cross – were exhibited at Easter and other major feasts. Each gallery was divided into two sections. The top part held a tabernacle, where the relics were shown, each framed by two of the spiral marble columns, while the lower areas contained triple-life-size sculptures of Saints Longinus, Veronica, Andrew and Helena (Constantine's mother), designed by Bernini.

Bernini's open canopy – you can see through and beyond it to St Peter's throne in the apse – is the crowning glory of this great church interior. It makes the crossing a place of dramatic power, dignifying the tomb of the figure from whom the popes claim their authority and framing the spot on which the Mass is celebrated. No wonder that – despite the fabulous wealth of the papacy – it has never been replaced. The structure powerfully conveys, in architectural form, the claim of St Peter's to be the seat of the Christian Temple and the site of a New Jerusalem.

***

By any account, St Peter's Basilica, the Süleymaniye Mosque, Hagia Sophia and the Temple Mount are among the greatest works of human architecture. At their core is the idea that a building could embody God's presence, and enable people to make the leap in understanding that is faith. They are all shaped, in distinctive ways, by the blueprint of the lost Temple in Jerusalem.

These are very different buildings; not least because of the powerful and sometimes contending religions they serve. At a time when religious disagreement is often magnified to the extent that it can be hard to grasp any connection between faiths, it's important to reflect on the shared inspiration behind some of the world's most wonderful buildings made in the service of the divine. The spiritual power of a Temple destroyed almost two thousand years ago has stimulated a series of equally exceptional – and just as inspiring – structures. It is said that faith can move mountains, but buildings like these create and sustain faith.

The Roman Forum

3

ROME: SELF-BELIEF

First Century CE

Rome's origins are suspiciously precise. On 21 April 753 BCE the twin brothers Romulus and Remus are said to have founded a new city on the site beside the River Tiber where, as infants, they had been suckled by a she-wolf. The twins were the children of Rhea Silvia, daughter of the deposed king of Alba Longa, and the god Mars, and they had been left in this isolated place to die by their great-uncle Amulius, because of a prophecy that they would overthrow him. Whatever the origins of Rome – and no fantasy novel could supply a stranger or more imaginative story than this 'history' – for several centuries no one could have believed that this unlikely settlement would ever amount to very much.

Romulus and Remus's bloodthirsty struggles over the seven hills that one day would become Rome were parochial and insignificant beside what was going on elsewhere in the Mediterranean basin and the Near East. The Greek and Phoenician city-states (poleis), as well as the Egyptians, were building impressive urban civilisations, providing secure food through agriculture or trade for their growing populations and protecting their peoples with armies and navies. The poleis were exceptionally effective, creating strong cities which used their trading networks and military resources to set up satellite states or colonies around the Mediterranean coast.

In comparison to the Romans, the Macedonians were better soldiers, the Phoenicians better sailors and the Athenians better businessmen. If anyone in the seven centuries before the Common Era had been asked to name the Italian state to watch, they perhaps would have pointed to Etruria, in modern Umbria and Tuscany, or Greek-founded cities such as Naples and Syracuse. But by the second century BCE the Republic of Rome headed a loose confederacy of Italian states. It had been propelled there by its disciplined armed forces and the Romans' firm belief that their city was divinely ordained to overcome all obstacles.

Rome's rise

A surprising combination of circumstances made Rome into a world power in the mid-second century. In 146 BCE Carthage, one of the most ancient and significant cities of the Eastern Mediterranean, was razed to the ground, as the culmination of the Third Punic war. The city was burned for seventeen days by its Roman conquerors, so that it could never rise again, and the entire population was enslaved. A hundred years later, the Roman poet Virgil would create the tragic love story of Dido, Queen of Carthage, and the Trojan prince Aeneas (supposed ancestor of Romulus and Remus) to retrospectively justify the historic enmity of the Romans and the Carthaginians. At a stroke, Rome had become the most powerful empire in the Mediterranean. Its forces had already taken over the former Carthaginian territories in southern Spain. Now they seized the north African seaboard. In the same year, victory at the decisive Battle of Corinth enabled the Romans to assume control of the former Macedonian Empire and all its affiliated territories on mainland Greece and in the Aegean.

For the next two centuries, the Romans continued to expand their empire so that it covered Europe, the Middle East, the Sahel and parts of Mesopotamia. They were blessed with reasonably stable government, an exceptionally strong military machine and an efficient bureaucratic regime that could weather numerous regime changes over the 150 years during which Rome moved from republican to imperial rule. Rome's strength derived from its rootedness in the original city community, and the nascent empire's recognition that its subject peoples needed to feel part of the system of government, as well as proud to be part of the Roman state. They were therefore granted some level of citizenship and formal voting rights – even if lack of residence in Rome meant they could never exercise them – in exchange for military service.

After 146 BCE, Rome's enormous territorial possessions meant that the city-state was an empire in all but name. Governors were appointed, but in spite of the excellence of Roman transportation and communication networks it wasn't possible for them always to keep in direct contact with the capital. As a result, governors had to be trusted to manage local affairs, with at least some autonomy. Such was the strength of the bond of Rome that in most cases this was effective.

Local communities remained Roman partly because of military might, no doubt, but also because of the tangible benefits that Roman civilisation offered, both material and philosophical. Romans across the empire bought into the idea of 'Romanitas' – a commitment to strong moral principles and to legal and social norms which ordered society according to divine authority. There were also unusually generous prospects for social mobility: it was possible to move from enslavement to wealth and prestigious public positions within just two generations.

Without Rome and its indomitable self-belief, the history of the western hemisphere would have been very different. Most of the fundamental problems of the European continent have their roots in the political, economic and legal structure – altered, but still omnipresent – of Imperial Rome and its successor states. Roman precedents continue to shape the expectations and norms of Western culture, wherever it has been established and in whatever circumstances, all over the world. The forms of cultural expression that the Romans embedded – many adapted from the ancient Greeks – are still with us, from theatre to political discourse, and from grand public architecture to naturalistic sculpture and painting.

Partly this is because of the conscious creation of Roman-inspired buildings and art in medieval and modern Europe, and because of the role that the Spanish, the Portuguese and the Roman Catholic Church played in Europe's South American colonies. The moving image also helps – fantasy empires, as envisioned in series such as *Game of Thrones*, often recall Roman-built structures. But it is also because Western education was dominated by Latin for centuries – by the poetry of Virgil, Ovid and Horace, the natural history of Pliny, the rhetoric and philosophy of Cicero, the medical theories of Galen and the architecture of Vitruvius. Latin was the language of education, and of communication. Well into the late eighteenth century most scientific works were published in Latin, so that they would achieve as large a readership as possible. Very few of us learn Latin, or study Roman literature and history, today, but our lives are still shaped to a surprising extent by the legacy of Imperial Rome.

From Republic to Empire

The territorial growth of Rome was marked by increasing political instability. From the end of the second century BCE the Republic was racked by civil wars and popular risings, including by the numerous slaves who serviced the needs of citizens. Leaders who commanded huge armies in the field and exercised unrestricted power in the provinces became reluctant to bow to the authority of the Senate at home. Political structures that had been adequate for a small city-state were unable to cope with the ambitions that came with the expansion of Rome's possessions across the Mediterranean basin. The huge economic inequalities that increasingly existed between the elite and the mass of the populace further exacerbated tensions.

Conflicts broke out sporadically between the oligarchs and leading soldiers who banded together for short periods, chiefly to promote their own interests. In 48 BCE Julius Caesar, the soldier and politician who had conquered the wealthy province of Gaul, was elected dictator for ten years. This office had previously been used within the Republic during periods of emergency. Four years later, Caesar provoked a crisis when he was declared dictator for life – his enemies feared that he was emperor in all but name. Caesar was assassinated, and the Roman state plunged into further turmoil. We have an insight into the intrigues and shifting alliances of this tempestuous time through the writings of Cicero, who supported Julius Caesar but was betrayed by his great-nephew and heir, Gaius Octavius, better known to history as Caesar Augustus.

Augustus was a politician and leader of singular ability. Following Caesar's death in 44 BCE, he ruled the Roman Empire with Mark Antony and Gaius Lepidus. When this triumvirate was destroyed by the personal ambitions of each member, it was the youngest man, Augustus, who came out on top. After the Battle of Actium in 31 BCE he restored the mechanisms of the Republic, and the Senate, magistrates and citizen assemblies once more controlled the government of Rome.

In practice, Augustus gradually assumed all the powers of state as the first emperor of Rome. He may have been, as is often said, a committed republican, but he was determined that Rome should not slide back into civil war after his death. The Ara Pacis, the Altar of Augustan Peace, is Augustus' manifesto for Rome's future. In the July of 13 BCE, the Senate voted to erect the altar and offer yearly sacrifices on it, to honour Augustus' return from the conquest of Spain. This impressive sculptural monument gives a visual record of the harmonious, righteous and godly state of empire, as seen by Augustus, and those who had benefited from his regime.

The Ara Pacis formed part of a complex of monuments on the Field of Mars. This was the largest expanse of land in the centre of Rome, on the east bank of the Tiber. It had long been considered to belong to the people, to be used for voting and military exercises, but during Augustus' rule it was transformed into a huge memorial for him and his family. The altar was on the eastern side, off the Via Flaminia (today's Via del Corso in the centre of the modern city). At the north end was Augustus' own tomb, begun by the emperor more than thirty years before his death. There was also an immense sundial, its pointer a giant Egyptian obelisk and the hours marked by large gilded bronze numbers on paving stones, which linked Augustus to the rhythm of the seasons.

As a group these monuments were intended to erase republicanism and establish the right of Augustus' descendants, the Claudian dynasty, to rule the city and its empire. They were the clearest expression of how Augustus had transformed Rome (as he claimed on his deathbed) from a city of brick to one of marble. The altar itself, approached up steps as part of a horseshoe-shaped platform, was the site for annual sacrifices offered by Rome's magistrates, priests and Vestal Virgins, the priestesses consecrated to Vesta, goddess of the hearth. It stood within a rectangular marble box which could be entered from the east and the west. The entrances were on the equinoctial line; their measurements were determined so that on Augustus' birthday, coincidentally, the day of the September equinox, the shadow cast by the obelisk from the sundial would fall on the centre of the altar. Only priests could enter the enclosure, the interior of which was decorated with garlands carved in relief. Presumably the spaces around the enclosure were crowded on the annual feast days with senators, state officials and members of the imperial family, including (certainly in the first years of the altar's existence) some of the personages carved on the outside of the walls that surrounded it.

The sculpted decoration of these external surfaces relates to and dignifies the altar within, where blood sacrifices of animals were performed as the most holy and worthy rites of the state religion. Some details of the iconography are open to interpretation, but the longer sides depicted two processions that move in a westerly direction towards the place of sacrifice and ritual. That on the northern side shows priests and the imperial household, including members of the princely colleges.

These comprised the fifteen men, appointed by the Senate, who guarded and consulted the sacred oracles known as the Sibylline Books, and who were more generally required to 'perform sacred actions'. Also the group of seven who arranged sacrificial banquets, or public feasts that were connected to religious holidays.

Augustus is said to be shown in this procession. His image is given space in the frieze and many of the participants look in his direction. He wears a laurel wreath that distinguishes him from the other priests, or flamines, around him, who have distinctive leather caps, and the lictor, who carries the ritual axe used to slaughter the victim. Other members of the imperial household and family have also been inserted among the procession of priests. A woman, who like Augustus stands slightly apart from the others, is probably his only daughter, Julia, the wife of Marcus Agrippa (who died the year after the Ara Pacis was begun). At this moment, some fifteen years before her eventual disgrace and exile, Julia was seen as the matriarch of the imperial dynasty. The presence of women and children was highly unusual in a monument of this sort, and alludes to the importance of succession and genealogy in Augustus' plans for Rome and its territories.

At Julia's feet is a small boy with long hair and a large necklace around his neck; he is perhaps a barbarian prince from the eastern borders of the empire. Subject kings were often forced to send their heirs as 'guests' to the imperial court as a pledge of loyalty. The far right of the procession contains many of the younger generation of Augustus' family. Touching details suggest the personal connection between them. Antonia the Younger, mother of the future Emperor Claudius, looks expressively at her husband, Drusus Germanicus, as she clasps the tiny hand of their eldest son, Germanicus. The other young members of the imperial family, the future Emperor Nero's father Gnaeus Domitius and his older sister Domitia, stand close to their relatives. In a sweet gesture, the child Gnaeus holds on to the military cloak of his uncle Drusus Germanicus, while his mother, the elder Antonia, reassuringly clasps his shoulder. Little Gnacus looks up to his sister, as if for more support, and although the more mature Domitia stands by herself, she is encircled protectively by her mother and father. These details which humanise Augustus' family are typical of sculpture from the early Roman Empire. It tended to emphasise the youth, beauty and kindness of the imperial clan, and by implication their fitness to govern. Many Western leaders, from Renaissance princes to Napoleon Bonaparte, have followed such Roman models, particularly when looking to legitimise their rule.

The frieze on the south side of the monument represents more Romans, men, women and children. They are life-size, moving slowly and with dignity, thinking of the religious rite they will observe. The women and children are at the back; the men in this part of the procession are members of the priestly colleges, wearing laurel wreaths and holding herbs, carrying the jugs and boxes used in the sacred ritual. At the front, another lictor carries the fasces, an axe held within a bundle of birch rods, a symbol of Roman power and authority. This amalgamation of religious and secular authority was a salient feature of both Republican and Imperial Rome, giving its rulers a sense of purpose and destiny.

Augustus and his family traced their descent from Romulus and Remus. The ceremonial front of the altar enclosure showed the twins and Aeneas, so naturalistically that again the separation between the divine and the human is reduced. On the side that the public approached the altar, a veiled goddess suckles two male children. Personifications of the winds of the land and sea caress her with soothing breezes. Her precise identification is unclear, but she seems to encompass the peaceful fertility and fecundity of the earth. She was joined by the goddess Roma, seated beside a pile of weapons and flanked by two young men personifying Virtue and Honour.

For all that the friezes have been heavily restored and have lost all the painted colour that would have made them seem real, the Ara Pacis still has an overwhelming sense of vitality. The lifelike details of the procession make the remote figure of Augustus into something human and believable. It's striking how the Ara Pacis swarms with energy. Even the decorative friezes on the lower levels of the altar are filled with non-human life, from acanthus leaves, grapes and spring saffron to swans, salamanders and snakes. Maybe the most extraordinary detail is a nest of baby birds, presumably fallen from a branch, squeaking with terror with wide open beaks as a snake slides towards them across the ground. One has already left and is trying to escape on its spindly legs. Perhaps the message, chiming with the rest of the complex, is that if you believe in divine destiny and in Rome, there is nothing to fear.

Building the Pax Romanorum

By the time of the Ara Pacis's construction, a Roman subject could have travelled across the empire and – despite substantial regional differences – believed they inhabited the same world. Many towns and cities in the provinces had their origins in colonies, settlements for veteran soldiers and their families, whether they were constructed on the site of an earlier settlement, like Colchester in south-east England, Nîmes in southern France and Pompeii in Campania, or new towns built from scratch, such as Timgad in Algeria and Florence in central Italy. Each colonist – and this was a model used by Western conquerors long before and after the first century – was given a plot of land within the settlement boundaries, with the intention that by their presence they would order and civilise the newly conquered land. What had been barracks became houses.

From the Scottish borders to Mesopotamia, similar architectural and urban forms made Roman subjects, whatever their origins, feel at ease. All towns followed a recognisable pattern. In each centre, you would expect to find a forum, with grand civic buildings and the baths and water fountains essential for the necessities of life. And wherever you were, sculptures, paintings and mosaics would recreate the stories of the gods and goddesses, melded with local traditions and customs. This was the structural glue that bound the empire together and created its sense of identity and belief.

Many Roman towns were built on greenfield sites, where there had been little or no previous settlement, unambiguous expressions of Rome's cultural superiority and dominance over its subject peoples. This sort of development was so frequent that it was worthwhile for Vitruvius to provide guidelines for town planning in his book *On Architecture*, in order to help budding architects. The treatise was dedicated to Augustus and famously argues that architecture should be characterised by the three fundamental qualities of strength, utility and beauty. Vitruvius' work gives a clear sense of what Roman builders considered the essential elements of a town. First, a healthy site is required, far away from marshes, with good agricultural and pasture land nearby. The town should have a regular street pattern that makes sense of its topography. For instance, the forum should either be in the middle of the settlement or next to the sea, depending on where the town is located. Ever one for practical details, Vitruvius recommends that the basilica should be along the warmest side of the forum, so that lawyers and merchants can continue to meet there during the winter.

One of the longest shadows cast by the confidence of Imperial Rome is that the architectural language it adopted is still recognisable in the monumental architecture of towns and cities across Europe (and, indeed, much of the world). Roman buildings made brilliant structural use of the arch, but they were ornamented with forms drawn from different orders or modes of design. The orders are most obviously distinguished by the decorative treatment of the heads of columns, termed capitals. From Greek examples, the Romans borrowed the plain Doric, the Ionic with its elegant scrolled top, and the Corinthian, notable for its stylised acanthus leaves. They additionally created the Composite order, which combines the Ionic's scrolls with the Corinthian's foliage, and the Tuscan, a smooth, simplified version of the Doric. These orders provided the building blocks of Western classical architecture and can be found, copied or adapted, in every kind of building from churches and museums to schools, parliaments and government offices. In the Western world and in its former colonies, such forms are an easily understood symbol of authority.

In a very different way, twenty-first-century modernist architecture, based on a mid-twentieth-century aesthetic that in many ways attempted to reject history, is as deeply indebted to the Romans. They invented concrete, which although scarcely used in the West for fifteen hundred years after the decline of Roman rule, is now a crucial material in contemporary architecture. The Romans first used concrete – far more alluring in the sunny, relatively dry Mediterranean than in dank and dark northern Europe – for functional structures like bridges and walls (it has been alleged that seawater, volcanic ash and quicklime were the secret ingredients that made Roman concrete so much more durable than its modern successor). It was concrete that enabled the Romans to create extraordinary vaulted domes which defied gravity, such as the Temple to all Gods, the Pantheon, with its great rotunda of brick-faced concrete, or the Baths of Caracalla. Roman structures made of masonry and concrete, from baths and aqueducts to windmills and roads, are dotted over the landscape of Europe and Eurasia. Using concrete, stone and mortar, the Romans tried to shape the world for their purposes.

The road

Most of us have heard the expression 'all roads lead to Rome', and having a good road network was key to the success of the Roman Empire. All planned Roman cities were built around the meeting of two roads, the Cardo Maximus, running from north to south, and the Decumanus Maximus, from east to west. Roman roads were of exceptional quality, and maintained unstintingly and diligently. Main roads were generally around four metres wide, consisting of well-fitted blocks of paving stone on a bed of pounded pebbles and earth. Kerbs lined both sides, and by the Augustan period, milestones were always erected. Called cippi, these were little columns which marked the distance to the Forum Romanum in the centre of Rome. In the Forum itself, Augustus had installed the Milliarium Aureum, a column of gilded bronze that gave the names of Italian cities and their distances from Rome. Latterly, it became a verbal map of the empire, holding the names of the provinces, their rulers, the means by which they had been conquered militarily and the garrisons that were held there. The great names of the first Roman roads – including the Via Appia and the Via Francigena – endured long after the fall of Rome. Even in distant Britannia, Watling Street, Ermine Street, Fosse Way and others, running across England, Wales and parts of Scotland, and still in use today, bear the imprint of the Roman conquerors who left sixteen hundred years ago. Driving or walking along a previously winding road or path, its sudden straightness reminds you of its Roman past. Coming upon these relics of Rome in now remote localities, like the North Yorkshire moors or the Cumbrian fells, is a poignant reminder of the former power of the Roman Empire, and its ability to turn natural features to its own ends.

The Forum

The original Forum, set in a marshy flat area on the southern end of the Field of Mars, between the Capitoline and Palatine Hills, symbolised Roman power and authority, and the evolving combination of religion, exchange and commerce which was at the heart of Rome's identity. Here stood several of the most revered and venerated spaces, central to Roman belief. These included the circular Temple of Vesta, where two symbols of Rome were housed (the sacred flame of Vesta and the Palladium, a wooden statue of Athena saved from the wreckage of Troy); the Shrine of Janus, god of thresholds, which was closed to symbolise the peace of empire; and the Lapis Niger (Black Stone) covering what was thought to be Romulus' grave.

In the Republican era, the Forum was the setting for some of the most important events of Roman history. The Senate

House, site of many speeches and debates, was on the edge of the Forum complex, and it was outside the Temple of Concord that Cicero delivered his powerful oration against corruption and the Catiline conspirators (who had aimed to overthrow the consuls) in 63 BCE. On the rostra, the traditional setting for open-air speeches, Mark Antony gave Julius Caesar's funeral oration and Caesar's body was burned. Here too, Augustus built the temple to a new god, his great-uncle the Divine Julius.

The Forum was the centre of Rome's administrative and commercial world. It housed the basilicas where lawyers and merchants met, and which were also the setting for lobbying between senators, politicians and foreign visitors. The Via Sacra (Sacred Way) which ran through the Forum was used both for religious processions as well as the more prosaic transactions of everyday life. As the empire grew and the Republic receded, the Forum maintained its significance as a ceremonial centre. It was in every emperor's interest to enhance its role as a backdrop for imperial rituals. Augustus, and practically all his successors, erected some grand structure there. Triumphal arches, dedicated to Augustus, Tiberius and Septimius Severus, mark the entrances to its central area, while the Arch of Titus on the high point of the Via Sacra commemorates the short-lived emperor's victory over the Jewish rebels in Jerusalem in 70 CE. Temples to Vespasian, Titus, Aemilius Pius and the Empress Faustina – among others – joined those of the traditional Roman pantheon.

Wherever you went, across the empire, you would find a forum, on the model of Rome itself, with at least one temple, generally dedicated to Capitoline Jupiter as well as to the local deity. Their construction and maintenance was the responsibility of the local elite. There would be enclosed arcades and a basilica, where business could be undertaken in good and bad weather. A comitium, where assemblies of citizens gathered, was standard. And on the edge of the Forum, or close to it, would be another central element of Roman identity, the public bath.

The bath

Visiting the baths was widely asserted to be one of the major benefits of the Roman way of life. Agrippa's baths, built by Augustus's heir on the Field of Mars itself, were the first to be designated for a principally public use, but bathing, like many aspects of Roman civilisation, had its origins in the Greek city-states. However, in Rome it developed in a completely new form, emphasising pleasure as well as hygiene, and open to both sexes (although not together) – something that would have been anathema to the Greeks. Bathing became a key element of popular culture, one that distinguished the civilised from the barbarian. Bath complexes have been found across Roman territories, supported by emperors, the state and by wealthy citizens, who paid for heating, decoration and free bathing days. Even Vindolanda, a fort town on Hadrian's Wall in Northumbria, had a miniature version of the cold, steam, warm and hot baths found in the luxurious heart of empire. The survival of a tiny wooden sandal shows that children were taken to the public baths.

One of the best preserved bath complexes is the Forum Baths in Pompeii, first constructed in the first century BCE when the town became a Roman colony, and rebuilt only fifteen years before the fatal earthquake in 79 CE. Like many Roman buildings, the full lavishness of the structure was invisible from outside. If you were male, you would come in from the street through a small passageway and make your way to the atrium, or hall, open to the elements – not a problem south of Naples – where you paid your entrance fee and young men exercised. It was considered helpful to build up a light sweat before bathing. Women entered their own bath complex through a separate entrance (in other bathhouses, women and men attended separately, at different times of day).

The apodyterium, which came next, was where you undressed. In the Old Baths, there are still holes on the wall marking the placement of clothes hooks. The room was painted, there were benches around the walls and the upper levels of the walls were covered in plastered stucco decoration. You could choose to immerse yourself in the plunge pool of the frigidarium, or to begin the sweating and cleansing process that began in the tepidarium. As its name suggests, this beautifully decorated room was heated to a pleasant ambient temperature by a bronze brazier, and an underfloor heating system, called a hypocaust, fuelled by wood-burning furnaces. It would have felt deliciously warm to sit on the three bronze benches. This calming room gave pleasure for the eyes as well as the body. At Pompeii, it is possible to see the remains of the wine-red walls, the stuccoed and painted ceiling, and the mosaic floor. It was an impressive barrel-vaulted space, with cupids disporting themselves on dolphins and seahorses in the waters, mythological figures such as the goddess Venus wafted along by the breezes, and Ganymede, the cup-bearer of the gods, being taken to Mount Olympus by Jupiter in the form of an eagle. Beautiful naked and bearded male statues leaning against pillars, termed telamons, apparently held up the vaults.

Suitably relaxed, the bather progressed into the calidarium, or hot room. Its floor was directly above the furnace. Behind this was a hollow brick wall, which enabled the hot air to spread more evenly. The ever-practical Vitruvius recommended that the vaults in the hot room should have a double structure, so that the high moisture would have less impact on the ceiling timbers. Like the tepidarium, this was a beautiful space. At one end of the room was a hot pool (piscina calida), and at the other a round marble basin called a labrum, in a barrel-vaulted space resembling the apses of later Christian churches. The basin held cold water, which was poured over each bather's head as they left. The hot-bath process normally ended with an invigorating plunge in the frigidarium. It was a circular structure with an impressively decorated and colourful ceiling. Energetic bathers would look up at the dome to see plaster cupids racing on horseback or on two-horse chariots, with niches depicting pretty gardens filled with chirping birds.

It was possible to spend large parts of the day at the baths. After a morning's work, Roman men went there to relax. Dinner invitations were handed out, and much formal and informal business was done. A politician would canvass support from the baths, for instance. Bathing was a social and sometimes an intellectual experience: some, such as the Baths of Diocletian in Rome, had libraries attached to them. Baths, as the surviving complexes from Pompeii demonstrate, were beautifully and expensively decorated. Some of the largest and most impressive surviving Roman sculptures, the Farnese Hercules and the Farnese Bull, now in the Archaeological Museum in Naples, were excavated from the grandiose Baths of Caracalla in Rome.

The writer Seneca, who lived above a bathhouse, satirised the noises and activities of these establishments, from the grunting of the enthusiastic exerciser, the man who likes to hear his own voice as he bathes and the deliberately messy diver, to the even more annoying shrieks of those touting for business – the hair-plucker, the cake seller and other hawkers of wares. The poet Martial tells of men who hung around the bathhouse until they received a dinner invitation. They were also a notorious place to meet lovers, and ingenious ways were found of smuggling the opposite sex into men's and women's baths. Pliny the Elder comments sententiously that earlier generations of Romans would have been horrified by this laxity. However, the stern edicts proscribing mixed bathing, regularly issued from the second century CE onwards by emperors including Hadrian and Marcus Aurelius, are sure proof that this practice continued.

A 'typical' Roman town?

Layers of history and of building can make it hard to appreciate the 'Romanness' of many surviving towns and cities, even those founded by the Romans, such as London and Lyons. Nowhere is this truer than in the imperial capital itself. Modern Rome is a hive of activity, as it was two thousand years ago when its million inhabitants made it the greatest city in the world. Although the Forum, the Colosseum, the Pantheon and many other important structures survive – and others remain in part – the remnants of the ancient metropolis jostle with buildings of every period, none more destructive than the 'Wedding Cake' memorial to Italy's first king, Vittorio Emanuele, on the slope of the Capitoline Hill. Augustus's Ara Pacis was moved by Mussolini from the central Via del Corso to a site that was less disruptive of the modern city, closer to the the eastern bank of the River Tiber. Although this has made it easier to visit, it is confusing not to see this monument in its original location.

What did it feel like to live in a Roman town? The terrible tragedy of the violent eruption of Mount Vesuvius in 79 CE that totally destroyed Pompeii and Herculaneum, killed all their inhabitants and covered the surviving buildings under layers of volcanic ash and pumice does mean that we have good evidence for life in a more typical Roman urban centre than the capital. Pompeii is situated on the idyllic coast surrounding Naples that was one of the playgrounds of the Roman elite. They built luxurious villas and frequented resorts like Baiae, Herculaneum, Sorrentum and the island of Capri, to enjoy leisure, good living and excellent weather throughout the year. Pompeii was more of a working town. It had been conquered by Rome during the Social Wars (91–87 BCE) and resettled by the general Sulla as a colony for his soldiers. By the first century CE it was a commercial centre, celebrated for the manufacture of garum, a fermented fish sauce which was one of the most distinctive and popular elements of Roman cookery. Together with the large slave-farmed estates (latifundia) in the neighbouring countryside, Pompeii provided the food and resources for the tourists and second-homers along the coastline of Campania.

Long known by locals, the ruins of Pompeii were 'discovered' in the late sixteenth century, Herculaneum in 1709, and some decades later systematic excavation began at both sites under the patronage of the king of Naples, Charles VII. Many Grand Tourists, members of the northern European elite who travelled to Italy to finish their education, visited Vesuvius and the excavations. Those with large pockets, like the English gentleman Charles Townley, returned to their countries with antiquities to decorate their homes. Less wealthy tourists such as the writer Johann Wolfgang von Goethe shared their impressions of a lost town whose ruins demonstrated a love of the arts and good design 'common to the whole people'. Successive impressions of Pompeii have shaped our views of the Roman world, from the sensational descriptions of the eruption by the painter Karl Briullov, and the novelists Edward Bulwer-Lytton and Robert Harris, to the more indolent recreations of 'life' in Pompeii, in baths, luxurious villas and gardens by the late nineteenth-century artist Lawrence Alma-Tadema. At Pompeii, the marvel is that, despite the destruction of the volcano and of several centuries of excavation, you still feel that you are in a Roman town.

Walking down one street, the Via dell'Abbondanzia (Street of Plenty), takes you through the highs and lows of the Roman urban experience. Most visitors to Pompeii would have crossed this street, as it runs from one of the principal town gates to the Forum, intersecting with the other main street, Via Stabiana, on the way. Near the gates were several large houses, but as the street approached the junction with Via Stabiana and one of the town's main bathhouses, the number of commercial operations increased. Shops, bars, taverns, brothels, inns and workshops were crammed into the central section of the street. Larger, grander houses were mixed in with shops as you neared the Forum, together with two more public structures, the complex dedicated to the priestess Eumachia, and the Comitium, a place of public assembly.

The street would have been continually busy. How people moved around would have conveyed their status. Slaves would have run or walked briskly, doing their master's bidding, while the free born could amble as they pleased. The very rich and aristocratic never stepped out alone, but were always preceded by an entourage of clients or freedmen. You didn't even need to look up from the ground to know where you were. Outside the grander residences were pink mosaic pavements formed from ceramic fragments, superior to the average paving stone. Identity and status were literally part of the ground on which you walked.

Painting: a perfected Rome

Comparisons between ancient Greek and Roman art and civilisation tend to pigeonhole the Romans as pragmatic makers and the Greeks as innovators who established the norms that the Romans were to follow. It is certainly true that the Romans were astonishing builders. But they were also pioneering visual artists. In painting, they were able to create even more compelling imaginary worlds, offering windows into improved and idealised versions of reality that express their confidence and self-assurance.

According to Pliny's *Natural History*, it was the painter Studius, at the end of the first century BCE, who 'first instituted that most delightful technique of painting walls with representations of villas, porticoes and landscape gardens'. Studius had worked in Rome, probably for Emperor Augustus's daughter Julia and her second husband Marcus Agrippa, and he developed a lively and spirited style of painting that, although indebted to Greek precedent, is uniquely its own. Roman wall-painting is notable for its illusionism, theatricality and love of details that fool the viewer into believing that they are seeing real objects, rather than painted simulacra that trick the eye.

Painting directly onto a plaster wall is difficult. Because the wet paint becomes part of the wall, you can't easily make changes as you work. And if the wall isn't free of moisture, your painting will disintegrate. Vitruvius writes that artists were encouraged to insert lead sheets into walls, to prevent dampness rising to the painted surface. The preservation issues mean that few Roman wall paintings have survived, and it's more than faintly ironic that the best-preserved examples owe their survival to the eruption of Vesuvius. A mile or so north of Pompeii lies Boscoreale, the 'Royal Wood', where the villa of Publius Fannius Synstor was located. Excavated in 1901, the villa was covered with strikingly coloured *trompe l'oeil* paintings that seem to date from the end of the Roman Republic, when painters in Studius' wake were striving to create convincingly three-dimensional fantasy worlds on flat surfaces. The quality of the painting meant that it was not updated by Fannius, who owned the villa about a century later.

One complete room is now in the Metropolitan Museum of Art in New York. Entering the Boscoreale cubiculum is a marvellous privilege. The lucky inhabitant of this bedroom, presumably the villa's owner or a close family member, would have been transported by the frescoes into a world of sublime dreams. Two Corinthian columns with illusionistic squares show where the bed would have been located. Along each of the long walls of the oblong room, you move from cityscapes through an enclosed garden towards a central shrine, each containing a statue of a goddess. The artist has used an early version of perspective, depending on receding lines which converge at multiple points along a central axis, in order to give depth to the flat surface. Large, decorative but closed doorways lead into strange building complexes, topped with balconies and little turrets that are almost mirror images of each other. It is beautiful, although confusing and strange.

The short wall, beside the bed, is perhaps the most wonderful. Again, you are invited to move from the corners into the centre. On either side, a fountain is invitingly placed in front of a grotto, partly covered by vines, on which birds are perching and trilling. Atop the rocky opening is an open colonnaded structure with vines laden with inviting grapes. The room is lit by a real window – the illusion being that a garden such as this awaited just outside. In the centre of the wall, broken up by the window, is a yellow panel. It seems to mimic either a carved low relief marble or a painting. On it are depicted houses, towers, colonnades, a bridge, fishing boats and possibly an aqueduct. On top of this work of fictious art sits a glass bowl, filled with appealing fresh fruit. Everything – fine art, peaceful birdsong, a well-maintained garden, even food – is ready for the sleeper when they awaken.

Painting of this quality and scale evaporated with the collapse of the Roman Empire. It would not be seen again for over a thousand years. And in its time, it could only have been accessible to the lucky few. Thanks to the chance survival of the villa under volcanic ash, and the movement of its paintings to a public museum, we can all experience the luxury, confidence and novelty of Rome. Although almost two thousand years old, this bedroom uses a visual language that is very familiar today. No one has ever managed to impose such artistic consistency as the Romans did. In buildings, in art, in film and even with our own screens we create visual illusions that remain profoundly indebted to the self-belief, tenacity and innovation of the Roman Empire.

Gold dinar of Harūn al-Rashīd

4

BAGHDAD: INNOVATION

Eighth Century CE

In the summer of the year 758, the most powerful man in the world spent 'the sweetest and gentlest night on earth' in a place where 'everything pleased him'. This was not a glittering palace or a magnificent temple, but a quiet spot beside a Christian church on the banks of the Tigris. The man was the Abbasid caliph Mansūr, and he was seeking the perfect place to build a new capital for the empire inaugurated by his brother Saffāh. Mansūr, a direct descendant of the Prophet Muhammad's paternal uncle Abbās (hence the Abbasids), was the surprising beneficiary of his family's sudden rise from prosperous obscurity in southern Jordan to rulers of most of the Muslim world, from North Africa to the Indus River in modern Pakistan. Having woken from his reviving sleep, the caliph is said to have declared, 'This is the site on which I will build.'

It was not simply the beauty of the place, on an 'island' of land between the rivers Tigris and Euphrates, that attracted Mansūr. Strategically and practically, there could hardly have been a better site for the foundation of the 'City of

Peace' (Madīnat as-Salām). It was right in the middle of the Abbasid territories, connected by water and land routes to the Mediterranean and the Persian Gulf, and to their military support base at Khurasan on the borders of China. It could dominate trade across the northern hemisphere, drawing goods and raw materials from underdeveloped Europe and sophisticated China. The great ninth- and tenth-century Arab historian and theologian al-Tabari, a long-term resident of Baghdad conveys Mansūr's confidence: 'This is the Tigris. There is no obstacle between us and China. Everything on the sea can come to us.'

Baghdad, like ancient Babylon before it, would exploit the fertile land between the rivers, irrigated by a further network of canals, to feed its population (perhaps eight hundred thousand strong within forty years of its foundation) and the caliph's army. Mesopotamia was by far the richest province of the Abbasid Empire. Its substantial tax revenues enabled the caliph to build his city, to furnish it with grand palaces and mosques, and – together with the city's elite – enjoy a lifestyle which made Baghdad the cultural capital and envy of the known world. This is the period that passed into legend as the setting of the *Arabian Nights*.

Mesopotamia's rich history as the fabled location of the Garden of Eden and heartland of the great Babylonian, Sassanian and Parthian Empires added a veneer of historical respectability to the brand-new capital of an *arriviste* empire. The crumbling ruins of Babylon were less than forty miles south on the Euphrates. Although there's no evidence that Mansūr visited the site, he must have been aware of its significance. Closer still was Ctesiphon, former capital of the Sassanian Empire. Mansūr is said to have contemplated demolishing the late sixth-century Emperor Xosrow Anōšīravān's palace, so that the bricks could be used in the construction of Baghdad, to underline the superiority of his Muslim empire. Only the cost of demolition saved the Tāq Kasrā, which is still today the largest single-span brick arch in the world. Memorably photographed from the air by Roald Dahl as a young trainee pilot in 1940, the surviving vault crowned the arcaded hall (iwān), in front of the throne room. Its ambition, innovation and technical brilliance inspired Mansūr and his successors as they strove to build a fitting capital.

Round City

From the start, Baghdad was envisioned as a sprawling metropolis. At its heart was the Round City, encircled by three rings of walls constructed of mud brick, for centuries the favoured building material in this part of the world. The striking circular design, based on the geometric proportions devised by the Greek philosopher Euclid, was as much a project of engineering as architecture. The weight of the whole structure, and each of its individual elements, was assessed to ensure that large towers and walls would not collapse. One story recounted by al-Tabari in the tenth century tells that when a section of wall was demolished, the workmen found a brick with a note saying that it weighed 117 ratls – about forty-six kilos. They weighed the brick and found that this was accurate. This tale, even if untrue, testifies to the attention to detail reflected in every aspect of this project.

The ninth-century writer al-Jahiz extolled the perfection of the city's form, as though it had been poured into a mould and cast: 'I have never seen a city of greater height, more perfect circularity, more endowed with superior merits or possessing more spacious gates or more perfect defences.' This made it an expression of paradise on earth. Less idealistically, it enabled the caliph to observe and control everything. The unfortunate combination of sieges and Mansūr's notorious parsimony (he would not fire the bricks for the city wall because of the cost of firewood) means that nothing survives of the Round City today.

Some evidence can be gleaned from a surviving palace at Ukhaydir, about 120 miles south, the fragmentary remains of the walls at Rafiqa in northern Syria, and from the Abbasid pleasure capital of Samarra. But the principal evidence for reconstructing Mansūr's lost city comes from texts – al-Khatīb al-Baghdadi's compendious eleventh-century *History of Baghdad*, the ninth-century geographer al-Yaʿqūbi's *Book of Countries* and al-Tabari's *History of the Prophets and Kings*. We are told that Mansūr made the workmen trace the plan of the city on the ground, using cinders from a fire. He then walked through the site to personally approve every inch of the ground plan, and is said to have laid the first brick with his own hand. Everything, from the form, materials and foundation date (30 July 762, chosen on the advice of the court astrologer Nawbaḫt) to the construction methods was decided by the caliph. As the city crystallised his theory of rule in physical form, every detail mattered.

In the central hub of the wheel were two major buildings on a large square – the Palace of the Golden Gate and the Great Mosque of al-Mansūr – along with a military barracks. Everything in Baghdad was centred on the palace. At its heart was the throne room and audience chamber, preceded by a vaulted hall, open on one side in the Persian fashion. The audience chamber was crowned by a green dome 130 feet high, supporting a statue of a horseman bearing a lance. It was said that this figure, placed at the highest point in the palace, could be seen from every location in the city. Later, it was alleged that the horseman had magical properties, and would turn his lance in the direction of approaching enemies. Be this as it may, he could not protect the Round City from attack, first during a civil war between two of Mansūr's great-grandsons and then during the Mongol invasions of 1258. The dome and the horseman were already no more: they had collapsed during the storms of March 941. Subsequently much of the Palace of the Golden Gate was pulled down to facilitate expansion of the mosque.

But before it was demolished, elements of this highly influential building were copied in the palaces of Muslim rulers across central and southern Asia. Delegations from the empire were received in the iwān, according to a strict protocol and order that was inherited by the Ottoman Empire. Mansūr and his heir Mahdi sat cross-legged on a raised platform covered with quilts and cushions. The audience chamber was a place for even more important pronouncements. Here governors were appointed and state proclamations read out. The chamber was used for public audiences, which in theory could be attended by everyone, whatever their rank, where they could ask for the caliph's help. The idea that the caliph should be able to intervene on behalf of the poor and dispossessed was a central tenet of orthodox Islamic rule.

The Great Mosque was built by Mansūr to stand next to his palace, signifying the symbiosis of religion and state. It had a simple design, reflecting what we know of Mansūr's orthodox spirituality. Unlike the palace, this was a functional building, animated by faith and activity rather than decoration. Made from unbaked clay bricks, it was a square building with a prayer hall, a large central courtyard and a portico running around its sides, supported by wooden columns. Mansūr was much involved in the practices of the mosque, regularly preaching to supplement and sustain his political authority. Over time, however, the caliph detached himself from the daily life of the mosque. By the 1160s, when the Jewish traveller Benjamin of Tudela visited Baghdad, it seems that Mansūr only came to the mosque once a year, at the end of Ramadan.

From the central square, four arcaded avenues radiated through three successive lines of wall to each of the city's gates, which led on to the key imperial cities of Kufa, Basra, Khurasan and Damascus. To leave or enter Baghdad, you had to pass through an immense vaulted gateway crowned by a dome. The iron gates were so heavy that many doormen were required to pull them open. Al-Tabari writes that the four external gates, and the ones that gave access to the Palace of the Golden Gate, had been made for King Solomon. The truth of this statement is less important than its symbolism. Mansūr and his successors were keen to demonstrate both their debt to the other People of the Book and the relative religious tolerance their regimes offered.

The building of Baghdad was as much about creating an Abbasid identity as it was about erecting a city. So it was important that those engaged in the construction were not slaves but people who chose to be there. The numbers attached to this city are often prone to exaggeration and it's unlikely, in spite of what al-Tabari and others tell us, that there were ever as many as a hundred thousand labourers and craftsmen on site. However, the city certainly drew workmen from all over the Abbasid territories. Part of the attraction was pay. Workers were reportedly paid one-twelfth of a dirham per day; a supervisor double this. When you consider that one dirham would buy thirty kilos of dates, now as then a very important foodstuff in the Middle East, this was a substantial wage. By remunerating his workers so well, Mansūr ensured that the most skilful and valuable people in his realms would move with their families to Baghdad. The new city would have every advantage, including talented inhabitants.

Reputation

Given the resources poured into the creation of Baghdad, it is not surprising that the city became the epitome of sophistication and innovation. The city was a melting pot, synthesising the civilisations of the Near East, the Mediterranean, the Sassanians and central Asia. The requirements of the court, and the noble families associated with it, created a demand for beautiful objects that enabled the necessities of life – eating, drinking, sleeping, washing and dressing – to be accomplished in the most luxurious fashion. Although the destruction of the Round City has deprived us of one of the world's greatest architectural and artistic sites, we are not entirely at sea in attempting to evoke the internal riches of its palaces, mosques and civic buildings. Literary sources, archaeological evidence from Samarra and surviving objects from across the Abbasid world enable us to piece together some of the opulent and commodious interiors in the great city founded by Mansūr.

The city's reputation spread as far as north-west Europe. In 802, Mansūr's grandson, Harūn al-Rashīd, exchanged gifts with Charlemagne, who had been crowned Emperor of the Romans two years earlier. Charlemagne's chroniclers, Einhard and Nokter the Stammerer, extol the magnificence of the court at Aachen in modern Germany, as well as the gifts of Spanish horses, Dutch hunting dogs and fine cloaks that the

emperor sent to Baghdad. These offerings paled into insignificance beside the riches the caliph sent to Europe – fabulous
textiles beyond anything that could be seen in Europe, brass
candelabra, an ivory chess set, perfume and balsam, a tent
with many-coloured curtains, and the *pièce de résistance*, an
elephant called Abul al-Abbas. Five years later, a water clock
arrived. This marked the hours with bronze balls dropping
into a bowl of water, a crash of cymbals and the appearance of
twelve horsemen out of doors. It was so sophisticated that certain members of the court thought that magic and sorcery must
be responsible for its workings. The caliph's gifts made a deep
impression on all who saw or heard of them. Charlemagne's
court, for all its relative refinement, was risibly provincial in
comparison to Baghdad.

Even golden Constantinople was found wanting. Al-
Khatib's *History of Baghdad* gives a long account of the
reception given to an embassy of Byzantine courtiers sent
by Emperor Constantine VII Porphyrogenitus to Baghdad in
the year 917 to reclaim captives taken in battle. The ambassadors were taken around the palace, where they saw seven
thousand eunuchs, seven thousand chamberlains and four
thousand additional Black servants. Store chambers were
thrown open so that they could admire the extent of the
caliph's wealth. Jewels, textiles, hangings, golden curtains,
carpets and other valuable possessions were laid out for them.
They were processed through a glorious succession of courts,
audience halls and gardens, among them a hall with one hundred lions and a pool made of tin, surrounded by a similarly
lined water channel, 'more lustrous than polished silver'. As
the culmination of the visit, they met Caliph al-Muqtadir, in
an audience lasting no more than a few minutes. The ambassadors were overwhelmed by the depth of wealth and power

Pieter Bruegel the Elder, *The Tower of Babel*, around 1560 CE

Proto-Cuneiform tablet with seal impressions, 3100–2900 BCE

The Cyrus Cylinder, after 539 BCE

1930s reconstruction of the Ishtar Gate completed using original bricks from c. 575 BCE

Panel with striding lion from the Processional Way, c. 604–562 BCE

The Lion of Babylon, 605–562 BCE

Detail of Adad and Marduk from the Ishtar Gate

Interior view of the
Dome of the Rock, built
between 685 and 692 BCE

The Baldacchino, St Peter's
Basilica, Rome, 1624–33 CE

Exterior view of Hagia
Sophia, completed 537 CE

Interior view of Hagia Sophia, completed 537 CE

Interior of the Süleymaniye Mosque, 1550–7 CE

Two of the 'Solomonic' columns brought by Constantine to Rome, installed on the sides of the tabernacle designed by Bernini housing relics of the True Cross, seen through Bernini's Baldacchino, St Peter's Basilica, Rome, 1629–40 CE

Raphael, *The Healing of the Lame Man,* c. 1515–16 CE

View of the exterior of the Ara Pacis Augustae, Rome, 13–9 BCE

Detail of floral frieze, Ara Pacis Augustae

Short wall of the Boscoreale cubiculum, Pompeii, c. 50–40 BCE

View of the Forum, Pompeii, with Vesuvius in the background, first century CE

Caldarium in the Forum Baths, Pompeii, c. 64 CE

Corbridge, Hadrian's Wall, c. 160–300 CE

Internal view of the Pantheon, Rome, 118–125 CE

Bowl with Kufic inscription, 'Made by Abu al-Taqi', ninth century CE

Haram wall painting fragments, Samarra, ninth century CE

Spanish textile fragment with wrestling lions and harpies, early twelfth century CE

Astrolabe by Khafif, apprentice of Àli ibn ʿĪsā, ninth century CE

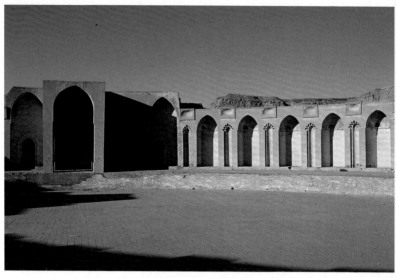

Residence of the Caliph Mu'tasim, Samarra, ninth century CE

Pair of teak doors carved in the bevelled style, ninth century CE

Scholars in the library of the House of Wisdom, from the *Maqamat al-Hariri*, 1236–7 CE

that was shown to them, a setting more appropriate to gods than mere mortals, and their resolve crumbled in the caliph's presence. Even accounting for the dramatic exaggeration common to such descriptions, where nothing deserves less than a superlative, there is no doubt that Baghdad was one of the most impressive and prosperous civilisations of the medieval world. It's no coincidence that many of the *Thousand and One Nights*, that collection of compelling tales recounted by the Princess Sheherazade to save her life (and probably first compiled in eighth-century Cairo), were set in the capital of the Abbasid Empire. Real historical figures including the quixotic but benevolent Caliph Harūn al-Rashīd, his powerful vizier Jafar al-Barmaki and the poet Abu Nuwas are mixed with fantasy in its pages. The enduring appeal of the *Thousand and One Nights* among people of various faiths, time periods and countries meant that well into the twentieth century Baghdad remained a byword for sophistication, innovation, power and wealth.

Moveable riches

Textiles, or *farsh* – rich brocaded silks, embroidered cloths, woven tapestries – were key elements of the ornate and richly coloured interior decoration of Abbasid palaces and homes. Because of their fragility, very few textiles have survived. Many of those that have owe their existence to the sacred value they held for European Christians. Their intricate patterns, stylised depiction of beasts and birds, and incorporation of words and script into borders were emulated, collected and copied across the Western world. They can be found in the treasuries and sacristies of cathedrals, as part of priestly vestments and the wrappings of sacred relics, and in the tombs of princes when they were laid to rest.

The obsession with fabrics can be explained by the Abbasid dynasty's origins as a campaigning army. Mansūr himself had spent much of his youth in tents, and he continued to live like this after Baghdad was built. His cousin Mohammed ibn Sulayman paints a compelling picture of visiting the caliph on a cold day when he was recovering from illness. He was taken to 'a tiny apartment consisting of one room with a portico on one side supported on one teak column separating it from the court. He had hung rush mats up in the porch as they do in mosques ... I went into his room and there was a felt mat and nothing else apart from his quilt, a pillow under a blanket.' Mansūr's son and heir Mahdi also lived with portable possessions, although they were distinctly more lavish. In the early 780s, the grand vizir was summoned to the caliph's private apartments. He found Mahdi in a room with rose-coloured cushions and textiles, looking out on to a fragrant rose garden, accompanied by a beautiful slave girl dressed in matching rose-coloured garments.

Further literary accounts, such as al-Shābushtī's eleventh-century *Book of the Monasteries* (Kitāb al-Diyārāt) mention the extensive floor coverings in the palaces of the Abbasid caliphs at Samarra. These were also features of middle-class dwellings. The ninth-century *Brocaded Book* (Kitāb al-Muwashshā) by al-Washshā describes the interiors of well-to-do citizens of Baghdad, focusing particularly on the curtains and pillows woven with quotations from poetry. Inscribed textiles, or *tiraz* (the name comes from the Persian word for embroidery), were highly important in the early Islamic world. They were produced in private (*khassa*) factories for the caliph and his court, and public (*'amma*) workshops for the upper classes, and for wider use. The caliph would bestow *tiraz* decorated with his name and the date and place of manufacture on loyal subjects, or those whose support he desired. These precious silks were so desirable that they were widely imitated, and even forged. the value placed on Iraqi textiles was demonstrated by the creation around the year 1100 CE, in Andalusia in southern Spain, of silk fabric, part of the shroud of a Spanish Christian bishop, whose inscription states, firmly against the material evidence, that it was made in Baghdad.

Baghdad and Samarra

Somewhat paradoxically, the best evidence for the art of Baghdad comes from Samarra. For less than sixty years, from 836 to 892, this city on the flat plain north of Baghdad was the capital of the empire. Civil unrest in Baghdad explained the move. Meaning 'he who sees it is delighted', Samarra was to be a new metropolis for Caliph Mu'tasim's pleasure, served by a canal network, ceremonial avenues, grand palaces and monumental mosques as well as with gardens, polo grounds and racecourses. Aerial photography conveys its massive scale, like a sprawling Midwestern American city. There was so much space that when a new building was planned, there was no need to knock down and rebuild. But it was equally possible for buildings literally to melt back into the clay from which they came.

Because modern Samarra developed on an adjoining site, much of the fabric of Abbasid Samarra has remained at least partially intact. As a result, it provides outstanding evidence of the artistic and archaeological innovations and achievements of the caliphate (and it could give so much more since, to date,

80 per cent of the site remains unexcavated). Thanks to the investigations begun by the pioneering German archaeologist Ernst Herzfeld in the early twentieth century, documented in his meticulous papers and drawings, as well as in millions of archaeological fragments and artefacts divided between museums across the world, it's possible to understand some of the riches of this fabulous site. However, like Babylon and many other Iraqi sites, it remains extremely vulnerable. One of its greatest elements, the al-Malwiyyah spiral minaret, was used as a military base during the Iraq War. It was damaged during a terrorist attack in 2005 and remains on the UNESCO 'at risk' register.

The principal palace in Samarra was the Dar al-Khilafa, or Palace of the Caliphate. It stood above the Tigris, surrounded by beautiful gardens that ran down to the river. The palace was built around a succession of courtyards and benefited from piped water, bathhouses and pavilions, toilets, stables, cellars and cooling water features. Polo fields, racecourses and quarters for the emperor's guards adjoined the palace. Only the triple-arched entrance gate, the Bab al-Amma, still stands, giving a sense of the palace's magnificence. It led to the public areas of the palace, which covered the southern part of the complex. Visitors would have travelled through a grand vaulted hall and several courtyards before reaching the domed audience chamber. It was even more impressive than the Palace of the Golden Gate in Baghdad, with no less than four iwāns leading off it. This grand cruciform space was used for public audiences, while private guests were entertained in adjoining smaller chambers.

Writing around the year 1000, al-Shabushti recorded earlier accounts of the throne room at Samarra in the 860s, glittering with huge images in gold and silver. The throne itself was made of gold, with lions and eagles 'just as the throne of Solomon King of David [sic] is described'. The room contained a fountain, lined with silver, with a golden tree so lifelike that birds perched and sang on it. The walls of the palace itself were covered with mosaics and gilded marble. These descriptions may seem hyperbolic, but at least part of them are corroborated by the archaeological evidence. Herzfeld and other scholars have devoted their lives to reconstructing the palace's staggeringly opulent internal fittings from the fragments they found crushed on the floors of the ruined interiors.

These rooms were brightly coloured, in varied shades that Herzfeld recorded in evocative terms like 'pistachio green', 'peacock', 'chickpea', 'sand', 'pearl' and 'tin'. The domed audience hall was covered with carved panels of stucco plaster and marble – rare in Iraq, and imported from quarries to the west – and with ceilings, beams, doors and frames of teak imported from the Indian subcontinent. These materials were carved and sometimes painted in semi-abstract, rhythmic and symmetrical patterns, formed of curved and slanted lines ending in spirals. This is known as the Samarran or bevelled style. There's a mesmeric dynamism in these forms, whose patterns are never-ending and have a hallucinogenic quality. Animals and natural shapes seem to come and go before your eyes in these intricate outlines.

The private quarters were as remarkable as the great hall. Some of the walls were covered with plaster or ceramic tiles, fired with bright colours and streaks of metallic glazes, showing plants, animals and Arabic letters. Others had intricate designs made with pieces of mother-of-pearl and clear mould-blown glass, and repeating bull's-eye decorations made from multi-coloured glass rods. The floors were beautiful to behold, with pavements made of tiles, black glass and marble, along with millefiori glass. You can imagine how these would shine and catch the eye in the strong sun of central Iraq, or intensify the cooling calm of the fountains and pools. The lighting of these spaces was subtle and varied, with glass windows coloured from aquamarine to amber tinting the marble and stucco surfaces.

Other archaeological finds give a sense of how these rooms were used: fragments of metal goblets, glass jars for storing perfume, bronze sticks for applying eye make-up, nails and metal fixings, ceramic plates and bowls for eating and drinking, and even an extraordinarily heavy white porcelain basin, imported from Tang dynasty China, were all found by Herzfeld and his team.

We should imagine that the palaces of Baghdad were similarly sumptuous. Like those of Samarra, they would have included many ceramic tiles and vessels. Those produced in Abbasid Iraq, principally at Samarra and the port city of Basra, are some of the most beautiful and innovative made in the medieval period anywhere in the world. The ceramics industry was sponsored by the caliph and his court to rival and surpass the Chinese porcelain brought by a tortuous sea route to the mouth of the Persian Gulf, and thence by land to Baghdad and Samarra. Ceramics can break, but they don't decompose, making them the best-preserved of artworks. They give us the clearest sense of how people lived, and what they valued, even if they survive in a fragmentary form.

Their forms and colours are testimony, in their multiplicity of forms and their hybridity, to the Abbasid caliphate's desire for synthesis. Shapes were taken from Sassanian metalwork, Chinese ceramics and metal cups. Others were simply invented by their makers. The typically Abbasid palmate and idealised natural forms, stylised animals and faces were copied across the Near East and Europe. But the two major innovations were technical.

Inspired by the tactile beauty of Chinese white porcelain – lovely to touch and to cradle in the hand, hardwearing yet delicately translucent – Iraqi potters tried to imitate its purity and simplicity. Without kaolin, the fine white clay from near Jingdezhen that is the magic ingredient required for bone china, or kilns with a reliable high-firing temperature, it was impossible to make porcelain. But they discovered that bowls made from yellow clay, when fired with an opaque white glaze made from tin, resembled it from a distance. Ten parts silica or quartz, one part glass frit and one part clay were mixed into a paste that was kneaded like bread dough. It soon became the preferred material of most Islamic potters, and this fritware was exported across the Mediterranean and Europe.

The Iraqi potters were evidently not completely satisfied with their pure white objects and so added colourful and painterly decoration, using cobalt blue imported from Iran. A ceramic artist would take a brush and paint an inscription in Arabic in a wet cobalt glaze onto a raw glazed white dish or bowl. The decoration was fixed in a single firing; during this process, the coloured layer developed a slightly blotted surface that is poetically called 'ink in snow'. Many of these objects, which are so close to modern taste, bear the artist's name and blessings on the user. Often these are hard to decipher. We feel tantalising close, and yet so far, from these extraordinary artistic achievements. They were also exported to China, where this technique of drawing with cobalt – now considered the archetypal Chinese art form – inspired a new tradition of 'blue on white' porcelain.

The resources and support of the Abbasid court also enabled potters to experiment with lustre, a bright metallic glaze often further decorated with silver and gold. Lustreware is exceedingly complex to make as it consists of applying metal oxides to a piece that has already been fired. The second firing takes place in a low-oxygen environment, and the kiln temperature needs to be carefully controlled. The resulting pots glisten with a sheen that can range from copper to gold, dependent on the metal oxides used. There would have been many failures before success was achieved. It would have been difficult, even in a region as rich as Abbasid Iraq, to have reliable quantities of wood for the kiln, as well as the technical skills required to maintain consistent temperatures for the double firing and the reduced oxygen for the lustre phase. The late twentieth-century British potter Alan Caiger-Smith took twenty-six trial firings before he achieved any lustre on his pots. And, as Caiger-Smith remarked, he was able to rely on medieval manuals, such as Abu'l Qasim's fourteenth-century treatise. The Abbasid innovators in this art form had nothing to go on but their own skill and intuition. The quantity and quality of the fragments from Samarra show how marvellously they succeeded.

House of Wisdom

One of the most compelling notions that developed in Abbasid Baghdad was that it represented a House of Wisdom, or a compendium of the best ideas from different eras and from different intellectual and religious perspectives. Its purpose was to stimulate and provoke further intellectual ferment and discovery, and is visualised in a thirteenth-century manuscript illumination by Yahya ibn Mahmud al-Wasiti. Turbaned scholars squat on the floor, listening to one of their number read from a large book. Behind them rises a large and beautiful open library. Each alcove is stacked with ordered piles of books. There is no doubt that the city was full of hundreds of thousands of such manuscripts. During the Mongol siege of 1258 they were thrown into the river in such numbers that the Tigris was said to have run black with ink.

But many historians would now say that the House of Wisdom, or Bayt al-Hikma, had no physical, and perhaps even no intellectual, status. What is seems to have been, in fact, was a court institution that the Abbasids inherited from the Sassanians, where Persian manuscripts were stored and sometimes translated. The intellectual ardour of Baghdad in the eighth, ninth and tenth centuries is more exciting than the concept of the House of Wisdom. Discovery and innovation were so intrinsic to the court culture of most of the caliphs that not just Baghdad, but many of the empire's cities, were vibrant centres of intellectual discovery. It's often said that ancient Greek and Roman literature owes its survival to the Italian Renaissance, but what was really key was the contribution of Islamic scholars during the Abbasid Empire.

The court and the mansions of princes were centres for the gathering of ideas. Mansūr stimulated an existing custom of translating texts from Pahlavi, and especially from Greek, into Arabic so all educated men could read them. This movement gained real impetus under Caliph Ma'mūn, who had returned to Baghdad from Merv in modern Turkmenistan after a disastrous civil war, which had continued even after he had murdered his brother and destroyed the only likely rival for the throne. Ma'mūn had to bind his empire and court together. One of his solutions was to create a court elite who were connected by their membership of an intellectual caste who valued learning, and who were able to square this with their faith. It was so successful that most of his successors copied his example.

Scholars were attracted to Baghdad because here, either under the patronage of the caliph and his family, or one of the great court families such as the Banū-Mūsa clan, it was possible to think, develop ideas and be paid – often extremely well – for one's labour. One of the most important parts of this endeavour was the movement to translate ancient Greek philosophical texts – including the work of Aristotle, Ptolemy, Euclid and Galen – into Arabic. This was motivated principally by reasons of utility: works of mathematics, astronomy, logic, medicine and other pursuits that had a practical application were chosen for translation. Without the translation movement, much of the learning of the ancient Mediterranean and Levant would have been lost to us.

There was a real sense that translation was a creative endeavour, whose purpose was to stimulate new thinking. Nowhere is this more evident than in the work of Ya'qūb ibn Ishāq al-Kindi, celebrated as the Philosopher of the Arabs. The translation activity of al-Kindi and his circle was part of their aim to use Aristotle's work to create an Islamic philosophical tradition, and to address the problem of how to reconcile faith and reason. Al-Kindi wrote on medicine, music, astronomy and mathematics, as well as philosophy. Many of his works were translated into Latin, and he was a key figure for medieval European intellectual development.

The success of the translation movement was evident in its gradual slowing down in the tenth century. It was no longer needed because it had catalysed so much intellectual excitement, from Avicenna in astronomy and 'Ali ibn al-'Abbas al-Majusi in medicine to Al-Battānī in mathematics and Ibn al-Haytam in physics. They were able to publish new works that revolutionised science by standing on the shoulders of – and indeed surpassing – Galen, Ptolemy and Aristotle.

Astrolabe – the world in your hand

The desire of Baghdadis not just to understand the world but to control and use it for God's purpose is exemplified by the astrolabe. In the tenth century the astronomer Abd Al-Rahman Al-Sufi worked out there were about a thousand uses for this valuable instrument. The principal ones related to the primary purposes of life. With an astrolabe, you could orient yourself to Mecca, and therefore pray. It enabled you to set a reliable timetable for the major events – secular as well as sacred – of life, including the payment of taxes and the planting of crops. Knowledge of the skies – what we now call astronomy – was an important aspect of Islamic civilisation, as it had been for the Babylonians. This was as much about seeking meaning as observing phenomena. It's worth remembering that the Abbasids, like their Greek and Roman predecessors, considered divination and astrology to be a legitimate scientific discipline. Mansūr had founded his capital on a day that was deemed to be auspicious, and ordinary people also made important decisions at times and dates decreed by the heavens.

Miniature and exquisite, an astrolabe is an understanding of the world in the palm of your hand. It is no coincidence that its Arabic name, derived from the Greek, is 'star holder'. Astrolabes were created in ancient Greece, but their development is one of the major achievements of the early Islamic world. Hipparchus, working around 150 BCE, is believed to have invented 'stereographic projection', or the means of representing the three-dimensional sky on a two-dimensional plate of metal. The earliest surviving astrolabes date from the ninth and tenth centuries, from Baghdad and Syria, so it is possible that Hipparchus' idea remained largely theoretical.

These are marvellous but functional objects, generally

made of brass or copper, sometimes with additional decoration in precious metals. A ring at the top enables the user to hang the astrolabe in a secure and level spot so that it doesn't swing around, and the throne makes it possible to hold the astrolabe vertically. The main element of the instrument is the *umm* (mother), or perimeter base. This holds the other parts of the astrolabe together, and other key information, such as the zodiac, times and days. One or more plates, sometimes engraved on both sides, are held within the *umm*. There might be different plates depending how far north or south you are – for instance, there would be one plate for Mecca and Baghdad, possibly another for Cairo and Cordoba.

The beauty of this versatile instrument is that it can be used anywhere – you just need to change the plate to one specific to your locality A rotating part, called the net (*rete*) in Latin, or the *'Ankabut* (spider) in Arabic, sits on top of the plates. Each of the pointers direct you to a different star, the sun and the brightest constellations in the sky. These pieces are held together with a pin (*faras*). On the back is the *al-idada*, or ruler. You line up the ruler with the sun (being careful not to look at it). Then you can use this to see stars, the constellations of the zodiac, and make readings, using the front. Or you can start with the zodiac or a star, and do this process in reverse to tell the time.

One of the earliest datable astrolabes is a modest instrument, made in the late ninth century by Khafīf, an apprentice of 'Alī ibn 'Īsā. The three plates of Khafīf's astrolabe cover the latitudes 33–36 to 41, appropriate for use in Syria, Iraq and Armenia. Baghdad sits on the 33rd parallel north, while 36 degrees north passes through the Mediterranean, the borders of modern Syria and Iraq, and was a key point for navigation in the Mediterranean in the pre-Copernican world. On the back of the plate are four quadrant scales and a shadow scale. Almost nothing is known about this maker. His teacher, 'Alī ibn 'Īsā, was a celebrated astronomer and geographer, active in Syria and also at the court of Caliph Ma'mūn. He famously measured the earth's circumference, on an expedition to the plain of Sinjar. But whoever Khafīf was, with his instrument he changed how men understood and managed their world. Well into the seventeenth century, its ease of use and portability made it part of the equipment of most mariners. The astrolabe helped many people – and not just the rich – to predict the weather, navigate the seas and understand the skies.

Dinar: innovation and trade in the service of God

Only words, not images, could legitimately be used in the service of God. It is for this reason that calligraphy (it literally means beautiful writing) is such an important element of Islamic art. The caliph claimed to rule one single Muslim community on God's behalf. And although the caliphate recognised the right of the other People of the Book to practise their faith, only Muslims could proselytise and preach. There was no better way than to proclaim the power and might of the only God than through coins, one of the very few mass-produced objects in use throughout the Abbasid Empire. Coins had existed for centuries, but the importance and novelty of the dinar lay in the quality of its materials, the beauty of its manufacture and its explicit honouring of God.

A golden dinar, struck in the year 172 (788 CE) is testament to the riches of the earthly kingdom of the fifth Abbasid caliph, Harūn al-Rashīd. It was a completely functional object, whose worth lay in its reliable value. The coin is skilfully made, and is a religious as well as a commercial token. It is inscribed front and back with two quotations from the Quran, proclaiming the indivisibility of God, and that Muhammad is his true messenger. Not only is there no God but God, but God has no partner. It is written in Kufic, a calligraphic script that was used for copying the Quran, or extracts from it. Because God's revelations were conveyed to Muhammad in the Arab language, words from the Quran in Arabic script are physical representations of the divine message. The use of Kufic therefore makes the coin into another manifestation of the power of God. Even those who could not read would recognise the elegant pattern, with its distinctive short vertical and longer horizontal strokes, and understand from its mere appearance that it represented God's presence. The word of the Quran is absolutely critical to the message of this piece of metal, the stamp of authority which had value throughout the empire.

Coins were monetary currency, but a dinar like this, with the actual word of the Prophet engraved on it, held spiritual value far beyond the domains of the ruler in question. It could be held in the hand, caressed and cherished, becoming a talisman of faith and identity separate from its monetary worth. The coins conveyed the idea of a single caliph ruling one Islamic empire according to the universal language of faith, Arabic, which could be found and recognised all over the local linguistic variations of the Abbasid Empire. This coin is a brilliant manifestation of empire in a form with financial and religious value that could convey the power and innovation of Abbasid rule in the service of God to those who would never see or experience it.

Misery and slavery

It is easy as well as compelling to see the undoubted advances of Abbasid Baghdad as a sign of human progress, and to mourn its destruction by the invading Mongols in 1258. But history is never this simple, and there was much cruelty and pain in this empire, as well as beauty, harmony and innovation. One of the most striking features of the archaeological fragments of Samarra are the human personalities that emerge from the damaged wall paintings that shattered and fell on the floors of the private apartments of the Dar al-Khilafa and other palaces. Half-naked women, with full breasts, sit in the middle of acanthus-leaf scrolls. Dancers twist and turn, moving sinuously and confidently. Creatures, including hares, camels, foxes and birds, run wildly – the Abbasid caliphs were dedicated hunters. The art historians Oleg and André Grabar have written of a 'family of kings' who – whatever their nation or religion – enjoyed a private and privileged way of life that other princes across the globe would have recognised. It was summarised by the eleventh-century Persian poet Manuchihri in the jingle 'sharāb u rahāb u kabāb' ('wine, music and meat').

The people we see in the tantalising pieces of wall painting from the Dar al-Khilafa, painted in assertive lines of black paint on plaster, engaging with us across the centuries, look in many respects like ourselves. They are portrayed in ways which are immediate and compelling. They are dark-eyed women and boys, with big eyebrows, firm lips and straight profiles. They look out, with a hint of melancholy, and with perfect anonymity. These people were the close private associates of the caliph, together with the nadīms, his noble drinking companions sitting with him as he ate and drank, entertaining and amusing him, doing his bidding by day or by night. We have no way of telling who any of these people were, yet they are convincing depictions of the real individuals who lived unsung lives in one of the world's greatest palaces. It seems surprising to get so close to people who have no presence in the documentary record that is history.

Islam prevents the enslavement of Muslims, and so the women of the Abbasid haram (the women and others under the caliph's protection in his household) – whether servants, dancing girls, sexual companions or a combination of these roles – came from outside the empire. Mansūr himself was the child of a Berber slave from North Africa. Berbers, Greeks and girls from former princely families in central Asia were perhaps the most regular members of the haram, and most of the caliphs' children were their progeny, not the official wives'. Apart from their beauty, the women of the haram were celebrated in stories, from the *Book of Songs* to the *Thousand and One Nights*, for their wit and talents as musicians, dancers and poets. They most resemble the hetaerae of ancient Athens, the geishas of Japan or the courtesans of Renaissance Venice. Here too, in an environment where most women had little agency or choice, becoming part of the caliph's haram could be an ambitious career move.

But their lives could be precarious. One story tells of the 'girl with the mole' who was sold to Harūn for the vast sum of seventy thousand dirhams, but because she told the caliph the truth about a former liaison, he gave her away to his servant Hammawayh. Another tale, told by Alī ibn Yaqtin, about the caliph Hādi (Harūn's elder brother), recounts the horrific fate of two girls who were caught making love. Their heads, still fragrant with perfume and entwined with jewels, were brought on a platter to the sultan and his boon companions. And it was allegedly a slave girl in the household of the caliph's mother

Khayzurān who suffocated Hādi with a pillow in September 786. Her fate will not have been a pleasant one.

***

What makes Abbasid Baghdad so human and so absorbing is the combination of the admirable and the good with the harsh and brutal. The objects that survive from this society – from archaeological fragments to astrolabes to ceramic vessels and coins – are as evocative as they are artistically impressive. Many of their innovations have become part of the fabric of our lives. Abbasid discoveries and interests still impact on us today, in our food, in the way we see the universe and in our valuing of knowledge, but also in our cruelty and suppression of others. Looking back at Baghdad in the eighth and ninth centuries, we see people and objects that connect us to the past in ways that are simultaneously inspiring and shocking. And we see ourselves, good and bad, in the mirror of history.

Jōchō, Amitabha Tathagata (Buddha seated), Byōdō-in
Buddhist temple, Uji

5

KYOTO: IDENTITY

Eleventh Century CE

In the early eleventh century, when King Cnut was supposedly ordering back the tide on the English coast, halfway across the globe, in another northern archipelago, the Lady Murasaki was composing the elegant *Tale of Genji* – the world's first novel – at the refined court of the Empress Shōshi. Like other great story cycles, such as the *Odyssey* or the *Ramayana*, the world of Genji is at once compelling and incomprehensible. Murasaki's story, told over more than fifty chapters, and with a confusing cast of characters, is centred around the eponymous Genji, a younger son of the Japanese emperor, his wives and lovers, and his supposed son, Kaoru. Murasaki's clever, perceptive pen takes us into a world ruled by elegance, where men and women devote their hours to writing poetry, admiring nature, staging elaborate competitions and dressing in ensembles of subtle, rainbow-coloured silk. Although Genji, the 'Shining Prince', is a fiction, his environment reflects the circumstances of the Japanese imperial court. How one held a brush, discussed painting or layered one's clothes determined the success or failure of a promising career. Once we have put aside our surprise that such issues were life-critical, it is evident that Murasaki invites her readers to pity those excluded from this privileged environment – including ourselves.

Heian Japan, unlike Anglo-Saxon England, has become a byword for peaceful sophistication and artistic independence. In 794, Emperor Kammu, dismayed by the inauspicious marshy site of his capital in inland Japan, sent two envoys to establish the merits of a new location on a fertile plain bordered by mountains and a great river, ideally situated, neither too far nor too close to the coast, in an area renowned for its rice production and eminently defensible against attack. As an imperial edict proclaimed, 'the joyfully flocking people and the singers of praise raise their different voices in identical words, naming this the Capital of Peace and Tranquillity'. Heiankyō – or Kyoto, as it has long been known – would remain Japan's capital for over a thousand years.

The word Heian is still used to denote the period of calm rule and government instituted by Kammu and upheld by his successors, as well as their advisors, members of the powerful Fujiwara clan (Fujiwara no Michinaga, the most powerful of them all, was one of the models for Murasaki's Genji; she herself belonged to a lesser branch of the family). Several centuries of isolation, a stable economic, political and administrative system, and the absence of armed conflict created the circumstances for one of the world's most remarkable cultural flowerings. This urban society concentrated its artistic endeavours on temple complexes and the arts that gave refinement to living, underpinned by a deep appreciation of the natural world.

Everything in Heian Japan emanated from Kyoto – and its values remain key to modern Japanese identity – so it is depressing that practically nothing of the original city survives.

Like Rome, it has been built and rebuilt for centuries, and much of the archaeological evidence is hidden under the densely populated modern city. It is also situated in an earthquake zone. Yet from a hotchpotch of sources – tenth-century governmental procedure documents, thirteenth-century maps, as well as literary evidence – it is possible to gain a sense of the city at its moment of greatest glory. Like Chang'an (modern Xi'an), capital of the Chinese Tang dynasty, it was laid out on a grid. Thirty-three north–south and thirty-nine east–west avenues crossed the city, intersecting at regular intervals. The largest single space, in the centre, was occupied by the Great Imperial Palace. Suzaku, the great avenue that ran north to south, and other lesser ones, provided unparalleled views to the mountains beyond. It is testament to the imperial regime's confidence, and sense of security, that Heian was wall-less. Only a small garden-like structure, the Southern Rampart Gate, the ceremonial entrance to the city, offered any separation between the urban and rural environments.

Kammu's decision to build a new city was itself a sign of political resolution and security. In the following centuries, Japan succeeded in separating itself politically and culturally from the Chinese mainland as the Tang Empire collapsed. Chinese culture had first reached the Japanese islands from the Korean Peninsula, and during the seventh to early ninth centuries the Japanese learnt extensively from the Chinese. From 838, the date of the last official mission to China, and for many centuries, Japan was a closed society. This stable culture, with no threats to its order and structure, was able to develop, for the rich at least, a civilisation where the admiration of beauty and the appreciation of beautiful things, natural or man-made, was paramount. While official delegations to China ceased, Japan developed a distinctive and enduring cultural identity which was largely based on Chinese precedent. In Heiankyō, respect for China's religion, ruling system, literature, art, music and customs empowered the Japanese to craft their own unique cultural voice, founded on the twin pillars of a cult of beauty that reflected divine harmony and reverence for the written word. Yet, in an imperfect world, such ideals could never be realised completely. Heiankyō was undoubtedly a city of beauty, peace and stability. But it was also a place of social control and, on occasion, oppression.

The art of religion

Japanese spiritual traditions have always been entwined with worship of the natural world as a manifestation of divine beauty and order. The islands' native religion, Shintoism, was based on spirits (kami) residing in either places or human beings. Like many other features of life in Heiankyō, Buddhism was an import from the mainland, but as it evolved, it further enhanced the high reverence for natural and man-made beauty already evident in Japanese religious practice. It also became polytheistic, connecting the various manifestations of the Buddha and his followers, bodhisattvas (beings destined to attain Buddhahood), tenbu (gods), and rakan (saints), to existing Japanese deities: for instance, Amida, the Buddha of Infinite Life and the Western Paradise, was associated with the sun goddess.

The Buddha's final scripture, the *Lotus Sutra*, assumed a special significance. Known in Japan from Chinese translations, (most influentially that undertaken in the late fourth century by Kumārajīva, a monk from the central Asian Kingdom of Kucha), the *Lotus Sutra* asserted that the creation and veneration of works of art was key to attaining enlightenment. It also encouraged the adoption and development of several strands of mystical – also called esoteric – Buddhism in Japan: the Shingon, Tendai and Pure Land (Jodo) traditions. Central to all these was the concept that by reciting mantras, performing the symbolic hand gestures known as mudras and imagining oneself as being awakened, it was possible to achieve enlightenment or Buddhahood even as soon as this life. This process could be further accelerated by good works, such as building and restoring temples, venerating and supporting shrines, chanting, reading and storing sutras.

The monk Kūkai, founder of the Shingon sect, had travelled to China in the early ninth century to study mystical Buddhism. He returned to Japan with sutras, poems and mandala paintings, and placed a special emphasis on the arts in his teaching, asserting that painting and sculpture revealed the state of perfection. The performance of religious ritual was considered an aesthetic experience, and art was made within a religious context that endowed both the process of making and the product with an aura of sanctity, both for professionals and amateurs. Excellence of manufacture was a major consideration in Japanese religious art, and Buddhist painters were attached to temples to make sacred images. In Japan, the mandala – essentially a diagram of the realms of existence – evolved into a highly sophisticated genre of painting that guided practitioners through the cosmic processes of death and reincarnation so that they could achieve nirvana, the state of enlightenment.

Pure Land Buddhists believed that temples and their artworks constituted virtuous stepping stones on the path to paradise and freedom from the cycle of birth and rebirth. These 'Lands of Happiness' were mere earthly visualisations of the Western Paradise, as described in the Visualisation Sutra (Kanmuryōjukyō), where the Lady Vaidehi begs Buddha for rebirth in a pure land (Sukhavati), far from 'this polluted and evil place teeming with hells, ghosts and animals'. Everything in these temple complexes – their landscape settings, buildings and contents – was made to enable worshippers to visualise paradise in their mind, and reach the promised land by enlightenment, rebirth and salvation through faith.

We can see this amalgamation of native and imported traditions to create a new art at the Byōdōin Temple in the picturesque river city of Uji. Byōdōin is one of the few architectural survivals from Heian Japan not damaged beyond repair by earthquakes and warfare, built in 1050 by Imperial Regent (Sesshō) Fujiwara no Yorimichi on the site of a family villa. Yorimichi, a devotee of Pure Land Buddhism, belonged to the Sekkanke (regent and councillors) line of the Fujiwara clan. For several centuries they managed to control the empire by marrying their daughters to successive imperial heirs. Yorimichi's father was Regent Fujiwara no Michinaga, one of the most powerful figures in medieval Japan. Like Michinaga and indeed many emperors, Yorimichi would end his life as a Buddhist monk.

At the centre of the temple complex is a three-chambered wooden structure on an artificial island, the Phoenix Hall (Hōōdō). Strikingly red and white, with lacquered doors and gable roofs, it seems almost to take flight like the mythical bird itself. The hall's central golden chapel is dominated by a monumental naturalistic carved statue of the Amida Buddha. Pillars decorated with contrasting red vermilion and deep blue lapis, further ornamented in gold, divide the walls. The Buddha sits with his legs crossed in the lotus position, on a throne made of criss-crossing rows of lotus leaves. The lotus was considered to have great affinity with the Buddha – its roots were in mud, as Buddha himself was born in the imperfect world, yet its leaves were in the pure air, as Buddha himself reached paradise. The Amida Buddha's hands are composed in a harmonious mudra, thumbs touching. It is to this state of equilibrium, producing a deep and all-encompassing concentration on truth, that followers of the Buddha aspire.

The Buddha wears a monk's robe, which slips from his shoulders to reveal a firm, stocky body. There is no sense here of what we might call a 'Buddha belly'. The regularity of his features and his carefully coiffed hair, each curl a tight knot, a stylised tuft on his forehead, again demonstrate the idealisation of a god in recognisably human form. His face is perfectly proportioned, eyebrows arching out from the nose, the eyes themselves impassive and half-lidded, his mouth somewhere between open and closed, representing the ideal of the middle way. Only his ears hint at a less perfect world. Siddhartha Gautama, the historical figure of the Buddha, had worn heavy jewelled earrings as a prince. After rejecting luxury, he kept his stretched earlobes as a symbol of how far he had journeyed on the path to improvement. Even within the strong conventions established for the representation of the Buddha, the sculpture in the Phoenix Hall is extraordinary for its grave but kindly and reassuring majesty.

A sense of divine power exercised benignly is further heighted by the warmth of the gilded throne. Comforting organic shapes – resembling the whorl of a snail's shell, or the crests of waves – constitute the carved screen or mandorla at the back of the throne, made using an openwork technique called sukashibori, with holes that pierce the wood. Light plays upon the gilded surface of the Buddha's body, so that he appears not just a copied representation of a sacred figure but a living, moving being. Tiny figures of hiten ('hovering celestials') emerge from the screen, framing the sacred form. Above the Buddha's head is a suspended canopy, resembling a circular crown formed of interconnected peonies called hōsōge ('Buddha-visage flowers'). The central section, a polished bronze mirror framed by lotus leaves, seems to crown the deity's head. It's as if Buddha has been delivered as a ray of sunshine.

Painting combines with sculpture, architecture and landscape to create a compelling vision of paradise, and of perfect form. The lower walls of the room are decorated with paintings of Heaven, chosen by the Lady Vaidehi as 'the place of Amida', the Western Paradise, as recounted by the Buddha in the Visualisation Sutra. He instructs her that, through ethical behaviour and the power of the Buddha, she and others will be able to see Paradise 'as though seeing one's own face in a mirror held in the hand'. Even those who have committed great sins and deserve a place in hell can be permitted a rebirth in Paradise, as long as they call on Amida and chant his name. The paintings – much damaged, and heavily restored following a devastating fire in 1698 – are based on the sixteen visualisations in the Sutra. Following the moment of rebirth (recounted in the thirteenth visualisation), on a lotus flower as its petals are opening to the sun, gazing at Amida rising above the lake in Paradise, the Sutra recounts – and the paintings on the internal doors depict – the nine grades of rebirth. Twelve describe, in hyper-real detail, the glories of Paradise, with its trees, earth and lake of jewels, to the gleaming gold figure of Amida with eyes the colour of the four oceans. The paintings in the Phoenix Hall are mostly concerned with depicting the nature and category of rebirth, and the three highest grades are given pride of place, flanking the front of the Amida statue itself. They are welcomed by Amida in a pool of light, accompanied by bodhisattvas and musicians.

On the upper walls of the room, surrounding the Buddha, are fifty-two sculptures of flying bodhisattvas or bosatsu. These enlightened beings represent the entourage of Amida in Paradise and on his visits to earth. Literature of the early twelfth century called them apsaras, cloud-born creatures that danced around the Buddha and proclaimed his virtues. There is indeed a sense of celestial delight in these elegant beings, carved so that they seem of one element with the clouds on which they sit. Male and female, dressed in religious and secular clothing, the bosatsu play musical instruments – lutes, drums, cymbals and flutes – dance, pray and meditate. Some balance precariously, others seem to fly into the atmosphere, using their clouds as if they are broomsticks. Their playfulness – like angels in the Western Christian tradition – contrasts strongly with the sublime gravitas of the Amida Buddha. You sense here the sculptors being able to indulge their individualism, and to experiment in a way that was lese-majesty for the Buddha himself.

The Amida Buddha and his heavenly companions were the work of the master sculptor Jōchō and a large body of skilled sculptors working under his direction. Jōchō, himself the son of an admired carver, set the standard for what imperial and aristocratic patrons desired, working exclusively for Fujiwara no Michinaga and his family, including Yorimichi and his sister, the Empress Shōshi. We know that he had a huge workshop, employing twenty master sculptors, each with five assistants under him, and that he was an extremely spiritual individual. Jōchō was given titles previously reserved to high-ranking priests: hokkyō ('bridge of the law'), and hōgen ('eye of the law'), and his work was considered to embody the highest religious virtues. From the completion of the sculpture in this temple, sculptural makers of sacred objects were considered to be communing with the divine, in a manner only shared by clerics. Until at least the late twelfth century, any sculptor who departed from this model ran the risk of their work being rejected. Down to the present day, traditional Japanese sculptors have valued the monumental, balanced and restrained style of Jōchō's works. Thanks to his example, the act of making became an act of worship in Japanese Buddhism.

Word and religion

Among the most sacred man-made objects were scrolls of the sutras, Buddha's exhortations to mankind to achieve rebirth, salvation and paradise. The *Lotus Sutra*, written and spoken in Chinese, was used in the service of national identity and state-protecting rites. As early as the seventh century, Buddhist nuns at Lotus Temples for the Vanquishing of Wrong-Doing recited the sutra to protect the emperor and the state, and to create a prosperous and enlightened nation. The government established an official department for sutra transcription, an act of prayer for the peace and security of the country. Copies of Buddha's words were given a similar status to Buddhist relics, so the act of copying each individual character was accompanied by obeisances and meditation. The sutra was also used to designate sacred areas. Two of the three most sacred sites on Mount Hiei, the home of Tendai Buddhism, contained reliquaries, each holding a thousand copies of the *Lotus Sutra*. (A special manuscript made by the visionary monk Ennin was kept at the third site.)

Lay people meditated and recited the *Lotus* and other key sutras, as well as – if they could – writing them themselves, as an act of worship. Calligraphy could be a religious and prayerful act because the self-discipline required to perform it was aligned to each writer's conceptual and craft skills. The monk Kūkai, a noted calligrapher, remarked that its role was to blend tradition and individualism, revealing the writer's personal interpretation and their understanding of nature. It was believed that sutra-copying could bring prosperity, bodily healing, protection from disaster and salvation for your soul and those of your ancestors – ultimately, rebirth in a Pure Land. Fujiwara no Michinaga's own copy of the *Lotus Sutra*, written in gold ink on indigo paper, was transcribed as part of a purposeful act of prayer and remembrance. The script is beautifully formed and precise; the contrast between the deep blue and the gold is rich and pleasing. In the year 1007, after purifying himself for a hundred days, Michinaga buried this and fourteen other scrolls of sutras in an engraved casket on the holy site of Mount Kinbu, under a gilt bronze sutra mound.

The *Chikubushima Sutra*, also a copy of the *Lotus Sutra*, made about forty years later, is an even more perfect synthesis of painting and writing with the brush. One handscroll, copying the introduction and the 'Expedient Means' chapter of the *Lotus Sutra*, survives. It was made for the Hogon-ji Temple on the beautiful and remote island of Chikubu on Lake Biwa, north-east of Kyoto. Chikubu has a long history as an important spiritual site: according to tradition, the Emperor Shomu received a divine message from the sun goddess, informing him that the island was the earthly home of Lady Benzaiten, goddess of prosperity, eloquence and music.

This scroll of the *Chikubushima Sutra* exudes an appropriate elegance and luxury. The lines for the text were ruled in gold ink on paper made from mulberry fibres; then the scribe took a brush wet successively with silver and gold ink to make a series of fluid drawings. Flowering plants, imaginary and auspicious peony-type flowers with large petals and huge stamens, clouds, birds and butterflies dance across the surface of the manuscript. Magical birds like elegant hummingbirds, with the addition of long swooping tail-feathers, fly upwards in a rough diagonal from right to left, while others float serenely upon the surface of the water. It's a stunning work of art, and yet it's subordinate to the writing of the characters.

Finally, and most importantly, came the words themselves. The Chinese symbols are emphatic and bold, in a deep black ink that stands out strongly against the decorated background. An inscription, by the celebrated seventeenth-century calligrapher Shôkadô Shôjô, states that the scribe was Minamoto Toshifusa, Minister of the Right, a high-ranking nobleman and renowned calligrapher, but there is no evidence for this.

Because writing evolved as an act of reverence and devotion, preparation and ritual are intrinsic to Japanese calligraphy. The poetic phrase 'the way of the brush', first applied to writing in the nineteenth century, reflects the traditions established a millennium earlier. In Heian Japan, the materials required for writing were carefully crafted and much prized. The first stage of the process was the sourcing of the paper, a luxury item reserved for the nobility, and expensive even for them. High-quality, low-absorbent paper was favoured by Japanese calligraphers, either made from mulberry or the inner bark of *gampi* bushes native to Japan. Next came the manufacture of the ink itself. Even today, Japanese calligraphers make their own ink. They are responsible for getting the consistency, colour and density right. They grind their inkstick on an inkstone, made from materials such as stone or pottery with abrasive surfaces, mixing the ink with small drops of water so that it pools in the well of the stone. Two factors – the quality of the inkstick and of the inkstone – are paramount.

The *suzuri bako*, or special box within which inkstones were kept, was often made from lacquered wood, because it kept moisture out. Typically this container would house the inkstone (*suzuri*), an inkstick holder, a small knife and paper – the 'four treasures of the study'. These functional objects became gorgeous, valuable possessions. They were crafted out of the best quality materials, further dignifying the process of writing. In particular, inkstones were richly decorated and carved, while the boxes themselves were inlaid with mother-of-pearl, or had *maki-e* ('sprinkled picture') lacquer.

Dipping a brush into the well of an inkstone, a calligrapher forms every character carefully. The execution of the script matters as much as the content. This can be difficult for Westerners to grasp because it is so antithetical to how we approach writing: using ready-made pens and affecting a spontaneity of expression that is supposed to reflect our frankness and openness.

In Heian Japan, beautiful writing not only brought the writer closer to the divine; in the rarefied world of the imperial court it moved them up the social ladder, making men more likely to obtain promotion and women high repute. Sei Shōnagon's witty *Pillow Book* – a collection of carefully crafted lists, ephemera and observations written while the author served the Empress Teishi – criticises Fujiwara no Nobutsune, an official in the Ministry of Ceremony, for his inability to write appropriately:

One day when Nobutsune was serving as Intendant in the Office of Palace Works he sent a sketch to one of the craftsmen explaining how a certain piece of work should be done. 'Kindly execute it in this fashion,' he added in Chinese characters. I happened to notice the piece of paper and it was the most preposterous writing I had ever seen. Next to his message I wrote, 'If you do the work in this style, you will certainly produce something odd.' The document found its way to the Imperial apartments and everyone who saw it was greatly amused. Nobutsune was furious and after this held a grudge against me.

The Pillow Book, named because it was apparently left by accident on a pillow, is one of the most witty, acerbic and timeless of books. Its celebrated lists include 'adorable things' and 'things that arouse a fond memory of the past', 'things that should be short' and 'things that should be large' (the latter category includes men's eyes, fruit and the petals of yellow roses). Its simplicity and charm make it immediately accessible, even if the court ceremonies and rituals described seem very odd. Shōnagon's anecdote about the pompous and out-of-place Nobutsune not only demonstrates her wit: it shows how writing was seen to reflect both one's identity and, just as importantly, one's rectitude and fitness (or otherwise) for official positions.

Crafting an identity

Calligraphy was a crucial element of the strong and enduring sense of Japanese identity created in the Heian period. At its heart was an act of cultural fusion: all the earliest writing in Japan, from the third century CE, was made with Chinese characters and script. This made sense, because it was already a well-established written language, and because it was much venerated as the script of faith and the most esteemed scholarship. For many centuries, the most prestigious education in Japan was based on the use of the Chinese alphabet for the Japanese language. Those intended for a court career learnt the heavy, sombre kan-ji script, called 'men's hand' because women were discouraged from learning it. It wasn't appropriate for anything but official or serious matters.

In the long term, this was a complicated solution because Chinese and Japanese are fundamentally different languages. The problems began when Japanese thinkers wanted to record their own histories, ideas and poetry in written form. A complicated fudge evolved, so that Chinese characters could be used to write vernacular Japanese. Over time, writers devised a better approach, transforming the Chinese art and system of writing into something that was uniquely Japanese. The end result was kana script, with two varieties, hiragana ('simple kana') and katakana ('fragmented kana'). A set of forty-six basic and twenty-five additional characters could be combined to represent the language's complexity and variations. A page of hiragana, with its swift, flowing lines, looks deceptively uncomplicated. Perhaps as many as six characters can be joined in a single sweep of the brush – to do this accurately takes confidence and bravura as well as long and painstaking practice. The results are incredibly fluent and beautiful to look at.

The principal benefit of the kana system was to facilitate the development of poetry in Japanese, enshrining an inherently Chinese custom at the heart of Heian culture. The *waka* – 'Japanese poem' – of thirty-one syllables became part of life for those in elite circles (a later offspring was the seventeen-syllable *haiku* form now known across the world).

Poetry, written in hiragana script so that it was open to men and women, was composed on every occasion. It was used to correspond, to express emotion and to mark occasions as varied as stages of a journey, a season, a new set of clothes or a developing love affair. Writing excellent poetry contributed to one's place in the social and political hierarchy: inclusion in the *Imperial Anthologies of Japanese Verse*, first compiled in 905 as the Kokinwakashū or Kokinshū ('Collection of poems from ancient and modern times'), was a much-sought-after accolade. Poems recorded the elegant but fiercely fought court competitions (*mono-awase*) that compared and judged pairs of natural or man-made objects, including plants, shells, incense-burners and fans. The outcomes of these contests charted the imperial favour shown to a clan or individual.

Most consistently, *waka* captured emotions – responses to natural phenomena, the beauties of particular locations or certain seasons – without providing explanations for them. For example, Ono no Komachi, one of the Rokkasen, or 'six poetry immortals', of the Heian period, compares her fading talents to cherry blossoms suffering in the rain, but does not feel the need to say why she felt that way. This left the door open for complex and nuanced interpretations of simple situations. In her eleventh-century *Sarashina Diary*, the court lady Sugawara no Takasue no Musume considered that the most momentous episode in her life was a pair of encounters with the distinguished courtier Minamoto no Sukemichi, at which they exchanged poems on the subject of the seasons.

Minamoto no Sukemichi's unusual recollection of the 'winter drizzle' they had experienced on a court veranda during a religious service, rather than conventional poetic praise for 'the snowy night at Ise', Japan's most important Shinto shrine, remained for Musume a sense of their deep connection. The next year, by chance, they met one early morning in the Imperial Palace. He recognised her voice, and exclaimed, 'That night of softly falling rain I do not forget, even for a moment! I yearn for it.' The diarist replied quickly, 'What intensity of memory clings to your heart? That gentle shower fell on the leaves – Only for a moment [our hearts touched].' There is such poignancy in these memories – every word of their exchange still seems fresh, despite a distance of over a thousand years. Sugawara no Takasue no Musume's abiding regret was that they did not meet again. Far more of their exchange was implied than was out in the open. The abiding power of *waka* poetry lay in its ambiguity, and its power to provoke empathy.

Poetry and painting

Painting, like calligraphy and poetry, was also admired and practised by the elite. It too was open to all manner of interpretations, although it took conventional forms. The Heian court housed an Imperial Bureau of Painting, based in the main compound of the Imperial Palace, but many courtiers painted as a hobby, using the convention of 'hikime kagihana' ('a line for an eye, a hook for a nose') which resulted in pretty basic, stylised images of aristocrats who all looked the same. But in the mid-twelfth century, members of the Fujiwara family began a new tradition of portraiture. It was so realistic that the high official Kujō Kanezane recorded his delight at having been absent for three imperial pilgrimages, because he'd therefore avoided being painted by Fujiwara no Takanobu, who was notorious for his naturalistic portraits of courtiers. Even the imaginary Genji, paragon of every Heian virtue, is adulated for his delicate, restrained but moving paintings of his suffering while in exile, accompanied by 'poetic impressions' of these landscapes. On this occasion – as in many in Murasaki's account of Genji's life – the prince amateur surpasses every professional artist.

At court, the genre of the 'screen poem' evolved. Folding screens or byōbu (a literal translation is 'wind-wall'), made of paper, fabric or bamboo were a staple of Heian domestic life, as they remain today, because they made it possible to introduce insulation and some privacy, as well as charm and aesthetic pleasure, into very crowded households, including those of the emperor himself. The first screen poem, written in response to a waterfall, was painted on a screen in the Imperial Palace. By the early tenth century, screen poems tended to depict cycles of the four seasons or the twelve months, the kernel of the poetic repertoire.

The earliest 'Japanese' form of painting, *yamato-e* (named after the mountain-enclosed plain in Nara province that was the heartland of Japan's first rulers), was used solely for paintings on folding screens or room partitions during the Heian period. *Yamato-e* depicted scenes from court life, moments from nature and places famed for their beauty – landscapes with recognisably Japanese features – and illustrations of Japanese writings and folk traditions rather than subjects drawn from Chinese literature. *Yamato-e* has become a loaded and somewhat nationalistic term, distinguishing Japanese painting from its Chinese antecedents. Yet even the most patriotic of commentators would agree that its sources were Chinese.

An eleventh-century screen, now in the Kyoto National Museum, is the earliest, and one of the best surviving examples, of Heian painting. For many centuries, this screen was housed at the Shingon sect Tô-ji Temple in Kyoto, where it was used as part of an ordination ceremony establishing karmic bonds with a Buddha. Originally, however, it would have been used in either the imperial household or an aristocratic residence.

The screen comprises six connected paintings, intended to work as an expansive landscape of mountains, clouds, water and woodlands, on a soft spring day. It presents an idealised view of countryside created by the compact between nature and mankind, whose contours are enhanced by the demands of human society. We see small pockets of civilisation brought together by hills, the outline of the coast and an expansive bay, and the lush green of the mountains and the plains. Although the paint surface is abraded, and colours have changed, the relationship between the brown-gold surface of the silk, the subtle brush painting and the blue-green of the landscape remains striking.

The focus of attention is a simple man-made structure on the two central panels, where an old man is about to put pen to paper. He has been identified as the Chinese poet Bo Juyi, whose work was very popular with Heian aristocrats. His hermitage appears to be made of wood, with bamboo columns, and he is seated on the veranda. Pulled-back curtains separate his sleeping and living quarters from the outside world. It is evidently a carefully maintained place of contemplation and repose, from the songbirds singing on the roof to the wisteria vines and spreading trees in the garden. We see a young nobleman arrive at the poet's retreat. He is approaching Bo Juyi's servant, having dismounted from his horse. Two further groups of mounted travellers can be seen in the distance, in the first and last panels. It is unclear whether they are also on their way to visit the sage, or if they are hunting in the countryside.

The screen combines an awareness of Chinese culture, and Chinese painting, with what was evolving into the *yamato-e* style, with a particularly Japanese sensibility. The figure of the poet, for instance, is evidently indebted to models from Chinese painting. And the mountain peaks, with their distinctive application of blue and green pigments, recall a Chinese genre called the 'blue-green landscape'. The bands of soft clouds, however, and the bright colours, are more reflective of Japanese taste. So is the very naturalistic depiction of the landscape immediately surrounding Bo Juyi's house, and the birds that are nestled low on the tree, and on the ground, in the fifth panel.

What is remarkable about this screen is that it shows us how the Japanese took Chinese examples and adapted them into a new, identifiably Japanese genre and manner of painting. It also takes us into the organised, compartmentalised world of the Heian aristocracy, with all its inherent contradictions. This was a highly sophisticated society which celebrated the glories of the seasons and the natural world, while at the same time valuing the occupations of the city far above those of the countryside. And although far-flung Japanese locations were praised for their natural beauty, no one at court wished to leave the sacred precincts of the Imperial Palace and actually experience them, except on short excursions.

Heiankyō and the arts of living

With such visual sources, as well as texts such as diaries and the *Tale of Genji*, and the rare illustrations of it and other stories, we can begin to reconstruct the lives of the 'haves', those privileged families whose lives were entwined with the court and the imperial bureaucracy, and the spaces they inhabited. While some temples and religious buildings have survived, such as the Phoenix Hall at Byōdōin, nothing remains of the wooden mansions of the Heian nobility. No domestic building in this stable and prosperous city, not even the Imperial Palace, was designed for longevity. Partly, as noted above, this was due to Japan's vulnerability to earthquakes and to the ever-changing nature of Kyoto. The ultimate reason, however, was that Heian culture did not value household architecture in itself. The rituals, ceremonies, clothing and moveable objects that shaped the life of the elite, as well as of their many servants and dependants, mattered far more than the buildings themselves.

Heian dwellings were timber-frame constructions, usually on a single level, elevated above the ground on posts. Most floors and gabled roofs were made from planks, although in the better establishments the roofs would have been made of cypress bark shingles. Palace complexes were known as *shindenzukuri*, from the *shinden* or central dwelling hall where the main inhabitant lived and slept. The *shinden* generally consisted of a large central chamber (*moya*), with four additional chambers (*hisashi*) under the eaves. Beyond these were open verandas running along the length and breadth of the building and connecting the *shinden* to any subsidiary halls, such as for married daughters and their families, who tended to live with their parents rather than their husbands.

Life within *shindenzukuri* was not noted for its comfort, in spite of its elegance. These were flimsy, draughty structures. They offered very limited protection from the elements: some relief during the hot and humid summers, but potential misery during the winter, when snow was not unusual, for an elite who dressed almost exclusively in silk (texts of the time comment, unflatteringly, on the red noses of people who could not afford continual heating with braziers). There was exceptionally little privacy. People lived on top of each other, and the acts of sleeping, flirting, making love, giving birth and performing bodily functions took place within the same space, or separated by temporary screens and partitions.

The smells and noises could be challenging. Only the leading members of the household would have had the limited privacy offered by a curtained sleeping area (*chōdai*), which did additional service as a sitting room. These spartan mansions and palaces were designed as simple backdrops for the arts of living. Vast sums of money, and as much time, were spent acquiring fine clothing, calligraphy and exquisitely crafted objects, and on horticulture. The Heian elite prized luxury, but it had to appear subtle, understated and natural, as if it had always been there.

Gardens, which provided sensory delight and variety, were highly valued. The meticulously planned grounds that were a major part of every grand house were more important than the architectural structures themselves. Each of the *shinden-zukuri* was planned around the vistas and openings onto the gardens, which were an extension of the living spaces. Access to the separate pavilions, their verandas and walkways was organised around the perfected views of the natural world that surrounded them.

Gardens were designed by nobles, but the work of creating them was left to *domin* ('earth people'), and the back-breaking maintenance to the *komori* ('tree guardians'). A twelfth-century novel, the *Heike-mongatari*, recounts a storm which hit a hilltop garden that had been planted with maple trees so as to enable the viewer to enjoy the autumn colours. The next morning the poor servants were sent out early, before their masters would awaken and draw their blinds, to sweep up the leaves and broken branches (at least they were allowed to heat up some warm sake when they had finished).

The main sanded courtyard, carefully raked, every grain

and stone perfect, with lakes, miniature hills and rockeries, showed to maximum advantage the seasonal glories of the Japanese garden, with its moments for flowering plum, cherry and wisteria in the spring; globeflowers (*yamabuki*) and white chrysanthemums in the summer and early autumn; colourful autumn leaves and plume grass (*susuki*); the bleakness of the winter landscape, with spectacular effects of snow and ice.

This played a similar role to that of paintings and sculpture in grand houses in the Western world, providing diversions and variety in lives that, although privileged, could be monotonous. In one of the oldest illustrations to the *Tale of Genji*, one of these gardens is glimpsed through the open door and windows. Tiny clumps of rocks and miniature shaped trees (bonsai were recorded in Japan as early as the ninth century), each slightly different, punctuate the outdoor space. Even more perfect gardens are found on screens. These landscapes were as composed and perfect as a picture, with variety in scale, dimensions and colours. These were also settings which were designed to look subtly different in response to even the smallest change in conditions: a ray of light, a shower of rain, or a gust of wind. Sei Shōnagon writes movingly of a clear morning in autumn, when despite the strong sun, dew was still dripping from the chrysanthemums in the garden outside her room. She was mesmerised by raindrops that hung on broken spider webs like 'threads of white pearls'. As she watched, the dew vanished from plants like the clover bushes, and they 'sprang up of their own accord'. Such observations speak to an extreme sensitivity to nature and weather, made possible because gardens were an integral part of daily life.

Clothing and appearance were also exceptionally important. Although we can't take everything in the *Tale of Genji* as fact, Genji himself and the other leading characters are always praised for their sartorial elegance and good taste. This was particularly true for women, as female attractiveness, of the mind as well as the body, was judged by clothing and hair. Conventions of beauty required that women's hair was black, straight, exquisitely brushed, and that it was grown very long. Six feet, far exceeding average height, was not unusual. Genji first noticed his beloved Murasaki, as a ten-year-old girl, because of her hair, spreading out like a fan on her shoulders. And when she was dying, it was again her hair, freshly washed, carefully combed and spread out around her, in striking contrast to her pale face, which drew his attention afresh to her extraordinary beauty. Faces were made up according to strict convention. The Heian ideal, as we read in poetry and see in pictures, was of an opaque white complexion, to contrast with black hair; teeth were specially blackened, to prevent them looking yellow against pale skin. Natural eyebrows were shaved off, to be replaced with painted black 'butterfly' brows, almost at the hairlines. And women's lips were painted into bright red rosebuds.

The set patterns of make-up and hair enabled dress to be the stage where individuality and taste were demonstrated, although with a sense of what was appropriate to the wearer's age and within the official court stipulations of status relating to certain fabrics and colours: blue, for instance, identified those who weren't of noble status, belonging to the sixth rank of the imperial court or below. Sumptuary laws, regulating and controlling costume, are a sure sign that lavishness was the norm among the aristocracy. Clothing, even undergarments, was almost exclusively in silk. The art of dress was found in delicate colour combinations and in careful layering, to reflect the wearer's sensitivity to the seasons of the year, or to particular moods or sensibilities. Such clothing was difficult to wear and – particularly for women, with their flowing, wide-sleeved robes – hard to move in, but the wearers drew comfort and status from its beauty and elegance. We can sense the delight of Sugawara no Takasue no Musume, the author of the *Sarashina Diary*, when she entered court at the advanced age of thirty-two, in the costumes she donned to fulfil her office as lady-in-waiting to Princess Yūshi, infant daughter of the Emperor Go-Suzaku. She describes excitedly how on her first occasion in service, she wore 'eight layers of gowns in the chrysanthemum colour combination alternating light and dark, with a jacket with a lustrous crimson silk'. The chrysanthemum colour combination was white with a lining of dark red-purple. The lining would be visible, meaning that there was beautiful layering of light and dark at the edges and openings of garments. Eight layers may seem cumbersome, but it was relatively modest in an environment where twelve was normal, and as many as forty could be possible.

Refinement, optimal materials and high quality of manufacture were also key for portable objects. A typical example is a small lacquered box (*tebako*) from the National Museum in Tokyo, about the size of a laptop, with a tight-fitting lid. Made of wood, the joints and joins (it was held together without nails, as is common in Japan) were strengthened by an application of lacquer. The box's round, bevelled edges and contours make it appear organic and natural in shape.

Making this seemingly effortlessly exquisite object was a complex task. The mere process of producing lacquer is lengthy and includes many phases. Sap tapped from *urushi*, the lacquer tree, is filtered, coloured and heat-treated before it can be used. Lacquer seems magical, being shiny and smooth, beautiful to the touch, and yet also very hard. It holds its colour and is supremely resistant to moisture, making it easy to clean and to maintain. Before the invention of plastic, no other material had anything like its qualities, making lacquered objects perfect for serving food and drink, or for keeping valued possessions free from damp, dirt or insects. This particular box would have been used to store toiletries, make-up, or paper – some of its owner's most valuable possessions in a society where personal jewellery was not worn. Like so much else, lacquer was introduced to Japan from China. But it became such a Japanese art that in Europe lacquering in the Asian manner is still known as 'Japanning'.

When the black base lacquer was set and burnished – a task which could involve the application and polishing of as many as fifty or sixty separate coats – a design of cartwheels within swirling waves of water was engraved on its surface. Then, once the box had been lacquered, the process of decoration could at last begin. The cartwheels were picked out with mother-of-pearl, a material that shimmers and catches the light, fixed with a combination of starch and glue. Once held in place, these pieces of cut shell were engraved to define the wagon spokes and the hub of each wheel, and to show how each wheel was made out of several pieces of wood. While still wet, the rest of the engraved lacquered surface was sprinkled with irregular particles of aogin, a blue-tinted gold and silver mixture that also responds to changing light. Subsequently, all this was covered with black lacquer. Painstakingly, meticulously, this layer was rubbed off until the hidden decoration was revealed. The resulting object is subtle and elegant, with a translucent, ever-moving surface. The joy of experiencing something very special continues if you open the box. The lid and internal surfaces are covered with flying birds and flowers, made using the same painstaking technique of *togadashi maki*, or 'sprinkled pictures'.

The cartwheel pattern is seen on many other Heian art forms, from the covers of sutra scrolls to mirrors and fine decorated paper. Carts pulled by oxen were the principal means of travel for the elite and their wooden wheels were preserved by soaking them in water (the observant Shōnagon comments that nothing is worse than travelling in a cart not properly maintained, with squeaky wheels). The skill of the box's maker was to turn something utilitarian into a series of exquisite designs. None of the cartwheels are exactly the same. They are in groups of twos or threes, and their gold and silver colouring is as varied as their organisation. Cleverly, at a corner, the angle is carefully considered so one feels you are looking down at the spoke of the wheel as it sits at the edge of the box. Swirling gold lines represent the water in which the wheels were soaked. The wheels themselves look ethereal, as if they are going to float away.

The genius of Heian culture was to make functional objects into art which didn't just give pleasure but shaped the course of life. None were more important than screens, blinds and curtains. In a society that formally segregated men and women, they enabled social contact and interaction between the sexes to continue. (On Shōnagon's list of 'hateful things' in *The Pillow Book* is a lover who bangs his tall, lacquered hat on something when he leaves, or who lifts up a head blind or sliding door with a rattle.) During the ritual competitions at court, the highest-ranking women would take part behind a screen, so that the rules of propriety could be respected. Appointments and assignations were arranged with screens and partitions, enabling men and women from different households to talk and share letters and poems without meeting each other's eyes. Blinds were lifted, and lowered, in what was often an elaborately staged flirtation. Every word and gesture that was exchanged, through these paper or fabric structures, was heard and discussed afterwards, by the participants and their companions.

In such situations, every subtle hint and inference mattered. Details such as the timbre of a voice, a delicate scent, the glimpse of a sleeve peeping under a blind, locks of long, clean, well-brushed hair, or a sheet of carefully chosen paper with beautiful script, took on a particular significance. These encounters were supposed to happen in accordance with generally accepted conventions. For instance, during Sugawara no Takasue no Musume's important chance meeting with courtier Minamoto no Sukemichi, the writer and her companions remained hidden behind blinds while they talked and exchanged verses with Minamoto. On such occasions, men and women could hear each other's voices and they talked openly – but everything but the women's silhouettes and perhaps the edges of their robes was hidden. This was clearly an enjoyable occasion when everyone kept to the rules. But at other times, such events could be brutal and frightening.

The complexity of these interiors, so apparently elegant, civilised and ordered, is evident in an early illustration to the *Tale of Genji*, made about a century after the writing of the text. The image accompanies Chapter 50, 'The Eastern Cottage', from the final section of the book, which tells of the adventures of Genji's supposed son, Kaoru, and his friend Niou, third son of an emperor and one of Genji's grandsons. Niou, 'the perfumed one', is married to the Lady Nakanokomi, a daughter of the Eighth Prince, who has a long-lost, much younger half-sister, Ukifume, stepdaughter of a provincial governor. Nakonokomi takes Ukifume into her household to hide and protect her. Both Niou and Kaoru fall in love with the young girl, but their passion is far from innocent. Ultimately, she becomes a nun to protect herself.

The picture shows six women in a space opening onto a veranda. One, behind a moveable blind decorated with trees, hills and mist that flutters in the wind, is reading intently, her hands clasped on a large book. This is Ukon, who Murasaki describes as reading to her mistress Nakanokomi and Ukifume. The two sisters are absorbed in listening, and in getting to know each other after so many years of separation. At the left, another woman, in green with yellow underrobes, sits elegantly on the floor, while in the foreground, at the far left, two more women converse, one pointing at the reader. All seems peaceful and relaxed. The little details are charming, such as the striped textile cushion that softens the transition from the veranda to the interior, the green dado rail along the back wall, and the garden that appears beyond the flimsy floor-to-ceiling windows. But a closer look reveals that most of the women are close to places where they can hide if necessary: beside screens, pillars and curtains. There is a potential need for protection and cover. No woman in such a household, whatever her rank or age, was fully in control of her body.

Shortly before the scene described in this picture, Niou 'came across' a girl he had not seen before, on the western veranda. Through an open door, partially blocked by a screen, beside a curtain backed by a blind, he saw the sleeves of a lavender robe, and a green-yellow cape. The girl wearing them was looking out at the garden. Peering at her around the side of the screen, Niou could see she was very pretty. 'Never one to hold back', he clutched her skirt, so that she could not move, and seated himself in the shadow of the screen. She could not see him, but he could see her, and she knew it, raising her fan to protect her face. He grasped her hand; she and her nurse were horrified, but there was nothing they could do. He was the man of the household. For some time he sat there, clothed in just a singlet, watching her closely. Murasaki recounts Ukifume's horror: she didn't move but was soaked in perspiration, as if she had woken from a nightmare. In spite of her half-sister's presence she would not be safe here. Once you understand this backstory it can be hard to view the peaceful scene with quite such composure.

In this painting, where nothing is said but much is implied, we reach the kernel of Heian identity. This was an ordered society with worthy ideals, imbued with an appreciation for beauty and the natural world. Here, cultural excellence and sensitivity were valued far above military might. In no other prosperous community has the ability to compose poetry or to paint a perfect picture enabled people to succeed in official life. Both Murasaki Shikibu and Sei Shōnagon owed their careers to their talents as poets and writers. But Heiankyō was certainly not a paradise for everyone. Women, despite the conventions and manners of the court, were deeply inferior to men. Most people outside the court or the noble households lived highly constricted, limited lives. And yet there is much to admire, to value and to emulate in this world of 'Peace and Tranquillity'. Niou, for all his desire for Ukifune, is unable to possess her. She chooses a different path which enables her to retain her autonomy. Ultimately, a sense of calm, order and beauty prevails.

View of the Hall of Supreme Harmony, the Forbidden City, Beijing

6

BEIJING: RESOLVE

1400–1450 CE

On 17 July 1402, Zhu Di was crowned the Yongle Emperor of the Great Ming, the third of the 'Bright' dynasty that had ruled China since 1368. With hindsight, the rule of Yongle, meaning 'Perpetual Joy', was the apogee of Chinese imperial rule. His empire was the greatest, in terms of land mass and population, anywhere in the world. Its territorial range included icy mountains, tropical beaches, windswept deserts and lush farmland, from the edges of the Gobi Desert to the borders of modern Vietnam. An estimated eighty-five million people lived under his direct rule. He had power, riches and authority that none of his contemporaries could match. And his reputation as a ruler stretched far further, across continents and time. In eighteenth-century Europe, the Irish writer Oliver Goldsmith, in his *A Citizen of the World*, a collection of satirical letters written by a fictional Chinese philosopher, Lien Chi Altangi, praised the 'Emperor Yonglo' [*sic*] who 'arose to revive the learning of the east'.

Although the Yongle Emperor's fame, in his lifetime, didn't quite reach the barbarous plains of Europe, products of his empire were revered halfway across the world. He sent out fleets called 'treasure voyages', manned by visionaries including the senior court servant Zheng He, to the edges of the Western Sea, today's Indian Ocean. As a tablet erected in Admiral Zheng's name in Fujian province in 1432 proclaims:

> We have traversed more than 100,000 li [50,000 kilometres] of immense water spaces and have beheld in the ocean huge waves like mountains rising in the sky, and we have set eyes on barbarian regions far away hidden in a blue transparency of light vapours, while our sails, loftily unfurled like clouds day and night, continued their course [as rapidly] as a star, traversing those savage waves as if we were treading a public thoroughfare.

One of the most spectacular of the many gifts that Zheng He conveyed to the Yongle Emperor in 1414 was a giraffe from the king of Bengal. These elegant creatures were prized and exceptionally rare diplomatic gifts all over Eurasia. It was described as a *qilin*, a mythical beast that, according to the foundational Chinese sage Confucius, only appeared when a wise ruler was on the throne. The arrival of three more giraffes, in 1415, 1419 and 1433, were further signs of divine benevolence. A hanging scroll dated 1414, and now in the Philadelphia Museum of Art, is inscribed with a poem attributing the appearance of the *qilin* to the fact that 'Your Majesty's virtue equals that of Heaven'.

From Prince Zhu Di to Emperor Yongle

No one had expected Zhu Di to rise to the position of emperor. He was the fourth son – of thirty-six sons and sixteen daughters – of Hongwu, the first Ming emperor, who had overthrown the Mongol rulers of the Yuan dynasty following a twenty-year conflict. Hongwu, meaning 'Vast Military Power', had been born into a poor tenant farming family in Anhui province in eastern China, and spent his early adulthood as a monk and an itinerant beggar. In the 1350s and 60s his skills as a commander enabled him to triumph in the skirmishing among small regional powers that resulted from the gradual Mongol withdrawal from China.

To end the horrific cycles of murder and conflict that were part of the succession struggles of many Eurasian empires, including the Yuan dynasty, the Hongwu Emperor had decreed that the title should pass down the male line, from eldest son to eldest son. His younger sons, including Zhu Di, were to act as a 'fence and a screen' for the emperor, his heir and the imperial capital of Nanjing. In this role, they were sent to rule as subordinate kings of provinces all over China, controlling sizeable armies to defend the realm against the Mongols, who remained a considerable threat. The most important province in military terms was allocated to Zhu Di. At the age of ten he became the prince of Yan, centred around the former Yuan capital of Daidu in northern China. A decade later, the prince moved to Daidu, by then known as 'Beiping', or Northern Peace. With the help of his father-in-law, the general Xu Da, Zhu Di campaigned against the remaining power of the 'Northern Yuan' kingdom. He was an able and effective leader, impressing his own troops and, more importantly, his father.

In 1392, the crown prince died. The balance of power, although Hongwu was still in charge, began to shift. After a gap of six months, the crown prince's eldest son, the fifteen-year-old Zhu Yunwen, was appointed heir apparent. It is possible that Hongwu had considered changing the succession and making Zhu Di his heir, but it was Zhu Yunwen who succeeded to the throne in 1398. Zhu Yunwen took the regnal name Jianwen ('establishing civility'), and he immediately began to limit the freedom of the imperial princes, including his uncles. In 1399 Zhu Di launched a well-planned and effective revolt, claiming it was essential to save his nephew from bad advisors. Three years later, after prolonged skirmishing and success in Shandong province, south of Beiping, Zhu Di made the bold decision to march on Nanjing. The imperial fleet went over to him, and in July 1402 the gates of the capital were opened for the conqueror. The Jianwen Emperor, his empress and their children were killed, apparently as the imperial palace went up in flames. His uncle made sure, in a detail as brutal as it was effective, that his nephew's name was excised from the official record.

Having used his power base in northern China to destroy his nephew, Zhu Di was particularly eager to prevent any similar challenges to his rule. Military power and authority became centred on the emperor's person. He led five campaigns against the Yuan Mongols on the steppes, although neither armies nor fortifications could keep these persistent fighters out (notoriously, his great-grandson, the Zhengtong Emperor, was captured by the Mongols in 1449). More successfully, the Yongle Emperor systematically reduced the military capacity of his male relatives. By 1441, when Zhu Di's grandson Prince Zhuang of Liang was buried in a magnificent tomb on his lands in Hubei province in central China, it is notable the only armour included in his grave goods was decorative and symbolic, not functional. It's very striking that – unlike early modern Japan, or Renaissance Europe – very few objects relating to war have survived from the Ming period. It may be that such items were made from materials which disintegrated.

But it's more likely that Ming society became increasingly focused on civil and cultural pursuits because members of the elite were rarely involved in direct military activity. The arts of peace (*wen*) were more valued than the arts of war (*wu*), because they were key to success at court.

The Northern Capital

Shortly after his assumption of the imperial throne, the Yongle Emperor made the significant decision to move his capital from Nanjing to Beiping, which was renamed Beijing (Northern Capital). It is not surprising that he felt more comfortable in the city that had been his power base for more than twenty years. This was a decision with profound implications for China, as the effective capital has remained there ever since (although the Hongwi Emperor, Yongle's son and successor, seems to have wished to return to Nanjing, his reign was so brief that its impact was negligible), with the exception of the period 1927–49, when the Republic of China purposely returned the capital to Nanjing, the original Ming stronghold.

Moving the capital north presented significant practical difficulties. Nanjing, in the Yangtze delta, was close to the main rice-growing areas and connected to a major water-based transport network. Beijing was not. But as emperor, Yongle could make unilateral decisions which brooked no disagreement or compromise. The Grand Canal linking Beijing and the southern port of Hangzhou was repaired and improved, enabling the movement of food and building materials to the new capital. Within two years of the start of the Yongle period, ten thousand households were ordered to move from Shanxi province in the west to Beijing. And two years after this, in 1406, new palaces and walls began to rise. Work was slow, because of a shortage of building materials and artisans, and in 1407 thousands of specialist workers – of whom at least seven thousand were prisoners – were drafted in to speed up activity. In 1409, sufficient progress had been made for Zhu Di himself to visit. In that year, work commenced on the Changling mausoleum fifty kilometres outside the city, the future burial site of the Yongle Emperor, his empress and his successors.

Many of the prisoners who were put to work rebuilding the city came from Vietnam, some four thousand kilometres to the south. They must have found the climate, with its harsh and freezing winters, hard to bear. Timber was brought by water from the distant provinces of Sichuan, Hunan and Guizhou, as well as from the mountains that surround the flat plain of the city on three sides. Tile and brick factories were set up in Beijing, to provide the materials for the walls, royal palaces, ritual altar sites, monasteries and temples, and houses for the new inhabitants, from courtiers to the humblest citizens and slaves. In spite of the difficulties of the site, and more than a certain reluctance from the southern Chinese who dominated the official bureaucracy, by 1417 the emperor was in residence and the construction of the imperial palace, known as the Forbidden City, had begun.

Inside the Forbidden City

Not only was the structure of the imperial palace designed to copy those at Nanjing, it was based (as had that palace been) on a set of eleventh-century ordnances, the 'Treatise on Architectural Methods or State Building Standards' (*Yingzao fashi*). The shortage of materials and skilled artisans meant that the architectural style of the early Ming period – in comparison with what we know of earlier structures – was highly simplified. It was a one-size-fits-all model which could be rolled out across the empire, and then decorated according to local proclivities. Although Yongle had lived as the young prince of Yan in part of the Beijing palace of the Ming's predecessors, the Mongol Yuan emperors, as emperor he wished to raze the buildings to the ground and to start from scratch.

The imperial palace has been built and rebuilt so consistently since the fifteenth century that probably no brick, stone, tile or timber is original, but many visual and written sources enable us to reconstruct aspects within it during the Yongle Emperor's reign. And all refurbishments have maintained the colours and materials of the original. In essence this is because the Purple Forbidden City, as it is formally known, is a structure with strong religious significance as the home of the emperor, the Son of Heaven. The name derives from a Confucian description of the emperor as the polar star – and purple (zi) is the first character forming 'polar star' in Chinese.

There are a number of contemporary bird's-eye depictions of the palace, as if we are looking down from the heavens. The walls are red, ornamented with friezes of red and blue, with striking roofs of yellow tiles that look golden from afar. Gold names on blue boards at the front of each building make their identity clear. Each structure is surrounded by billowing clouds – of course, the emperors, after their death, became gods, and even at this moment they were closer than anyone else to the divine. Entrance to each successive quarter, moving from the public to the entirely private, is controlled by a series of gates and bridges. At the front are the grandest public halls, where time is denoted by drums and bells. An unknown official stands in his court robes at the left of the first bridge. He holds a scroll in his hand and looks straight out at us. He must have been important to have been standing within the enclosing gate of the palace compound.

Even now, when the centre of power has moved elsewhere in the city, the Forbidden City remains a place of huge symbolic significance. The Tiananmen Gate of 'Heavenly Peace' that leads to the palace complex marks the north end of the eponymous square, which today houses the Mausoleum of Mao Zedong, the National Museum of China and the Great Hall of the People. Moving into the palace from Tiananmen, you meet the canal of the Tongzi moat before reaching the Meridian Gate, the entrance into the Forbidden City proper. Inside the gate is a vast square, paved with white reflective stones and featuring five curving marble bridges over the Golden Water. Each represents one of the five Confucian virtues – humanity, duty, wisdom, trustworthiness and ritual correctness. (The precepts of Confucius are an enduring survival in Chinese moral and cultural life.)

After the bridges, the visitor approaches the gate and then the Hall of Supreme Harmony, known in Ming times as the Hall of Offering to Heaven, the throne room. It has an odd number of bays, or 'the space between' the pillars, as is usual in Chinese traditional architecture, because even numbers were considered inauspicious. But because this is the throne room, there are many more than usual. Three was the norm in Chinese domestic architecture; here there are eleven. The hall is raised on a marble platform, the Dragon Pavement, in the i-shaped character Gong. The platform is practical – it raises the timbers above the ground and prevents damp – but it also enables the building to seem greater than it is, and to impress the superiority of the Son of Heaven on his subjects. This courtyard was the most public part of the palace, reserved for men only. Here the emperor and the male members of his court would perform state ceremonies and religious rituals, such as the celebration of the emperor's birthday, the New Year ceremonies and enthronements. The emperor's progress across the courtyard was marked by a special pathway, with a ramp taking the sovereign, borne in a sedan chair, to the top of the Dragon Pavement, carved with the imperial symbols of dragons chasing pearls through clouds, mountains and waves.

When the Yongle Emperor appeared in public, 'drums, cornets, cymbals and bells' sounded, and two thousand musicians sang in harmony to his praise. In 1420, an embassy to Beijing from the Timurid ruler Shahrukh, led by his son Baysunghur, included the artist Ghiyath al-Din. As instructed by Baysunghur, al-Din kept a diary of his five-month stay in the Ming dominions, noting his thoughts on the landscape, tourist sites, governmental structures and buildings. He was evidently bowled over by Beijing, which he describes as 'a city of inordinate magnitude, made all of stone', although not forgetting the apparently one hundred thousand scaffolds still attached to the city's walls. Al-Din noted the size of the imperial palace; the apparently vast courtyards with flags of regularly cut stone that could hold up to a hundred thousand people at a time; the special paths for the emperor himself; the dominance of the colour yellow, worn only by the emperor, who sat in halls with yellow wooden pillars and yellow tiled roofs, drinking yellow-coloured wine, using golden furniture and turmeric-coloured silk textiles, all perfumed by exquisite incense burners. He admired the quality of the construction and the furnishings, commenting 'the masters of stone cutting, carpentry, painting and tile-making of that region have no peers'.

Image of the emperor

The Yongle Emperor, as we see him in a series of images that he must have approved or commissioned, is apparently benign. Yet the overall impression is of an emasculating eminence and power, contrary to reports of his actual physical presence. According to Ghiyath al-Din, he was of medium height 'with neither large or small features'. Of note, however, was his facial hair. His beard and moustache were said to grow so opulently, they could be 'braided into three or four plaits'. Full beards were associated in Ming culture with masculinity, exemplifying power (*yang*), an energy and force that was a symbol of vigour and maturity. A silk screen hanging, showing the emperor on a life-size scale, depicts him in all the accoutrements of imperial status. It is one of a series of works created for the performance of ancestral rites within the imperial family, and was presumably painted shortly after the emperor's death. These pictures would have been very rarely displayed – probably around the Chinese New Year – and only to close family members. Their purpose was to inspire awe and devotion in the beholder. Veneration of ancestors, and particularly the respect that sons owed their fathers, was a key element of Confucius's teachings.

Much about these works conforms to the conventions of imperial life and court ritual. All are painted on silk scrolls with a yellow background, with ink and coloured pigments. In each case, the emperor wears the black winged cap that was a sign of royal status (examples have been found in excavations of royal tombs, such as that of Zhu Tan, Prince Huang of Lu), and the yellow silk robes that were reserved for the emperor and his official consort, emblazoned with at least one embroidered silk medallion of an open-mouthed dragon showing large sharp teeth and a slavering tongue, and brandishing pointed talons, rising into the heavens. The dragon chases a flaming pearl, a sign of infinite possibility. The Yongle Emperor adopted the dragon as an imperial symbol because he also held the power of life and death, with absolute authority over his subjects, and a divine responsibility to provide them with the stuff of life. The dragon's most important function was to be in control of water supplies, having the ability to destroy whole populations through drought or flood, and to make life possible through the rain that produced crops. As Chinese dragons were believed to spend the winter in the sea, flying upwards to the sky in spring, forming clouds and making rain, they represented the generative qualities of life.

This is an image of a powerful figure: poised, determined and ready to act. He is also, as befits the father of the nation, portrayed as reasonably benevolent. We see him slightly turned to his left, giving the impression that he is listening carefully in a measured adjudication. The painting is stylised, and yet it represents an individual (unlike much imperial portraiture). His facial features are distinct from his father's, and subtly different from those of his son and grandson, who both have slightly forked beards. Although divine, he is evidently a man, as his moustaches curl with movement, and the individual hairs of his beard are slightly parted to reveal the dragon roundel on his robe below. Yet there is no doubting his authority. He is seated on the dragon throne that was symbolic of the Chinese imperial position and the status of emperor. The back and arms of the chair are flanked by dragon heads with bulging eyes. Each has a golden ring through its mouth, symbolic of the emperor's power to direct even the uncontrollable forces of nature.

The dragon thrones on which the Hongwu, Yongle, Hongxi and Xuande Emperors sit are subtly different in this series of imperial portraits. Interestingly, those of the Yongle Emperor and his Xuande Emperor grandson – the pair had a close relationship – are the most alike, with carved dragon ornaments on each corner and finial. The portrait of the Yongle Emperor shows him as strongly Chinese, while also heir to the multinational Mongol empire his father had conquered. Just as he is recorded as eating non-Chinese foodstuffs, such as Korean rice cakes, and commissioning non-Chinese furnishings for his palace, his person and throne are ornamented with objects and patterns derived from the cultures he emulated and wished to control. As well as dragons, the carpet and base of the throne include motifs from central Asian, Tibetan and Islamic art, including the stylised flowers of every season found in Timurid and Mughal miniatures and carpets. The Yongle Emperor fingers a golden bejewelled belt around his middle, perhaps to signify his authority over trade in these precious materials.

Such jewel-encrusted golden belts were made by craftsmen working in the imperial Jewellery Service, to be distributed as a sign of special favour to princes of the imperial family. A rare surviving example, comparable to that worn by the Yongle Emperor in this portrait, was discovered in the tomb of his grandson, Prince Zhuang of Liang. The preponderance of rubies reflects the special significance of this rare precious stone for the Ming emperors, for whom red represented their family's particular right to rule. Their personal surname, Zhu, sounds like the word for 'crimson'.

Private life in the imperial palace

Beyond the Hall of Supreme Harmony were the inner, private parts of the palace, reserved for the emperor, his children, wives and concubines, and their servants. The imperial family's private attendants were eunuchs, either young men captured in war like the future Admiral Zheng He or those who had voluntarily undergone this sacrifice in order to gain access to the emperor's most special circle.

Every building in the central imperial complex was arranged axially, with the emperor's own quarters, the Palace of Heavenly Purity, in the south and the empress's Palace of Earthly Tranquillity on the northern side. Between the two structures stood the far smaller Hall of Celestial and Terrestrial Union, where marriages and other family ceremonies took place. On the west and east sides of this inner court were six identical walled compounds. These were the residences of the emperor's consorts, his lesser wives. Together, each group of six forms the Chinese character K'un: ☷. This is one of the eight trigrams of ancient Chinese philosophy, symbolising the mother and earth, a metaphor for the traditionally female roles of fecundity and care that were envisaged for the inhabitants of these buildings.

Life in the private quarters of the imperial palace was exceptionally luxurious. Just as the founding emperor had gathered specialist artisans in Nanjing to build a new palace, so did the Yongle Emperor and his successors in Beijing, where, until it became an official capital, such objects were said to have been made by imperial servants 'following the chariot', or the travelling persona of the emperor. The furnishings and luxury objects were made centrally by a number of household agencies controlled by eunuchs. These included the Silver Workshop, the Royal Household Department of Sweetmeats and Delicacies, the Jewellery Service for personal adornments of precious metals and stones, and the Directorate of Imperial Accoutrements for even more specialised products such as

enamelled cloisonné jars and lacquered objects. From 1416 to
1436, the Orchard Factory, as the imperial lacquer workshops,
a subdivision of Imperial Accoutrements, were known, were
situated in the north-west corner of the palace, run by Zhang
Degang and Bao Liang from Jiaxing in Zhejiang province.
Such was demand for the products of the Orchard – tables,
chairs, beds, carved dishes for serving food, treasure boxes,
even swings for the imperial children – that several thousand
lacquer specialists from southern China (the tree that provides
the lacquer sap cannot grow in the north of the country) were
conscripted to work for the Beijing court for four years as part
of the imperial tax system.

A silk workshop wove satins and plain watered silk for imperial use; a further workshop, in another part of the compound,
made silks for presentation to trusted servants, for diplomatic
use, or for religious functions. In Nanjing, which remained an
official imperial residence, a further weaving and dying workshop was maintained at the site of the tomb of the founding
Ming emperor and his consort, employing three thousand
staff, with an additional shop with fourteen hundred workers
for ceremonial robes.

Every aspect of this luxury production was strictly controlled, even though it was on an exceedingly grand scale. A
script mark, denoting the reign of the emperor under which
the object in question was made, was used, during the Yongle
and Xuande eras to mark lacquer, textiles, bronzes and cloisonné enamels.

The reign of the Xuande Emperor witnessed a new genre
of painting, one that showed the emperor, his servants and
his family enjoying their leisure activities. Perhaps the purpose was to convince the viewer – presumably officials and
princes outside Beijing or Nanjing – that the direction of the

government was in good hands. The business of ruling was so secure that these men – and sometimes women – could allow themselves to take some time off. Certainly, the manufacture of these paintings until the late fifteenth century, and the inauguration of a related genre, showing senior officials relaxing in their gardens, suggests there was a market for these works. Here we see the emperor taking his ease: hunting (amazingly, only killing beasts in the lucky colours of black and white), enjoying the Lunar New Year, playing board games with his household, watching quails fighting, and sitting enthroned under a wooden pavilion while his wives, concubines and children pick and water flowers or play in the palace gardens. Men and women of the educated classes were expected to take an interest in the fine arts – music-making (zither for men; the lute for women), chess, calligraphy and painting. The ability to pursue these talents was a sign of how far civilisation had come: that the arts of peace far outweighed the arts of war. The Xuande Emperor in particular was an accomplished artist. An emperor who had time to concentrate on his painting had come a long way.

Ceramics and resolution

Ceramics were the most renowned aspect of artistic creation under the early Ming emperors. From the Yongle period, all ceramics produced at the imperial kilns in Jingdezhen were inscribed with a mark indicating the ruling emperor. Nothing is more valued or celebrated in this genre today than blue and white Ming porcelain. It has become shorthand for luxury, and one of the first global brands. The name of the country, China, has become synonymous with the objects themselves.

In English, we call all clay-fired items china, wherever they were manufactured. Objects – cups, wine vessels, bowls, flasks, flower pots, plates, ewers, gourds, bird-feeders, basins, writing boxes and even candlesticks – were made on a scale that rivals modern production methods, but were of a far greater quality. It is impossible not to admire the tenacity and sense of purpose that led to the perfection of this complex and difficult art form.

Vast resources were poured into ceramic production under the early Ming emperors. From 1402, the start of the Yongle reign, there were twelve kilns in Jingdezhen working under the direct supervision of the Ministry of Works. Jobs were shared between them to deliver greater efficiencies. Each aspect of the process, including the preparation of clay, the design and shaping of objects, their decoration, firing, packing and trans-portation, was organised centrally. These factories had existed before the Ming emperors, under the Yuan dynasty, but their increase in scale under the Ming dynasty was staggering. In the year 1443 alone the kilns received an order for 443,500 items – and this was only for the dragon and phoenix designs. As the repertoire by that date included the four seasons, birds on branches, cherry blossoms, Islamic-inspired flowers and clouds (to name but a few), it is likely that annual production at Jingdezhen would have exceeded several million objects.

Why were ceramics commissioned in such vast numbers? Partly, it was because of the demands of the court. However, recent research suggests that they were not used to serve food and drink to the emperor himself, but instead for those who represented him across Ming China. The imperial mark stamped on each item showed that these members of the imperial family or senior officials were effective regents for the imperial presence.

The Ming emperors were shaping their identity through

their Chineseness, but also through their ability to assume the accoutrements of other princely states, and of princes whom they admired. The forms of early Ming porcelain during the Yongle and Xuande eras could imitate objects and motifs from other cultures that the emperor and his officials valued, or that they wished to capture and incorporate into their territories. There are a number of surviving vessels which replicate totally different forms, including brass-inlaid metalwork and glass from the Middle East and Levant. One, in the British Museum, is a tankard with a sturdy neck and globular body. The raised ridges at the rim, separating the collar from the body, look as if they're copying an object that was made in sheet metal, where the shape would be made stronger with a thickened section around the neck. Or perhaps even jade – vessels of such shapes are recorded in the collection of Timur Beg, Prince of Samarkand. The Ming tankard has an undulating scroll pattern of a lotus at various stages in the growth cycle, with leaves, buds and full flowers, in blue that varies in colour in a controlled and deliberate way. Within the full flowers, lines of a blue so deep it's almost black alternate with lighter, more washy ones. You can see the control and talent of the decorator in the way that the lines vary: some heavy, others delicate and thin. You feel that you can experience their pleasure in work done well, in the blobs of sticky cobalt glaze that coagulate on the edges of petals and leaves.

To look at these objects is to marvel at the talent, precision, innovation and determination of their makers. As anyone who has tried to throw a pot will know, it is a task that involves a combination of the hand and eye, and control of one's own body to get the object to stay moving on the potting wheel. At Jingdezhen and the other pottery sites, huge numbers were involved. Hundreds of labourers and craftsmen worked at the kilns; thousands of trees were cut down for wood to fuel the high and reliable temperatures needed in the kilns. Firing clay is a tricky and dangerous process. Firing porcelain, which requires temperatures of up to 1500° C, is even more complex.

Sourcing the raw material wasn't difficult – there is clay all over China – but finding the right quality was key. Fortunately Jingdezhen is less than two hundred kilometres away from large deposits of white-firing kaolinic clays. Potters in the early Ming period experimented, developing new recipes for clay that included more kaolin and less iron, which enabled them to make thinner vessels, and ones that could hold new glazes, so that the porcelain glistened more than before. In order to produce more, and to make objects of greater variety in one firing, they developed new kilns. These egg-shaped kilns were used in Jingdezhen up to the 1950s. They could be fired and cooled in forty-eight hours; they could be easily repaired if (as sometimes happened) objects exploded during firing; and they enabled the potter to vary the firing temperature within the kiln.

The items most in demand were ceramic vessels of pure monochrome colours to be used at the altars where they made sacrifices for the good of the realm – red for the Sun, white for the Moon, blue for the Heavens and yellow for the Earth. Getting hold of the right glazes, however, was extremely difficult. But the Hongwu and Yongle Emperors were adamant. To achieve the strong contrast between deep blue and glistening white, it is necessary to have the best quality cobalt, a pigment made from mixing cobalt oxide with molten glass. The cobalt used in the imperial kilns was imported from Iran. It was higher quality than the local variant and could more easily be manipulated to achieve painterly effects, such as the deliberate varying and shading of blue outlines in order to imitate the washy effects of the fan, scroll and album paintings that were practised at court.

The technical innovations are astonishing. Perhaps the most complex was the creation of a deep crimson colour known as xianhong, 'fresh red'. This glaze, a copper solution, is notoriously unstable. If the copper – an auspicious material – spread into the surrounding glaze, the painting became hazy. It was hard to reach a balance between a glaze that suspended the copper pigment and one that gave clear definition. It is a highly fugitive colourant. Furthermore, it has to be thick, of the right composition and fired to an exact temperature. Attempts to produce a red glaze during the fourteenth century had failed. For reasons that are not clear, the expertise in firing copper red was lost after 1435. Perhaps it was the skill of one individual, who died. The red-glazed vessels made after this date – the death of the Xuande Emperor – have a rather pallid, liverish and very unattractive colour. The new emperor was requested to cancel all orders for red glazes 'as all attempts ended in failure'.

Over time, experimentation made it clear that using a sticky lime-alkali glaze and a shortened but higher firing temperature reduced the risk of glaze running, and produced a greater stability of colour. It proved impossible, however, to completely stop a glaze from running, and consequently most pieces of red copper early Ming porcelain have variations in colour. Excavations at Jingdezhen have shown that around 80 per cent of red pieces were discarded after firing as they didn't meet the exacting standards of quality control. In one item, a cup now in the Victoria and Albert Museum, made in the Yongle Emperor's reign, you can see the deep red across the object, except on the rim, where the sharp edge has meant that the colour has bled away from it. This thin white border – although unintentional – is also very beautiful. The hot glaze bubbles, and sometimes bursts, on the surface of the vessel to produce what's known as an orange peel effect. The burst circles of the glaze create a delicious speckled colour and a texture and sheen that resembles fruit-heavy jam, with a deep raspberry colour. This type of cup is called a *quanbei* – an 'urging cup'. When you lifted the cup to make a toast, you were meant to exhort your drinking companions to do the same. It stands only ten centimetres high on a small squat stem with a large bowl, ideal for swirling and swilling your alcoholic beverage and for enjoying the moment.

A cup of the same proportions and design in the British Museum is a showcase of all the latest technologies. The mark of the Xuande Emperor dates it to between 1426 and 1435. The shape was innovative and hard to model, with a heavy basin balanced on a small stem. Bright red dragons, incised in a red glaze, ride blue waves with huge white crests around the outside of the cup and its base. Inside, an *anhua* (secret decoration) worked in raised slip shows two five-clawed dragons chasing their tails and a flaming pearl. This detail, meant for the emperor himself, was only visible when he raised the cup to the light. This stunning decoration would greet him as he drank, so that on the outside and inside of your cup he had his soulmate, the dragon, before his eyes, in his hands and under his control.

Tenacity and pragmatism

A major part of the emperor's duties was the performance of state religious rituals. The Ming dynasty ruled over an ethnically and religiously diverse empire, but the emperor himself was the prime official of the state religion, combining the 'three teachings' of Confucianism, Buddhism and Daoism. Most of his subjects also followed this path. Individual doctrine was less important than what it enabled you to do. For all his exceptional qualities, we can see this pragmatism in the life of Admiral Zheng He. Born Ma He (all Chinese Muslims took the surname Ma) into an observant Muslim family in Yunnan province in 1371, he was enslaved in the civil unrest that followed the fall of the Yuan dynasty in 1368. Throughout his life of service to the future Yongle Emperor, Zheng He remained close to Islamic communities, visiting and worshipping at mosques. But he was also a realist: at his final mooring at Changle in Fujian province in 1431, he dedicated a stone stele to the popular local goddess Tianfei, the 'celestial consort' beloved by sailors who believed she would save them from trouble at sea when they called her name. He also made donations to a Buddhist monastery in the city, including a bronze bell with an inscription asking for long life, good luck and safety at sea.

Zheng He's activity was sensible, to preserve the optimism and morale of his sailors. Like other senior eunuchs, he was open to the mix of Chinese and Tibetan Buddhism that dominated the court life of his era. He commissioned printings of the Chinese Buddhist canon for ten monasteries, including Changle, and one in his home province, and a particularly luxurious illustrated copy of the Lotus Sutra, written in gold on blue paper (like the *Chikubushima Sutra* we have already seen), which still survives.

In Nanjing, Zheng He oversaw work on two very different religious sites while acting as garrison commander between his last two voyages. In 1426 he successfully petitioned the emperor to take charge of the refurbishment of the state altars, which had become neglected after the court's removal

to Beijing. He also undertook, at imperial command, repairs to
the Nanjing mosque, using the craftsmen and resources of the
eunuch offices in the city. But his major work was for a religious
foundation that had nothing to do with his natal religion or his
explicit responsibilities as a servant to the state religion. It was
under his supervision that one of the most important structures of the early Ming period was completed. The Da Baon
Monastery of Filial Gratitude had been begun by the Yongle
Emperor as a thank-offering to his parents. As a ruler always
conscious of the unorthodox start to his reign, filial gratitude
is a theme that ran through his pious works. Buddhist priests
travelled to Nanjing from all over China to conduct services
at the monastery, including a group of Tibetan monks who
made a three-year journey to hold a requiem for the emperor's
parents, the Hongwu Emperor and Empress Wu. Private ceremonies were also performed by the court, including the Yongle
Emperor himself.

The centrepiece of the monastic complex was a nine-storey
tower, known in later centuries as the Porcelain Pagoda, set
in the centre of the monastic courts between two mountain
peaks, as we can see from several eighteenth- and nineteenth-
century prints. According to the seventeenth-century French
mathematician Louis Le Comte, it was 'the best contrived and
noblest structure in the East'. Made of clay brought from Anhui
and fired locally, and porcelain tiles carefully shipped from
Jingdezhen, the pagoda shone like a lighthouse as the sunlight reflected off its white surfaces. At night, it gave an even
stronger impression of the power of religion, as light shone
from 146 oil lamps set into interior and exterior niches. Strings
of bells and chains tinkled in the wind. Called one of the 'Seven
Wonders of the World', it was destroyed during the unrest of
the mid-nineteenth century. In 2015 it was reconstructed in

Nanjing, but despite its great scale and ambition it seems to lack the elegance of the original. Brightly coloured, with glazed tiles impressively coloured in red, green and yellow as well as white, it would have been something never to forget. The arched doors of the pagoda were turned into 'gates of glory', a Nepalese Buddhist motif formed of coloured tiles representing images of elephants, winged goats, serpent deities, lions, crocodiles and other cult animals. Each of the four openings on the nine floors of the pagoda was decorated with these tiles. They reproduced the iconography of the 'revolving' sutra cabinet in the scripture hall at the Zhihua Si temple in Beijing.

Export and admiration

During the fifteenth century, Ming porcelain was so valued in the Mediterranean basin that, despite its origins in China, it was used to present offerings to the infant Jesus. A few extremely rich and recondite individuals, including the Ottoman sultans and the celebrated Italian collector Isabella d'Este, Marchioness of Mantua, had such wares in their possession. Andrea Mantegna, court painter to the teenage Isabella and her husband, included a Yongle period blue and white bowl in an *Adoration of the Magi*, now in the Getty Museum, made in the final years of Mantegna's life. The oldest and most important of the three wise men uses the bowl to offer gold coins to Christ, who almost touches the lip of the cup with his left foot. The object's distinctive shape is mirrored in small white glazed cups excavated at Jingdezhen, and it's likely that Mantegna was deliberately copying a cup in the Mantuan court collection. Mantegna's brother-in-law Giovanni Bellini, working fifteen years later for Isabella's brother, Alfonso d'Este, Duke of Ferrara, includes three large blue and white porcelain bowls, bearing the scrolling decoration found on many fifteenth-century Ming ceramics in *The Feast of the Gods*, a depiction of a lavish banquet hosted by Jupiter and Juno, king and queen of the Roman pantheon. We know that Alfonso and Isabella's mother, Eleonora of Aragon, owned Chinese ceramics, which Alfonso likely inherited.

Luxury Chinese goods were highly valued across the northern hemisphere, from the sophisticated courts of the Timurids, Safavids and Ottomans to the city states and kingdoms of Western Europe. Fine manuscripts of the *Shahnama*, the great Persian epic poem, and the Quran, were made at the Timurid court of Herat in modern Afghanistan, using heavy Chinese paper dyed in many colours and decorated with gold. Henry V, the English king, was buried in 1422 with a funeral shield backed with Chinese silk. Lorenzo de' Medici, the de facto ruler of Florence, who could buy anything he wanted, coveted Chinese porcelain. Fifty-one pieces are recorded in the inventory of his palace taken after his death in 1492, twenty of which were a gift from the sultan of Egypt in 1487.

The status of early Ming porcelain was high in courts and elite circles across Eurasia. An illustration from the *Shahnama*, illuminated in Shiraz in the mid-1440s, shows three Ming courtiers and local servants carrying early Ming wares. These seem to have been diplomatic gifts. Shipwrecks along the shores of South-East Asia and the Kenyan coast have uncovered not just fine blue and white ware, but more basic Ming ceramics, made for the everyday market. It's been estimated that until the 1420s Chinese ceramics made up between a third and a half of such cargos; by the middle years of the fifteenth century, local markets were producing their own very effective imitations. Copies in local materials of Chinese ceramics are found from Samarkand to Vietnam, Thailand to Egypt.

The spread of Ming, however, continued. The celebrated ceramics have been discovered all over the globe, including in a Peruvian cathedral and a Czech hospital, and in shipwreck sites as far afield as South America, Southern Africa, California and even Australia. The Ming emperors, like their most famous export, were no longer struggling to maintain their territories or their impact. An upstart dynasty ruled one of the world's richest empires without serious challengers. Resolve and perseverance had led to security. Chinese artistic culture and heritage identity today, for all its richness and variety, remains in debt to a medium and a man who lived six hundred years ago.

The city of Florence from the hills with Brunelleschi's Dome

7

FLORENCE: COMPETITION

1430–1500

If you climb the steep hills above Florence and look down on the city, a view unfolds before you that has changed remarkably little in the last five hundred years. Nestled on the banks of the Arno, surrounded by the hills and mountains of northern Tuscany, Florence is a city of towers, from those of civic buildings including the town hall (Palazzo Vecchio) and the former prison (Bargello), to religious foundations such as the churches and convents of Santa Croce and Santa Maria Novella.

Yet all these magnificent buildings pale into insignificance beside a vast brick dome which looms above them, designed by the goldsmith, architect and engineer Filippo Brunelleschi in the early fifteenth century. This is the roof of Florence's Santa Maria del Fiore. For all of its life, it has been known simply as *il Duomo*, the Dome. Brunelleschi's contemporary, the architect and thinker Leon Battista Alberti, praised this 'enormous construction towering above the heavens, vast enough to cover the whole Tuscan population with its shadow'.

With this project Brunelleschi achieved what had been

thought impossible. For several centuries, there had been a huge gaping hole in the roof of Florence's cathedral. No architect had been able to join the separate bays of the building together, partly because it stood 180 feet above the ground, and because the hole itself was almost 150 feet wide. But Brunelleschi's semi-circular cupola looks effortlessly elegant, as if it had always been intended to crown this enormous structure.

Literally underpinning this was some audacious but risky engineering. The dome consists of two shells: an external one which is the roof that still dominates Florence's skyline, and an inner one visible from within the cathedral. This ingenious system meant that the load would be spread, making it less likely to collapse. Furthermore, rather than being made of stone – usual for a building of this importance and prestige – much of Brunelleschi's dome was built from a lighter and more adaptable material: brick.

Brunelleschi's imaginative design and creative use of materials enabled his structure to stand, against the odds. It's clear that he wished to emulate the architects of ancient Rome, and for his dome to be recognised as an ambitious feat of engineering comparable to the Colosseum, the Pantheon and the viaducts and aqueducts that safely carried people and water far above ground level. But Brunelleschi was also motivated by a spirit of artistic and intellectual idealism – to do better and differently than any of his predecessors. As a textbook example of artistic innovation, his dome has come to represent not just Florence but the artistic movement the city has come to encapsulate.

Florence and the European Renaissance

Since the fifteenth century, the Renaissance has been seen as a defining moment of European cultural life. As its name suggests, it was built on a rebirth. Inspired by the legacy of classical Greece and Rome, artists, writers and thinkers tried consciously to reboot cultural life in Western Europe, using the distant past to understand the modern world. Today, historians tend to downplay the Renaissance, arguing that the classical world had never stopped being fundamental to European culture. Contemporary sources, however, make it clear that many people thought something new was happening, particularly among intellectuals and artists. Renaissance art and architecture, like that of ancient Rome, was inspired by nature, and based on rules of ideal proportion. Mathematical perspective – developed by Islamic thinkers in Baghdad and southern Spain – and Christianity were new elements in the mix. Renaissance artists used these stimuli to create paintings, sculpture and buildings that set the standard for how visual artists were to work for centuries, in cities and states across Europe, and in Europe's colonies all over the world.

And although Renaissance culture was developing everywhere, there was little doubt that something particularly exciting was happening in Florence. The city was a honeypot, attracting painters, sculptors and architects who wanted to learn the Florentine style and find well-remunerated work. These gifted individuals included the painter Masaccio, who made pictorial form seem rounded and three-dimensional, the sculptors Lorenzo Ghiberti and Donatello, who conjured deep emotion out of bronze and stone, Fra Angelico, the monk who painted paradise, and Brunelleschi himself.

These artists and their immediate successors, who included Botticelli, Leonardo and Michelangelo, aspired to produce works of art that were grounded in reality, and which connected the present to early Christianity and ancient Rome. Gold backgrounds, intended to give a sense of the divine, largely disappeared from Christian art. Holy figures, like Christ and the Virgin, looked like their Florentine commissioners, or how they wished to be seen – practically every Virgin Mary is blonde, the ideal of female physical perfection in Renaissance Italy. Stories from the Bible as well as from classical literature were set in hilly landscapes punctuated by small fortified towns that closely resembled the countryside around Florence.

Fifteenth-century Florentine architecture, painting and sculpture gives a strong sense that man, God and nature are in equilibrium, and that all is right with the world. This was, however, an attractive fiction. Idealism and innovation alone can't explain the Renaissance in Florence, or indeed anywhere else. Rivalry and competition, two less positive but recognisably human emotions, were key to its success. Take Brunelleschi's dome: its design and construction were intrinsically linked to the architect's deep-seated hatred of Lorenzo Ghiberti. Their mutual animosity predated the dome by two decades.

In 1400, artists from all over Tuscany had competed to create a set of bronze doors for the city's Baptistry. Bronze had been the preferred medium of ancient Greek and Roman sculptors, and in the early fifteenth century this gave it a prestige above every other material. But to make a life-size sculpture in bronze, let along two enormous doors, was a huge technical challenge. The competition was run by a powerful trade organisation, the Clothfinishers' Guild, fierce rivals of the Woolworkers, who controlled artistic commissions for the cathedral, next to the baptistry. Each contestant was given four brass tablets and was asked to melt them down and sculpt and cast a bronze relief of Abraham preparing to kill his only son, Isaac, at God's command. This competition piece was to be exactly the size of one of the twenty-eight narrative panels that would ultimately make up the doors.

Ultimately, the decision came down to a choice between two young and superbly talented goldsmiths – Brunelleschi and Ghiberti. It's evident that the judging committee was as concerned about their ability to deliver as it was excited by their drive and ambition. Brunelleschi was the slightly older and more experienced of the two. He was the safer choice, for all that his panel was spatially innovative. However, Brunelleschi's relief employed an old-fashioned technique of bronze casting. This involved making each of the figures and some other elements separately and attaching them to a metal backing with pins. It was less elegant than Ghiberti's solution, which was essentially to create the panel as one element – only the tiny figure of Isaac made ready for sacrifice was a separate piece. Crucially, Ghiberti's idea was more technically efficient, and, because it used less bronze, significantly cheaper. But neither he nor the guild had been entirely sure his method would work.

It's still unclear if Ghiberti entirely won the competition. According to one account, the Guild wanted the two artists to work together. Ghiberti's own highly partial recollection, written many years later in his autobiographical *Commentaries*, relates that a small majority of the votes went to him. But what Brunelleschi did next suggests that the first story is true. Unable to contemplate collaborating with Ghiberti, he left for Rome in the company of his friend Donatello. It was during his lengthy absence from Florence that he learnt to understand the construction methods of the ancient Romans. Their use of brick was critical for how Brunelleschi would come, twenty years later, to build his Dome.

Meanwhile, Ghiberti took to working on his doors. They were much admired and led to an even more remarkable commission: two further doors, of glittering gilt-bronze, telling stories from the Old Testament, which Michelangelo was to dub the Gates of Paradise. Brunelleschi did not share his fellow citizens' adulation of Ghiberti. It's clear that his desire to worst the man he saw as his artistic nemesis spurred his ambition and his will to succeed with the dome. The Woolworkers' Guild were quick to exploit this, to get more out of their chosen architect and to trump their rivals the Clothfinishers' success with the baptistry.

In 1420, when Brunelleschi became supervisor of the Dome project, it was on the condition that he shared it with Ghiberti. The Guild gambled that this would spur Brunelleschi, notorious for his slowness, to complete the job in hand. Posterity shows that they were right: within three years Ghiberti's annual salary (but not his title) was downgraded, reflecting the real progress that Brunelleschi was making. Slowly but surely, the dome was built, brick by brick.

Challenge and one-upmanship dominated artistic life in Renaissance Florence: from the guilds and companies that regulated artistic training and activity to the workshops within which artists worked, and the public bodies and private individuals who awarded most artistic commissions. There were intrinsic reasons for this state of affairs. First, the sheer number of aspiring artists in the city required them to be unusually driven and single-minded in order to succeed. Those who couldn't tended to move elsewhere. Second, Florentine artistic life depended on collective commissioning. Everyone who ordered art – families, monasteries and convents, religious brotherhoods, guilds, the communal government – instigated at the very least a discussion and at most a competition to choose their artist. And finally, Florence itself and its structures were based on rivalry and competition. This, and the desire to excel, was the glue that bound the city and its artists together.

Prosperity and political insecurity

Brunelleschi's Dome is one of many examples of the spirit of enterprise that created the Florentine Renaissance, both from the viewpoint of those who made it and from those who paid for it. Competitiveness underpinned life in Florence, the world's first truly capitalist economy. Since the late Middle Ages the city's merchants had controlled large swathes of the European textile trade, but a shift from trading in wool to trading in money made Florence into the continent's financial capital. Two factors – that the city's currency, the gold florin, was the dollar of the fifteenth century, and Florentine bankers developed bills of exchange (meaning that debts could be paid, money could be lent and credit offered without cash) – made Florence the birthplace of modern banking. This was literally a godsend for Christian businessmen, as, for the first time, it permitted trade in money without committing the sin of usury, or charging interest on a loan.

This meant that Florence and many Florentines became incredibly rich. Their banking networks stretched all over Europe, led by merchants including the Medici family, who eventually came to rule the city. Because the banks lent money to everyone with pretentions to power, they enjoyed influence throughout the continent. Immigrants and income poured into Florence, but the city's fabulous wealth aggravated its political instability. Florence was a plum ripe for picking by the aggressive rulers of larger states, including the pope, the duke of Milan, the Republic of Venice, and even the king of France. All these regimes supported Florentine factions that promoted their interests, making the city difficult to govern and vulnerable to attack. During the fifteenth century, foreign armies threatened Florence with invasion on at least eight occasions, with actual invasions in 1494 and 1530.

Florentine domestic government was also notoriously insecure. Between 1400 and 1530, roughly the timespan of the Renaissance, the city underwent more than seven regime changes and its internal stability was threatened on at least five occasions by potential civil disobedience, often fomented by outside agitators. In contrast, the Republic of Venice maintained a steady and consistent form of government from the late thirteenth century to 1797.

Several Italian urban republics had risen to prominence during the eleventh and twelfth centuries. Rather than resembling modern republican states, they were more like the oil- and gas-rich oligarchies of today's Arabian Peninsula. Foreigners, women, clergy and the working classes were excluded from political life. In Florence, only men who owned property above a certain threshold, who were over thirty and who belonged to one of the city's seven major guilds could stand for public office. By the fifteenth century, Florence's retention of a governmental system of elected officials for all state positions, chosen by lot every few months, appeared not merely old-fashioned but self-destructive. The system was prone to exploitation by the city's elite, who called themselves patricians. In practice, only their candidates were elected.

Political instability meant that Florence's merchants and bankers had strong reasons to devote themselves to cultural activities. Commissioning art and architecture was a surrogate for exercising power, whether within the existing structure of the republic, the guilds or on their own initiative. These men were financially secure but socially and politically competitive, and they had appetites, interests, obligations and pleasures to satisfy. A further comfort was their belief that expenditure on art and architecture was not a choice but a duty.

The leading European philosophers of the day, in tune

with Christian as well as ancient Greek and Roman thought, argued that the wealthy had a social responsibility to beautify their surroundings and those of their fellow men. This doctrine, called 'magnificence', meant that improving churches, convents, monasteries, public buildings and even private residences was considered morally beneficial. Not only did this change Florence's appearance for the better, but it drew attention to the patron's magnanimity, enabling them to fulfil essential religious obligations, as well as providing a livelihood for many craftsmen and their families.

As one merchant, Giovanni Rucellai, wrote, such endeavours 'have given and give me the greatest satisfaction and pleasure, because in part they serve the honour of God as well as the honour of the city and the commemoration of myself'. Rucellai's range of expenditure was entirely typical of his class. He rebuilt his house, his local parish of San Pancrazio, where he was to be buried, the façade of the church of Santa Maria Novella and his villa outside the city. As a member of the Bankers' Guild he also contributed to civic endeavours: through the guild, Rucellai endowed San Pancrazio and supported the dowries of four poor girls a year.

This particular mixture of political and social competition, combined with piety and pride, characterises much Florentine art of the early Renaissance. Perhaps it is clearest of all in the principal chapel of Santa Maria Novella. In the late 1480s, Domenico Ghirlandaio and his assistants – including a very young Michelangelo – painted an elaborate series of frescoes in this echoing space. Ghirlandaio's client was the well-connected patrician Giovanni Tornabuoni, a leading executive of the Medici Bank, treasurer to the pope and uncle to Lorenzo de' Medici.

Ghirlandaio was one of Italy's most sought-after artists. He had worked for Florence's government and leading men, and for external dignitaries, including the pope. In the Tornabuoni chapel we see the patron's family and friends in glorious colour and on a life-size scale, associating on an equal basis with the Holy Family and saints. An inscription – perhaps written by Giovanni Tornabuoni, certainly chosen by him – celebrates the chapel's inauguration 'in the year 1490, when the most beautiful city, graced by treasures, victories, arts and buildings, enjoyed wealth, health and peace'. There could be no clearer demonstration of why Florence's leading men commissioned art.

Relatively little has changed here since Giovanni Tornabuoni's day. The chapel's lofty Gothic walls are covered from floor to ceiling (including the windows) with the lives of the Virgin Mary and John the Baptist, the patron's name saint. Appropriately for a man who owed his advancement to his family connections, Giovanni's name saint was Jesus' cousin. It is striking how often Ghirlandaio inserts Giovanni and his family into the most important moments of the saints' lives. With his son Lorenzo, his nephew Piero de' Medici and political, banking and intellectual associates, Giovanni Tornabuoni watches Zechariah, St John's father, announce his name.

Giovanni's daughters, and his beautiful pregnant daughter-in-law Giovanna degli Albizzi, are on hand to rejoice at the Virgin Mary's birth, bringing restorative fruit and drinks to her mother Anne, who rests from her labour in an opulent bedchamber decorated with lavishly gilded woodcarving in the height of contemporary fashion. Giovanna, who shortly afterwards died giving birth to her child, a boy, witnesses the Virgin Mary's visit to her cousin Elizabeth, the moment when both holy women became aware that their sons were quickening (moving) in their wombs.

The message of the chapel is clear: religious observance and strong family connections bring prosperity. And prosperity is something which the wealthy have an obligation to share. In Giovanni Tornabuoni's will, he made provisions for massive choir stalls for the Dominican friars, windows, an altarpiece, a covering for the great cross, tombs for the family, candles and memorial Masses to be said for his soul and those of his closest relatives. In the Tornabuoni chapel, the world of fifteenth-century Florence still feels alive, as it does in chapels, convents and monasteries all over the city.

Private architecture, public power

The presence of Tornabuoni's family and associates on the walls of his family chapel reflects the factionalism of Florentine public life. During the fourteenth and early fifteenth centuries, several families, including the Albizzi, the Pazzi and the Strozzi, vied to control the city. By the early fifteenth century the Medici, the family of bankers originally from northern Tuscany, held power. Cosimo, the head of the family, was Florence's richest and most powerful man.

Cosimo's excellent political instincts and wealth were to give his family an enduring status. In 1433, his political enemies engineered his banishment from Florence, on the crime of elevating his position above that of ordinary citizens. The following year he was back: the absence of the Medici Bank had had a drastic effect on the Florentine economy. His rivals were expelled from the city. Many were never to return. For the next sixty-one years Cosimo, his son Piero and grandson Lorenzo were the de facto rulers of Florence. Their power as international bankers, with clients including the pope, made them hard to dislodge. A century later, Cosimo's descendants became the Grand Dukes of Tuscany, and would rule Florence until 1737.

Yet republicanism died a slow death in the city. During the fifteenth century, the Medici were mindful of the fact that their rule was only tolerated because the alternative – anarchy and civil disorder – was even less palatable to their peers. Although Lorenzo bore the soubriquet 'the Magnificent', he was never the undisputed leader of the city, only the 'master of the workshop', as a contemporary pithily characterised his authority. There were numerous serious threats to the family's rule. In 1478, Lorenzo's brother Giuliano was assassinated in Florence's cathedral, in front of a ten-thousand-strong congregation, by a group of conspirators led by the Pazzi family, supported with money and arms by the pope. And in 1494, the family were expelled from the city after two years of chaotic government led by Lorenzo's arrogant son Piero. In this uncertain world, artistic patronage was a convincing way of asserting even an illusory authority.

Nothing better illustrates the shifting power dynamics of Florence than the palaces built by the Medici and their rivals. Fifteenth-century Florence underwent a building boom comparable to early twenty-first-century London. Many of these palaces were consciously indebted to ancient Roman architecture, so that their commissioners could show their superiority over their fellow men. For instance, the statesman Bartolomeo Scala, who used his talents to pull himself from poverty to high status, built himself a small but exquisite palace, designed by the innovative architect Giuliano da Sangallo.

The Palazzo Scala opens from the street onto a small courtyard decorated with delicately carved relief sculptures. A closer look shows that they are made of plaster, the cheapest of materials, and represent the most violent, unpleasant subjects. Men and beasts fight for supremacy, scratching and biting to gain the upper hand. These highly crafted representations of brutality, created from sand, lime and water, were intended to demonstrate Scala's ascendency – more clearly than words ever could – over his fellow men, and of men over animals.

In Florence, private architecture became a surrogate for political aspirations and authority. A decade after his triumphal return to the city in 1434, Cosimo de' Medici felt sufficiently comfortable to build a new family palace on the Via Larga, or 'wide street', a stone's throw from Brunelleschi's newly completed Dome. Cosimo and his sons bought up property surrounding their old palace in the parish of San Lorenzo, their power base in the city. Their architect, Michelozzo, levelled the existing structures, and an elegant building in the avant-garde classical style rose slowly from the ground.

Although the palace has only three floors, optical illusion makes it seem taller. Michelozzo cleverly exploited the transition between the large stone blocks of the lowest level (made using an ancient Roman architectural technique called rustication), and the two upper storeys, where each stone is cut on every side (ashlar masonry). Even today, the palace seems to dwarf its neighbours, and presents an imposing front to the outside world. This is a place you could defend against civic unrest, if you had to. The stone benches marking the periphery of the palace were not installed to make this into a civic space. Rather, they were intended for those who supported, or were supported financially by, the Medici: what an ancient Roman magnate would have called his clients. These seats projected Medici family power into the public sphere.

All this show emphasised that the family were not straightforwardly the city's rulers. Unlike civic palaces, such as the

Palazzo della Signoria, the seat of Florence's rulers, there was no open space in front of the Palazzo Medici. In Florence, such areas were reserved for churches and buildings with a clear public purpose. To propose a square before the Medici Palace would have destroyed the republican fiction that was so important to Florentines. At least superficially, the Medici Palace stays within the bounds of private architecture. It is a square-ish structure, relatively compact, confined within the existing fabric of the city, sharing walls with neighbours.

Sixteen years later, a far grander private house began to rise on the other side of the Arno. Built on the site of a former stone colony, it soon loomed over everything nearby, even the local church of Santo Spirito, designed by Brunelleschi himself. This palace was commissioned by another banker, Luca Pitti, an aspirant to political power and traditionally a Medici supporter. Construction began in 1458, the year that Pitti led a coup against the Florentine government that was meant to increase Medici authority. It halted around 1466, when he and four others plotted – unsuccessfully – to remove Piero de' Medici from power. The Pitti Palace reflects his power in Florence at this moment. It's been much altered and greatly expanded, but if you look at the central seven bays and three doors which constitute the original façade, you will see that the architect, Brunelleschi's pupil Luca Fancelli, was essentially asked to design a supersize Medici Palace.

Pitti is said to have asked his architect to make the internal courtyard of his palace large enough to swallow up the whole Palazzo Medici. This was in keeping with the dreams of someone who saw himself as the kingmaker of Florentine politics. The building has the same rusticated stones that are such a conspicuous feature of the Medici Palace, but here they became, in the words of the French historian Hippolyte Taine, not just building blocks but 'chunks of rocks and sections of mountains'.

A third Florentine palace, the Palazzo Strozzi, is more ambitious still. It was designed by Benedetto da Maiano for the merchant Filippo Strozzi. Strozzi's opposition to the Medici wasn't personal – it was a family obligation. The two clans had long loathed each other, and when the Medici gained the upper hand in 1433, they set about removing their rivals from Florence. Filippo, aged five, was sent into exile, together with most of his male relatives. His formidable mother Alessandra maintained his interests in the city until he was allowed to return thirty-three years later.

Filippo came back to Florence exceptionally rich and the head of the Strozzi family, but unable to take a major role in public affairs. Tellingly, his personal motto was 'Be Mild' (*Mitis esto*). In the late 1480s, towards the end of his life, Filippo felt sufficiently confident to assert his family's status in Florence. He devoted his activity as a patron of art and architecture to making the Strozzi name visible in the city, for instance in his burial chapel in Santa Maria Novella, next to that of Giovanni Tornabuoni.

Filippo's most significant undertaking, however, was the new Strozzi Palace. He spent about a third of his income on its construction alone. The foundations were laid in 1489, but Filippo and his brothers had been planning it for many years, purchasing and subsequently demolishing property surrounding the existing family home on Via Tornabuoni in the centre of the city. As a result, the Strozzi Palace – unlike the Medici – is a free-standing building, far taller than any private building in the vicinity. It presents a symmetrical and ordered front to the world on all four sides. Each is emblazoned with the family arms and Filippo's own armorial device of three crescents.

The Strozzi Palace's power derives from its height, together with the massive stone blocks that make up its façade. This is enhanced by the transition from rough to refined architectural orders as you move up the building, from the ground floor with its huge doorway and small square windows to the delicate arched openings of the upper levels. The palace is imposing, but it is also accessible. Two large doors, at front and back, open the interior courtyard to the street, and by association to the world. This building suggests that if the Strozzi held the reins of power, they would use their authority for the public good. Stones and mortar speak louder than words.

Palace interiors: spend, spend, spend

The exteriors of these palaces were undeniably impressive. Yet this was nothing in comparison to the riches found within their walls. By the middle of the fifteenth century, the production and display of luxury goods was a way of life for wealthy Florentines. To live elegantly, surrounded by fine art and furniture, linen and tableware, was an outer reflection of a refined and worthy mind. As we have seen, contemporary social and political theory opined that private magnificence benefited society more widely. It provided a livelihood for the virtuous, hard-working artisans who were the backbone of civil society. The ornate contents of these grand family palaces were in stark contrast to the imposing but spartan interiors of public buildings, such as the Palazzo della Signoria, which housed those Florentines chosen to hold state office. Here they wore simple clothes, slept together in a basic dormitory and ate at a communal table.

This sudden shift from sobriety to ostentation was another reflection of financial prosperity and political competition. In the early fifteenth century, Florentines put most of their private resources into artistic projects – churches, monasteries, public fountains, hospitals and the like – which would more obviously benefit those outside the immediate family circle. By the end of the century they were spending more on their homes. Through inventories, made as part of the inheritance process, we can trace this explosion in material goods. In 1418, for instance, there were only six chairs in the Medici family's principal Florentine residence. In 1492, when a comprehensive inventory was made of the moveable contents of the Medici Palace following Lorenzo the Magnificent's death, all of the rooms used by the family contained chairs, and much more besides. The clerk who compiled the list estimated the financial value of the palace's contents at 79,618 florins. At a time when fifty florins could keep a family for a year, this was a staggering sum. The Medici Palace was unique in the quality and quantity of its decoration, but because it fitted into a general pattern in Florence, it's worth looking at it in more detail.

Contemporaries recorded their impression of the building in awed terms. Entering from the street, the perfectly judged proportions of the central courtyard made it seem larger than it was. When visitors' eyes turned, inevitably, towards the light, their eyes were caught by the Medici family's emblem, seven balls, or *palle*, interspersed with circular sculptural reliefs. Most of these were copies of cameos and engraved jewels in the Medici collection. These tiny, intricately carved hard stones, often decorated with portraits of emperors and stories from Greek and Roman mythology, were prized everywhere in Europe for their sophistication and subject matter (the Medici family's collection was second only to that formed by Pope Paul II). In 1492, these were among the highest-value items in the palace. An onyx cameo carved with a scene of Noah's Ark was valued at two thousand florins, twenty times more than the most expensive painting, Fra Angelico's *Adoration of the Kings*. Placing large facsimiles of these precious decorated stones in the courtyard, the most public place in the palace, was a further way of highlighting the family's wealth and status.

In the middle of the courtyard stood Donatello's sculpture of David, the puny Old Testament hero who defeated the giant Goliath with a slingshot. Florentines saw David, and Judith, who had made Holofernes, her people's enemy, drunk, and then beheaded him, as emblems of their state's capacity to overcome far greater powers. David represented a series of firsts. It was the first representation of a naked man, and the first free-standing bronze sculpture created since the fall of the Roman Empire in the fourth century CE. It was also the first time an individual Florentine family had dared to use a symbol of the city's identity for their own purposes.

Donatello's statue, made for a private house, is markedly different from earlier Florentine representations of David because it is both political and strongly sensuous. Feathers from the wing of Goliath's helmet caress David's inner thigh. This surprised contemporaries, but they were most shocked by the governmental aspirations that the sculpture brought out into the open. A notorious inscription on the pedestal identified the Medici family's interests with those of the Florentine state: 'The victor is whoever defends the fatherland. God crushes the wrath of an enormous foe. Behold! A boy overcame a great tyrant. Conquer, O citizens!' Twenty years later a second bronze by Donatello, *Judith*, joined *David* in the palace courtyard. Commissioning such works for a private setting remained highly controversial. Even some Medici allies thought it overstepped the mark. One of the first acts of the republican government that overthrew the Medici in 1494 was to move both sculptures to Florence's main public space, the Piazza della Signoria. They were rein-stalled outside the town hall, the Palazzo della Signoria, as guardians of civic responsibility rather than tyranny.

Guests permitted to move from the courtyard to the interior of the Palazzo Medici entered a palace that surpassed those of many kings. Lorenzo's ground-floor chamber, next to the garden, contained three enormous paintings by Paolo Uccello depicting Florence's victory at the Battle of San Romano in 1432 (appro-priated by Lorenzo and claimed back by their rightful owners after the Medici regime fell), together with pictures of battles and hunts, as well as tapestries. Seven brass candelabra provided reliable lighting at any time of day or night, picking out details of the paintings and the fine intarsia decoration – different woods worked into pictures or patterns – which adorned two imposing beds, one for daytime rest, the other for sleep. Walnut panelling, ornamented with more intarsia, including a twenty-nine-foot built-in cabinet and a series of display shelves, lined the walls. The cabinet was filled with exceptionally rare and valuable Chinese porcelain, one of Lorenzo's private passions.

The very best rooms were found on the first floor, or *piano nobile*. Most striking of all was the family's private chapel, a privilege generally reserved for royalty. Those allowed into this inner sanctum marvelled at the cycle of wall paintings by Benozzo Gozzoli that showed the Medici family in the train of the Three Kings as they travelled across the Near East to find the infant Jesus. Cosimo, Piero and his second son Giuliano ride in the procession. Since the fifteenth century, many have believed that Lorenzo, Cosimo's eldest grandson, wasn't just a member of the entourage, but the Young King himself. Power is represented as this family's right, passing from father to son.

Aside from the chapel, the first floor of the palace accom-modated spaces for eating, for rest and for welcoming guests.

The most public of these was the *Sala Grande*, adorned with three large canvases of the *Labours of Hercules* by Antonio and Piero del Pollaiuolo, *St John the Baptist* by Andrea del Castagno and *Lions in a Cage* by Pesellino. All of these subjects – like David and Judith in the courtyard – were symbols of Florentine state identity. This floor also contained three separate suites of rooms, one for Lorenzo, the others for his two elder sons, Piero and Giovanni. Each consisted of a *camera* (chamber), *antecamera* (an ancillary room next to the chamber), and a third space, a *studiolo* (study) or a bathroom. The *camera* was a multi-purpose room, where men slept, conceived their legitimate heirs and entertained privileged guests. Like many of his contemporaries, Lorenzo de' Medici did his most important business in his *camera*.

Lorenzo's most intimate apartment was his study, a smallish room originally built for his father Piero. The floor and ceiling were decorated with ceramic tiles and roundels made by the sculptor Luca della Robbia (inventor of the lustrous ceramic glazes that bear his name), while the walls held more intarsia cabinets for Lorenzo's treasures, including clocks, cameos, small paintings, vases and rings. In 1492, the vases alone were valued at 17,850 florins. Lorenzo was proud that other rulers knew of his inner sanctum: its decor was imitated by at least one other Italian leader, the military commander Federico da Montefeltro.

Spend and innovation

Everyone who could followed the Medici pattern. Without exception, the men of Florence's top three hundred families spent small fortunes on art, furnishings and fabrics, particularly to mark their marriage alliances. To some extent this

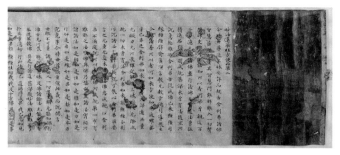

Lotus Sutra, chapter on 'Expedient Means' (*Chikubushima Sutra*), eleventh century CE

Phoenix Hall/Hōōdō, Byōdō-in, Uji, 1050–3 CE

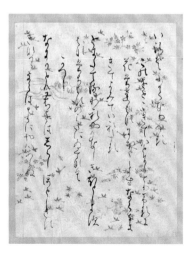

Page from the collection of poems by Lady Ise (Ise shū), early twelfth century CE

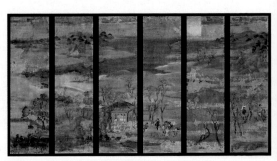

Landscape screen, pigment on silk, probably eleventh century CE

'The Eastern Cottage' from *The Tale of Genji*, early twelfth century CE

Lacquered wood toiletry case decorated with cart wheels in a stream, twelfth century CE

The Yongle Emperor in
the Dragon Chair, probably
fifteenth century CE

Tribute giraffe with attendant,
sixteenth century CE

Portrait of an official in front of the Forbidden City, Beijing, fifteenth century CE

Royal reception in a landscape, from a *Shahnama* (Book of Kings) of Firdausi, 1444 CE

Stem porcelain cup, with incised dragons in red against blue waves, 1426–35 CE

Blue and white porcelain jug in the shape of a tankard, early fifteenth century CE

Red-glazed porcelain wine cup, 1403–25 CE

Palazzo Medici, Florence, 1444–60 CE

Palazzo Strozzi, Florence, begun 1489 CE, completed 1548

Donatello, *David*, c. 1440 CE

Sandro Botticelli, *Primavera*, c. 1480 CE

Raphael, *The Madonna of the Pinks*, c. 1506–7 CE

Masaccio, *The Holy Trinity, with the Virgin, St John and donors*, 1427–8 CE

Leonardo da Vinci, *Study for the Battle of Anghiari*, c. 1503 CE

was true in prosperous cities all over Europe – then, as now, marriage was a good moment to decorate your house. But what made Florence into the continent's artistic capital was Florentines' desire to commission not just the best, or the most expensive, but the most innovative works. This was a means of showing your superiority over your neighbours.

Thanks to this competitive pressure, Florentines developed new genres for art. One of these was narrative painting that didn't tell Christian stories. Secular painting as we know it developed out of the rather prosaic habit of decorating furniture and wall panelling with stories drawn from ancient mythology and history, or from more modern poetry. Men tended to commission such works for their chambers around the time of their first marriage. We often think of art made for a purely functional purpose as having little worth, but it's clear from inventories that these paintings had a high financial value, and that they were cherished. Thousands of Florentine furniture paintings survive in museums and private collections across the world. They range from poor quality works to some of the most-loved pictures of Western art. Take Sandro Botticelli's *Primavera*, a mythological painting of vast erudition and sophistication inspired by a range of Greek, Latin and Italian literature. It is first recorded in a 1499 inventory of the possessions of Lorenzo de' Medici's ward and cousin, Lorenzo de' Pierfrancesco. He commissioned it around about the time of his betrothal to the Tuscan noblewoman Semiramide Appiano for the room where they would consummate their marriage. *Primavera* was probably made to hang above a day bed. It was thought that if women looked at beautiful images at the moment of conception, they would have sons – in this male-dominated society, boys were positive additions, while girls were considered expensive liabilities.

Yet if Botticelli's *Primavera* had an ostensibly simple purpose, there's nothing straightforward about it. More ink has been spilt over this picture than almost any other in the history of art. It shows male and female figures standing on a flower-strewn bank in the midst of an orange grove. The fruit in the trees, resembling the *palle* of the Medici family's heraldic device, would have wittily connected the picture to the commissioning family. In the *Primavera*, Botticelli represents the nymph Chloris being raped by the wind god Zephyr; her transformation into the goddess Flora; Venus, the goddess of love and marriage, blessing the Three Graces; and Mercury, messenger of the gods, putting the clouds of winter to flight. It's hard to make sense of this, but it's least confusing if you move from right to left, from the creation of spring represented by Chloris' metamorphosis into the goddess of fertility to the figure of Mercury protecting the Garden of Love.

There are many texts behind Botticelli's painting. Its mood was inspired by a contemporary Latin poem, the *Rusticus*, about the joys of country life, composed by the humanist scholar Angelo Poliziano, tutor to Lorenzo de' Pierfrancesco and his Medici cousins. The story of Zephyr and Flora comes from the *Fasti*, Ovid's long poem about the months and festivals of the Roman calendar, while spring's arrival is indebted to a more scientific ancient Latin text, Lucretius' *De Rerum Natura* (On the Nature of Things).

What's remarkable about the painting is that it's both deeply erudite and connected to everyday life. Its magical, unreal mood recalls some of the most popular love poetry of the day – verses by the medieval Italian poets Dante, Boccaccio and Petrarch, which every Florentine knew from childhood. Perhaps it's closest of all to Lorenzo de' Medici's poetry, and a song he wrote which extols the beauty of youth and happiness, but warns it's here today, gone tomorrow. Botticelli's gods and goddesses are at once part of the real world as well as the products of his and his patron's rich imaginations. The dance steps they take would have been familiar to fifteenth-century Florentines, as would have been the leafy bower that frames them (during spring, young men cut down green boughs and attached them to the doors of the women they admired).

Other elements, however, are far stranger. The grassy meadow with more than 130 identifiable species of flowers – all of them present in Tuscany – resembles no known place, but the *millefleur* or 'thousand flowers' tapestries exported from Flanders. The Graces are clothed in versions of the under-shirts and jewels worn by prosperous unmarried women. Their costumes are see-through and little about their physical appearance is left to the viewer's imagination, yet we know that real women from the elite were fully clothed and veiled when they went out on the streets of Renaissance Florence.

The wonder of *Primavera* is that no one can understand all of its elements, but that everyone who has seen it has grasped that it's a picture about spring, and love. Botticelli's artistic talent enabled him to meld his different inspirations into something that works in visual form, so that the painting becomes more than just the sum of its parts. As a result you don't need to know any of this background to understand that *Primavera* is a testament to beauty, passion, renewal and the continuing cycle of nature, as well as to rape and tragedy. We care about the painting, not the sources that inspired it.

The genius of Botticelli and other Florentine painters was in developing a simple form of household decoration into something which could tell complicated stories quickly, and which could talk to people across many centuries and continents. This was an unlikely beginning of a rich tradition of secular painting in post-Roman Western art, from the works of Rubens and Velázquez to Manet and Cy Twombly. And much of this springs from the desire of wealthy Florentines to have the best of the best painted furniture in their bedrooms.

Florence, the honeypot

In the early 1470s, when an aspiring artist called Leonardo arrived in Florence from the small town of Vinci, the city boasted more artists than butchers. This number included celebrated artists, such as the sculptor and painter Andrea del Verrocchio with whom Leonardo – ultimately the most famous of all – had come to train, and legions of their less successful collaborators and assistants, on whom their work absolutely depended. Florence was home to hundreds of painters, sculptors, potters and architects because cultural patronage was a viable way for Florentines to show their superiority over others. At that time there was nowhere in Europe where an artist could potentially make more money, because everyone in the city, from the richest to the poorest, was in the market for art.

As a result, artists from across Italy and beyond moved to train and work in Florence. There were Spaniards, Neapolitans, Flemings, Germans – many of whose names, even after years in the city, still identified them as being from somewhere else. Some came simply for the commercial opportunities, but just as many were attracted by the city's reputation for artistic innovation. These artists wanted to make buildings, paintings and sculpture which exuded the strong sense of harmony and order that characterises Florentine Renaissance art.

Central to this was the development of one-point linear perspective. This simple and effective means of creating spatial recession underpins modern visual culture. For centuries, every school in the Western world has taught it. We all learnt as children how to use a single vanishing point, placed on a horizon line, together with a series of orthogonals to create the illusion of spatial depth and three dimensions on a two-dimensional surface. Still and moving images depend on perspective, and because it's one of the building blocks of the modern world it's almost impossible to think of it as new or radical. But once it was – and the breakthrough moment came in early fifteenth-century Florence.

One morning around the year 1420, Brunelleschi stood outside the front doors of the cathedral he knew so well, with an image of the building in his hand. This sketch had been made using linear perspective. He put a small hole in its centre and attached a handle to it – holding this before his face, but facing away from him. Taking a mirror, Brunelleschi held it behind the image. Through the small hole he had made, he saw the image reflected in the mirror. What was in the reflection looked exactly like what he saw before him. Brunelleschi's brilliant and simple experiment meant that painters, sculptors and architects could now make flat objects imitate the real world.

Other artists were quick to pick up on this revolutionary idea, among them Brunelleschi's friend Donatello and the young painter Masaccio – very likely also a personal friend. The pilaster-framed arch which surrounds Masaccio's *Trinity* fresco in the church of Santa Maria Novella closely resembles the arcade that Brunelleschi had built for the Hospital of the Holy Innocents. The vanishing point is on the ledge that the donors kneel on. From this, orthogonal lines travel up to the outlines of the coffers in the ceiling. Masaccio's contemporaries were amazed by the palpable realism of this painting, the first to incorporate Brunelleschi's theory of perspective.

Yet at this moment this idea was not set in stone. In fact, Masaccio's *Trinity* doesn't strictly obey the rules of one-point perspective – in all likelihood because the painting would look better that way.

The idea itself had been born far from Florence. It was the great tenth-century Baghdadi mathematician and geometrician Abu Ali al-Hasan Ibn al-Haytham (known in the West as Alhazen) who discovered light rays and developed a theory of vision based on geometric abstraction. This argued that rays of light radiated from points on the surface of an object, converging in the eye as a form (sūra). Ibn al-Haytham's theory was an inversion of the ancient Greek and Roman theory of extromission, which held that light rays emerged from the eye. He also addressed the relationship between the specific qualities of an object and the mental or conceptual representation of it. Alhazen, however, never conceived that you could use this theory to construct realistic, human-centred representations of the world. Nor, more significantly, that you would ever want to: images that envision and control the world through the eye remain contrary to mainstream Islamic thought. Curiously, the Western reception of his *Book of Optics* created a pictorial theory, single-point perspective, that made the human gaze the 'pivotal point' of perception and encouraged artists to depict this in paintings. In the fifteenth century, only a Western Christian like Brunelleschi – who believed that images that looked real took you closer to God – could have conceived of such a thing.

The most avant-garde theology of his day argued that Christians should try to imitate Jesus – his sacrifices, his actions and his piety. Three-dimensional and perspectival images and sculpture became so successful because they reflected the zeitgeist. How better could you behave like

Christ than if you had convincingly lifelike depictions of him before your eyes, set in spaces that seemed real, and chimed with the reality of contemporary life, its settings and its contexts?

Within a few decades, one-point perspective had spread throughout Europe. The Florentine nobleman and architect Leon Battista Alberti's treatise *On Painting* played an important role in this. Alberti's book is extremely close to Brunelleschi, Donatello and Masaccio's practical explorations of perspective. Because it was translated into Latin, the international language of scholarship, many outside Florence got to hear of the idea. Art, however, was the main conduit. Donatello – the most admired Italian sculptor of his generation – disseminated the concept around Italy in the many years he spent working outside Florence. Other artists visited Florence to learn this new skill. Typical of those who sought to use perspective was the Venetian Jacopo Bellini, who lived and worked in the city with his master, Gentile da Fabriano, in the mid-1420s. His remarkable pair of drawing books, filled with perspectival visions of cities and landscapes, were inspired by his Florentine sojourn.

Eighty years later, artists were still coming to Florence. One of the most celebrated incomers was the painter and architect Raffaello Sanzio, or Raphael. Born in Urbino in the isolated Marche, and son of the court painter, Raphael was one of those rare individuals endowed with talent, charm and energy in equal measure. He spent four formative years in Florence, developing a more dynamic style shaped by the art of his contemporaries, who included Fra Bartolomeo and Michelangelo. But the artist who made the greatest impression on him was Leonardo da Vinci, who belonged to an older generation. Before Florence, Raphael's paintings were undeniably beautiful, but they lacked punch. The opportunity to see, copy and probably discuss the works of Leonardo and Michelangelo with their creators transformed his painting. For the first time, there is a sense of movement in his art, as well as harmony. Even in a tiny painting like the *Madonna of the Pinks*, we sense the twist of the Virgin as she reaches to clasp the Christ Child's hand, as well as his inching closer to his mother. This ability to make a static moment into something alive, which seems to move before the viewer's eyes, is something that Raphael learnt from his study of Leonardo's work. For the first time, Raphael's paintings convey psychological depth. This combination of meaning and form, which he was to develop further during his years in Rome as the favourite artist of successive popes, made his works so admired in subsequent centuries.

Art and diplomacy

Just as artists were drawn to Florence, successive Florentine governments exported their art to their known world. Florence was the first modern state to consistently use art as a political and diplomatic commodity. After 1434, this process was controlled by the Medici family. Cosimo, his sons and grandsons made up for what they lacked in authority with diplomatic tact. Because Florence was a small and prosperous state, always under threat from political giants, they used soft power as a means of keeping their military rivals outside the city's gates.

Cosimo de' Medici's favourite artist, the sculptor Donatello, was greatly in demand outside Florence because of his unrivalled mastery of the new technique for making bronze sculptures that were free-standing and you could walk around.

When not working for Cosimo or for Florentine institutions, Donatello and his work was exported throughout Italy. Several complicated and expensive projects kept him out of Florence for decades. The Sienese, who disliked the Florentines as much as the Scots hated the English, kept him busy on their civic baptistery. Here he produced his most revolutionary work, a relief sculpture of Herod's Feast, using linear perspective to tell the story of St John's execution, but without actually showing the grisly event. Even Sienese artists and patrons – justly proud of their own local traditions, and, in addition, hugely distrustful of Florence – were sufficiently impressed to adapt and change in Donatello's wake.

But this was nothing compared to the impact of his ten-year stay in the great university city of Padua, near Venice. The Franciscan friars who ran the Santo, one of Europe's great pilgrimage sites (dedicated to the patron saint of lost causes, Anthony of Padua), commissioned him to make a series of ever more ambitious works in bronze: from a large crucifix to a life-size sculpture of their former military commander, the 'Honeyed Cat' (*Gattamelata*), on horseback, and then the massive high altar in the centre of the church.

Donatello set up a large studio in Padua to meet this demand. Artists were keen to assist him, and to understand his work. His innovative depiction of space, his use of perspective and his mastery of three-dimensional form made a deep impression on his contemporaries. Padua became a centre for bronze casting, specialising in exquisite collectors' items such as inkwells and miniature sculptures that were coveted all over Europe. The enormous marble tombs and sculptures dominating Venetian Renaissance churches, in which effigies of the great and the good are set in triumphal arches, are also indebted to Donatello. But his example additionally changed the work of many artists who weren't sculptors, including two exceptional painters, the brothers-in-law Andrea Mantegna and Giovanni Bellini.

Mantegna excelled in making whatever he depicted – whether the lives of Roman emperors or saints, or arcane myths – seem believable. To do this he filled his paintings with elaborate stage sets inspired by Donatello's relief sculptures for the high altar of the Santo. Bellini, a much less showy artist, specialised in intense paintings of Christian subjects, such as the Virgin Mary and her infant son, or Christ after his crucifixion. His earliest works are so close to Donatello that they are almost copies of his sculptures in a different medium. The psychological depth and realism of Bellini's portraits and small religious paintings began with his intimate study of Donatello in Padua.

It's likely that Donatello's reputation outside Florence encouraged the Medici to use the city's artists in the service of politics and diplomacy. Cosimo's sons Piero and Giovanni used this to improve relations with the strategically important Kingdom of Naples, in the south of Italy. They were clever negotiators and realised that artistic innovation was where they had the upper hand. But it was Piero's eldest son, Lorenzo, who made Florence's cultural supremacy into a key element of foreign policy. From this point Florentine artists and their work travelled everywhere. They went to the furthest ends of Europe – from the Tudor court in England to Hungary in the east – producing art that helped to bolster new or precarious governments that were important for Florentine trade.

Their greatest achievement, however, was to help secure the continued existence of Florence itself. In 1478, the aftermath of the Pazzi conspiracy set Florence at loggerheads with the papacy and with Naples. Only brinkmanship and a risky one-man mission by Lorenzo de' Medici to Naples saved the day. Lorenzo brokered peace with Pope Sixtus IV by sending the best Florentine painters to Rome. Sandro Botticelli, Domenico Ghirlandaio and Cosimo Rosselli were dispatched in the spring of 1481 to join the Umbrian painters Pietro Perugino and Bernardino Pinturicchio in painting the pope's private chapel in the Vatican – known to posterity as the Sistine Chapel, famed for Michelangelo's frescoes on the roof and altar wall, which were begun twenty years later.

The chapel's side walls were painted with scenes from the lives of Moses and Christ, chosen to assert the pope's supremacy over all other Christian leaders (this was a strange twist of fate for Botticelli, who three years earlier had painted images of the executed Pazzi conspirators). Posterity has not always judged them kindly – the Anglo-German Romantic painter Henry Fuseli lambasted their 'mediocrity, tinsel ostentation and tasteless diligence'. To be sure, the overriding impression is a sea of showy ultramarine and gold. Yet for all the criticism, the scheme contains some of Botticelli and Ghirlandaio's greatest narrative paintings, and the frescoes are undeniably impressive. John Ruskin, the Victorian writer and critic who changed British taste with his love for Turner, the Pre-Raphaelites and the early Renaissance, far preferred them to Michelangelo's Sistine ceiling.

The sense that this commission was undertaken by the Florentine state is reinforced by the fact that as soon as the artists returned to Florence, they were set to work, together with Antonio and Piero del Pollaiuolo, in the Sala dei Gigli in the town hall. The other painter who joined them, Botticelli's former pupil Filippino Lippi, was subsequently dispatched to Rome. It was no doubt thanks to Lorenzo de' Medici's backing that this quirky, eccentric painter was accepted by the conservative Roman cardinal Oliviero Carafa to decorate his burial chapel in the basilica of Santa Maria sopra Minerva. He would probably have preferred something less original, but the ready application of precious metals and semi-precious lapis lazuli seems to have satisfied him. At any rate, this commission was less about the art than Lorenzo de' Medici's efforts to have his thirteen-year-old son Giovanni – later Pope Leo X – made a cardinal. As late as June 1488, Carafa had opposed Giovanni's election, but by December, sweetened by Filippino Lippi's paintings, he was prepared to support the Medici candidacy. Giovanni was the first Medici cardinal, and his election was a strong step forward in Lorenzo's efforts to maintain the family's power after his death.

Florence enlisted artistic diplomacy to maintain foreign relations as far afield as Turkey. Sultan Mehmed II had aided Lorenzo de' Medici by returning the surviving Pazzi conspirator from Constantinople to face retribution in Florence. In turn, Lorenzo flattered Mehmed – who saw himself as a reincarnation of Alexander the Great – by recognising him as the legitimate ruler of the territories that the sultan's forces had conquered in the Eastern Mediterranean. Lorenzo commissioned his household sculptor Bertoldo di Giovanni to make a medallic portrait of the sultan that is wholly European.

This is a strange object for an Islamic ruler, whose religion frowned on the production of figurative art. The obverse, or front, of the medal shows an image of the sultan as if portrayed from life, wearing the Ottoman crescent round his neck. The reverse depicts a naked youth standing on a pedestal, carried forward on a chariot, holding the end of a rope binding three female captives together. These represent the former Greek possessions that Mehmed had conquered – Asia, Trebizond and Greater Greece – all recorded in the inscription on the medal's obverse.

As Florence's political standing worsened, the city's artists played an ever more crucial role in its foreign policy. In 1494, the French king Charles VIII invaded Italy. The political theorist and Florentine statesman Niccolò Machiavelli was right to see this as a watershed for Italian politics. King Charles's armies marched south to Naples, subduing everything in their wake. Italy became the battleground of Europe.

During the ensuing decades of war and instability, art and artists were used as political collateral. In 1494, when the Charles VIII occupied Florence, the city hoped to pacify his troops by lodging him in the rich surroundings of the Medici Palace. Three years later, when the Florentine republic was reinstated, Michelangelo, Leonardo da Vinci and other renowned artists were given important state commissions which were in essence propaganda, celebrating the might of Florence's independent government. Michelangelo's mammoth statue of David, carved from a huge slab of marble previously deemed of too poor quality to use, was placed beside the Palazzo della Signoria. It symbolised the republic's determination, like the teenage Israelite with his sling, to slay the modern-day Goliaths that threatened the Florentine state.

Together with Leonardo, Michelangelo was commissioned to paint the hall where Florence's Great Council met with episodes from the Battle of Anghiari, a famous victory over Milan. The demands of diplomacy meant that neither artist ever completed their work. In 1506, Leonardo returned to Milan – where he had previously lived and worked for almost twenty years – at the request of the city's French viceroy, Charles d'Amboise. He never returned to Florence. A year before, Michelangelo, a lifelong republican, had been dispatched to Rome to work for Pope Julius II.

Despite a stormy relationship with the warrior pope, Michelangelo remained in the papal capital, working with tenacity on his tomb. The structure we see today in the Roman basilica of San Pietro in Vincoli is a relatively modest affair compared to the free-standing funerary monument that Michelangelo intended, carved of the best Carrara marble and incorporating almost fifty independent statues. Had it been completed, it would have been more like a work of architecture than a sculpture in its scale and ambition. For more than forty years, long after Julius's death, Michelangelo struggled with what became 'the tragedy of the tomb'. There was always something else that his patrons – including the pope – insisted took priority.

The first of many such projects was Pope Julius's insistence that Michelangelo decorate the ceiling of the Sistine Chapel with scenes from the Old Testament. Michelangelo infinitely preferred sculpture to painting. His own accounts of the Sistine commission make no secret of his dislike of this task, and the discomfort it caused him, crouched like a beast, suspended a couple of feet from the ceiling. For all Michelangelo's agony, this is one of the few works of art that has never ceased to astonish everyone who sees it.

On the Sistine ceiling, Michelangelo told the stories of man's early life with clarity, creating powerful images of humanity that still influence how we think about the world. Michelangelo's idealisation of the male body – taut, muscled and powerful – has found thousands of echoes, from high art to popular culture. Who can forget the creation of man, where the tiniest of gaps between Adam's outstretched hand and God's finger represents the relationship of man to divinity, tantalisingly close but so far away. Yet at least one contemporary thought the ceiling was the work of Michelangelo's hated rival, the younger, charming, more socially assured Raphael – at the time everyone's favourite artist.

It is unlikely that Michelangelo – an anguished, self-driven and highly patriotic soul – would have stayed the course in Rome had he not believed his actions were materially supporting the country he loved. Leonardo was similarly devoted to his adopted city. A far more adept courtier than Michelangelo, he undertook a spectacularly dangerous assignment several years after the Anghiari fiasco. In 1483, when Leonardo had first left Florence for Milan, he had boasted to Duke Ludovico Sforza, the city's ruler, of his ability to design bronze cannons and fortifications, and how he preferred this sort of work to painting.

In the troubled years of the early sixteenth century, this combination of skills meant that Leonardo became a diplomatic pawn, passed from ruler to ruler. During the autumn of 1502 he found himself in central Italy, with Cesare Borgia, son of the ruling pope, Alexander VI, and Niccolò Machiavelli, who was a scarcely disguised spy. Borgia was a rapacious warlord who was trying to carve out his own kingdom and ensure that it would last after his father's death. He is the ruler whom Machiavelli admired and loathed most, in equal measure; the hero figure of his ruthless treatise on government, *The Prince*, is based on Borgia.

Leonardo was employed as Borgia's chief engineer. His job was to reinforce the defences of Cesare's new possessions and to devise new fighting machines. The military leader hoped that Leonardo's genius would enable him to take the prosperous city of Bologna, but suspected that he was – like Machiavelli – a Florentine agent. As Borgia's entourage moved around the Romagna and the Upper Arno Valley, he ensured that both men saw at first hand how mercilessly he could crush his enemies. They were present at the coastal town of Senigallia, when Cesare smiled upon his former friends then garrotted them. Borgia intended that witnessing such events would nip further treachery in the bud.

By this point Leonardo had become a commodity as valuable as his art. When Giovanni de' Medici became Pope Leo X in 1513, Leonardo was one of the influential Florentines called to his court in Rome. He passed his Roman years in the pope's palace in the Vatican, accompanied by his pupils Salaì and Melzi. Most of his time seems to have been occupied with scientific experiments, even dissection, and little with painting. Three years later, when Leo X was engaged in peace talks with the French king Francis I, Leonardo was persuaded (possibly at the pope's behest) to enter Francis's employ. He was to die, supposedly in the monarch's arms, near Amboise in 1519. The illegitimate son of a lawyer and a peasant girl had come far. Leonardo, like Michelangelo, had made his own way, but neither artistic superstar was immune to being used for the greater good of the Florentine state.

How Florentine art changed the world

In 1530, the Florentine Republic was crushed by the combined forces of Europe's most powerful men, the pope and Holy Roman emperor. No less a figure than Michelangelo had taken responsibility for the city's fortifications and defences. At this point, despite the continued opposition of many Florentines, the Medici family became the city's hereditary rulers. Although their courts were never short of artists, they were stronger on protocol and tradition than innovation. Florence was now politically secure, and as there was no longer any need for the elite to prove themselves through commissioning art, the city became more culturally conservative. It never regained the creative fervour of the fifteenth century.

Yet it was from the mid-sixteenth century onwards that Florentine Renaissance art made its greatest impact. This was thanks to Giorgio Vasari, whom Cosimo, the first Medici grand duke, employed as his artistic fixer. Born in the Tuscan town of Arezzo, Vasari was a good painter and architect, but an exceptional propagandist and administrator, and the founding father of art history. His *Lives of the Artists*, first published in 1550, was a series of biographies of the artists he most admired. Practically all Vasari's chosen subjects were Florentine or central Italian. For this faithful Medici servant, the art of Florence had to be the best in the world.

Vasari claimed that the Italian Renaissance – first in Florence, then in Rome – was the pinnacle of artistic achievement. His *Lives* chronicle three ages of artistic production, starting from those who were good but lived in challenging times, moving on to those for whom hard work and good luck couldn't make up for relative deficiencies of talent, and followed by a trio of semi-divine superstars – Michelangelo, Leonardo and Raphael. For centuries Western artists were encouraged to take these three as their model, particularly the charming, patron-friendly Raphael. And those who commissioned art were urged to cast themselves in the mould of Lorenzo de' Medici. In Vasari's words, Lorenzo's rule was 'truly a Golden Age for men of talent'.

In 1563, the first real academy of art and design was founded in Florence. Vasari's input and support was key to its success. The Company and Academy of the Arts of Design merged the trade guilds that had previously regulated Florentine artists' activity with a training college for aspiring artists. Mature artists were invited to become academicians, which gave them status, and to participate in teaching. The Academy delivered a more formalised and intellectual education than the practical apprenticeships that artists had previously undertaken. Its curriculum was based on two of Vasari's key ideas. One was *disegno*: the ability to make a drawing, but also to invent a compelling idea. The other was the importance of competition. Vasari's studies of fifteenth- and early sixteenth-century Florence had convinced him that this was a key component of artistic excellence.

The Florence Academy was not the only such body to exist in sixteenth-century Europe. However, its prestige, and its association with the Medici and with Vasari, meant that it set the standard for academic artistic training. Vasari's ideas and writings proved fundamental for artistic education in Europe and her colonies well into the twentieth century. Love them or hate them, they are the bedrock of modern art and of art theories. Giorgio Vasari, not even a Florentine by birth, played the greatest single role in chronicling and recording the Florentine Renaissance. It is thanks to him that fifteenth-century Florence's innovation and creativity are still known and celebrated. As much as the art itself, Vasari's writings meant that Florentine Renaissance art, and the competitive spirit behind it, changed the world.

Equestrian oba and attendants

8

BENIN: COMMUNITY

1500–1700

Four thousand miles south of Florence, on the tropical plain north of the creeks of the Niger Delta in West Africa, lies one of the early modern world's greatest but least known artistic centres. From the thirteenth century Benin City was the capital of a mighty military and commercial empire that stretched from Dahomey in the west to the River Niger in the east. The Kingdom of Benin, ruled by its god-king, the oba, had evolved from a loose federation of small settlements and towns into the dominant power of West Africa. Its wealth and authority derived from its control of trade between the inland peoples of Sub-Saharan Africa and the Atlantic coast. Benin used this prosperity to create a stable community that was envied by many visitors, and to produce the Benin Bronzes, some of the most admired and evocative art of the sixteenth and seventeenth centuries. In their technical complexity and brilliance these works rival and sometimes surpass the revered sculpture of Renaissance Europe.

And yet, unlike Florence or Rome, Benin is not a byword for artistic excellence. Partly this is due to its incorporation within modern Nigeria, one of Africa's largest and most diverse post-colonial states. But principally it is because of the whole-sale destruction of Benin City, the overthrow of its government and the systematic looting of its artistic treasures by the British Punitive Expedition in February 1897. Ostensibly the motive was revenge for the recent murder of British officials and to put an end to alleged human sacrifice, but the attack had been long contemplated. It was one of a series of moves against smaller kingdoms intended to facilitate British control over West Africa and its natural resources. Even by the standards of nineteenth-century European colonialism, the 1897 expedition, led by Admiral Sir Harry Rawson of the Royal Navy, was unusually cruel. The city and its population were decimated by the attackers' superior weaponry and artillery. Victor Roth, a doctor who accompanied the expedition, wrote: 'Dead and mutilated bodies seemed to be everywhere – by God! May I never see such sights again!'

The Punitive Expedition and its aftermath

Later accounts by British officials make it explicit that their agenda was the destruction of this complex, layered and living community, because it tied the past, the present and the future together in one continuum. The burning of the oba's palace was claimed to be accidental, but it may have been a deliberate fire whose scale got out of control. The reasons for this wholesale devastation were cultural, political and financial. To break the oba's power and to permit the British to trade, it was essential to destroy the altars and places where his ancestors were revered and worshipped. Tragically, the work of many centuries was dismantled in a few weeks. Benin was stripped of its artistic assets with frightening completeness.

A series of photos show members of the expedition squatting and sitting in several of the palace's principal courtyards. They resemble a group of overgrown Boy Scouts, except that they are surrounded by huge piles of carved ivories, bronze statues and bronze reliefs. Many of the objects were sold by the British to defray the costs of the expedition. Others were divided among the members of the invading force, or left the country in the aftermath of this chaos. As a result, objects from Benin are now scattered in museums over the world, mainly in Europe and North America. The greatest concentration is still to be found in the British Museum, 'donated' by the Foreign Office or purchased from and given by members of the Benin expedition. Many questions are now being asked about their acquisition, and indeed their presence in Western collections at all.

Benin's origins

The Kingdom of Benin was defined as those lands where the oba controlled the life and death of his subjects. Oral tradition tells of the Ogiso dynasty, 'Rulers of the Sky', who founded Benin City. When their reign failed in the late thirteenth century, it is said that a group of chiefs requested a new monarch from the Yoruba ruler of Ife, to the north-west of Benin. According to one account, the Oni of Ife sent his son Oranmiyan to Benin, where he fathered a son by the daughter of a local chief. This boy is said to have been enthroned as King Eweka I around the year 1300. Whatever the truth, it is evident that Eweka was of both Edo and Yoruba heritage.

Eweka's successors further consolidated the authority of the oba. His son Ewedo insisted that his chiefs stand rather than sit before him. Ewedo's successor, Oguola, is said to have been the first to invest in the complex and marvellous network of earth-works that still (although in highly debased form) surrounds Benin City. If not quite the largest earthworks in the world or longer than the Great Wall of China, as has been claimed, they were built on a highly substantial scale, perhaps measuring as much as 145 kilo-metres in length. These powerful structures attested to the Edo people's close relationship with the land and their environment. From the fifteenth to the early seventeenth century, a series of great warrior kings – Ewuare, Ozolua, Esigie, Orhogbua and Ehengbuda – rebuilt the city, and established the artistic forms and religious ceremonies that endure in Benin to this day.

Ewuare, a contemporary of the Medici, his son Ozolua and grandson Esigie, brought Benin to the height of its powers. Ewuare established the administrative structure of the state, and instituted the rituals and ceremonies that created a national identity, centred on reverence for the oba. He also devised the costumes and regalia in the prized materials of brass and coral which remain important sources of the mon-arch's power. Esigie, who ruled in the early sixteenth century, took the throne from his brother Arhuaran and defended Benin City from an attack from the Idah kingdom. A series of military conquests, a firm alliance with the Portuguese and the talents of his mother, Idia, enabled him to extend the territory of Benin. Esigie's augmentation of the rituals instituted by Ewuare enabled him to enhance the authority of the oba and the legitimacy of his own rule.

Benin City

Ewuare was responsible for the urban design of Benin, and the kingdom's complex administrative bureaucracy was reflected in the city's layout. He is said to have burnt down the existing settlement in the coup of 1440 that deposed his brother, so that a new city could rise like a phoenix from its ashes. A very broad street ran through Benin, separating it into Ogbe, the king's area at the south-west of the city, and Ore Nokhua. Ogbe contained the oba's palace, the palace associations and the homes of the palace chiefs. The town chiefs, members of the artists' guilds, priests, herbalists, hunters and other ceremonial specialists lived in Ore Nokhua. Within this area, people were divided by occupation. Just outside the wall to the north was the former village of Uselu, where the queen mother and crown prince had their palaces.

The city's orderliness, beauty and cleanliness were much commented on by visitors. A Dutch traveller of the early seventeenth century, thought to be Dierick Ruiters, recorded in 1602 that the city was defended by wooden gates and guards around the clock. There was 'a great broad street, not paved, which seemeth to be seven or eight times broader than the Warmoes [Warmoesstraat] street in Amsterdam'. Olfert Dapper, an Amsterdammer who did not visit Benin, but who used others' accounts in his *Accurate Description of the African Regions*, published in 1668, wrote that Benin had 'thirty very broad streets, each about 120 feet wide', which ran at right angles to each other. The city was therefore laid out on a grid plan, like so many settlements built from scratch.

Houses were built along the streets, on adjoining plots 'as here in Europe'. They were well made, of red clay, with roofs of reeds, straw and leaves, and were substantial dwellings, although they were only one storey high, with separate quarters for the husband, the women of the household (*oderie*) and the young men (*yekogobe*). Every house had a well – unlike the houses of many contemporary Europeans. Those of the nobility were enormous, and according to Dapper had external surfaces that gleamed 'like mirrors'. The roads had underground drainage to carry away storm water, and there were designated areas for animals to graze. Markets took place twice a day and there was always food to eat. Overall, the picture given is of a well-ordered, affluent city. It was also far safer than many other cities. Lourenço Pinto, a Portuguese sea captain who visited in 1694, recalled that not only was Benin far larger than Lisbon, 'It is so well governed that theft is unknown and the people live in such security that they have no doors to their houses.' The fate that befell this structured, safe community was one that could not have been imagined by these visitors to the city.

The oba, god-king

Before the catastrophe of 1897, the oba's domination of Benin City reflected his absolute rule, and control over life, law, religion, politics and commerce. According to the Tudor translator Richard Eden, in an account included in Richard Hakluyt's influential late sixteenth-century compendium of English voyagers: 'when his noble men are in his presence, they never looke upon him in the face, but sit cowring ... with their elbows upon their knees, and their hands before their faces, not looking up until the king commanded them ... Likewise when they depart from him, they turn not their backs toward him, but goe creeping backward with like reverence.' The oba was the channel through which the powers of his ancestors continued to protect the Edo people and ensured their survival into the future. The royal palace contained shrines to each of his predecessors, where regular sacrifices were made to protect the nation and confirm the oba's spiritual authority. The oba's power was further enhanced by his control of the royal relics, particularly the coral crown and brass staffs which held spiritual power.

The Sun King, the seventeenth-century Louis XIV of France, claimed 'I am the State' (*L'État, c'est moi*), at least in part because this was not a truth universally acknowledged. The oba of Benin needed to make no such assertion because no one would have denied his divinity. John Adams, an eighteenth-century English visitor to Benin, noted that the oba was 'the principal object of adoration in his dominions ... a god himself, whose subjects both obey and adore him as such', with higher status even than the pope in contemporary Catholic Europe. On land, the oba was a god, the terrestrial counterpart to Okolun, the son of the creator god who was responsible for the seas and for prosperity, and the most venerated deity in Benin's pantheon. He was known to the Edo people, in a strong oral tradition recorded by the anthropologist R. E. Bradbury in the late twentieth century, as the 'Child of the Sky whom we pray not to fall and cover us, Child of the Earth whom we implore not to swallow us up'. It was believed that because the oba was divine, he did not need to sleep or eat, and was therefore omnipresent. And it was right that all the good things came to him.

Benin's structure

Benin was divided into tribute units or fiefs, each of which was overseen by an official in the capital on the oba's behalf. All villages were required to send cowrie shells, livestock and agricultural products to the oba as tribute, and provide soldiers if required. The oba controlled trade in slaves, pepper and other important goods, so that the revenues went directly to support his court and government. All intercourse and exchange with foreigners was mediated through the oba. Most significant of all, he was entitled to a tusk from every elephant slaughtered in his domains. This meant he possessed one of the world's largest sources of white gold – ivory – prized from Beijing to Britain.

Of course, Benin, like all court cultures, was subject to shifting alliances. Much of the structure was established by Ewuare, who also devised the ritual on which it depended. Consecutive obas managed, largely successfully, to control the state by operating this tried and tested policy of divide and rule. The primary principle was that the exercise of power was dispersed among three groups, so that no single faction had enough authority or influence to mount a challenge. In the king's private quarters, the palace chiefs (Eghaevbo Nogbe) held sway. These hereditary aristocrats looked after the administration of the palace and the oba's personal life: the Iweguae were the oba's personal staff and the Ibiwe served his wives and children, while the Iwebo chiefs took care of the king's regalia, the craft guilds that made them and trade with non-Edo peoples.

The town chiefs (Eghaevbo Nore) were formally incorporated into the government by Ewuare. Unlike the palace chiefs, they normally achieved their position by their own efforts rather than by birth. They collected tribute, recruited military support and served as intermediaries between the oba and the villages. Their number included the Iyase, one of the oba's two principal military commanders. According to tradition and oral history, the Iyase tended to oppose the oba, it seems to maintain a check on his power.

A third group, the Uzama, were descendants of the elders who had sent for a new king from Ife. Their number included the Oliha, who guarded the shrine that protected the kingdom, the crown prince (Edaiken) and the Ezomo, who shared command of the army with the Iyase of the town chiefs. Because their titles and power predated the oba they always posed a potential threat to his authority.

The other important figure in the hierarchy was the queen mother (Iyoba), whose power was equivalent to that of the major chiefs. The first queen mother was Esigie's mother Idia. He instituted her cult partly to honour her, and partly to consolidate his authority and that of his clan. During rituals designed to rid the kingdom of malignant forces oppressing the kingdom, the oba would wear an ivory mask of the Iyoba to channel her spiritual power.

The oba's rule might appear ordered and benevolent, but it depended on the total subjection of the kingdom and of the tribute peoples beyond to his authority, and acknowledgement of his divine right to govern. What opportunities existed depended on following established customs and were only open to men. Women's roles were limited to childbearing and caring. They were confined to designated areas in family compounds, and during menstruation they were deemed to be unclean and were made to live outside the house. Since most men took more than one wife, households were often riven by tensions between wives and their individual children. Childless women were the most powerless of all the peoples of Benin.

The palace

At the heart of the city was the royal palace. According to Olfert Dapper, it was 'easily as big as the town of Haarlem'. Even accounting for exaggeration, it was evidently on a very large scale, a sprawling complex of individual palaces, houses and offices housing the oba, his wives, children and servants. Chief Ekhator Omoregie, who recorded his childhood memories of the palace before its destruction in 1897, remembered its compound as an irregular pentagon that dominated the king's side of Benin City. It is likely that it had not changed radically since the fifteenth century, when the functions and purpose of the monarch had been established. As well as the oba's private apartments and the service quarters there were public audience rooms, spaces for religious rituals and state ceremonies, and for palace administrators.

A combination of visual and textual evidence allows us to tentatively reconstruct how the palace looked. It was both grand and imposing. To enter, it was necessary to pass through one of several substantial gates. As David van Nyendael, a merchant with the Dutch West India Company who is documented in Benin in September 1701 noted, some were surmounted by tall turrets, and further ornamented by brass birds and snakes. This account is corroborated by a bronze plaque returned to Nigerian ownership by the Staatliche Museen zu Berlin. It shows four of the oba's officials, standing in pairs on either side of a doorway. The pillars of the door are composed of stacked carved heads of bearded Europeans. A pyramidic tower rises up above the doorway, while a large snake sinuously curves down to the bottom of the roof, its eyes staring balefully and directly at us.

Another plaque, in the British Museum, is very similar, with a pitched roof, turret and snake. At the top, where the plaque has been damaged, are a bird's feet. The first edition of Dapper's account of Benin was accompanied by an engraving of the oba and his court engaged in a ceremonial procession in front of the palace, with the wider city and its orderly streets stretching out behind them. Three turrets, with pyramid-shaped tops, reach up into the sky, crowned by birds with outstretched wings.

These are the houses in the king's court, the most private space of the palace. The purpose of these bronze birds of prophecy on the palace roof was to warn of danger. We know from other descriptions and images, including an altar box in the shape of a palace building, that these birds had curved beaks and outstretched wings. They are remarkably like the plaques, so Dapper's account was presumably based on a description from someone who knew the city.

It seems that the palace complex was set up around atrium courtyards; some had galleries with wooden pillars supporting the roof. Dapper described each of these 'beautiful and long square galleries' as being 'about as big as the Exchange at Amsterdam'; as many as five hundred people could be crowded into the seating that ran around the walls.

He also recounts how, in a larger gallery, the pillars were covered with cast copper, engraved with depictions of battle scenes and the deeds of war. Practically all the surviving bronze plaques show signs of nails and fixings being driven into them, so if Dapper's account is correct, most (if not all) of them would have been in this highly impressive room. Members of the British Punitive Expedition noted that the doors, openings and rafters of the council chambers and private quarters were lined with sheets of hammered brass and carved ivory figures. The two brass plaques mentioned above, with carved figures on either side of an opening, give an insight into these arrangements. The pillars, whether covered with ivory or brass, would look as if they were made out of the two most precious materials in the economy of Benin. They were impressive but also intimidating, a visual manifestation of the oba's absolute power.

Religion and the state

The courtyards also housed the ancestor shrines that were of crucial importance to the health of the nation. The first act of every oba was to institute a shrine to his father, to honour his achievements, to create a living connection with his spirit and to ensure his support of the kingdom. These were semi-circular baked mud platforms, rubbed smooth so that they shone like polished stone. An early nineteenth-century visitor recorded that there were at least twenty-five to thirty such shrines in the palace. They were covered with specially commissioned heads of male ancestors of each oba, each supporting a massive carved ivory tusk. David van Nyendael recorded his impressions of a shrine with 'eleven men's heads cast in copper ... and upon each one of them is an elephant's tooth'. Contemporary practice and photos from the 1890s suggest that the heads were generally arranged symmetrically in pairs. They are a reminder that the oba's head – his brain – is critical to guiding the nation. At the centre of each altar was a miniature brass altar, with a standing figure of the dead oba, holding some of his insignia and accompanied by attendants. Brass bells and rattle staffs were also placed on the altar, to awaken the departed oba's spirit, along with cast figures of horsemen and messengers, together with ceremonial swords, and Neolithic thunderstones or axe heads. The Edo people still believe that they are hurled to the ground by Ogiuwu, the god of death, in anger. The axe heads' presence recalled the power of death, reserved for gods and to the oba himself.

Numerous state rituals enforced the oba's connection with his ancestors and reinforced his personal capacity to serve as an intermediary between them and the peoples of Benin. None was more special than the state ceremony of Igue, when life-giving charms were placed on parts of the oba's body to preserve him during the year. Sacrifices of domestic animals as well as wild ones, particularly the sacred leopard, were made to the oba's head. It finished with a rite in which children ran out of the city with torches to expel evil spirits, returning with 'leaves of hope' (ewere). Ugie Erha Oba, where the king receives the homage of all office holders, reiterated the oba's inherited and divine authority to rule. The oba appeared in his full ceremonial regalia and the chiefs demonstrated their fealty to him in a series of sword dances and mock battles. The oba made a sacrifice on his father's altar to his father's memory, and to the earth in which his divine predecessors are buried.

It is not surprising that these festivals – in their continuing forms – also commemorate unsuccessful threats to obas of the past. One of these was Ugie Oro, instituted by the sixteenth-century Oba Esigie to mark a victory over the Idah people. Esigie's rule was repeatedly challenged because he had overthrown his brother, their father's eldest son, but subsequently he was revered as one of Benin's greatest rulers. Several leading courtiers had refused to support Esigie in his defence of Benin City. Ugie Oro demonstrates that they were full of empty noise, like the ibis which had prophesied the king's defeat. Esigie shot the bird and used it as his standard in the decisive battle he won. As part of the festival, these same courtiers processed around the city, striking the ground at particular moments with bronze staffs topped by a bird to show that they now deferred to Esigie's wisdom.

Art and kingship

The great arts of Benin are interlinked with the oba, for whom they were made, and whose authority they upheld. The craftsmen who made them were the oba's servants. They lived in designated parts of the city, working in family groups like many of their contemporaries in Renaissance Europe. In one square alone, the Portuguese visitor Lourenço Pinto counted 120 metalworking shops, 'all working continuously'.

The craftsmen worked under the organisation of a guild for each material; the most prestigious were the Igun Eronmwon (bronze casters) and Igbesanmwan (ivory and wood carvers). Membership of the guilds was hereditary, a precious position handed down from father to son – the head of the bronze casters had a status equivalent to a general. Because their skills were so special, and because in the wrong hands they could be dangerous, these craftsmen were only allowed to work for other clients with the oba's express position. If their work satisfied the king and his courtiers, they could be well rewarded, with gifts of commodities including food, slaves and wives. While the guilds were separate, they often made artworks that were displayed together, such as on the ancestor altars in the oba's palace.

These craftsmen worked in the precious materials of metal, ivory and coral. All metals held spiritual value, but those with greater permanence and endurance were particularly valued. As a local proverb puts it, 'brass never rusts, lead never rots'. The Benin Bronzes are actually made of brass. This was preferred above every other metal for its shiny surface and reddish hue, attributes which were believed to repel malevolent deities. Ivory also was believed to have divine qualities. Its whiteness and purity connected it to Okolun, the great but tempestuous god of the waters, whose dangerous instability needed to be propitiated with valuable gifts. Like shining brass, the polished sheen of worked ivory was believed to be hateful to evil spirits. Most of the surviving objects from Benin are made from one or other of these materials. They are unforgettable for the quality of their production, and the insight they give into the values and customs of a highly sophisticated and civilised society.

The Benin Bronzes

West Africans had invented the smelting of bronze and the casting of brass as long ago as the tenth century CE. One oral tradition recorded in the mid-twentieth century attributes its introduction in Benin to Oba Oguola, who ruled in the late thirteenth century. He is said to have asked the Yoruba ruler of Ife to send him a brass caster, named as Igueghae. Archaeological digs in Benin City have indeed confirmed the presence of metal casting by this date, and it may have begun even earlier. Certainly, by the late fifteenth century it was a well-established practice. The raw material, an alloy of copper and zinc, came from ingots traded by the Portuguese in bracelets called manillas, which were made in the Rhineland in their millions. The reliefs seen by Dapper's informant, together with the heads and sculptural groups on the altars, were all made from this melted brass. The king himself is said to have taken part in their creation: the ritual construction of the altar to the oba's father demanded that he began the casting process – either pouring the bronze or, as is more likely, supervising the work.

More than 850 brass reliefs survive from the palace. They were made between the late fifteenth and early eighteenth centuries to decorate the pillars in the principal audience court. Most were commissioned by Oba Esigie and his son and successor Orhogbua. Esigie's rule was more difficult than his son's – there were threats to his power and he had to work hard to establish his undisputed authority. The plaques from

Esigie's reign are both simpler in their manufacture and more celebratory of courtiers and warriors than glorifying the king. Each plaque has a meaning by itself, but they also contributed to a greater story of the power of the oba and the regime he headed. Did the plaque commission cement Esigie's authority? Certainly, by the end of his reign, and throughout Orhogbua's, the court was a more reliable support of the monarchy.

The plaques' display on pillars framed the actual oba, his courtiers and warriors in the audience courtyard, giving his subjects examples of how to behave, both at court and when outside Benin City on military campaign. By 1800 the reliefs had been removed to a storeroom, where one scholar has described them as functioning as a 'card index' of court hierarchy, belief and custom. Whenever there was a dispute about etiquette or tradition, the reliefs could be relied upon to solve the problem.

The kingdom of Benin was strictly hierarchical. In the plaques, power and authority is denoted by each figure's relative size. The hierarchy is evident – simply put, nobles and generals are bigger than pages, pages are larger than servants, and no one is as tall or as dominant as the oba. He is in the centre of every plaque on which he appears. As a whole, the bronze reliefs tell the history, society, culture of Benin, and its relationship with the outside world, in visual form. They also demonstrate how this evolved, from the fifteenth to the sixteenth centuries. There are certain themes that recur across the plaques – warfare, the oba's autocratic power, his ability to delegate authority and to take it away. They give this story solely from the king's side. No women or scenes from domestic life appear on the reliefs.

Mudfish and leopards, the animal signifiers of the oba's qualities, abound. The first represented his divinity and riches, derived from rivers and the ocean, in the form of coral and trade from overseas. The leopard stood for the oba's ultimate authority, like the swift king of the jungle. Leopards were sacred creatures – graceful, powerful and cruel, but decisive and strong – whose attributes reflected the leadership qualities valued by the sixteenth-century obas. Ozolu was given the name 'the leopard cub with strong claws' because of his prowess as a warrior. In a number of plaques the oba is shown holding two tamed leopards by their tails or wearing a belt of mudfish.

A relief now in the Metropolitan Museum of Art in New York portrays the oba in some of the unique regalia of his office. He wears a beaded crown and collar made of coral. The wing-like projections on either side of his crown are said to represent the whiskers of the mudfish. Its unusual capacity to move between the sea and rivers, the land and water, was compared to the oba's ability to live between the divine and human worlds. Mudfish could also be dangerous – some species release an electric charge as a sting. On other reliefs the oba is shown with his legs transformed into mudfish. Only a divine being could partly be a mudfish or control them. The background motif of a four-petalled water hyacinth, repeated over the background of this plaque, like many others, further emphasises the oba's control over the waters.

In the Met relief, the oba's chest is adorned with a number of necklaces, made of coral and agate beads. Agate pendants hang from his crown. An elaborate belt and hip decoration, with a mask on his proper left side, holds together the intricately arranged fabric wrapper – presumably a rare imported Portuguese or Indian cloth – that covers his lower body. His arms, which clasp the hands of the pair of attendants nearest to him, are covered with wristbands of coral. Similar decorations

can be seen at the top of his feet. The next most important figures are the two men at the far edges of the plaque, who protect
the oba's head with ceremonial decorated shields, and who also
wear patterned wrappers and hip masks. The oba rides a horse,
and is attended by two emada, teenage boys who acted as
pages. Horses were not native to West Africa, and presumably
this beast was imported by the Portuguese.

The page at the left holds a ceremonial sword, the eben, used
in ritual by the oba's senior officials. He may belong to the order
of Ooton priests. His opposite number has ritual scar patterns
(iwu) on his torso, identifying him as a subject of the oba. Three
tiny figures, in the two top corners and the third literally at the
oba's feet, must be palace servants. Their size and the absence
of any special regalia denote their lack of status. Two of these
underlings carry an epokin, a small barrel-shaped container
used to carry gifts. The messaging of the plaque is, however,
more subtle than you might think. The oba, for all his power,
cannot stand alone. Partly this is because he was weighed
down by the godlike regalia he had won in his conflict with
Olokun, but also because supreme power could only be exercised with proper support from the oba's subjects.

Manufacture

The Benin Bronzes were made using the highly complex 'lost
wax' casting process. This begins with a wax mould around
a core of clay. Every detail that the artist wishes to be visible
on the finished object is modelled or incised into the wax.
Channels, called sprues (for the eventual pouring in of the
molten metal) and risers (so noxious gases can escape), are
attached to the mould. It is then covered in more clay, first

layers with a consistency like pancake batter, then a more solid material, known as an 'investment'. The clay mould is then baked in an extremely hot firing oven. Because wax has a low melting temperature, it turns into liquid and runs out of the mould, leaving a void.

Using the sprues, the artist pours hot molten brass into the void, and waits for the metal to harden and cool. The clay is then broken to reveal the brass object, identical to the lost wax model. The metal sprues are filed away, and the object is polished until its surface is smooth and all signs of the channels are gone. Anything made by this method is unique, because the wax disappears and the clay case cannot be reused.

The Benin craftsmen evolved and innovated as they became more skilled and comfortable with a difficult and sometimes dangerous art form. To begin with, they made low-relief bronzes, with relatively few details that rise off the surface. They also followed a formula for their casts. Those with human figures tend to depict groups of three people, with the oba (the largest and the most important) in the centre. Gradually, they introduced more elements of high relief. It may reflect the artists' awareness, as they went on, that high relief would be easier to see across a large courtyard – the details of the human figures in particular would be easier to make out – and would give the casts greater depth, making them seem more three-dimensional. However, high relief involves even more complex management of the molten metal, ensuring that it reaches all elements of the form in the lost wax void before cooling.

The narrative of the later figures also more directly praises the might and authority of the king, showing men carrying out rituals and processions. The artistry and technical assurance of the reliefs was scarcely comprehensible to Europeans of the early twentieth century accustomed to thinking of Africans as primitive peoples. Felix von Luschan, who published the first Western scholarly account of the Benin reliefs in 1919, wrote: 'These Benin works stand among the highest heights of European casting. Benvenuto Cellini could not have a made a better cast himself, not anyone before or after him, even to the present day. These bronzes reach the very heights of what is technically possible.'

Women

The lives of Benin's women were as restricted and limited as those of their Florentine contemporaries. Only one female in Benin had an explicit role in the power hierarchy, the queen mother, the Iyoba. The title originated with Idia, Esigie's mother. Idia was a determined mother who made difficult decisions. When her husband died, two of his sons were vying for power. She used everything at her disposal to secure her son Esigie's place on the throne.

It was thanks to Idia's political authority and astuteness, as well as her mystical and medical powers on the battlefield, that Esigie was able to hold on to his position as oba, to defeat his brother Arhuaran and the neighbouring Igala people. From the time of Idia, the queen mother was allocated her own separate palace, with her own staff. She was the only woman permitted to use symbols of royal power, such as the ceremonial *eben* and *ada* swords, and to wear coral. Her horn-shaped coral-bead headdress, with the towering ede projection on top, is comparable to the projection on top of the oba's own crown, making explicit her role in the creation of the god-king. The Iyoba was allowed to commission bronze and ivory objects for sacred use from the guilds of bronze casters and ivory carvers under the oba's control.

Busts of the queen mother are among the most remarkable of all free-standing Benin Bronzes. Esigie is said to have established the tradition of casting heads of this type, to be placed on altars in the palace and also in the queen mother's residence. These sculptures of power and ritual are more strikingly naturalistic and characterful than many of the Benin Bronzes. The five that survive from the sixteenth century do not seem to represent the same person. A determined and steely identity emanates from one bust, slightly less than life size, acquired by the Berlin Museums after the Punitive Expedition and now returned to Nigerian ownership. The head and neck stand on a bronze base, itself part of the same object, decorated with relief representations of river fish, to demonstrate the queen mother's control of the watery elements associated with trade and prosperity. In this bust the Iyoba is wearing the horned crown and with coral beads arranged over her ears. Two vertical marks on her forehead denote a ritual scarification, again associated with her powerful position. This is a measured portrayal of a mature, beautiful woman, with a high forehead, large expressive eyes and a straight nose. Her lips are pursed, and she gazes ahead intently. This is not someone to trifle with. She has a striking dignity and conviction accentuated by her status, but which seems to come from her inner being.

Two masks of the queen mother convey the same sense of rightful authority. We know that these pendants were worn by the oba during rituals to expel evil spirits from his kingdom. One in the British Museum is remarkable for the directness and purpose of the Iyoba's gaze. Her features are beautifully regular, her eyes evenly spaced across her forehead, her nose positioned in perfect symmetry above her full lips. This mask conveys a powerful impression of Idia's strength and self-belief. Her quasi-divine status is denoted by her extraordinary tiara, composed of stylised European faces, with long beards, hats and staring eyes. They are images of Portuguese men, the first Europeans to be received at the Benin court, whose ability to live between land and water meant that they were believed – like mudfish – to inhabit the spirit world. Who could conquer this woman, and who would wish to challenge the king that she had installed?

A wider community – Benin and Europe

The Portuguese had begun trading with Benin in the 1480s, when they were seeking new sources of pepper to undercut the Ottoman Empire's monopoly on spices from Asia. This agreement, initiated by Ozolua, who had recently succeeded his father as oba, was a mutually beneficial arrangement between equals. Trade quickly expanded to include ivory, pepper, leopard skins and people sold by the Kingdom of Benin in return for European cloth and metal. It is not surprising that the Portuguese themselves became part of Benin's artistic repertoire. Not only did they provide the manillas that were the raw material for the kingdom's brass reliefs, but they gave the oba access to the terrifying but effective power of gunpowder and muskets. In 1515, it was with Portuguese assistance that Ozolua's son and successor, Esigie, was able to drive the Attah of Idah from the walls of Benin City to the far bank of the River Niger. The success of this operation enabled Benin to continue undefeated until the Punitive Expedition of 1897.

The oba and his personal representatives, led by the Unwague, the head of the palace chiefs, personally controlled trade with the Europeans. But this was about more than economics. The Portuguese sought to enter Benin City in search of

Prester John, the legendary Christian king, who was supposed to live somewhere in the continent's interior. Subsequently, they had high hopes of converting the oba and his people to Christianity. Esigie's son Orhogbua and some other high-ranking young men were baptised and taught to read and write in Portuguese, while the oba permitted the construction of three churches in the city. The Edo hierarchy, intrigued by the European's white faces, linked their new associates with the pale-faced Olokun. Because they came from across the sea, bearing rich and valued goods, it was straightforward to fit them into existing belief structures around Olokun, both god of the sea and the generator of earthly wealth. Just as Benin dignitaries, such as the Chief of Ughoton, the oba's ambassador to João II of Portugal – judged in Lisbon as 'a man of good speech and natural wisdom' – were a source of interest and respect at the Portuguese court, so were the Portuguese in Benin. A subset of the Benin Bronzes are independent sculptures of European men, with pointy chins, beards and long faces, in the act of firing muskets. Similar figures appear on the relief plaques that adorned the oba's audience chamber.

Perhaps the most fascinating of these cross-cultural items is a group of ivory salt cellars. In the sixteenth century, to facilitate diplomatic relations, the oba gave his craftsmen permission to produce objects that would be valued by their European visitors. In Europe, ivory had long been used for sacred objects, such as miniature altarpieces, and for the domestic implements of the elite, from combs to table settings. But by the sixteenth century, the wealthiest Europeans were starting to create cabinets of curiosity, which brought together strange and valuable objects from across the world. This was a metaphor for their international connections, and increasingly their control of peoples and states far from home.

Fifteen salt cellars, made for the Portuguese in a court work-shop in Benin City, survive in Western collections. These were made exclusively for foreign trade, as this was not a category of object used by the people of Benin. In Europe, the salt cellar had long had a role in elite gatherings. We still understand the phrase 'above or below the salt' to describe social status. Elaborate or precious salts were brought out for special occasions and dinners at court and noble households, as well as in high-status educational establishments and trading companies, bringing honour to their owners and distinction and amusement to their table. The Benin salt cellars would have been valued for their exotic, non-European provenance and appearance, and as novelties. In one, you would have lifted the top, which is in the shape of a boat sitting on top of an orb, to get access to the seasoning. The lid accounts for about a third of the entire object – in contrast, European-made salt cellars usually had a shallower top.

The Benin craftsman must have either known Portuguese people or been shown images of them (he had evidently not seen a boat, as its timbers resemble the roof shingles of the oba's palace rather than the real planks of a ship's hull). Those depicted on the salt cellar, such as the man holding a staff who looks out from the crow's nest on top of the boat, are in great contrast to images of the oba and his subjects. These alien men have thin, drawn faces accentuated by their long beards. Two of the figures are of higher status; they are wearing elaborately decorated buttoned doublets with flaring shoulders and sleeves, and hose patterned with rosettes, and each has a crucifix hanging on a string of large beads on the front of his chest.

Their heads are covered with high-crowned hats, decorated with a jaunty feather, and they clutch spears before them, while holding onto the hilts of the swords at their sides. Their companions are in the act of pulling their swords from their scabbards, giving a sense of movement which contrasts with the static majesty of the higher-status figures. It has been suggested that the latter are based on portraits of Afonso de Albuquerque, the second governor of Goa, who would have sailed around the West African coast. However, all these people are essentially portrayed as caricatures. The Portuguese owner of the salt cellar would have been both fascinated and amused by how he and his countrymen were seen by a set of people very different from them.

**

Today, Benin City is a busy metropolis, home to more than 1.5 million people. But, tragically, there is at present little to distinguish Benin from a swathe of similar conurbations in West Africa. For over 120 years, the city and kingdom of Benin have lived with the impact of the Punitive Expedition, when the work of many centuries was dismantled in the space of a few weeks. The fate of the Benin Bronzes, and the question of whether they should be returned to Benin, are now subjects of lively debate. A number of private owners and public collections have returned objects to the Court of Benin and the Nigerian government. Many others have announced their intention to do so. Some have offered to lend objects to the Edo Museum of West African Art, designed by the Ghanaian-British architect Sir David Adjaye for a site beside the oba's palace.

This raises new and different issues of community. Even if the wrongs of the past are being righted, and the horror and destruction of the Punitive Expedition are fully acknowledged, can artefacts acquired in this way have a legitimate home in public institutions outside Benin? How can such museums – often in a position to tell a global narrative of interaction, continuity and change between societies and civilisation – maintain their moral equilibrium if their collections have been formed by European colonialism? Should all the objects looted in 1897 be returned to their place of origin, to be used in the way their makers and commissioners intended, by their descendants? These questions are profound, hard to answer, and there are many points of view. In finding a way forward, we should principally be mindful of respecting the sense of community and identity that motivated the original makers and commissioners of Benin's unique cultural inheritance.

Amsterdam Town Hall (now Royal Palace)

9

AMSTERDAM: TOLERANCE

1650–1700

Where else on earth could you find,
as easily as you do here, all the con-
veniences of life and all the curiosities
you could hope to see? In what other
country could you find such complete
freedom, or sleep with less anxiety,
or find armies at the ready to protect
you, or find fewer poisonings, or acts
of treason or slander?

Descartes, letter to Balzac,
5 May 1631

The French philosopher René Descartes – he of 'I think therefore I am' fame, and a resident of Amsterdam in the 1630s – put
his finger on it. In Amsterdam, everything is possible, and it
can be done pleasantly and tolerantly. There are still few more
enjoyable places to wander than the ring of canals and streets of

central Amsterdam familiar to Descartes. Perhaps it is because all this comforting stability and prosperity has always stood on a knife edge. Day by day, minute by minute, Amsterdam continues to slip back into the watery elements which are the source of its trading wealth. Not even the most ingenious dams can halt this process. The city is here today, but it may well be gone tomorrow, so it's not surprising that Amsterdam's people have sought pleasure, gratification, relaxation and self-fulfilment in a bewildering variety of ways. Equally, they have been encouraging and tolerant of this diversity.

At no time was this truer than in the middle of the seventeenth century, the zenith of Amsterdam's wealth, power and influence. Here it was possible to believe and write what you wanted, and to indulge yourself in every imaginable way, with riches, goods, ideas and pleasures from all around the world. The per capita income was the highest in Europe. Not surprisingly, it's a period that historians and the Dutch people have long eulogised as the 'golden age', where freedom and tolerance brought prosperity, full bellies and culture to everyone.

Seventeenth-century Amsterdam witnessed an extraordinary flowering of the moveable art forms of paintings, drawing and prints. There was a painter for about every two thousand people. Some were jobbing artists, but this number also included those whose reputation has never faded – Rembrandt van Rijn and his many successful pupils, including Gerrit Dou, Govert Flinck and Ferdinand Bol; Pieter de Hooch, the archetypal painter of domestic interiors; Meindert Hobbema, whose work van Gogh loved; the maritime artist – and Rembrandt's friend – Jan van de Capelle. Purchasing quality art, generally an elite activity, was in everyone's reach. It's been estimated that by the mid-seventeenth century even artisan families owned an average of seven works.

The English merchant and traveller Peter Mundy, visiting Amsterdam in the 1640s, was astonished that 'Butchers and bakers ... yea many tymes blacksmithes. Coblers, etts., will have some picture or other by their Forge and in their stalle. Such is the generall Notion, enclination and delight that these Countrie Native(s) have to paintings.' The market for historical art today is still overwhelmingly dominated by paintings made, traded and collected in seventeenth-century Holland.

The rise of Amsterdam

Amsterdam's rise had been meteoric. In the year 1500 it was a small city, twelve thousand strong, with a recently acquired set of stone walls. It owed its existence to a dam that protected the low-lying but fertile land from the waters of the rivers Amstel and Ij, and the Zuiderzee on the north-western edge of Europe. By 1650 Amsterdam was the Western world's financial and commercial capital, a hub of artistic, scientific and technological innovation, with an estimated 150,000 inhabitants. A particular combination of factors, including geology, religion and conflict, was responsible. But the key, as the Leiden and Amsterdam merchant and economist Pieter de la Court noted, was stable government and a global trading network.

In the late fifteenth century the silting of Bruges's harbour had moved most waterborne trade in north-western Europe to Antwerp, at the mouth of the River Scheldt. Antwerp became the political and economic heart of the Netherlands, the seventeen provinces ruled by the Habsburg prince Philip II of Spain. Simmering unhappiness about being ruled from abroad, exacerbated by the religious discontents of the European Reformation, led to rebellion, and the bloody Dutch

Revolt. When it became evident that Antwerp was staying in Habsburg hands, the nascent Dutch Republic, formed of the seven rebellious provinces, took every opportunity to destroy Antwerp's trading supremacy. They blockaded the Scheldt and welcomed the industrious Jewish and Protestant families who fled north. Most settled in Holland, the largest, richest and most cosmopolitan part of the new nation.

At the same time Dutch shipwrights were inventing the *fluyt*, a cargo ship that required a small crew, and which – because of its longer keel – was able to sail and dock in shallower waters than its competitors. By the early seventeenth century the Dutch were Europe's greatest shipbuilders. Increasingly this production was concentrated around Amsterdam because the city's harbours and docks were large, deep and safe. Success bred success. The northern suburb of Zaan became one of the first modern industrialised areas in the world, with mechanised windmills processing a range of goods. Amsterdam was quickly becoming the most important centre of prosperous and highly urbanised Holland. The city had already crafted an export market based on its economic staples – cured fish, dairy products, dyestuffs – which meant that it could always import enough grain to feed its people.

Now it took international trade to another level. The city was the driving force behind the VOC (Vereenigde Oostindische Compagnie), the first trans-national trading company, founded in 1602. Its navy dominated the world's seaways and controlled the movement of goods from Asia to Europe, establishing trading colonies from Taiwan to New Amsterdam on the island of Manhattan. By 1650, sixteen thousand merchant ships flew the Dutch flag. The VOC was empowered to act as the representative of the Dutch government outside Europe. It had autonomy to govern its colonies, issue coinage, administer justice and even negotiate with foreign powers. Amsterdam's Bourse, the first modern trading exchange, was created in 1613 to facilitate the activities of the VOC. It was remarkable for the number and speed of transactions. Formal trading was restricted to one hour a day (hence the speed), initially on a bridge, but lively discussion and exchange continued from morning to night in the coffee shops and taverns on Kalverstraat and the plaza in Damrak. International business became the most lucrative of occupations. Of Amsterdam's top tax payers in 1631, 253 were overseas merchants. Only sixty were industrialists or working exclusively in the domestic market.

As a whole, the Netherlands was governed by a nominated States-General, with a stadtholder or prince, nominally the servant of the States. Each province had its own States-General too. But Amsterdam was largely free to rule itself. Like most other cities, it was run by a group of male citizens, the regent class. They belonged to wealthy families, many connected by marriage, who were able to step aside from day-to-day business life, who were moderate in their politics and religion and who shared a paternalistic commitment to the worse off. Both the town council (*vroedschap*) and the aldermen (*schepenen*) were drawn from this group. Each year the councillors elected four burgomasters who governed the city, while the other councillors, in committees, directed key areas of the city's administration, including the civic guard and the maintenance of canals and dams. The active merchants and businessmen were of slightly lower social status. They exerted their influence on the boards of trading companies, guilds and charities. As a group, these individuals identified the city's interests as their own. Increasingly, they saw themselves as autonomous from the wider Dutch Republic, and God's favourites. In 1648, the stadtholder sent an army to Amsterdam to enforce his authority. It was believed that divine favour could be inferred from the army's disappearance in the Amsterdam mist, and the prince's untimely death from smallpox.

By the early seventeenth century Amsterdam was bursting at the seams. In the eastern part was the Jewish quarter, home to some of the most recent and most prosperous immigrants, Sephardim from Antwerp, and Ashkenazim from central Europe. In 1613, the city launched a programme of canal building, adding a ring of three new waterways around the city. The wealthy competed for building sites on the banks of the 'three canals', the grand Herengracht, the slightly less prestigious (in spite of its name) Kaisergracht and the Prinsengracht. Poorer citizens fought for space in streets of the Jordaan, at the city's western edge, abutting the harbours, timberyards and docks that spread along the banks of the Isselmeer. The mass of the citizenry consisted of shopkeepers, small tradesmen and artisans, including shipbuilders, sailors and carpenters.

Rulers

Amsterdam's Stadhuis, in Damrak, overlooking a busy shipping basin, was begun in 1648, the year the Spanish finally recognised the legitimacy of the Dutch state. It is a clear expression of the elite's pride in their city, and their fitness to govern it. They wanted the 'eighth wonder of the world', and in the Haarlem-born architect Jacob van Campen's design they got something which was radically different from most of Amsterdam. The Stadhuis was built of gleaming white imported stone, not locally made red brick. It was resplendent with elaborate architectural decoration – including columns, capitals, cornices, cupolas and tympanums – inspired by

Vitruvius' *Ten Books on Architecture*, and the classical Roman buildings that were known to van Campen and his major sculptural collaborator, Artus Quellinus. This stylistic choice trumpeted that the councillors and aldermen were as virtuous as the morally upright ancient Romans. The city hall towered over the low-lying buildings of Amsterdam. Standing five storeys tall, topped by an oval cupola and extending over twenty-three horizontal bays, it was no mean feat of engineering (and luck) that it didn't just sink into the marshy ground.

The new Stadhuis embodied the functions of good city government, as the leading Amsterdammers saw it. All the principal elements of state bureaucracy – courts, prisons, taxation offices, markets, a bank, a police office, an armoury – were kept inside its walls. Everything about the building celebrated Amsterdam's ambition, and the benevolent power exercised by its rulers. The exterior acknowledged Amsterdam's ambivalent relationship with the sea. The city's survival depended on keeping the ocean under control, but its great wealth came from waterborne trade. An enormous sculpture of Peace on the front façade shows the gods of the sea paying homage to the Maid of Amsterdam, a mythical personification of the city. On the rear of the building the four continents, flanked by the river gods of the Amstel and the Ij, bow before the Maid as they present her with lavish tributes. Amsterdam's dominance of world trade is emphasised by the presence of Atlas, bowed by the weight of the globe, on the top of the building. In Greek mythology, Atlas was punished for his revolt against the gods by being condemned to hold up the sky on his shoulders for eternity.

The enormous building reinforced Amsterdam's right to exploit the known world. At its heart was the 120-foot barrel-vaulted Citizens' Hall (Burgerzall). It's hardly coincidental, given van Campen and the burgomasters' ambitions, that the room shares the only recorded dimensions of a room designed by Vitruvius himself. It was illuminated by three separate levels of windows and two interior light wells, so that even in the dark of the northern hemisphere winter the room was filled with sun. Illumination here means understanding: the Amsterdammers who entered this space could have been in no doubt that theirs was the way of the truth and the light.

As they walked across the Burgerzaal, they stepped upon three maps of the world, and the night sky as seen from Amsterdam, etched in stone on the floor. They lifted their eyes to see personifications of the four elements of earth, air, fire and water, and the Roman gods, representing the planets of the solar system. All were presided over by the Maid, ruling the known universe as well as her city. The message was loud and clear: the men of Amsterdam were to exercise their control over the heavens, the earth and the oceans, their peoples and animals, as a manifestation of their divinely ordained favour.

The rest of the building was decorated liberally with paintings that demonstrated the councillors and aldermen's intention to execute their authority wisely, if paternalistically. Patrons and painters – principally the talented and admired Govert Flinck, who died shortly after signing the contract that gave him sole responsibility for the Stadhuis decoration – plundered the stories of the Old and New Testaments, the Roman Republic before the time of Christ and the history of early Holland to render their manifesto of government in visual form. They wished to show, despite quite compelling evidence to the contrary, that Amsterdam was no upstart, but deeply embedded in European and Christian history.

Obscure episodes from the history of the Batavians, a Germanic tribe who were believed to have inhabited Holland during the Roman era, formed part of the decoration of the great hall. Rembrandt himself was commissioned to paint the conspiracy of Claudius Civilis, a one-eyed chieftain who led a rebellion against the Roman governor of Batavia. Claudius had been eulogised by the leaders of the Dutch Revolt and had entered into the canon of Dutch identity. Rembrandt's large canvas was quietly removed after less than a year, probably because it was not sufficiently heroic or decorous (it now belongs to the Royal Swedish Academy of Fine Arts). A strong mystical light suffuses the composition, centred on the conspirators' oath. The Batavians look barbarous, even slightly frightening – hardly a model for the respectable Amsterdam burghers.

Those paintings that enjoyed success eulogised the virtues of public-minded individuals, who placed the common good above their own interests, and who could make decisions on behalf of those who lacked the intellectual or moral qualities to act in their own best interest – women, children, the ungodly poor and non-European peoples. Such as, for instance, Gaius Fabritius Lucinus, painted by Ferdinand Bol in 1656, who could neither be bribed, nor intimidated by a martial elephant. Or the elder statesman Quintus Fabius Maximus, who dismounted from his horse to greet his son because of the public office the young man held, as depicted by Jan Lievens.

There was a definite Protestant as well as nationalist theme. The Protestant Dutch saw many parallels between themselves and God's Chosen People, the Israelites, which partly explains their tolerance of Jewish people, unlike practically every other state in Europe at the time. Not only had the Dutch been delivered from the Babylonian Captivity of Spanish rule, but they had been rewarded by their constancy to God's message by being endowed with immense wealth. Amsterdam's rulers were not, however, to be swayed by mere money. They were urged to follow the example of the Roman consul Marcus Curius Dentatus, who spurned the gold and silver treasures offered by Samnite envoys in favour of home-grown turnips. It was their duty to make difficult but correct decisions. For this they needed no less than divine inspiration. Nowhere was this more evident than in the Council Chamber, where Flinck portrayed King Solomon praying for wisdom. Magistrates would look at this before they entered the courtroom to give judgment, where it was hoped that theirs would be equally wise and fair. As a whole, Amsterdam's Stadhuis stood as a new, improved Palace of Solomon – a seat of impartial Protestant justice, exemplifying the merits of Christian government.

Amsterdam's elite had a strong sense of their social responsibilities, and of their role in maintaining civic harmony. This is expressed in group portraits of syndics, patrons of charities and guilds. Guilds were a central part of civic life in Amsterdam as they had been in Renaissance Florence, because they controlled the parameters of particular trades and commercial activities. By Rembrandt's time, there was a clear formula that artists were to follow: these pictures consisted of a line of behatted officials, often seated at a table, the monotony perhaps broken up slightly with the presence of a standing bare-headed servant. It is rare for mass portraits of the rich and powerful to be artistically exciting, or of interest to anyone but the sitters' nearest and dearest.

But in this inherently conservative genre Rembrandt created some of his most exciting and compelling pictures, which both satisfied his sitters and had an edge of psychological drama. One of these is his 1662 portrait, *The Sampling Officials of the Amsterdam Drapers' Guild*. Cloth was a substantial industry in Amsterdam, centred on the production of a felt-like fabric called *laken*, woven from wool. These officials regulated the prices and quality of dyed cloth, to maintain fairness in the industry. Rembrandt turns what could be an everyday – if important – scene into one with narrative and purpose.

Whoever looks at this picture enters the restricted, secluded world of the cloth samplers, choosing the right bales, with the right number of threads, ensuring that trade is carried out on fair principles and that neither buyer nor seller is short-changed. In order to preserve a sense of impartiality, the sampling officials met in a closed meeting room with a south-facing window, on the second floor of their guild headquarters, the Staalhof. Rembrandt, appropriately, shows the room bathed with light, entering from the left.

We are invited into the private realm of rich, kindly and sensitive men, making good decisions on our behalf. Five men sit or stand around a table spread with a valuable Persian carpet, too precious to place on the floor. The staalmeesters tested and assessed the cloth with their hands, so hands as well as voices are much to the fore in this picture. At the far right, van der Meije clutches the cloth sample under discussion. There is a disagreement going on, between the seated Master of the Guild, van Doeyenburg, pointing to a book held by his colleague de Neve, and the man to his left, Jansz, a celebrated art collector, who is in the process of standing up. But someone has come into the room. All the men, save the Master and their servant Bols, who stands at the back of the painting, are visibly perturbed by this interruption. They look directly at the inter-loper; van Loon, on the far the left, swivels in his chair towards the interloper – is it us, the artist, or someone else? Some are kindly disposed, while others are annoyed by the interaction. Van der Meije clutches his gloves, as if he is about to get up and go. The Master of the Guild continues his argument with his neighbour; while Bols, like a good servant, looks blank and inscrutable.

The wonder of Rembrandt's painting is that he makes us care about the lives and reactions of these officials. In this work, he asserts that their prosperous but relatively humdrum lives are as worthy of recording as more conventionally elevated subjects, such as those depicted on the walls of the Stadhuis. Rembrandt's genius draws us into this discussion, so that we wish to know its outcome. The picture appears to be a snapshot of real events, but it's a very composed and planned work of art. Three hundred years later, we don't wholly understand what is going on, but we want to find out.

The house

Peace, prosperity and order are all reflected in the comforting, conservative images of houses and streets that were popular among the upper classes of Amsterdam and the other wealthy cities of Holland. They are exemplified in the work of Jan van der Heyden, whose Amsterdam townscapes show quiet canals and clean cobbled streets punctuated by green trees, with red-brick gabled houses and churches; it is also in the calm courtyards of Pieter de Hooch, trained in Delft and settled in Amsterdam, and the work of an artist who has become even more successful in the centuries since his death, Johannes Vermeer.

Vermeer's *A Street in Delft*, painted in the late 1650s, shows a prosaic scene. It has been raining, and the weather is changeable. Grey clouds, mixed with white, reveal small patches of blue. The clouds scud quickly across the sky. There are some shafts of sunlight, but mainly the light is diffused. It reflects off the imperfectly applied, sometimes dirty limewash that covers the lower levels of the brick townhouse. Vermeer enhances the sense of the everyday by cutting off the edges of the buildings. Although this planning is deliberate, it's been done so that it seems inconsequential. You feel that you are walking through this scene. You are invited to look at, but not to engage with, the woman sitting sewing in the doorway while she supervises the children who are playing out of sight but not of earshot. This is not because they would not speak to you, but because they are occupied with such dull activities that you would not feel inclined to give them more than a glance. Another woman, seen through an open passageway, is reaching into a water butt. She is doing the laundry, as we can tell from the soapy water that runs along the open drain, across the street and presumably into the canal, which seems to be where we are standing.

There is nothing to keep you here. But it's the normality and banality of this scene that gives it its beauty. You wonder, why did Vermeer choose to paint it? Perhaps it is the restraint that is so appealing. This is a conservative, middle-of-the-road house, home to ordinary but sociable people. The wooden benches underneath the windows are for sitting on – the northern European equivalent of rocking on the veranda. Vermeer evokes smells as well as sounds and images. The greenish vine (which now looks blue, because the yellow pigment it was mixed with has changed colour) that covers the smaller house on the left of the painting is just forming grapes. Everything would have smelt fresh; you can imagine the steam rising off the road, as happens on warm spring and summer days.

The main house is attractive, reasonably well maintained, but modest. This is not a grand residence. It may be late medieval: it's certainly in an architectural style that by the seventeenth century was old-fashioned. The bricks have recently been repointed, and there are some strange, jagged repairs. It's been suggested that these are the result of the powerful explosion that devastated Delft when one of the city's gunpowder stores accidentally blew up in October 1654. It may not be an actual place but a convincingly realistic composite, an imaginary view which perfectly expresses the ideal of the Dutch city and the household that is its microcosm. Children occupy themselves happily, while women go about their domestic duties. The scene is quiet and contented. There is nothing to shock, or to worry about. All is right in the world.

Inside the house

On the outside, Dutch life seemed as prosaic, safe and comfortable as Vermeer's street scene. The Dutch in the seventeenth century were celebrated throughout Europe for the calm and settled nature of their family life. Their society was in many respects far more liberal than most others across the continent. Respectable women were allowed to leave the house far more than was permitted elsewhere. On marriage, women retained rights over their property. They could even undertake business activities, and make commercial transactions and sign legal documents in their own right. In a lower social sphere, women worked at market stalls and in shops – generally as part of family businesses – as well as the many who were employed in domestic service. The role of women, mistresses and maids, was seen as paramount in creating the godly, respectable household and, by extension, the state.

No one expressed this more influentially than 'Father Cats', the poet, moralist and statesman Jacob Cats. He wrote a series of immensely popular emblem books, which told people how to behave – including *Houwelick* (Marriage) of 1625, *Spiegel van den ouden ende nieuwen tijdt* (Mirror of Old and New Times) of 1632 and *Trou-ringh* (Wedding Ring) of 1637. These works consisted of woodcuts or engravings, illustrating a moral, mostly in verse. Cats satirised the slovenly home, the unsupervised servant, the mistress who didn't take care of her children. All these symbolised the problems of an unregulated country. If all households were properly run, so would be the state. Marriage was, as Cats described it, 'a smithy of men, a foundation of cities, a nursery of high government'. This belief helps to explain the quantity of Dutch paintings that deal with the concerns of household and daily life. History paintings were popular in Amsterdam, but the most successful pictorial compositions – found in every house, whether as a painting, print or drawing – were moralised and often very witty every-day scenes.

It's often unclear what is going on in these works. One of Vermeer's last paintings, *Woman Writing a Letter with her Maid* (now in Dublin), shows a woman bent deep over her sheet of paper as she concentrates. A red seal, some sealing wax and what appears to be a manual of how to write letters are scattered on the black and white floor in front of her desk. A maid stands beside her, looking out of the partially open window. Is she encouraging her mistress, or warning her of the dangers of corresponding with people outside the household? The ambiguity is intentional. You make of the picture what you bring to it.

A significant subgroup of these paintings depict – out of comic value but also worry – what happened when things didn't quite go to plan. The lazy maid, neglecting her duty in order to eat, drink or flirt, or the wife who gave herself over to pleasure with men, music and song, were staple subjects for painters, who revelled in depicting the rich sheen of the satins, silks and furs worn by these shameless hussies, their gleaming wine and beer glasses, comfortable houses and tables laden with poultry, hothouse fruit, seafood, sweet confits and nuts. Both genres are combined in Nicholas Maes's *The Idle Servant*. Maes was a pupil of Rembrandt who specialised in small-scale images of domestic life. A smiling young woman, wearing an expensive black jacket with fur cuffs, gestures ruefully at her maid, who has fallen asleep in the middle of her work, presumably preparing the feast of food and drink that several well-dressed people are enjoying in the dining room behind. Pots, pans and kitchen utensils lie at the servant's feet. On a chest behind her, a cat sinks its teeth into a dead goose, ready for cooking, which is about to topple over and land on the sleeping woman's head.

Perhaps the most successful painter of these scenes was Jan Steen, the landscape painter Jan van Goyen's son-in-law. Like Hogarth in London a century later, Steen was brilliantly able to combine morals with humour. In *The Merry Family*, three generations have come together to sing and make music, often a powerful symbol of harmony. On the surface, this looks like an enjoyable family occasion, with grandparents, parents and children enjoying innocent pleasures. However, the general merriment has been heightened by the presence of alcohol, leading to some raucous and probably not very tuneful noise. The father holds his goblet of white wine up to the light while he sings and plays the fiddle; a nanny lets a small boy take a swig of strong drink from the spout of a goblet; a child takes a break from his horn playing to smoke his pipe. A piece of paper hanging from the mantelpiece reads 'As the old sing, so shall the young twitter.' The message is clear: how can we expect the young to behave, if their elders set them a bad example? The viewers and owners of such works evidently enjoyed them, either out of a smug sense of superiority or from the vicarious thrill of living on the edge. They cannot be seen as a truthful representation of daily life, any more than Jacob Cats's amusing moral lessons point to the degeneracy of most Dutch men and women of his day.

We can, however, get some idea of how people lived from house inventories, usually compiled when their owner died, there was a legal dispute or when a family fell on troubled times. In July 1656 a clerk from the Amsterdam Chamber of Insolvency, the Desolate Boedelkamer, spent two days in Rembrandt's house on the prosperous Sint Antoniesbreestraat, to assess the value of the bankrupt artist's possessions. There were paintings, drawings and prints, by Rembrandt and others; sculptures, both ancient and modern; weapons and suits of armour; Mughal miniatures; Japanese and East Indian curiosities; what's described as a 'giant's head'; numerous shells and branches of coral; and more day-to-day objects such as fine Spanish chairs with velvet seats, cushion covers, bedsteads, pots, pans, tablecloths and even – the last items in the inventory – 'a few collars and cuffs'.

Interesting, and sometimes depressing, as these bald lists of possessions are, they don't give as true a sense of life as people wished it to be lived as one of the most surprising genres of artistic production to survive from seventeenth-century Amsterdam: the adult woman's dolls house. Like Rembrandt, men had cabinets of curiosities; women indulged their fantasies in miniature houses, as lavish as their wealth permitted. These were too important and cherished to allow children to play with them.

The most outstanding to survive is the dolls house that Petronella Oortman maintained from her second marriage until her death. In 1686 Petronella married the prosperous silk merchant Johannes Brandt, after the death of her first husband and daughter. Like her new husband, she had grown up in wealth. Her father was a gunsmith, and the family lived on the banks of the Singel canal, originally Amsterdam's moat. Petronella was at this time thirty, still capable of childbearing, but by no means a girl herself.

Everything in the house has been carefully made and planned. It celebrates the rooms and the features that we assume were most important to Petronella. There is a lying-in room, where the woman of the house would spend the first six weeks in comfort after a child's birth; a laundry and linen room for drying, ironing and storing clothes; spaces for Petronella's servants to sleep (each had their own bed, chair and chamber pot); and thoughtful details like foot warmers, so that everyone, not only the most important, could stay warm in the damp Amsterdam winter. Some surprising features are missing. There is a large show kitchen, where inlaid cabinets of precious wood show off a miniature collection of real Chinese export china. Yet the kitchen in Petronella's real house was a tiny space, even though we know that Dutch families of the status of the Oortmans and the Brandts lavished time and money on entertainment, and on the construction of elaborate meals and dishes at home.

The house stands about two metres high, on a tortoiseshell frame inlaid with pewter, made for her by a French cabinet maker (probably a Protestant refugee from France, where the Edict of Nantes had expelled all remaining non-conformists in 1695). All the pieces in the house were made to scale. Years after Petronella's death, her husband and their daughter Hendrina proudly showed the house to a visitor, marvelling at its artistry. In some ways it serves as a portrait of her, and in particular how she wanted people to remember how she'd lived. Hendrina thought that her mother had spent as much as thirty thousand guilders on her house. This was as much as a grand house in a good area of Amsterdam would have cost. Perhaps in keeping with the belittling of women's objects, Petronella's miniature house was valued at only seven hundred guilders when her husband made an inventory of his possessions.

Plenty

The luxury trades and items represented in Petronella's dolls house – from tea, coffee and spices to paintings, fine silks and marquetry – flourished, and the super-rich lived in townhouses filled to the brim with valuable possessions. The most tangible (and the most tactile) signs of this were the millions of pieces of blue and white Chinese porcelain which were imported to the Netherlands, and onwards to other European countries.

Ownership of these beautiful vessels remained an aristocratic privilege for over a century – everywhere except the Netherlands. Chinese porcelain wasn't quite the stuff of ordinary life, but it permeated middle-class culture. The challenge for the Dutch was to make these objects both desirable and pricey, but not so unaffordable that they were beyond the reach of the middle classes, to stimulate trade. Initially they were made as utilitarian items, but as their value increased they became show objects to be stood on sideboards, and so valuable that it was cheaper to commission a painting of one than to buy the real thing. Kraak ware, named after the ships in which it was transported, is easily recognisable. Every item is divided into separate decorative panels, each containing a design element such as stylised flowers, feathers or other patterns.

As we have seen, from the late sixteenth century the kilns at Jingdezhen predominantly worked for the overseas market, making specifically Western forms, such as mustard pots, candlesticks and butter dishes, in a material much prized by Europeans. The imitations that began to be produced in Delft and other centres in Holland were exported over northern Europe, and as far afield as Japan, South Africa and the West Indies. Chinese blue and white ware, reinvented as a Dutch art form, is even today used to project Dutch nationalism and sense of identity. Think of the souvenirs you may have purchased to bring home from the Netherlands: at least one is likely to have been a sweet tin imprinted with a design from a blue and white tile.

The other recognisably Dutch everyday luxury was painting. Relative to other countries, the Netherlands were able to support a huge number of artists. Making art became a more desirable career, because it was possible to make a living from it. A fully trained artist, recognised as a master by the guild, could earn in the region of 1,150 and 1,400 guilders a year, more than double the annual salary of a master carpenter. And celebrated painters were able to live on the same level as the Dutch elite, if (and it was a big if) they were able to manage their money.

Artistic dynasties, such as the landscape painters the van Ruisdaels and the Konincks, were supplemented by those hailing from more varied backgrounds. Rembrandt's parents were Leiden millers of sufficient wealth to have enrolled their talented boy at the city's Latin school, and then the university; his friend the Amsterdam marine painter Jan van de Capelle painted as a dilettante, living off the proceeds of an inherited cloth-dying business; while Rembrandt's most successful student, Govert Flinck, was the son of a wealthy merchant from

Cleves, who further bettered himself by marrying the heiress of a VOC director. Others had less privileged beginnings: the landscape painter Meindert Hobbema was a carpenter's son who had spent some of his early years in a municipal orphanage.

Because of the extreme competition and volatility of market-driven taste, life as an artist could be precarious. Many careers show the pendulum swinging from the high to the low life, as fashions and tastes changed, with surprising speed. Rembrandt, notoriously, went bankrupt, partly because of financial incompetence, partly because the darker moods and colours of his later works were not as attractive to buyers as the more academic pictures of his former pupils. In 1658 he moved from a grand merchant's house to modest rented accommodation in the Jordaan. Four years later his affairs were so low that he was compelled to sell his dead wife Saskia's grave plot (the marking stone in the Oude Kerk that you see today was only added in 1953). Others fared even worse: Emanuel de Witte's idealised views of peaceful churches give no sign of his turbulent life. In 1659 his younger second wife and teenage daughter were arrested for theft. De Witte was forced to work for the dealer Joris de Wijs in return for bed, board and an annual salary of eight hundred guilders. Ultimately, he hanged himself from a canal bridge. Jan van Goyen, perhaps the most gifted Dutch landscape painter of the seventeenth century – and whose paintings have remained commercially successful ever since – never recovered from his speculations in tulip bulbs when that market crashed disastrously in 1637. When he died nineteen years later he was still in debt. Vermeer and his family in nearby Delft were among the many artists to suffer a complete reverse in their fortunes following the 'Disaster Year' (Rampjaar) of 1672. Shortly after his death in 1675 Vermeer's desperate widow bartered *Woman Writing a Letter, with her Maid* and *The Milkmaid* to clear the family's debt of four hundred guilders at the local bakery. Most seventeenth-century Dutch artists tried to diversify, and supplement their income with other sources. Hobbema, for instance, combined painting with the more reliably remunerated post of wine-gauger – measuring imported barrels of wine for taxation purposes – for Amsterdam from 1668.

Perhaps the most emphatic images of this prosperity are the ornamental and extravagant still lifes of food and drink that were made for the city's art market. Pieter Claesz's *Still Life with a Turkey Pie* is a lavish rendition of conspicuous consumption that the banqueters have unaccountably abandoned. A fine white tablecloth of the best linen has been spread to protect an even finer table carpet. Luscious green olives, the perfect appetiser, glisten in a porcelain bowl beside clear white wine served in a grand goblet of Rhenish glass (the protuberances on the stem made them easy to hold). Rather than mussels, the more expensive oysters have been prepared for the feast. They are ready to be eaten, with the relish of the excitingly peeled lemon leaving a trail of sweet-smelling zest behind. Fruit and nuts, including grapes still alive on the vine, are invitingly shown in a blue and white dish of kraak ware, and half-eaten pigs of oranges and shelled nuts are strewn around the table. A spoon sits atop a broken fruit pie, its crust glistening white with crystals of sieved Brazilian cane sugar, tempting you to pick it up and take a bite. The finest sea salt spills onto a plate, while a mixture of ground and corn pepper is in a curled horn of paper.

It's not clear what the need is for the nautilus shell – presumably a salt cellar – except to flaunt the opulence of the table setting. Not for nothing were these paintings known as *pronken*, or show-off pictures. Dominating the picture is a pie, adorned with the head, neck and extravagant plumage of a turkey, at this time still a luxury meat. The Dutch were famed for their pie crusts into which birds and poultry were stuffed, in decreasing sizes, from the turkey or swan down to the songbird whose organs were a tasty morsel. This still life is full of movement, implied or otherwise. Strangest of all is the reflection in the shiny pewter plate at the bottom left. A lemon, a bread roll and a window are all that can be seen. The most modest of repasts is reflected in this sumptuous feast. The artist has signed his name on the knife that juts out from the creamy linen into our space.

Each of these drinks and foodstuffs had a meaning, which once you learnt the visual language was very obvious. A peeled lemon not only smelt beautiful, but it stood for the passing of time (it's been estimated that lemons appear in more than half of all Dutch paintings from the middle of the seventeenth century). White wine, in fine Roemer glasses, was a luxury product, but it often spoiled and went sour; hence, it was a perfect metaphor for the transience and imperfection of human life. But the transparency of the glass also made it a symbol of openness, friendship and sometimes love, handed around a merry company in a vessel made for sharing. Open oysters – and mussels – could signify a loose woman, ready for the taking. Grapes were a symbol of fertility, but also, when combined with bread, stood for the body and blood of Christ, and his Eucharistic sacrifice.

There was a long tradition in the Netherlands of painting food – as there was also in the Habsburgs' Spanish lands. To begin with, these northern still lifes were associated explicitly with Christian stories, such as the wedding feast at Cana, where Christ changed water into wine, or the supper at Emmaus, when weary travellers recognised the risen Christ.

By the early seventeenth century, a combination of Protestant objection to sacred images and a desire to celebrate the physical and earthy world meant that these biblical fig leaves were no longer required.

While paintings like Claesz's are more fantasy that reality, it's clear that the inhabitants of Amsterdam did not lack the good things of life. Holland and the other United Provinces were probably the only place in Europe where hunger wasn't a staple of everyday life. Well into the eighteenth century, foreign visitors found it hard to believe the plethora of foodstuffs available. Things were made much easier by the fertility of the Dutch lowlands, and the early adaptation of market gardening. There was a virtuous circle between the city and its periphery. The city was a brilliant market for fruit and vegetables, while it was the quantity and quality of human and animal waste it produced (more genteelly known as 'night soil') that enabled the Dutch flood plains to be so productive. There was a consistency of diet between the elite and the labouring classes. Even the very poor were extremely well fed. The accounts of the poorhouse in Leiden, between Amsterdam and The Hague, show that the residents had a balanced diet incorporating every major food group, including meat – the middle classes of practically no other city in the world would have eaten so well. It has been alleged that so common was wild salmon – elsewhere one of the greatest of delicacies – that servants begged their masters to feed it to them no more than twice a week.

The tolerance of plenty

As a whole, Amsterdam's inhabitants had a higher standard of living than was seen anywhere else in the world. The milk and honey continued to flow over the course of the seventeenth century. By the 1670s, lighting was being introduced to streets, the canals and waterways were regularly maintained and subsidies continued to be paid to orphanages and almshouses for the maintenance of the poor. Each religious community was held responsible for the care of its own poor, but the city paid regular subsidies to maintain their poorhouses and the religious buildings themselves. Education of some sort was open to a large proportion of children, including girls. Members of the burgher and merchant class were even able – like aristocrats elsewhere – to travel abroad for their education. The Athenaeum, the precursor of the University of Amsterdam, and the Latin school, provided an excellent, well-rounded formation for the male children of the wealthy and cultivated.

Amsterdam set the fashions and trends for other Europeans. Coffee and tea, those staples of modern life, were largely imported to the West via Amsterdam. With these beverages went discussion and dissent, fuelled by the active printing presses. By the 1660s the city had overtaken Antwerp as Europe's biggest centre of printing. In Amsterdam, it was possible to publish all sorts of works that would have been illegal elsewhere – from anti-Catholic propaganda and extreme anti-establishment Protestant tracts to Jewish religious literature. Free speech and frank opinions were encouraged, yet the conservative elite worried that this might well lead to a world turned upside down.

For all the trauma of the Spanish Wars, Holland, and particularly Amsterdam, was renowned for its tolerance in matters of faith. By the 1630s, Amsterdam was home not just to Calvinist Protestants who had fled the southern Netherlands but Sephardi Jews originally from Portugal and Spain, Ashkenazim leaving the anti-Jewish heartlands of central Europe, and

Christians of all persuasions, including Catholics, French Huguenots, English Baptists, Anabaptists and other radicals, including the Pilgrim Fathers. Here, the philosophers René Descartes and Baruch Spinoza felt safe to develop their controversial theories concerning identity and the existence of God. Even pleasure was allowed to flourish. Theatres, infamously closed in England under the Commonwealth, were allowed to open. During their official closure for five years following the 'Disaster Year' (Rampjaar) of 1672, the city authorities turned a blind eye to visiting companies.

The majority of migrants came for economic reasons, but they were evidently influenced by the tacit protection that was offered to 'practising' Catholics, Jews and members of separatist sects because of the financial benefit they could bring the city. Troublemakers, like the Quakers or the Fifth Monarchists (feared by the authorities for their revolutionary leanings), or the impoverished of any religion, were discouraged from making Amsterdam their home. Toleration was extended to those who were prepared, at least in word, to conform to the Dutch Reformed Church – in essence the state religion – and who made an economic contribution to the body politic, including strong international trading connections.

From 1657, Jews were acknowledged as Dutch citizens. In Amsterdam, they made themselves so indispensable to the economic life of the city that between 1669 and 1675 the government approved the construction of two synagogues, and took an active interest in the well-being of the Sephardic and Ashkenazi communities. And although there was more discrimination against Catholics, who were excluded from full citizenship if they outwardly professed their faith, it was possible to practise Catholicism more discreetly. Very few Amsterdammers had no connections to the 'Old Faith', as in the sixteenth century the city had been a Catholic stronghold. While few, such as the poet Joost van den Vondel, were prepared to openly declare their Catholicism, many more, like Rembrandt, came from Catholic or partly Catholic families.

Underbelly

What happened to those who slipped through the cracks? Amsterdam was good at looking after its own poor, but what became of those peoples across the world whose unremunerated work was at the heart of Amsterdam's prosperity? The wealth of seventeenth-century Dutch citizens largely derived from their maritime and military power in South-East Asia. Dutch capitalists had connections with the Amsterdam trading system and with producers all over the world, who became tied into servicing Dutch domestic needs rather than their own. If you were a European who wanted to understand the wider world, it was likely you would turn to a Dutchman. Amsterdam was also the West's centre of maps and cartography. The Dutch liked to present themselves as mediating between Europe and the rest of the world, but a more nuanced view would be that they controlled the 'world system' which was concentrating wealth in the hands of small number of Western Europeans.

We can see this exploitation in the apparently paradisical paintings of the Haarlem artist Frans Post. They show the forests and tropical lands of eastern Brazil as a place of primitivism and perfection, like the Garden of Eden before the Fall of Man. Post was a friend of Frans Hals, and his brother Pieter was one of the most significant Dutch architects of the seventeenth century. In 1636 Post travelled to Brazil, accompanying Johan Maurits, Count of Nassau, who governed the former

Portuguese territories in the far north-east of the country, now called New Holland, on behalf of the Dutch West India Company (WIC). He was to spend eight years working with Maurits, making a series of drawings, the basis of a book of engravings of the Dutch territories dedicated to his patron. In 1654, when Recife fell to the Portuguese, the WIC abandoned Brazil for more lucrative and less resource-heavy trade in the Caribbean.

Although Maurits went to New Holland with a number of 'experts' including the two Post brothers, his principal task was to map the land and to re-establish the Portuguese sugar cane plantations worked by thousands of Black African slaves who had been transported across the Middle Passage against their will. Their life was so hard that most died within a year of crossing the Atlantic. Sugar production was such a priority that when Maurits arrived in 1637, one of his first actions was to enable slaves to have access to manioc and calabash plants. This was not from altruism but so they could cultivate enough food to work. At the same time, the WIC's navy conquered the Portuguese strongholds in Ghana and Angola, intending to dominate the slave trade as well as the South American territories it served.

Post's career was made by his South American sojourn, and practically all his surviving paintings are Brazilian landscapes. The significant market for these works coincides with the Dutch dominance of the seas and of international trade in the 1650s and 60s. Post's paintings were attractive to collectors all over Europe, and are found as far afield as France, Scandinavia, Italy and Germany. In 1679, the year of his death, a picture was purchased by the Earl of Dysart, directly from the artist, and is still hanging at Ham House, just outside London, today.

Most of Post's Brazilian pictures were made long after his

return from the country in 1646. They show the plants, animals, topography and human inhabitants of this extraordinary place. As a whole his paintings are slight variations on a theme. Without exception they present a nostalgic and rose-tinted vision of the short-lived Dutch colony, with ruins of Portuguese churches and apparently idyllic tropical landscapes, filled with iguanas, sloths, armadillos and palms, cacti and papayas. On closer inspection, these are scenes of frightful industrial exploitation. The seemingly happy workers, in their exotic clothing, are slaves. They are shown working on the plantations, in sugar mills, or outside the 'big house'. In a painting now in Dublin exotic animals and trees are shown alongside slaves stoking the boilers of a furnace house, placing cane on a drying platform, leading a cart. Two European men supervise their activity.

The Brazilian experience was short-lived, but it exemplifies the Dutch colonial attitude across the non-European territories they controlled. These places existed in order to be exploited for the people back home in Holland. Post's paintings are symbolic of the broad-mindedness that only existed for those who were fortunate enough to be Dutch, or who were able to help the Dutch elite, revolving around the merchants and traders of Amsterdam. The famous tolerance of the city of Amsterdam, its openness to ideas and to difference, was only skin deep.

Johann Melchior Dinglinger, Georg Friedrich Dinglinger,
Georg Christoph Dinglinger, Johann Benjamin Thomae and
assistants, *The Grand Moghul's Throne*

10

DELHI: ENVY

1670–1730

In 1708, the German goldsmith Johann Melchior Dinglinger, assisted by his brothers Georg Friedrich and Georg Christoph and a team of assistants, completed their masterwork, *The Grand Moghul's Throne*, destined for the renowned European collector Augustus the Strong. It is an incredibly intricate object that presents the Mughal Emperor Aurangzeb ('Ornament of the Throne') receiving the homage of his subjects and the good wishes of his fellow world rulers on his birthday. Dinglinger's creation comprises a silver and gold architectural stage set, 132 separate figures, each no more than five centimetres tall and many of them originally moveable, and thirty-two gifts. It took seven years to make, and incorporated more than five thousand precious jewels and cameos. It remains a somewhat overwhelming vision of how contemporary Europeans saw the ruler of India, a figure they believed to be the richest person on earth. Dinglinger was so proud of his achievement that he signed it no less than three times.

Admiring *The Grand Moghul's Throne* is one of the most memorable parts of any visit to the Green Vault, Augustus's private collection of precious things, first opened to the public in Dresden in 1724. Dinglinger's vision is based on as full evidence about the Mughal court as he could glean from the accounts of Europeans who had travelled to India. When he delivered the work to Augustus in 1708, he included his own description of the object, several pages long, based on his extensive research. As a result, this object constitutes a fascinating insight into one culture's perception of another.

The emperor, he explains, sits enthroned on a crimson cushion, underneath a red canopy emblazoned with stars. This glittering structure is a recreation of the renowned Peacock Throne, made for Aurangzeb's father Shah Jahan. Aurangzeb's subjects and visitors move towards him in a choreographed procession, prostrating themselves at the foot of the throne. The shining sun behind the throne is a double reference to the emblem of Caesar Augustus and the Mughals' belief in their own divinity. The Hindu deities in the mini pagodas that crown each section of the architectural backdrop allude to the majority religion of the Mughal Empire, while the screaming demons and dragons hint at religious difference (Aurangzeb was a far more devout Muslim than his immediate ancestors, who had tried to emphasise the commonalities between the major world faiths).

At the front of the stage, Dinglinger continues, is a set of scales, with piles of silver and gold pieces before it. The emperor's birthday celebrations included the ceremonial weighing of the imperial person. Accounts of the ceremony relate that the gold, silver, clothes and spices were given to courtiers, while perishable food (not recreated by the Dinglingers) and money was donated to the poor. Nearly all the figures are crafted from pure gold, their costumes picked out in delicate enamel work. Four main groups of visitors, in litters or on an elephant, bring, in theatrical procession, a series of special gifts, including a clock (once functioning), vessels and vases, daggers, mini swords, an atlas, several votive hands and a rearing horse. The only element that Dinglinger did not research was a miniature version of the gold coffee service he had previously made for Augustus.

The patron of this magnificent item, Augustus II, Elector of Saxony, and from 1697 (save between 1704 and 1707) also King of Poland, was one of Europe's power makers and breakers. He was fascinated by manufacture, devoting substantial resources to alchemy, the hopeless challenge of transforming base materials into gold, and to the more successful enterprise of making the first true European hard-paste porcelain at his manufactory in Meissen Castle. Thanks to his Saxon mines, Augustus was exceptionally rich by contemporary European standards. At the same time that he commissioned Dinglinger's masterpiece, he was rebuilding two palaces and maintaining a standing army of thirty thousand men. But his resources, unlike the apparently bottomless coffers of the Mughal emperors, were not limitless. It took him five years to pay off the fifty-eight thousand thalers – large silver coins – owed to the Dinglingers.

What were Dinglinger's motivations in making this work? As a goldsmith and jeweller, the resources, materials and opulence of the Mughal imperial workshops would have greatly interested him. Augustus the Strong would also have found the example of Aurangzeb extremely compelling. Not only was he the richest ruler in the world, he was the commander of armies on a scale that European kings could only dream of. His position as a Muslim ruling over a largely Hindu population would have resonated with Augustus, who had had to convert to Catholicism to become King of Poland. So would have his staunch absolutism – admired by many eighteenth-century

Western monarchs, including Augustus. There is clear envy in the fascination that the Mughals held for Augustus, Dinglingler and their European contemporaries. Why else would the Mughal court be infantilised by recreating it on a miniature scale?

The Mughals

The Mughal dynasty ruled over the greatest Islamic state of the Indian subcontinent. Its founder Babur was descended from two celebrated central Asian emperors, Timur-i Leng and Jengiz Khan. In 1494, aged eleven, Babur inherited the small kingdom of Ferghana, but his desire to capture Timur's capital Samarkand meant that he lost his own throne. This bitter experience led Babur to turn his attention south, towards northern India, briefly ruled by Timur and therefore legitimate prey for one of his descendants. Babur's impressions of a 'disorderly Hindustan' filled with 'masses of gold and silver' are recorded in his remarkably frank memoirs, the *Baburnama*. He spent the best part of two decades campaigning in India, finally taking the two principal cities, Agra and Delhi, in 1526, but died before he could bring his Indian territories together into a kingdom.

His son Humayan, not as skilled a soldier or ruler as his father, struggled to keep his Afghan and Rajput rivals in check. In 1540 he was expelled from India, seeking refuge and support in Sindh, Marwar and Iran. Humayan only fully regained his father's Indian possessions six months before his own death in 1556. It was left to his son, Akbar the Great, to consolidate the Mughal Empire. Akbar was an exceptional character. Stocky, determined and energetic, he inherited a precarious kingdom but secured an empire that consisted of two-thirds of the Indian subcontinent, stretching from Kabul in the north to Berar and Orissa in the south, Gujarat in the west to the Bay of Bengal in the east. Akbar established a strong military and administrative structure for the empire, underpinned by religious tolerance. This enabled him to rely on an infrastructure mainly staffed by Hindus. He amassed enormous revenues that he was able to spend on his army and his court, particularly on buildings, manuscripts, metalwork, jewellery and textiles.

Akbar ensured that his son Jahangir, the 'World Seizer', would rule the wealthiest empire in the world. In 1616, an English visitor described the court as 'the treasury of the world'. Cash and precious goods were held in one of twelve treasuries of the royal household. One was reserved for unmounted precious stones, while others held the imperial family's jewels and jewelled objects, including golden thrones and drinking cups. In such circumstances, the arts could flourish. It is not surprising that Jahangir was a renowned connoisseur, with an active interest in paintings, gardens and architecture. He adored exquisite things, from miniature painting to intricately worked jade and jewellery. In keeping with the increased separation of his court from the people, Jahangir's architectural commissions were focused on the private sphere, including gardens, hunting lodges and private retreats. Sadly, little of this survives. Jahangir's passion and knowledge of the arts ring out strongly in the account that he – like his father and grandfather – wrote of his rule.

Jahangir's son Prince Khurram, who ruled as Shah Jahan, began his reign in 1628 with even greater advantages. He controlled most of the subcontinent, his armies were enormous and well ordered, and he possessed unparalleled wealth. In 1647, the historian Abdul Hamid Lahori assessed the *jama* or revenue of the empire at eight thousand million dams (a small copper coin), one thousand million more than at the end of Jahangir's rule. Like many of the Mughal emperors, Shah Jahan had had a tempestuous relationship with his father. Jahangir (correctly) viewed his son as a threat, while Shah Jahan resented his father's reliance on his principal wife, Nur Jahan, and on the bottle. On his accession he determined to erase the visible symbols of his father's reign.

It is probably for this reason that Shah Jahan was the Mughal dynasty's greatest patron of architecture. While his father had focused his artistic patronage on the more private world of the court, Shah Jahan built impressive and highly visible structures, from the Taj Mahal to a new capital, Shahjahanabad. These were expressions of his identity and belief, as well as of the persona of the emperor. He even obliterated his father's image in a number of paintings. In several illuminations, Jahangir's head was replaced by that of his son, so subtly that had the artists not signed their work it would be hard to discern. A painting by the artist Bichitr, made during Shah Jahan's reign, even removes Jahangir from the succession. It shows Akbar, Jahangir and Shahjahan with their three chief ministers. In the centre, Akbar hands a jewelled crown directly to his grandson. In 1658 such a fate was to befall Shah Jahan himself: his third son, who ruled as Aurangzeb, hunted down and executed his brothers and nephews, and imprisoned his father for the rest of his life.

Tragically, the structure of Mughal rule often meant the brutal destruction of family ties. There was no system of primogeniture for inheritance. This meant that each time an emperor approached the end of his life, the imperial family was torn apart by murderous conflict. Strength, cunning and luck decided which prince would succeed his father. The succession was particularly vicious when there were several adult princes of ability and ambition. This goes a long way to explain the tortured relationships of Jahangir, Shah Jahan and Aurangzeb with their fathers, sons and brothers.

The miniature paintings beloved of the Mughal court have a winning combination of stylised elegance and naturalism. They depict the hierarchy, order and opulence of the emperor's court, its customs, luxury and love of exotic creatures or objects, from zebras to white-skinned peoples. The absorption of influences from Persian, Indian and European art and literature reflects the early emperors' openness to ideas that would help a Muslim dynasty rule a predominantly Hindu country. Creating *muraqqa* (albums) was a Timurid custom, derived from the revered court culture of fifteenth-century Iran. They were a means of celebrating tradition, but also, because painting was subordinate to calligraphy and not displayed in public, they could express personal as well as imperial sentiment.

One of the most important *muraqqa* is the Shah Jahan album, a collection of calligraphy, poetry, portraits, illuminations and nature studies, now divided between the Metropolitan Museum in New York and the Freer Gallery of Art in Washington DC. It was owned by Jahangir and his two successors as emperor, but most of its contents were brought together by Shah Jahan. It is fitting that one of its most touching and evocative pages depicts the future emperor with his eldest and favourite son, Darah Shikoh. The two princes are portrayed by the painter Nanha – a fact noted by a description in Jahangir's hand – in a moment of rare privacy and relaxation. They are seated alone on a gilded dais; the five-year-old boy kneels between his father's knees, while Shah Jahan's body is supported by a large bolster, beautifully embroidered with plants and people in the Iranian style. As in most Mughal portraits, the sitters are shown in profile, although they have turned to the viewer, presumably the future emperor himself. Shah Jahan, a noted gemmologist, holds a tray of stones, one of which he is appraising. These are no ordinary rocks, but some of the unmounted gems stored in the appropriate treasury of the imperial household.

This is at once a depiction of parental tenderness and love as well as of power and wealth. Shah Jahan is festooned with pearls, rubies and sapphires. He is perfectly coiffed, his visible sideburn cut and combed into elegant curls, his moustache and eyebrows elegantly shaped. Although not yet emperor, he is already haloed like a divinity. His official chronicler, Lahori, noted that when the emperor, in the public viewing platform at Agra, presented himself to his subjects in the morning light, there seemed to be two suns. One was light from the real sun, reflected on the curved and gilded *bangla* roof. The second was the emperor, who seemed as if crowned with a halo like that seen in this miniature. Shah Jahan's halo recalls those placed around Christian holy figures, and indeed a scene of Christ's deposition also forms part of the Shah Jahan album. Although a more conventional Muslim than his father and grandfather, he remained receptive to other religions, if they could strengthen his rule.

Shah Jahan's love for Dara Shikoh, who grew up to become an intellectual and mystic (before being murdered by his younger brother), is well documented. The little boy is dressed like an adult in a miniature court costume, with a turban, earrings, and a dagger slid into his belt. Strings of pearls hang around his neck; another, combined with rubies and sapphires, decorates his turban. He holds a peacock fan, or chowrie, and a jewelled turban ornament in his hands. From a distance, the ornament looks like a flower, underlining the blend of naturalism and stylisation typical of Mughal art, and the extreme sophistication of this court, where valuable jewels were items for children's play. Panegyric poetry describes the court as an earthly paradise. Appropriately, the splendid border, almost as important as the illumination itself, situates the meeting of father and son in a stylised garden of narcissi, roses, poppies and peaches, populated by symbolic birds including peacocks, pigeons, partridges, birds of paradise and demoiselle and Indian cranes.

Paradise

Such ordered, perfected gardens represented paradise to the Mughal emperors. Paradise itself is a Persian Zoroastrian concept, but the idea of a lush, temperate and safe space translated easily into other world religions, including Islam and Christianity. For the Mughals, used to campaigning and living on the arid steppes of central Asia and the sun-beaten Indian plain, the irrigated garden became a treasured place of retreat. Gardens provided welcome respite from the heat of the day. Babur, founder of the Mughal dynasty, created gardens everywhere he went. In the *Baburnama*, he encouraged his descendants to follow his example.

Mughal gardens stimulated every sense. They were closely planted, so that users could enjoy the sensation of walking in the shade, even in a place of hot sun. They were full of enticing smells, and delicious food. A seventeenth-century European visitor to Lahore, the East India Company official William Finch, wrote of the overwhelming sensory experience of visiting such a space:

> In the midst of a garden is a very stately recreational terrace
> with fair buildings overhead, and a tank in the centre, with
> large and goodly galleries along the four sides thereof, sup-
> ported with high stone pillars. Adjoining to this is a garden
> of the King's, in which are very good apples (but small), mul-
> berry white and red, almonds, peaches, figs, grapes, quinces,
> oranges, lemons, pomegranates, roses, stock-flowers, mari-
> golds, wall-flowers, irises, pinks white and red, with divers
> sorts of Indian flowers.

Finch describes a Char Bagh, or quartered garden, the
Mughal paradise on earth. The central tank of water alluded
to the celestial basin of abundance (al-Kawthar) promised
to Muhammad, while the four water channels served by the
tank, which divided the garden into quarters, stood for the four
rivers of the Muslim Paradise.

Heaven's Gate

Paradisical imagery was particularly important to Shah Jahan.
It is evident in almost all of the buildings and spaces that he
commissioned and built. Nowhere is it so important as in the
Taj Mahal. Like the Eiffel Tower, the Sydney Opera House
or the Acropolis, the Taj, 'Crown of the Palace', has become
a symbol of national identity (though an ambiguous one for
Hindus), widely identifiable even by those who have never
seen it. The white marble mausoleum, crowned with a great
dome and with a willowy minaret at each corner, is only a
part of a forty-two-acre complex, divided by walls from the
outside world.

The Taj Mahal is a monument to enduring love, created to

honour Shah Jahan's beloved wife Mumtaz Mahal. On 17 June 1631, the empress went into labour. The emperor's daily game of chess with his eldest daughter, Jahan Ara, was interrupted when the teenager was called to her mother's bedside. Fear and panic descended upon the emperor, his family and the beleaguered medical attendants. Jahan Ara showered jewels on the poor, hoping to propitiate God, while Shah Jahan is reported to have shed 'tears like rainwater'. The empress died giving birth to her fourteenth child, Gauhar Ara. When the emperor returned to court, so the story goes, his hair had turned white, his back was bent and his face careworn. We are told that the dying empress asked her husband not to marry again and to 'build over me a mausoleum that the like of it may not be seen anywhere else in the world'.

Mumtaz's body was buried temporarily near where she died, within a walled garden at Burhanpur in the Deccan, while her grieving widower conceived a satisfactory monument to their love and eternal salvation. For this purpose he purchased a plot of land on the Yamuna River as it flows through Agra, the Indian heart of the Mughal Empire. In 1643, when Shah Jahan celebrated the twelfth anniversary of his wife's death, the tomb was almost completed. It extended beyond the central monument and gardens into a series of tombs for the emperor's lesser wives, accommodation for the tomb attendants and several bazaars and caravanserais where visitors could stay. Income from these – together with the revenues from thirty surrounding villages – paid for the tomb's upkeep.

The scale of the monument is breathtaking – with its gardens, it would swallow up the entirety of Great St Peter's in Rome, and Bernini's piazza before it. Entering through a red sandstone gatehouse, the imperial retinue would gather in a lush courtyard that serves as the forecourt of the tomb. Facing them, as they looked north towards the tomb itself, was an imposing sandstone arched gateway, about thirty metres high, leading into a walled garden, crowned at each corner with *chattris* or domed pavilions. The *pishtaq*, the rectangular frame surrounding the deeply recessed central arch, is inscribed with texts from the Quran chosen by the calligrapher Amanat Khan, inscribed in black lettering set into white marble, inviting the faithful to enter Paradise.

At the centre of the walled garden is a large marble tank. Channels of water, symbolising the four rivers of the Muslim paradise, divide the space into quarters, making it a Char Bagh. Today it resembles a municipal park, but it would have once had the lush vegetation that we read of in descriptions of Mughal gardens, so that the building and the planting worked in harmony. The court architect Ustad Ahmad Lahori called the garden 'this replica of the garden of Paradise'. Even given the hyperbole prevalent in Persian and Mughal literature, this is a powerful image. Mumtaz Mahal's domed tomb stands on a large plinth of marble raised above the gardens, a marble minaret at each of its four corners. This unusual feature is found at the Gur-i-Amir at Samarkand, home of the Mughals' Timurid ancestors, and also at Emperor Jahangir's tomb in Lahore. The symmetry and simplicity of the structure is one of the monument's most striking features. Every detail proclaims the promise of resurrection and the wonders of paradise, from the four *pishtaqs* inscribed with relevant verses from the Quran to the many surfaces covered with flowers. In Persian mystic poetry these are connected with the appearance of the beloved, as well as with paradise.

Directly across the river was the Moonlight Garden (*Mahtabbagh*), laid out as a mirror to the Taj and planned around an octagonal water basin proportionate in size to the Taj itself. Here Shah Jahan could contemplate his wife's burial place in the evening cool. Alternate plantings of cypresses and fruit trees represented the twinned concepts of eternity and life. From this viewpoint, the Taj would unfold slowly, in a series of ever-varied views, dependent on the changing appearance of the sky and river as reflected on the building's marble surface.

Shah Jahan's vision for his wife's tomb was that it represented the universe, where all of human civilisation was conjoined in the service of God. All those associated with the tomb – including the emperor himself, the calligrapher Amanat Khan, the builders Makramat Khan and ꞌAbd al Karim – were highly educated in literature, theology, astrology and mathematics. The interior of the dome is carved to resemble the cells of a honeycomb, with multi-faceted miniature vaults that reflect the sun. This form, the *muqarnas*, is a particular characteristic of Islamic architecture. The effect is to make the dome seem like the sun itself. Eight *pishtaq* arches divide the two-storey space into equal geometric elements at ground level, each crowned by a further, smaller arch. Light enters from the upper windows, channelled through a cut marble screen (*jail*), and through openings covered by the *chhatris* on the external dome. The eight surrounding chambers represent the eight gates of Paradise according to Islamic tradition.

The inner sanctum is further protected by a circular carved marble screen, entered through two identical archways. This is a marble version of a type of screen usually made from a more malleable material like wood or gold to separate the women of a household from men outside the immediate family (it replaced a gold screen, designed by Shah Jahan's goldsmith Bebedal Khan, because the emperor feared it could be looted). Light shines through its marble surfaces, and reflects off the white, blue and red *pietra dura* floral patterns on the arches and columns.

Mumtaz Mahal's ceremonial tomb is at the heart of the complex, under the central point of the dome. Her husband's mausoleum is at her side, slightly to the west. Historians will doubtless continue to debate whether the emperor – who spent the last years of his life as his son's prisoner in Agra Fort – intended to be interred here. It is interesting that the same arrangement is seen in another tomb, the 'Baby Taj' made for the empress's great-uncle and -aunt, commissioned by their daughter Nur Jahan. Yet Mumtaz Mahal's monument is lower than that of her husband. This is common in Mughal tradition; her tomb, flat and covered in inscriptions, alludes to a convention that the wife was the tablet on which the husband would write. Appropriately, therefore, a marble writing box sits on the top of Shah Jahan's cenotaph. In the crypt in the lower level, where the pair's bodies are actually interred, we see similarly oriented and placed marble structures. Full flowering plants only appear on the platform of Mumtaz Mahal's ceremonial cenotaph, while they are over all the surfaces of the emperor's tombs. Here in the centre of the Taj, a monument to love, power and God, the paradisical imagery reaches its climax.

Parchin kari, the setting of semi-precious stones into carved marble, was used to create these flowers and plants. Sculptors employed red jasper, lapis lazuli from Afghanistan, turquoise from Sri Lanka, crystal and jade from China to create in stone the effect of painting. In the words of the poet Abu Talib Kalim, 'the chisel has become the pen of Mani' (the ideal painter in Persian lore) and the stone tomb looks 'the image of a flower garden' lacking only smells. Carved from carnelian and amber, it is so lifelike that the dead empress will want to 'clasp the flower pictures to her heart'. Some of the blooms are combinations of earthly species, to show their divine perfection. But many real flowers are also present: narcissi, tulips, lilies, clematis, honeysuckle, chrysanthemum, lotus, carnations, cornflowers, poppies and pomegranates, among others. The paradise represented here is far from an exclusively Indian one, with plants from Europe and South America as well as Asia, evocative of the Mughals' origins and their wider territorial ambitions. Their materials mean that these blooms will endure for eternity.

The language of flowers compliments the Quranic quotations that cover the Taj Mahal complex. They were selected by Shah Jahan's favoured calligrapher, Amanat Khan ('Trustworthy Noble') as an iconographic programme for the tomb. According to tradition, Muhammad ascended to the seven levels of paradise on the sacred journey called the Mi'raj (literally meaning ladder), a spiritual gateway to heaven. Over the entrance gate to the complex are inscribed the words of the great apocalyptic Sura 89, which following an evocation of the horrors of the Day of Judgement ends on a more peaceful and comforting note, urging the 'soul at peace' to return to God, 'well-pleased and well-pleasing unto Him! Enter thou among My servants – And enter thou My Paradise!'

In the Taj Mahal the emperor was creating not a tomb but the entrance to Paradise. It has been argued that the complex represents the Islamic conception of the Day of Judgement and Resurrection, when the faithful will rise again, and gather at the place of judgement before the Divine Throne. The gardens and walkways are symbolic replicas of the gateway by which Muhammad entered Paradise. In the centre of the garden, the raised tank represents the celestial tank of abundance, while the tomb itself is the Throne of God, with the minarets as pillars of the throne. Medieval Islamic cosmology described the Throne of God in sufficient detail that a visualisation could be made. The throne, or 'arsh, is enormous, placed on a plinth, the kursi. Under the plinth are the sacred gardens of Paradise, protected by Rizwan, the gatekeeper, and filled with beautiful palaces and other delights. The faithful will enter Paradise on the Day of Judgement, and approach the base of the throne, where they will contemplate the Vision of God.

Seeing the dome from afar, symbolically suspended as it were between heaven and earth, recalls Muhammad's own account of his vision of paradise: 'I saw there His Throne, which seemed joined to Heaven in such a manner that it appeared that Heaven and the Throne were created together.' It is even possible that Shah Jahan and his architects were aware of Christian images of the Heavenly Jerusalem. Certainly such works were present at the Mughal court. An illustration by Nanha and Manohar of the Day of Judgement, based on a late-sixteenth-century Flemish engraving of the Christian Last Judgement, forms part of a manuscript of Mir 'Ali Shir's *Khamsa* (now in the Royal Collection, Windsor Castle) described by Jahangir as one of his most precious books, and by 1628 in the possession of Shah Jahan.

The earthly paradise

If the Taj Mahal was the gate to the heavenly paradise, Shahjahanabad, to the north of Delhi, was paradise on earth. In 1639, at an auspiciously chosen point, Shah Jahan commenced building not just a new palace but an entirely new walled city, a physical manifestation of his imperial rule. Like many absolute rulers, his answer to buildings that didn't work was to start again. The new build would avoid all the problems of Agra, where sudden growth had created a shambolic urban environment, with poorly built housing and bazaars crammed into every available corner. Shahjahanabad was therefore constructed with space for all the activities of the modern city: housing, shopping and trade, justice, worship and recreation. The site was imposing, on a bluff overlooking the Jumna River, beside the fortified hill of Nurgarh, a stopping point on an important trade route.

The palace now known as the Red Fort or the Blessed Fortress (*Qila Mubarak*) was formally dedicated in April 1648. Built of red sandstone following Akbar's building traditions, the walls stretched from the river in a sprawling rectangle, enclosing nearly 125 acres of land. The fort was restricted to the emperor and the women of the royal household, as well as the courtiers and servants who catered to their every need. As this number included the many workshops producing food, fine paintings, jade objects, daggers, textiles, paper, perfumes and so much more, it has been estimated that as many as fifty-seven thousand people lived within the palace. Everyone else, even the emperor's own sons, dwelt in the city outside.

Within fifteen years, this new city had some four hundred thousand inhabitants. An existing canal, connected to the Jumna north of the city, was improved and renamed the River of Paradise; separate branches served the city and royal palace with fresh water. The city branch, bordered by shady tree-lined avenues, ran in parallel to the ceremonial route into the fort. It was flanked by bazaars, with caravanserai for merchants and travellers. A square where the light of the moon was reflected in a pool was given the romantic name of *Chandni-Chowk*, Moon Plaza (the name, but little else, survives in what is now one of central Delhi's busiest areas). Jahan Ara, the emperor's eldest daughter, was responsible for this development. Many of the leading women of the court followed her example to endow complexes of bazaars, gardens and mosques in Shahjahanabad.

Impressive though these were, they were eclipsed by the emperor's gifts to the city, the Purani ᶜIdgah (of which little remains) and the Jamiᶜ Mosque. This red sandstone 'world-reflecting' mosque, crowned by three bulbous domes and towering minarets, and sitting high on a hill south-west of the fort's main gate, still dominates its surroundings.

The emperor's quarters within the Red Fort are conscious meldings of Hindu, Persian and Timurid traditions. Visitors moved through a covered bazaar to an enclosed courtyard where music announced the arrival of the emperor and important courtiers. From here, one approached the public audience chamber (Diwan-i ᶜAmm), an open hall of red sandstone nine bays wide. The bays are constructed of cusped arches, an architectural form much used by Shah Jahan because it incorporated Hindu, Buddhist and Muslim elements. A marble canopied throne, open on every side, stands in the central bay of the back wall.

Although the arched *bangla* shape of the throne is Indian, it is more than possible that the emperor and his advisors took inspiration from contemporary European art. Certainly, the impact of the king seated under his canopy would not have been dissimilar to the sight of the pope underneath Bernini's baldacchino. The carved hard-stone decoration on the columns and the plinth is more directly European in feel than the flowers of the Taj Mahal (seventeenth-century Italians were masters of *pietra dura*, carving in hard stone, similar in technique if not in feel to *parchin kari*). Panels of birds, lions and other animals, some Indian, some Italian, decorate the back wall. At the top is a representation of the Greek musician Orpheus, taming the wild beasts with his lyre. This carefully curated assemblage of ideas and motifs proclaimed the emperor's rule over the natural as well as the human world. When he sat in audience, arrayed in fine jewels and clothing, he appeared to have the aura and accoutrements of a god. His panegyrists considered he surpassed not just the Umayyad and Abbasid caliphs of Cairo and Baghdad in his splendour, but the awe-inspiring dignity of the ancient Mesopotamian emperors too. Mulla Tughra Mashhadi, an Iranian emigré poet attached to Jahangir and Shah Jahan's courts, even venerated the Red Fort over the still magnificent ruins of the immense vaulted throne room at Ctesiphon on the Tigris: 'Two hundred Arches of Ctesphion do not make a single brick of the city walls of Delhi.'

At the back of the fort, a group of white marble pavilions on the riverfront provided accommodation for the emperor and his family. They were as cool and restful as possible – Shahjahanabad was punishingly hot in summer – and full of symbols that emphasised the imperial family's centrality to the Mughal state. A marble basin in the shape of the pure and transcendent lotus, under the central open canopy of the Shah Burj pavilion, held the water to be channelled through the private apartments. The canopy indicated that this space was reserved for the exclusive use of the emperor and his children, so the water, source of all life, seemed to emanate from the imperial bodies themselves.

In the emperor's private room, the *khwabagh* (sleep place), a lengthy Persian inscription compares the fort to the mansions of heaven. To emphasise the 'natural' state of Shah Jahan's rule, the scales of justice, surrounded by a chain of flowering plants, surmount the intricate marble screen in the centre of the room, over the actual water flowing through the Canal of Paradise. In the private audience hall, the perfection of the glittering silver ceiling (removed by looters in the eighteenth century), marble piers embellished with floral sprays of jewels and gold, and the celebrated Peacock Throne echoed the Persian inscription on the walls of the central space: 'If there be a paradise on earth, this is it, this is it, this is it.'

The Peacock Throne had set the pattern for the architectural initiatives of Shah Jahan's reign. Following his coronation, the emperor had selected diamonds and other precious stones worth ten million rupees for his first major commission. It was fashioned by Sa'id Gilani, the poet and goldsmith known as the Peerless One (*Bibadal Khan*) and others over the course of seven years, and unveiled on 22 March 1635, the seventh anniversary of the emperor's accession – a doubly fortuitous moment, marking the Persian spring festival of Nauruz and Eid at the end of Ramadan.

The French jewel merchant Jean-Baptiste Tavernier, who spent two months at the court in 1665 as Aurangzeb's guest, has left us a lengthy description of the intricate design of the throne, created from more than 2,600 pounds of solid gold. There are other accounts, by the French traveller François Bernier, and Shah Jahan's court historians, Abdul Hamid Lahori and Inayat Khan, and although some details of each account differ, we have enough information to give an adequate sense of the opulent extravagance of this extraordinary construction. The golden rectangular frame resembled an elaborate gazebo, standing on four legs. Every inch was covered with decorations created from rubies, diamonds, emeralds and pearls. Several jewelled steps led up to the emperor's seat, surrounded by twelve jewelled columns which supported an internal canopy. The individual jewels included a huge ruby worth more than a hundred thousand rupees, a gift to the Emperor Jahangir from Shah Abbas of Persia. Above the canopy was, according to Tavernier, the famous peacock 'with an elevated tail made of blue sapphires and other coloured stones, the body being gold inlaid with precious stones, having a large ruby on the breast, from which hangs a pear-shaped pearl of fifty carats', with two bouquets of multi-coloured flowers, made from gold and jewels. Lahori's description suggests an even more elaborate object, with twenty-four peacocks, two at the top of each pillar, and several important historical diamonds, including the Koh-i-Noor, today part of the British Crown Jewels. In spite of these discrepancies, it is fortunate that we have these accounts, as the great 'Ornamental Throne' (*Takht-Murassa*) is gone, its structure melted down and its jewels dispersed around the world.

For all the grandness of the Red Fort, there is an air of sadness about it. What was a bustling court is now a tourist destination. The life of the place has left it, and its greatest object was destroyed over two hundred and fifty years ago. Yet we can still sense its vibrancy, and the people of the place, through the surviving objects that animated it and other places, that were held in human hands and which provoked love, but also jealousy and envy.

Take the Mughal skill in crafting exquisite but useful objects from nephrite jade, one of the hardest and smoothest of all stones. Imported from remote Khotan in China, it was probably the Mughal emperors' favourite of the many precious stones available to them, and one that they stockpiled. By the seventeenth and eighteenth centuries the Mughal workshops' skill was recognised outside Hindustan, even in Europe and China where there had long been a market for exotic objects in this material. Nephrite jade was valued because of its rarity, its expense and the talent that was involved in working it. It felt lovely in the hand, suited to being touched and stroked. Because of its molecular structure and chemical composition, it can be turned into apparently fluid shapes, ones that seem made by nature itself. Like rock crystal, nephrite jade cannot be carved. It has to be worked with diamond drills and small wheels, known as lap wheels. The smooth surface is achieved by abrasion, and the decoration by incision.

The Emperor Jahangir possessed several nephrite jade wine cups and bowls inscribed with his name. They were probably made by Sa'id Gilani, designer of the Peacock Throne, and used by Jahangir at what are said to have been his happiest moments, drinking and conversing after the work of the day was done (less optimistic reports comment that he was frequently incapacitated by drink). One of these objects, now in the British Museum, bears an inscription hoping that the 'water of life' will be in the cup, so that it will be the 'water of Khizr, life prolonging'. Khizr was a Muslim sage mentioned in the Quran, who, according to the Persian epic the *Shahnama*, guided Alexander the Great across the desert to find the fountain that gave eternal youth. The inscription on another cup, now in the Victoria and Albert Museum, is even more explicit, comparing the world 'filled with light by the radiance' of the justice brought by the 'Conquering Shah', to the transformation of the jade cup into a ruby through 'the reflection of his spinel-coloured wine'.

Despite bitter arguments between father and son, often differing opinions about alcohol, which came to a head when Jahangir forced the then Prince Khurram (a more devout Muslim than his father) to drink wine, one of the most precious of Shah Jahan's personal possessions to survive is a wine cup. While Jahangir's wine cup is in the shape of earlier Timurid pieces, Shah Jahan's is a novelty. Like so much of the art of his realm, it takes a plant-based form, and turns it by the effort of the human hand into something even more wonderful. The implication is that, under his rule, we live in paradise. Measuring roughly fourteen centimetres by seventeen, Shah Jahan's cup is small enough to be held in two hands, and caressed, before raising it to one's mouth. We can imagine how the liquid would have lapped against the sides of the bowl, and the contrast that the colour would have made against the milky white of the jade. Its transformed colour, and internal division into four natural and irregular lobes, turn the cup from a hard mineral into a living gourd-like shape. This form, copied from Chinese art, stands on a base of lotus flowers surrounded by acanthus leaves, which acts as a pedestal for the cup. The lotus is a traditional Indian symbol, reflecting the heartland of the Mughal Empire. The ram's-head handle recalls Hindu animal portraiture as well as the fantastical forms used by European Baroque silver- and goldsmiths. The pedestal base, and the acanthus leaves, were European ideas, and both are found on the buildings of Shah Jahan in Agra and Shahjahanabad, and on the Taj Mahal.

The cup was made in 1657, the last year of Shah Jahan's reign, while he was imprisoned by his third son in Agra. It is dated year 1067 of the Islamic calendar, and regnal year 31, when it entered the emperor's treasury. It is inscribed with his title, Second Lord of the Conjunction. This follows the conventions of royal titles in the Persian-speaking world to which the Mughals belonged, and specifically alludes to Timur, who styled himself Lord of the Conjunction. The cup, an object of great value, executed with confidence, reflects the Mughals' openness to the world outside their kingdom. Their ability to assimilate other ideas was a sign of their strength. They were not frightened of taking ways of thinking or technologies that worked. Their success was in blending them together to make something truly Mughal.

Envy from abroad

Mughal India was self-sufficient in almost everything, but still relied on precious metals, goods and people from the West. These included gold and silver (India imported the majority of Spanish South American silver); Jesuits and their learning (from Akbar to Dara Shikoh, Muslim princes discoursed with missionaries); gunsmiths, musket-makers and artillerymen for their skill in weaponry; diplomats for their exotic gifts, including clocks and telescopes, and access to brother kings abroad; and merchants and traders for the bullion they provided. In 1615, the East India Company persuaded King James I to send Sir Thomas Roe as royal envoy to the Mughal court. In his dispatches from his four-year stay in India, we have lively descriptions of life under Jahangir, including drinking with the emperor to celebrate his birthday in August 1616. He found the wine stronger 'than ever I tasted, so that it made me sneeze, whereat he [Jahangir] laughed'. Such evenings were good times to do business with the emperor, 'who then was for the most part very pleasant, and full of talk unto those who were around him, and so continued till he fell asleep (oft times by drinking)'.

The exceptional wealth of Mughal India impressed even a sceptical observer such as Sir Thomas, who recorded that although he inhabited 'a house of Mudd', he lived 'in many wayes in more state, and with many more servants than any Ambassador in Europe'. Conversely, European visitors made very little impression on the established Mughal order, except as exotic curiosities to be recorded in the paintings collected by the emperors and their courtiers. Many European travellers' accounts survive, as do Mughal objects in European collections. Yet very few Indians made the return journey, and none wrote down their impressions of it. They were more interested in the Islamic states, especially Safavid Persia and the Ottoman Empire. The Mughals assumed that any threat to their rule would come from these quarters.

Slowly but steadily, from the sixteenth century onwards, Europeans established trading stations along the Indian coast, lured by the spices, textiles and ceramics that were considered the luxury products of 'the Indies'. By the early eighteenth century, these trading positions were well established and there were Europeans in every major town in the subcontinent. The Portuguese were the first, followed by the English, the Dutch, the French and the Danish. Most of the trade was in textiles. Cheap striped cotton 'Guinea-cloths' were sought for barter in West Africa, and for dressing the enslaved people on the West Indian plantations; higher-grade painted and dyed chintzes, gauze muslins and 'Cambay embroideries' of chain stitch on cotton went to the Middle East and Europe.

During the seventeenth century, not just aristocrats and the super-rich but the more modestly prosperous middle classes coveted Indian textiles for their houses and for their clothing – from Cambay and Surat on the west coast, Bengal in the far east of the subcontinent and the Coromandel coast in the south-east. Samuel Pepys recorded in his diary of 5 September 1663 giving his wife 'a chintze ... that is painted Indian callicoe for to line her new study which is very pretty'. Chintz was extremely popular because it was colourful and exotic, and the colours did not fade. Perhaps because of legislation designed to limit its export in Britain and France, it remained very fashionable for interior decoration and dress well into the eighteenth century.

*

While Mughal India remained stable, Europeans were satisfied with their good trading relations with this wealthy, armed and territorially expanding state. In 1689, Aurangzeb looked unassailable. His rebel son was a refugee at the Safavid court in Iran; he had conquered the Deccan, Bijapur, the diamond state of Golconda and the Maratha kingdom. All of India except the Tamilian region in the far south was under Mughal rule. But from the 1690s, as Aurangzeb struggled with loss and defeat, pouring every resource into his army but no longer winning every battle, everything began to change. The Europeans were always conscious of their superiority at sea. Around their port-trading centres they established city-states, such as British Bombay and Madras, Dutch Pulicat and French Pondicherry.

Not only were these states under the control of the foreign companies, they sheltered refugees from devastated war zones and even, on occasion, provided a focus for revolt against the Mughal state. As a result the Dutch, French and British East India Companies, closely aligned to their countries' governments, developed the ability to challenge the Mughal emperor, and to negotiate successfully with him and his officials. Ultimately, the British East India Company was to hold sway over large swathes of the subcontinent. It kept its own armies, its own fleet – the East Indiamen – and enjoyed a trade monopoly.

Aurangzeb died in 1707, debilitated by illness, wearied by conflict and disappointed in his children. In the years of chaos that followed, the centralised structure of an empire established on the twin pillars of efficient taxation and administration very speedily collapsed. Devastated by war, famine and regional struggles between Aurangzeb's sons, their rivals and successors, the empire was quick to diminish and disintegrate. By 1857, when the last Mughal emperor, Bahadur Shah

Zafar II, was ousted by the British, he presided over little more than a court and capital city.

The first hyenas to attack the imperial carcass, however, had come from closer at hand. In 1739, the Iranian emperor Nadir Shah took the opportunity to sack Delhi. The city was pillaged, many of its inhabitants were murdered and everything moveable was stripped. The twelve treasuries were plundered, and the greatest possessions of the Mughal dynasty, including the Peacock Throne and its thousands of precious stones (as well as the skilled craftsmen who could build Nadir Shah a new Delhi), were taken back to Persia.

Nadir Shah's greed was indiscriminate and vast in scale, but the sentiment was shared by most of those who came to the subcontinent, particularly the British. Although the Peacock Throne and so much else is gone, we can still visualise the splendour of the Mughal world in the court miniatures of Mansur, Nanha and others. We experience it in the architecture and internal decoration of the Taj Mahal, Red Fort and new city of Shahjahanabad. And we sense it in those precious hand-held objects made for the imperial family, in their palaces and the cloud cities of great tented encampments in which they moved across their domains. Poignantly, it is largely due to the rapacious and envious foreigners that coveted its wealth that many of the surviving treasures of Mughal India can be enjoyed in collections and museums across the world.

Trafalgar Square from the south

11

LONDON: AVARICE

1800–1900

Towards the end of the eighteenth century, the Kingdom of Great Britain, formed following the union of Scotland and England in 1707 (to which Ireland was forcibly added in 1801), became the commercial powerhouse of Europe. Agricultural and industrial innovations at home, from the Spinning Jenny to crop rotation, were key. So was Britain's financial system, which lent strength to its commercial and military ventures as well as its steadily expanding international role. If the ships of the Royal Navy, East India Company and Merchant Navy did not yet 'rule the waves', to paraphrase the patriotic anthem 'Rule, Britannia!', the British certainly dominated swathes of North America, southern Africa, India, Australia and the Atlantic and Indian Oceans. The brutal triangle of the North Atlantic Passage trade route was firmly instituted, taking enslaved West Africans to the islands of the West Indies. They laboured on plantations to produce sugar, tobacco and rice that was transported to Britain, from where cloth was traded back to West Africa. In India, the East India Company was able to seize power and resources from the declining Mughal Empire and its successor states.

It was possible to amass great wealth as an industrialist and speculator in the United Kingdom. But truly immense fortunes were the preserve of those with interests in the Caribbean or India. Those whose constitutions could stand the notoriously hot and humid climates of both regions – life expectancy in India was three monsoons – returned to their wet, temperate islands with fabulous riches. The Indian nabobs, and the West Indian 'creoles' or 'planters' were envied for their wealth, but mocked for their impolite and uncivilised manners. We can see both types in William Thackeray's 1848 novel *Vanity Fair*, set in the Napoleonic Wars and their aftermath. The rich 'mahogany charmer' Miss Swartz, whose fortune doesn't quite cancel out her West Indian origins, is criticised for her excessive 'tropical ardour', while Jos Sedley, an official of the East India Company, is called 'that great hectoring Nabob' and satirised for his gluttony, indolence and cowardice.

Once home, the planters and nabobs purchased large rural estates and tried to live between country and town. Inevitably they gravitated to London, by far the largest city of the British Isles, where they bought great mansions and filled them with the showiest and most prestigious furnishings and art that money could buy. By the early nineteenth century the capital was a city dominated by commercial interest, opportunity and innovation, where everything was possible. The poor as well as the rich migrated to the megapolis, hoping that they would find the streets paved with gold. In London you could acquire anything – it didn't matter if the rest of the world was ruthlessly exploited to satisfy this desire. Or you could sink without trace. Depending on your point of view, London was either the pulsating, productive heart of empire or the Great Wen, a diseased cyst dissipating the strength of the country, in the memorable image of the campaigning writer William Cobbett.

London after Napoleon

The post-Napoleonic settlement of 1815 had formalised Britain's status as Europe's greatest power. But unlike the empires of Russia, Austria-Hungary or even defeated France, the country lacked the dignified infrastructure worthy of its position. Many of George III's subjects owned finer London residences than Buckingham Palace, and the prime minister inhabited merely a larger version of the usual London townhouse. This was no grand planned city with impressive buildings and streetscapes of international repute, with facilities to match. Parliament met in a decaying medieval palace; the civil service was largely housed in rabbit holes of offices along Whitehall; while the world's commercial centre was crammed into a maze of streets dating back to the Roman Empire. The elderly King, oppressed by illness, was certainly not concerned by these matters. But his son was obsessed by the *brutta figura* of this dearth of pomp and circumstance.

As Regent, George IV had commissioned John Nash to beautify the northern part of central London, and to connect his palace, Carlton House on the edge of St James's Park, with Marylebone (now Regent's) Park about a mile and a half away. As the extravagant prince got closer to the throne, he and Nash turned their attention to the heart of the city. Central London as we see it today is a palimpsest of ordered avenues and increasingly bombastic buildings begun by Nash, superimposed on an organic structure of winding streets and pathways that connected the original City of London to the towns and villages of Westminster, Chelsea, Marylebone, Paddington and others. In a very British way, the pace and rhetoric of change was piecemeal and sporadic.

In 1822, the French writer Chateaubriand, on his first visit to London for thirty years, praised the 'wide streets lined with palaces'. Although a lot has changed, if you walk the length of John Nash's Regent Street from Waterloo Place to Oxford Circus, you feel recognisably in the London that Chateaubriand evoked with its palaces of prosperity and commerce. A planned series of eye-catching views culminates in the circular Church of All Souls Langham Place (next to the BBC's headquarters), transforming an infelicitous but necessary turn to connect Regent Street to the existing Portland Place into an exciting vista.

Impressive as Regent Street remains, it was in many ways a smokescreen. A couple of minutes away were the crowded, messy streets of Soho, home to immigrant communities, impecunious writers, artists, prostitutes, drunkards and other undesirables. No writer captured this underbelly of London life better than Charles Dickens. Many of his sprawling, ungainly novels chronicle the stark poverty and destitution of the streets, of areas like Seven Dials, Limehouse and Saffron Hill. Dickens had known life from the wrong side. His father went bankrupt, and at the age of twelve he was forced to leave school and work in a factory. In his writings Dickens angrily contrasts the desolation of the decrepit, filthy buildings and their desperate inhabitants with the opulence and grandeur of clubland, Mayfair and Westminster and the smug, often uncaring, rich.

Trafalgar Square: the heart of empire

Central to the vision of John Nash and his patron was a ceremonial heart for the city and the nation, a proper setting for the exercise of governmental responsibility and public munificence worthy of Great Britain's wealth and status. As early as 1812, Nash had suggested the building of a square or crescent at Charing Cross, in the absolute middle of London, accessible to all. The Regent Street Act of 1813 made provision for such a feature. It was only in 1820, when it was agreed to move the Royal Mews to Buckingham Palace, that this became a possibility. Nash was invited to prepare a plan for the new square on the site of the mews, on ground rising gently from the marshy plain of Westminster. It was already bounded on its upper east side by James Gibbs's eighteenth-century neoclassical church of St Martin-in-the-Fields. Hubert Le Sueur's statue of Charles I on horseback, cast in 1633 and installed in 1678, provided a border to the south.

The square was to include a National Gallery, and a Parthenon-like structure in the centre for the Royal Academy. An avenue at the north-east, next to St Martin's, would lead to the British Museum in Bloomsbury. Two plinths were erected on the corners of the terrace, intended for grand statues of leaders on horseback, a convention that dated back to ancient Greece and Rome. Trafalgar Square, as it became, is a partial manifesto of London's identity as a city of empire, where military and naval might combined with commercial success enabled people to benefit from the fruits of culture.

Little of the magnificence of Nash's plan was delivered. The square itself, formally named in 1830 for Nelson's 1805 victory, was only opened in 1844. By that time Nash was long dead, having been replaced by William Wilkins (architect of the National Gallery), and then, in 1840, by Charles Barry, architect of the Houses of Parliament. It was thanks to Barry that the square bears its current appearance, with an elevated terrace and two high plinths for sculpture at the north, low walls along the east and west sides and two enormous quatrefoil granite basins (intended for fountains). Yet the structures that arose were haphazard. Of all Nash's plans, only the National Gallery was delivered – a disparaged and much criticised building.

The square has evolved into one of the most controversial and varied public spaces in London. It commemorates the British establishment, and the victory of Britain's armed forces overseas. It is a place of public rejoicing, and countless sporting triumphs have been celebrated here. It was the popular focus of Britain's victory celebrations in 1945, at the end of the Second World War. But throughout its life Trafalgar Square has also been the site of peaceful dissent, from the Chartist agitation for social and political reform in the great Year of Revolution, 1848, the rallies for women's suffrage before the First World War, the anti-nuclear marches of the 1960s, the poll tax riots of 1990, the Iraq War demonstrations of 2003, anti-Brexit campaigns, and the Black Lives Matter protests of 2020.

Nelson

Trafalgar Square is dominated by Nelson's Column, a popular symbol of Britain's naval, military and colonial triumph. A public monument to the hero of Trafalgar was first mooted at his state funeral in 1806. Twenty-two years later, in 1838, the competition to design a monument to Nelson was won by William Railton, otherwise known as a designer of modest rectories and churches. This result was so surprising that the competition – whose judges included the Duke of Wellington, victor of Waterloo – was re-run, but with the same result.

Railton designed a grand fluted Corinthian column, to stand on a granite base, with steps down to the square flanked by four lions. It was not fully delivered and was reduced in scale because of spiralling costs. The first lions were rejected, and today's grand set – on which generations of London children have sat – only went up more than twenty years later, designed by Queen Victoria's favourite artist, Sir Edwin Landseer. Nevertheless, it's a very impressive monument. An early photograph by William Henry Fox Talbot shows the column under construction at the south end of Trafalgar Square. The massive base – as tall as the hotel to the east of the square – is covered by wooden scaffolding made of huge vertical uprights. An engine, moving on a railway, raised the enormous blocks of Devon granite that constituted the column. Each side of the base contains a dignified bronze relief of Nelson's exploits – the Battles of Copenhagen, the Nile, and Cape St Vincent, and of course the hero's death in action at Trafalgar. Beneath are inscribed Nelson's famous words: 'England expects that every man will do his duty.' Three-quarters of the costs were met by public subscription.

E. H. Baily's statue of Nelson is 172 feet up in the air, topping a bronze capital decorated with swirling acanthus-leaf patterns. Edward Mogg's *New Picture of London and Visitor's Guide to its Sights*, published in 1844, trumpeted its scale: taller than both Trajan's Column in Rome and Napoleon's Column in Paris, a mere nineteen feet smaller than the Monument to the Fire of London in the City. The *Illustrated London News* praised Baily's ability to produce 'a portrait in stone, not an idealisation of a hero'. In October 1843 his statue was put on display and seen by a hundred thousand people in two days, before being lifted into place. His sandstone sculpture shows Nelson stepping forward confidently, his right foot protruding slightly over the edge. The admiral wears his uniform, with knee breeches, stockings, a vice admiral's coat adorned with four orders of chivalry, an epaulette on each shoulder and a sash across his front. Most splendid of all is his bicorne hat, topped with a glittering diamond plume called a chelengk, a gift from Sultan Selim III following the 1798 Battle of the Nile (it rotated when fully wound up). Nelson's left hand grasps the hilt of his ceremonial sword, his empty right sleeve held proudly across his chest. There is a huge coil of rope around his legs. Impressive from close quarters and from afar, Nelson's Column remains one of the most identifiable symbols of London.

One of the square's two sculptural plinths would remain empty until the late 1990s. The other found its occupant the same year as Nelson's Column, but George IV was hardly a natural fit. His decade of rule had been marred by extravagance and scandal. As the *Times* editorial on his death put it: 'There never was an individual less regretted by his fellow-creatures than this deceased king … If he ever had a friend – a devoted friend in any rank of life – we protest that the name of him or her never reached us.' Prinny, as the king was not so affectionately known, was satirised for indulging all the sensual pleasures, from sex to food and drink. If Brighton Pavilion, his overblown Indian palace by the sea, shows how he really was, this statue shows the man he wanted to be: slim, handsome, militarily successful and a munificent patron of the arts. He is shown riding bareback, something which only the most skilful of horsemen could do, to imply his effortless and natural command of country and state – not a judgement shared by his former subjects. The bronze had been made by Francis Chantry, the most successful establishment sculptor of early nineteenth-century Britain, for the Marble Arch that Nash designed as the ceremonial entrance to Buckingham Palace. The structure now stands on a traffic island at the top of Hyde Park. In a typical example of British parsimony, the expensive bronze statue of this most unpopular king was repurposed for use in Trafalgar Square.

In the early 1850s, two further plinths to Barry's design were installed at the southern corners. They hold statues to two generals, praised in their day but now controversial. General Sir Charles James Napier, who died in 1853, was a long-serving officer and public servant, hero of the Peninsular Wars, governor of British colonial possessions and Commander-in-Chief of the British army in India. The statue was paid for by public subscription, most of the monies coming from the army rank and file. A good story, you might think. But Napier is also notorious for having quelled several rebellions in north-western India, and for having captured Sindh province, in excess of his orders. Damned by a contemporary art critic as 'the worst public statue in England', George Gammon Adams's standing statue of the general in ceremonial dress, clasping his sword to his chest, is notable only for its ordinariness. Adams was a successful maker of medals and portrait busts who on two occasions was denied election to the Royal Academy; and it shows.

Henry Havelock, on the opposite corner, stands proudly astride his plinth, his proper right foot (like Nelson's) protruding slightly over the edge. One hand is placed squarely on his hip, while the other holds the hilt of his sword, presenting him as a man of action. The statue was erected not just as a monument to Havelock, but also to 'his brave companions in arms during the campaign in India'. He is an even more divisive figure than Napier. The euphemistically named 'campaign' is better known in Britain as the Indian Mutiny, or the First Indian War of Independence, when a large part of the Indian army rebelled against the British authorities. Havelock died of dysentery at Lucknow in 1857, having retaken the city, and was regarded a hero. In India, however, he is considered a brutal murderer, whose indiscriminate reprisals at Cawnpore and Lucknow may have resulted in as many as a hundred thousand deaths. William Behnes's bronze was taken after a photograph, as it was commissioned and erected some years after Havelock's death. It is now a highly controversial monument.

Art and empire: the National Gallery and the Royal Academy

The National Gallery, at the north end of Trafalgar Square, is the backdrop to many views of the square. It was one of a series of initiatives intended to give London the accoutrements of a major capital, creating respectable places for public leisure, from theatres and parks to art galleries. However, the gallery's foundation was fortuitous rather than strategic. A rich collector died; the prime minister of the time was an art lover; Parliament was happy enough to approve the relatively modest sum of sixty thousand pounds for its purchase. For fifteen years, the 'National Gallery' was in the late collector's house on Pall Mall, before the government, shamed by criticism, commissioned William Wilkins to build suitable premises for the National Gallery and the Royal Academy on the north terrace of the new square. He got the job largely because he made extraordinary claims about how little money he needed to do the work.

The ambitious concept was to combine the functions of a public museum and an art school, which would transform the nation's cultural and moral health, giving enjoyment to all. The derisory scale of Wilkins's building, for all its grand façade with an imposing portico and dome, meant that it was almost designed to fail. William IV vilified it as a 'nasty pokey hole', and Sir Robert Peel condemned its inadequacies on 'the best site in Europe'. There was simply not enough space – only six rooms for the National Gallery's rapidly growing collection, and only five exhibiting galleries for the Royal Academy. Three decades and two government enquiries into the National Gallery later, the Royal Academy had moved out.

Arts – market for painting

The relatively brief period when the Academy shared premises with the National Gallery transformed painting in Britain. At Trafalgar Square, the students at the Royal Academy Schools had immediate access to the museum's collection, including its innovative group of 'primitive' paintings. These were made by artists such as Jan van Eyck and Giovanni Bellini, who pre-dated the trio of High Renaissance geniuses, Leonardo, Michelangelo and Raphael. The students, like the influential art critic John Ruskin, were excited by their accurate observation of people and landscapes, their cold and sometimes brutal realism, and their use of everyday objects to convey symbolic meaning. Van Eyck's *Arnolfini Portrait*, acquired in 1842, the first Netherlandish painting in the collection, depicts an Italian merchant and his wife. They are shown warts and all; the man is extremely thin, with pinched features and a huge nose. Every detail in the picture, from the orange on the windowsill and the terrier's bristly hairs to the roughly rendered plaster walls and the reflection in the convex mirror, is depicted with meticulous precision. This was so unlike the bland perfection of Raphael, the model for young artists for centuries. Among the most talented of the early Royal Academy students was the child prodigy John Everett Millais and his friends, William Holman

Hunt and Dante Gabriel Rossetti. They called themselves Pre-Raphaelites because of their rejection of the academic art exemplified by Raphael.

The Pre-Raphaelites were radical in their approach to art, but most of them sought commercial success. At the very least, they needed to secure an income for themselves and their families. Their marketing strategies were clever: they ensured that reproductive prints were made after their paintings and, although they criticised academic painting, they still wished to be included in the Royal Academy's annual exhibition. This open-submission show, inaugurated in 1780, quickly became an important event of the London social season. Presence in the exhibition opened plenty of commercial opportunities. Britain's prosperity meant that more people than ever were purchasing art, and the art market was moving from an aristocratic to a middle-class phenomenon. Professionals and businessmen bought paintings to decorate their homes in selling exhibitions held in cities across the nation, often organised by regional art academies. The Royal Academy exhibition, because of its location, its prestige and its range, offered the greatest market, not just in direct sales but in terms of the reproductive copies that were made of the most popular and discussed exhibits.

In 1852, Millais and Hunt exhibited two paintings of completely different subjects, *Ophelia* and *The Hireling Shepherd*, which they had painted in tandem. Millais's *Ophelia* is now one of the most loved paintings in Britain. The subject is Shakespeare's tragic and hapless heroine, who dies after rejection by her lover Hamlet. Shakespeare leaves us uncertain as to whether Ophelia's demise was an accident or a deliberate act of self-harm. The story was immensely popular among the Victorians, who loved the sentiment and tragedy of Ophelia's untimely death (her evident beauty of body and mind also helped). At least fifty paintings of Ophelia were exhibited at the Royal Academy during the nineteenth century. It was the perfect subject for an artist who wanted an orthodox career. But although Millais was to end his working life as President of the Royal Academy, his *Ophelia* is anything but conventional.

In June 1851 Millais and Hunt had bought identically sized canvases and taken the train to Old Malden, then in the middle of the Surrey countryside. For three months they suffered the privations of wind, biting flies and damp feet, working eleven-hour days to paint their chosen sites in painstaking and exacting detail. Ophelia's landscape was painted in Six Acre Meadow on the west bank of the Hogsmill River. As is typical of Pre-Raphaelite art, the painted setting seems more naturalistic than the actual place. Strong colours and outlines make each element stand out, as if illuminated by unflinching daylight: the willow tree with its broken branch, the poppies, pansies, daisies and roses that float before Ophelia, the deep green of the weedy water and the slightly faded violets around her neck.

Millais's Ophelia didn't need to endure the privations of rural Surrey; urban life brought a particular chill to her suffering. The artist was the first to admit that 'Miss Siddal had a trying experience'. The artist and model Elizabeth Siddal, then aged nineteen, posed for Millais in a 'really splendid lady's ancient dress, all flowered over in silver embroidery'. He described buying this 'old and dirty' garment for the considerable sum (to him) of four pounds. We have to hope it was cleaned before the model put it on. So that Ophelia's waterlogged garments would hang correctly, Siddal agreed to pose in a tin bath. Millais promised that it would be kept at an even, warm temperature, thanks to lamps underneath the tub which warmed its metal base. So preoccupied by the act of painting, he forgot, the lamps went out and she caught pneumonia. Although Siddal did not complain herself, her father sent her medical bills to the artist.

Ultimately, the combination of innovation and tradition made Millais's *Ophelia* a big success. Within twenty years, it had become a favourite for display in middle-class homes. James Stephenson's large print after the painting, first published in 1866, was intended to be sold mounted and framed, ready to be hung on the wall. By this date Millais's work was no longer considered radical, but acceptable and popular, enabling the artist to provide for his large family. In 1885, when he was knighted, his conversion to an establishment figure was complete. William Holman Hunt was to become an artist of even greater renown, famous across the British Empire for a single composition that was to define his career and mainstream Victorian spirituality. In 1854, he exhibited a smallish painting inspired by the Gospel of St John at the Royal Academy. *The Light of the World*, made the previous year for Hunt's patrons Martha and Thomas Combe, was lambasted by most critics, but saved by John Ruskin who called it 'one of the very noblest works of sacred art ever produced'.

The painting shows the moment before dawn, when the coloured sky silhouetted against the trees shows that light is coming. The diffused light of the morning star illuminates the only figure. A male figure dressed in diaphanous white, cloaked in an iridescent red cape, stands at a door and knocks with his right hand. He holds a lantern that gleams with light, shining out of the darkness. His crown, adorned with plump berries that look like drops of blood, and the halo around his head, together with his priestly robes, proclaim him as Jesus Christ. His kindly eyes and patient expression indicate that he has been knocking for some time. Plants have grown up on the threshold, meaning that the door has been little used. Decaying windfall apples lie at Christ's feet, like the unproductive weeds, a further sign that life without the light of God is ultimately barren and unfulfilling. In later life, Hunt recalled: 'I painted the picture with what I thought, unworthy though I was, to be divine command, and not simply a good subject.'

In 1860, the *Illustrated London News* eulogised it as 'one of the most perfect things modern art has produced'. Through the medium of engraving, *The Light of the World* became one of the most popular images of the Victorian age, part of common culture. Widely reproduced and copied, it inspired poems and hymns, and was found across tens of thousands of homes and churches in the British Isles and across the growing empire. Because the subject appealed to Christians of most denominations, it found great success as a subject for stained-glass windows for churches – over two hundred survive in Australia alone.

In the 1890s Hunt, angered that Keble College, Oxford, which had been bequeathed the painting by Martha Combe in 1891, were charging visitors to see his picture, pondered the creation of another version. In 1900, at the age of seventy-three, he set to work on a life-size painting, with the intention that it should be accessible to everyone, for free, for spiritual and moral improvement. As Hunt was now almost blind, much of the actual work was done by his long-term assistant Edward Robert Hughes. In 1904, bearing the twin dates 1851 and 1900, *The Light of the World* was unveiled at the Fine Art Society in Bond Street.

Here entered Charles Booth. The industrialist, philan-thropist and researcher into poverty had been brought up a Unitarian Christian. Although an agnostic, he believed that exposure to great religious art was instrumental in improving society's morals. He bought the picture, on the understanding it would travel around the British Empire before being donated to the new Tate Gallery in London. In 1905, the picture embarked on a tour of Canada, Australia, New Zealand and South Africa. It was sensationally successful in the southern hemisphere – the organisers estimated that four-fifths of the total population of Australasia saw it. When it returned to Britain in 1908, it was clear that a mere art gallery was an inadequate location. *The Light of the World* was installed in the Middlesex Chapel at St Paul's Cathedral, the national pantheon of nineteenth-century Britain, housing memorials to such respected figures as Lord Nelson, the Duke of Wellington, Arthur Sullivan, J. M. W. Turner and Hunt's friend John Everett Millais. When Hunt died two years later, his ashes were also interred at St Paul's.

Bourgeois consumption

The intense interest that a picture like *The Light of the World* could generate was itself a product of social change. Art was one of the many reasonably but not excessively expensive products with which the British decorated their homes, to display their wealth and also their gentility. By the 1860s, the middle classes of London were living in pleasant semi-suburbs like Holloway, Clapham and Stoke Newington, connected to central London by the railway and horse-drawn omnibuses. (The expression 'the man on the Clapham omnibus', to denote an average citizen, was in general usage until the late twentieth century.) Their lives are satirised in the Grossmith brothers' *Diary of a Nobody* (1892), which describes the tribulations of the ever-slighted and slightly pompous clerk Mr Pooter and his wife Carrie, who live in The Laurels, 'a nice six-roomed residence' in Holloway. As Pooter's fictitious diary narrates, life was good. Property and domestic help were inexpensive. Most houses were equipped with the latest gadgets, from gas lighting and metal cooking stoves to indoor bathrooms and flushing toilets. They were decorated in the current fashion: heavy curtains, patterned wallpaper, massive dark furniture, house plants and richly decorated upholstery – sometimes further embellished by the woman of the house herself – were much in evidence. Luxury goods like pianos, ornaments and paintings were advertised in women's magazines.

The women in such environments were encouraged to be the 'angel in the house'. Their inactivity and commitment to indolent, luxury pursuits were a sign of their husband's ability to provide for them. Women prided themselves on their impractical clothes, their white hands and their elaborate hairstyles. Their job was to create an oasis for their husbands, a soothing interior in which to relax after the troubles of the day. This sort of environment is, ironically enough, seen in Hunt's *The Awakening Conscience* (1853), conceived as the opposite to *The Light of the World*. A woman, installed by her lover in a house in St John's Wood, realises her future as an outcast. This is in spite of the bourgeois comfort of her home, with a piano, a golden clock, rich furniture and woven carpets.

St Pancras

Such opulence came from trade, imperialism and transport, the three strands of British commercial success. Nowhere is this confidence more evident than in that great triumph of industrial architecture, St Pancras station and the Midland Grand Hotel. This was at the head of the third, and most important, of the railway lines in London, coming respectively from Lincolnshire and Yorkshire, the Midlands and from Liverpool and Manchester. The red brick of its elevation, topped with pointed tiled roofs and terraces, looms over the Euston Road.

Practically all the materials came from the industrial heartlands of the Midlands, a stipulation of the railway company that commissioned the station and railway. The fine decorative bricks were made by Edward Gripper's Nottingham Patent Brick Company and Tucker & Son of Loughborough, while the ironwork underpinning the structure was manufactured by the Butterley Iron Company in the Erewash Valley between Nottingham and Derby. The stone for the foundations, as well as decorative details including the pillars, columns and window frames, included Bramley Fall, or Derbyshire gritstone, Ancaster and Ketton limestone, and Mansfield red sandstone. Gleaming terracotta tiles, fired in bright colours and patterns, are still in fine condition. Even the most basic detail was constructed with an eye for everyday beauty as well function. Only the brick in the undercroft beneath the station was made on site – even the lime mortar which held the building materials together hailed from the Midlands.

The Gothic arched windows, divided by columns, are indebted to the storehouses and vaults of late medieval Venice and Florence; the stepped brick façades recall the townhouses and civic halls of Bruges and Amsterdam. The massive clock tower on the corner, a reference to all these successful city-states, anchors the building. The architect, Sir George Gilbert Scott, is saying in three dimensions what many of his contemporaries believed: that London was the true inheritor of these European predecessors, lauded in the nineteenth century for their commercial acumen, democratic government and moral rectitude. But the architecture makes even more grandiose claims for the purpose of the station complex, and for the superiority of London over everywhere else in the world. Elements from the greatest medieval European cathedrals – from Westminster Abbey, Salisbury and Winchester to Caen and Amiens – are incorporated within the tiles and brickwork.

In the booking hall, where passengers purchased their tickets, the capitals supporting the arches include figures of navvies, dressed in working men's clothing, holding models of wheeled locomotives. This building, with its impressive wealth of architectural detail, from secular and religious sources, is a powerful statement of the importance of trade, capitalism and industrialisation. This is brilliantly met by the structure that greeted those who moved through into the station proper. The railway shed, with an unprecedented clear span of 240 feet, and over 690 feet long, is risk-taking and audacious. William Barlow, the chief engineer of the Midland Railway, essentially created the span of a bridge in an indoor vaulted and glazed space. It remains one of the widest and largest spaces ever enclosed.

Visitors to the train shed are unaware that, rather than standing on the ground, they are on a platform well above street level. This was to prevent the lines out of the station blocking the canal network, still a crucial part of London's transport infrastructure at the time. The great transparent vault springs from the platform level. Twenty-five huge iron trusses, set at regular intervals and built into massive red-brick piers support a glass roof that takes you into the skies, among the scudding clouds and changing weather that are such a feature of London life. From the platform, each of these trusses seems skeletal. The effect is that God rather than mankind is bringing us through the act of travel, into the heavens. Surely this building – and the purposes it served – could only be divinely inspired and ordained?

The Albert Memorial

George Gilbert Scott was, in his own words, 'the apostle … of the multitude'. Born in remote Buckinghamshire in 1811, he was 'the foremost builder of his day', as an obituary in the *Builder* magazine put it. His greatest building is the Midland Grand Hotel at St Pancras. Yet the structure that is most representative of Victorian Britain, its ideals, its opulence, self-confidence and dependence on the rest of the world, is his Albert Memorial.

Albert, Prince of Saxe-Coburg Gotha, had married his first cousin Victoria, Queen of Great Britain and Ireland, in February 1840, when they were both only twenty. Victoria was deeply in love and devoted to Albert. She found him incredibly attractive; she gave birth to their first of nine children only nine months after their wedding night. She admired his intellect, his education and his gravitas. In many matters she deferred to him, although she had a very clear sense of her duties and autonomy as monarch. Victoria's desire to give him a status beyond that of her husband was a source of disagreement with her government and ministers, but in June 1857 he formally became Prince Consort. Albert was Victoria's most trusted advisor, and she never fully recovered from his death from typhoid fever in December 1861. She wore black, in mourning for the rest of her life, and hardly appeared in public for almost a decade. Within a month of Albert's death, a committee had been established to build the monument 'in the common sense of the word' that the queen desired. Only in April 1863 was Gilbert Scott's design formally approved, following lengthy discussion between the monarch and the government about the costs.

Scott was inspired, as he wrote, to construct a memorial that recalled the Eleanor crosses, erected by an earlier grieving monarch, Edward I, in the 1290s to mark the nightly resting points as his consort's body was moved to its burial place in Westminster Abbey. He was also influenced by the great churches and monuments in the medieval Gothic style that he had seen on his travels through France, Germany and Italy. The closest antecedent to the memorial wasn't the Eleanor crosses themselves but the open-air monuments to the Scaliger rulers of Verona in northern Italy, which were admired by many influential British Victorians, in particular John Ruskin.

The construction and decoration of the monument was much more complex than its design. Scott's proposal was for a ciborium – a canopy-like structure sometimes used to house the body of Christ during the Eucharist – under which a statue of the prince consort was to be placed. Ciboria, in the medieval world, were richly adorned, and although strongly architectural in feeling, were not free-standing buildings but interior decoration. Scott's novelty was to propose such a structure outdoors, and for it to house not a sacred image, such as the Virgin Mary and the Christ Child, but a mortal man. By this, Scott inferred that not just the queen, but also her consort, acted 'by the grace of God'.

The placement of the Albert Memorial was highly symbolic. In 1851, a decade before his death, Albert had presided over the huge success of the Great Exhibition, a celebration of modern technology and design (and especially that of Great Britain and her dominions) that had taken place in the specially constructed Crystal Palace in Hyde Park. The commercial success of the exhibition had enabled the Royal Commission for the Great Exhibition to purchase much of South Kensington along the north–south axis now known as Exhibition Road, to turn this into a centre of research and the arts. Imperial College, the South Kensington Museum, the Royal Colleges of Music and Art and a plethora of smaller royal institutes were established in this area. Victoria's – and her advisors' – desire was for the memorial, on the ridge in Kensington Gardens above these institutions, to effectively preside over Albert's legacy.

The monument as a whole celebrated his contribution to the arts of music, poetry, painting, architecture and sculpture, symbolised by the marble Frieze of Parnassus on the lower level of the structure. The frieze is crowned by four monumental groups – Agriculture, Commerce, Manufactures and Engineering – one at each corner. Scott's idea was to demonstrate the Prince Consort's long-held belief that industry was constantly improved by the intellectual high arts. But a colonial element was also key. At the base of the steps, beside the gilded fence that separated the monument from the public space of the park, were personifications of the major world continents, Africa, the Americas, Asia and Europe. As at the Great Exhibition, the meaning was plain: the riches of the world were placed at Great Britain's feet, to turn into objects and industries more precious than the raw materials themselves.

The crowning glory was the larger-than-life statue of the prince. Originally intended for the queen's favourite sculptor, Baron Carlo Marochetti, the commission passed on his death to a safe pair of hands, the highly regarded Irish-born Royal Academician John Henry Foley. It's impossible to miss Prince Albert, glittering with gold leaf, if you walk in Hyde Park and

Memorial head of a queen mother (Iyoba),
early sixteenth century CE

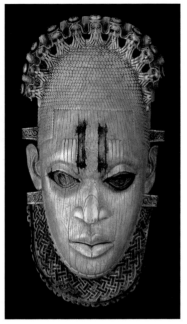

Ivory mask of Queen Idia,
sixteenth century CE

Plaque with four page figures in
front of the palace compound,
sixteenth–seventeenth century CE

Olfert Dapper, View of the city of Benin with the royal palace, Nigeria (detail), 1668 CE

Members of the British expedition to Benin City with objects from the Royal Palace, 1897 CE

Ivory salt cellar with European figures, 1525–1600 CE

Rembrandt van Rijn, *The Sampling Officials of the Amsterdam Drapers' Guild,* 1662 CE

Nicolas Maes, *Interior with a Sleeping Maid and her Mistress* ('The Idle Servant'), 1665 CE

Johannes Vermeer, *View of Houses in Delft,* c. 1658 CE

Jan Steen, *The Merry Family,* 1668 CE

Pieter Claesz, *Still Life with a Turkey Pie*, 1627 CE

Dolls house of Petronella Oortman, after 1686–1710 CE

Franz Post, *Brazilian Landscape*, 1660s CE

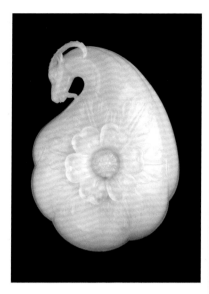

Shah Jahan's lotus wine cup in
white nephrite jade, 1657 CE

Nanha (painter) and Mir 'Ali Haravi
(calligrapher), the Emperor Shah
Jahan with his son Dara Shikoh, from
the Shah Jahan album, c. 1620 CE

The Taj Mahal,
Agra, 1631–48 CE

Interior dome of the
Taj Mahal, 1631–48 CE

Interior view of the Taj Mahal,
looking down on the screen
and the ceremonial tombs of
Mumtaz Mahal and Shah Jahan,
1631–48 CE

The Private Audience Chamber, Red Fort,
Delhi, 1639–48 CE

The Marble Throne, Public Audience
Chamber, Red Fort, Delhi, 1639–48 CE

John Everett Millais, *Ophelia*, 1851–2 CE

Jan van Eyck, *Portrait of Giovanni (?) Arnolfini and his Wife*, 1434 CE

William Holman Hunt, *The Light of the World*, St Paul's Cathedral, 1900–4 CE

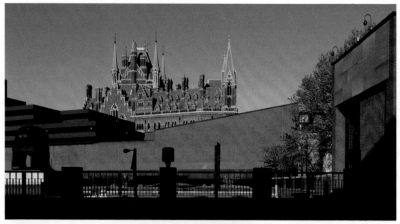

The Midland Grand Hotel from the south, 1865–76 CE

The railway shed, St Pancras station, 1864–68 CE

The Albert Memorial, Kensington Gardens, opened 1872 CE

Gustave Doré, *Over London, By Rail*, 1869–72 CE

Kensington Gardens today. Smiling courteously, the ever-young prince, who died aged only forty-two, looks towards the cultural and intellectual institutions of 'Albertopolis'. He wears court dress, and the Order of the Garter, the British monarchy's most illustrious decoration, is resplendent on his chest. His right hand holds – like the tablet of an Old Testament figure – a huge copy of the Great Exhibition catalogue of 1851, with an engraved image of the Crystal Palace in the centre.

There is something slightly uncomfortable about this image of a man who aspired to serve the public yet appears in his monument as a benign and gilded autocrat. It's important to remember that Victoria, although bound by the constraints of constitutional monarchy, resisted, like her husband, attempts to reduce the authority of her position. As her reign went on, statues of the queen as empress and divinely appointed sovereign were to be found increasingly over her domains, in Great Britain and overseas. None, however, ever reached the overwhelming dimensions of the Albert Memorial, an impressively over-the-top testament to the love that Victoria bore her husband, and which she felt, with never-decreasing acrimony, should have been shared by all her subjects.

Gustave Doré

In 1869, the French artist Gustave Doré embarked with the writer William Blanchard Jerrold on an ambitious project to record the highs and lows of the British capital. *London, a Pilgrimage* was published in 1872 to provide an illustrated record of the 'shadows and sunlight' of the city. This endeavour, partly inspired by the huge success of Rudolph Ackermann's *The Microcosm of London*, published over fifty years earlier, was to dominate their activity for three years. Jerrold was a successful journalist and editor; Doré was celebrated across the Western world for his powers as an illustrator. Under the terms of their publishing contract, they spent three months a year walking the streets of the city, by day and by night, on an annual retainer of ten thousand pounds. For their safety, they were often accompanied on their nocturnal excursions by plain-clothes policemen.

The experience was a searing one. Doré and Jerrold were horrified and transfixed by the brutal squalor and deprivation experienced by many of London's poor – lacking food, clothing, housing, education and any form of sensory pleasure beyond drinking or drug-taking. *London, a Pilgrimage* graphically demonstrates the gulf that separated the haves and have-nots in the city. Prosperous boys from Westminster School are shown being confirmed in the Abbey; the Goldsmiths Company enjoy a dinner in their grand hall and elegant race-goers attend the Derby, while the poor huddle for warmth in a night shelter, escape briefly from the horrors of their lives in a seedy opium den or by dancing to a mechanical organ in a dilapidated court, and undertake dangerous, back-breaking work in factories, the wharves or on the streets.

At the time, Jerrold's text was criticised for its superficiality, Doré's illustrations for their inaccuracy in detail (he disliked sketching in public) and for some exaggeration. Both were, however, aware that, at the time of writing and drawing, some of the worst exigencies of the London poor were beginning – slowly – to be addressed. It would take a long time: children evacuated from inner London during the Second World War were still notable for their stunted growth, a product of poor diet and environmental pollution over many generations.

Doré's emotional, sometimes searing images are the visual

counterpoint of Dickens's anguished fictional accounts of the London poor, such as *Oliver Twist* and *David Copperfield*, Mr Boffin from *Our Mutual Friend* and Jo, the sweeper-boy in *Bleak House*, and the equally affecting reportage of Henry Mayhew and Charles Booth among the London poor. He employed line engraving, with a sharing reach like social media today, to present an at times compassionate, at others horrified, account of London life. Doré adopted the tried and tested visual language of the greatest European print-makers – Dürer, Rembrandt and Piranesi – to convey the actuality of London around 1870, in images that are contemporary and universal. He used a visual repertoire that was very familiar to his viewers, enabling them to see women and their babies huddling together in the lee of an ugly modern bridge, for instance, as modern versions of the Holy Family on their flight to Egypt. But Doré's principal weapon was a highly sophisticated manipulation of light and shadow. Light here is a metaphor for spiritual as well as economic poverty and wealth. The life of the prosperous always takes place in well-illuminated spaces. In contrast, the poor's piteous existence is underscored by their lack of regular light. By day or night, they inhabit a half-light – in factories, on the streets or in dingy hovels that the sun never enters.

In Doré's mind, even the respectable, working poor had highly restricted and limited lives. The engraving *Over London – by rail* presents a nightmarish vision of workers living in identically mean brick houses, seen through a huge archway – presumably one of the railway bridges of the traditional working-class districts of south and east London. The railway was the technological innovation that was to change London and the wider world. The city's urban patterns became defined by the railway; its architecture was to shape their look and feel. Huge brick bridges and viaducts, often running high above ground level, carried commuters into the metropolis. Under the streets, tunnels connected a growing network of stations.

By framing his scene with the railway arch, Doré intentionally recalled Piranesi's highly influential *Carceri*, or prisons, implying that contemporary London is a site of hellish imprisonment. In Doré's interpretation, the human is dominated and diminished by the enormous, functional but emotionless industrial architecture. The houses are tall, thin and uniform. Their tiny back yards are filled with sagging washing lines of damp laundry – it's a mystery it could dry at all in this oppressive atmosphere – and crowds of people, sitting or standing in these cramped (but private) outdoor spaces. In the distance a steam train, belching out clouds of noxious smoke that billow towards us, speeds across a railway viaduct. The strong contrasts provided by the powerful lighting and black line and white space, make this a powerful evocation of a dystopian world, powered by excess, greed and a complete disregard of the have-nots.

The topography of wealth

A century and a half later, London's architectural fabric perpetuates class distinctions, even though the social and economic context of the city has greatly changed. For many years, as I walked daily to work, I traversed the lows and highs of Victorian London. In the late nineteenth century, my London street was one of the more squalid parts of the metropolis. I know this because of the diaries and 'poor maps' compiled by Charles Booth and his researchers. The 'very poor' lived here:

'builders' labourers; casuals; pros[titutes] ... barefoot dirty children ... the school board officer doing his rounds after truants'.
Not only was there a nasty smell, but bread, meat and paper
were found all over the street. A series of circular holes in the
bricks outside my front door are evidence that people milled
around during the day and twisted coins into the fabric by way
of a pastime. Round the corner were those who Booth called
the 'semi criminal' poor. And across the street, now an estate of
late twentieth-century houses, was Lambeth Hospital and the
workhouse. Here the young Charlie Chaplin, and many others,
bedded down in the communal wards.

Moving towards the Thames you pass the lower-middle-
class area of Walcot Square, with its charming 1840s houses,
miniature copies of grander establishments. This is where
Dickens's Mr Guppy, a lawyer's clerk who we are meant to
laugh at for his social simplicity, would have set up house
with the heroine Esther, had she agreed to be his wife in *Bleak
House*. The grand late Georgian houses of Kennington Road
had become subdivided into rented accommodation for music
hall artists, like Chaplin's parents, who worked in the establishments around Waterloo. Closer to the river, fine 1930s social
housing estates are on the site of Victorian factories. The South
Bank was a centre of pottery and artificial stone manufacture,
and power generation – noxious and noisy trades, whose rubbish was dumped in the river. The Thames had always been the
great drain of London, but the industrialisation and population
growth of the late eighteenth and early nineteenth centuries
made it into a breeding ground for typhoid and cholera.

On the north side of the river there is a distinct change of
mood. Here we enter the city of politicians, bureaucrats and
decision-makers. The Gothic Palace of Westminster, with
Big Ben and its clock tower, looms over Westminster Bridge.

Northumberland Avenue and its grandiose Edwardian buildings, on the site of one of the old noble palaces of Westminster, leads to Trafalgar Square. The heart of empire remains just over a mile from one of the poorest and most deprived parts of London. Over a hundred years after the death of Queen Victoria, the architecture of London is still defined, for good and for ill, by her brief dominance of the world economy.

The Secession Building, Karlsplatz

12

VIENNA: FREEDOM

1900–1914

To visit Vienna in 1900 was to be part of one of the most exciting, diverse and confused urban centres the world has known.
If cities have identities, early twentieth-century Vienna suffered
from a split personality. It was home both to the stultifyingly
ceremonial and traditional Austro-Hungarian court, where the
heir apparent was stigmatised for marrying a 'mere' countess,
and the psychoanalytical thought of Sigmund Freud and his
revolutionary theories of dreams. Ultra-conservatives mixed
with anarchists and radicals in its streets, cafés, theatres and
concert halls. The city encompassed an extraordinary variety
and breadth of ideas, peoples and attitudes. This was intoxicating or terrifying, depending on your point of view – and
sometimes both.

Vienna was the capital of the Austrian Empire, half of the
sprawling Habsburg domains ruled by Franz Josef, Emperor of
Austria and King of Hungary, which spread from northern Italy
to Ukraine. It was the largest and most significant city in central
Europe. By 1910, it had a population of over two million, as the
aspirational, both rich and poor, made their way to Vienna from

across the Austro-Hungarian territories. Most of those who lived there had been born elsewhere. The influx of new money and people meant that the city was a dynamic, seething organism. It was home to one of the largest Jewish communities in the world: in the early twentieth century, around 8 per cent of the Viennese population was Jewish. The majority were industrial or sweat-shop workers, or ran small businesses, and their community was concentrated in Leopoldtstadt, in the east of the city. But the community also included figures as significant as lawyer Hans Kelsen (who wrote the Austrian constitution of 1920), doctors Robert Bárány and Otto Loewi, Sigmund Freud, biologist Karl Landsteiner, the Ephrussi family of bankers and the anatomist Emil Zuckerkandl and his wife Berta Szeps, who ran a celebrated literary salon from their home.

The Ringstrasse

Travelling along the Ringstrasse, it is possible to forget Vienna's troubled twentieth-century history: its loss of empire, incorpo-ration into the Nazi state and position on the edge of Western Europe during the Cold War. This magnificent circular boule-vard, as grandiose as it is wide, embodies the pride of the Austrian Empire and its capital city in the late nineteenth cen-tury. The Ringstrasse was begun in 1858 on the site of Vienna's former military fortifications, under the emperor's sponsorship. It was to provide all the amenities required by a modern capital, and to link the inner Burg or citadel of Vienna with the new and increasingly industrialised suburbs. A further ambition was to impress Franz Josef's ever more dissatisfied subjects with the munificence and benefits of empire. The centrepiece of the project was the Kaiserforum, a monumental group of buildings that added the Neue Burg to the Hofburg, Franz Josef's principal palace, which was flanked by two enormous imperial museums on Maria-Theresia Platz, the Naturalhistorisches Museum facing the Kunsthistorisches Museum.

All the public institutions needed by a modern imperial city could be found along the four kilometres of the Ringstrasse – there was also the Rathaus (Town Hall), the Parliament, the Votivkirche, university, Burgtheater (Civic Theatre), Akademie der Bildenden Künste (Fine Art Academy) and the MAK (Museum of Applied Arts). The street also incorporated the celebrated structures of the past, from the Hofburg to the Karlskirche. New palaces and apartments for the rich, built in the 'New Renaissance' idiom that characterises mid-nineteenth-century Vienna, filled in the gaps. It is not for nothing that the Ringstrasse is one of the most important urban development schemes ever undertaken in Europe. In comparison, the civic improvements that George IV and John Nash proposed in London seem paltry and insignificant.

Vienna was at once a court, a financial and industrial centre. The elegance and sophistication of the Innere Stadt and Schönbrunn Palace just outside the city contrasted with the grimness of the industrial areas. These were home to factories, engineering plants, the railways and power generation plants. Most workers lived past the Linienwall, beyond the city's inner suburbs, in cramped rooms in tenement blocks near the factories, far from the wealthy establishments where many poorer women laboured in domestic service.

Conservatism and tradition

The newly prosperous middle classes, who had climbed their way from rural poverty to a degree of affluence, were keen to separate themselves from the poor, and if they could not join the nobility, then at least ape their dress, habits and preferred occupations. They complained of the noisy, disorderly life of the working classes, from occasional riots and strikes to the interruption their journeys into work caused to the harmonious life of the city (Vienna had no underground railway until the 1960s). They also wished to separate themselves from the dangerous world of politics, and return to the certain comforts of quiet, conventional domesticity.

Biedermeier, a term coined to satirise a representative of this new German-speaking urban middle class, was associated more positively with their aspirations. Heavy, well-crafted furniture, crowded but comfortable interiors with upholstered sofas and gently ticking clocks, paintings emphasising the quiet tranquillity and simple pleasures of domestic life, and the beauty of the Viennese woods – these are the essential features of Biedermeier style. A classic example is Ferdinand Georg Waldmüller's 1857 painting *On Corpus Christi Morning* in the Belvedere Gallery, Vienna. A group of children are getting ready for the Feast of Corpus Christi, an important moment in the calendar of Catholic Austria. Four girls stand proudly in their special white frocks, while a boisterous boy is ready to lead the procession. A kindly old man and several barefoot children watch the chosen ones as their mothers fuss over them. Bright early summer sunlight makes everything, even the ragged poor, the bare earth and the shabby masonry, look contented and beautiful. Another artist might have inserted criticism or social commentary into this scene. But in the hands of Waldmüller, it becomes a nostalgic reverie for a quiet, traditional, semi-rural life that would have been unfamiliar to those who bought and enjoyed his paintings.

Waldmüller and other popular artists portrayed the cosy,

gemütlich side of Vienna. Then there was the radical, angry and politically engaged world best exemplified by the painter Oskar Kokoschka, branded a madman for his expressive and violent brush strokes, and his determination to right the wrongs of women in a male-dominated society (although writing and performing a play called *Murder, the Hope of Women* might not have been the perfect way to go about it). Both sets of people and opinions met in the city's coffee houses. These were described by the novelist Stefan Zweig as 'a sort of democratic club, open to everyone for the price of a cheap cup of coffee, where any guest can sit for hours with their little offering, to talk, write, play cards, receive post and above all consume an unlimited number of newspapers and journals.'

Indeed, Viennese society could be remarkably porous and varied. The Gallias, a wealthy assimilated Jewish family, were a case in point. Adolf Gallia, a lawyer, invested in the radical newspaper *Die Zeit*, while his brother Moritz was appointed an imperial councillor. But Moritz was not that conservative. He and his wife Hermine patronised avant-garde artists, among them Klimt (who painted Hermine) and the designer Josef Hoffmann, who provided most of the furnishings for their apartment in the prosperous Wohllebengasse. Their friends included both conventional and more extremist figures, such as the prominent socialist and feminist Elisabeth Luzzatto.

Franz Josef and Sisi

The tensions and differences in the city of Vienna were also reflected in the personalities of the emperor and empress. Born in Vienna in 1830, and destined (at least by his mother) for greatness, Franz Josef had become Emperor of Austria in December 1848, aged only eighteen. A man of tradition and inherent conservatism, as well as of ambition, his initial desire was to unify the German-speaking peoples under his leadership, and subsequently, when that failed, to preserve the territories he had inherited and prevent the break-up of the Habsburg lands. He felt a strong duty to perform his role as emperor, which led him never to deviate from the path set for him.

In 1854, Franz Josef married his first cousin Elisabeth of Bavaria, known as Sisi (or Sissi), her childhood nickname. She was only sixteen. He had been meant to choose her older sister Helene, but the girls were in mourning when he met them, and Sisi's charisma and beauty (the dark blonde teenager looked better in black than her brown-haired sister) turned his head.

For many, Sisi – made yet more famous by an immensely popular series of 1950s films starring Romy Schneider – epitomises the glamour and nostalgic reassurance of the Habsburg Empire after the cataclysms of the earlier twentieth century. Images of Sisi, painted by the society portraitist Franz Xaver Winterhalter, cover countless chocolate boxes and souvenirs. In 2022, a Netflix series about the empress was the platform's top non-English language performer. Winterhalter's portraits of Sisi conform to the idea of the fairy-tale princess. Tragically, this apparently perfect beauty led a troubled life. In September 1898, aged sixty, she was assassinated by an anarchist. By this time, she had lost one child to illness and another – her only son – to suicide. In 1889, in a scandal that shocked the world, Archduke Rudolf, the heir to the throne, killed his twenty-three-year-old lover Mary Vetsera and then himself.

None of this trauma is evident in a full-length portrait by Winterhalter, made for the imperial state apartments in the Hofburg, where it still hangs side by side with one of Franz

Josef in formal court dress. The twenty-eight-year-old empress stands at the edge of a terrace. Columns stretch out to the right, and in front of her we have to imagine steps that take us down to the sunlit grass and trees below. Her clothing, however, would make it impossible for her to travel any distance. She is dressed in a white satin evening gown, overlaid with diaphanous layers of white tulle. Designed by the Parisian couturier Worth, who dressed the leading ladies of Europe – who were also painted by Winterhalter – the dress's double crinoline skirt was like a carapace that trapped the wearer. Diamonds and thousands of silver foil stars have been applied to the satin, so that the empress would shimmer like a cloud of fireflies when she moved. Sisi turns to the beholder, imperiously but courteously, holding a slightly extended fan in her hands, an expected accoutrement of high-status evening wear in the 1860s. Her long hair, adorned with white edelweiss diamond stars designed by the court jeweller Koechert, is a living, moving diadem. The effect is stunning. 'Empress style' hair ornaments were popularised in the mid-nineteenth century, but most women had to rely on false or borrowed hair and paste jewellery, lacking the long flowing locks and real jewels possessed by Sisi.

In this painting, dated 1865, Sisi looks the epitome of an empress. Beautiful, elegant, worthy of our admiration, but on a higher level than mere mortals, and spectacularly removed from the troubles of the world. At this time, the Austro-Hungarian Empire was facing political challenges that it had never known before, both from within – many of its subjects began to agitate for self-determination – and from powerful threats abroad, particularly from the emperors of Russia and Germany. In 1867, the Dual Monarchy – an explicit union between the Austrian Empire (the 'Lands represented in the Imperial Council') and the Kingdom of Hungary – was established to neutralise some of this discontent. It produced a bureaucratic system of labyrinthine proportions, but only postponed the inevitable crisis. There were also existential dangers, some of them emanating from the figurehead of the empress herself.

Almost immediately after her marriage, Sisi, a mercurial free spirit, became deeply unhappy. The stifling atmosphere of the Austro-Hungarian court, with a devoted but rule-bound husband, and a domineering mother-in-law aunt who was (as a wit of the time remarked) 'the only man in the Hofburg', oppressed her. Sisi was to suffer from depression for most of her adult life.

Demoralised by what she perceived to be the tyranny of rigid court protocol, she tried to spend as much time as possible away from Vienna, seeing little of her husband and children. She endeavoured to develop ways of understanding and improving her mental health, and reducing her levels of anxiety. Many of these strategies were focused on one of the few aspects of her life she could control: her physical appearance. In order to preserve her youthful looks, she exercised and dieted obsessively, spending hours daily on horseback and doing gymnastics, using weights and restricting her diet to a bizarre cocktail of egg whites, fruit purée and raw meat juice. Sisi subjected her body to repeated treatments and tortures, including wearing specially designed firm leather corsets to keep her waist to a maximum of nineteen inches – something she retained well into her fifties.

Sisi was a highly complex character, obsessed with her appearance but also unfulfilled by such a superficial life. Her hair was her crowning glory, and although she was prepared to spend two hours a day having it dressed, she worried that while having her hair brushed her 'mind escape[d] through the hair onto the fingers of [her] hairdresser'. To prevent boredom and introspection she filled this time with learning languages. The empress also travelled incessantly in search of variety and a mental calm, and wrote complex, beautiful and personal poetry. Her family did not find her easy to live with, but she was a highly intelligent woman, unsuited temperamentally for the regimented, restricted and convention-bound life she was required to live.

Freud and the language of dreams

Sisi's attempts to control her life sprung from a desire to alleviate inner turmoil and uncertainty. These motivations were very familiar to Sigmund Freud, although his methods for understanding the human unconscious, and for treating the symptoms of mental instability, were quite different. Freud, the founder of psychoanalysis, had been educated in Vienna and in Paris, where he had studied in the clinic of the great pathologist Charcot at the mental hospital, the Salpêtrière. He developed the theory that hysterical symptoms, to which characters like Sisi, living with little control over their lives, were particularly prone, were connected to psychiatric rather than physical causes.

In Freud's assessment, humans were driven by the id, ego and super-ego, the three elements of the mind that made up an individual's personality – the manifestation of the power struggle going on deep within our beings. Therefore, we are all 'actors in the drama of [our] own minds, pushed by desire, pulled by coincidence'. Hysteria could be treated by talking out the ideas that disturbed and troubled Freud's patients, including under hypnosis, because these ideas were embedded so deeply in patients' unconscious they could not be expressed in norms acceptable to society. 'The psychoanalyst,' he said to an early patient, Sergei Pankejeff, 'like the archaeologist in his excavations, must uncover layer after layer of the patient's psyche, before coming to the deepest, most valuable treasures.'

It was by understanding unconscious desires, and by confronting uncomfortable ideas of sexuality, violence and aggression, that someone could be cured. Dreams, Freud was convinced, could be interpreted, although like Egyptian hieroglyphs they needed much study and the development of the appropriate tools. His *The Interpretation of Dreams*, first published in 1900, legitimised the study and analysis of dreams, as representations of our true unsuppressed feelings, and as valid manifestations of unmediated human emotion. These were complex, and included the expression of sadism and other fantasies that could never be articulated in ordinary life. If these desires were not understood or acknowledged, we could not be in full comprehension of our deep psyches, and therefore would be unable to tap into and exploit the full extent of our creativity.

Freud was fascinated by art and by artists. He believed that interrogating their practices and motivations would help understand the human mind. Sleep, dreams and the power of animalic sexual identity were more broadly explored across every art and literary form in late nineteenth-century Vienna. This was partly because there was connection and discussion between scientists, artists and writers. Gustav Klimt, who had been academically trained and who initially, like Winterhalter, simply followed a conventional artistic career, became exposed to innovative medical ideas at the house of Emil and Berta Zuckerkandl. Through this connection he read Darwin, studied biology and was able to attend lectures in the medical school of the University of Vienna, whose head, Carl von Rokitansky, was guided by the motto 'truths are hidden from the surface'. This could be a leitmotif for Klimt's own work. In different ways, it also impacted on a group of younger artists, including the composer (and painter) Arnold Schönberg and the painters Richard Gerstl, Kokoschka and Egon Schiele. These artists disturbed and sometimes frightened their contemporaries through their single-minded quest for the artistic freedom to confront the most difficult issues of life: sexuality, attraction, the subconscious and death.

Klimt and the Secession

In 1897, Klimt and eighteen others, including the architect Josef Hoffmann and the all-round designer Kolomon Moser, formed a new movement, the Union of Austrian Fine Artists, or Vereinigung Bildender Künstler Österreichs. They became more commonly known as the Secession because they declared that they were removing themselves – seceding – from the conservatism of the Künstlerhaus, the principal body for artists in Vienna. This was inspired by the way that the ordinary people (*plebs*) of ancient Rome had, on occasion, rejected the rule of the patricians, and detached themselves from public life (*secessio plebs*). Unlike the plebs, who had physically removed themselves from Rome and refused to undertake military service, the Secession's rebellion was more abstract. They wanted to set themselves free, to be in tune with the spirit of their age as well as with human nature through the centuries. It was one of several artists' associations to share such aspirations, especially in German-speaking Europe, but the Vienna Secession was particularly successful because of its longevity and its situation in one of the world's most tumultuous and varied cities.

Klimt's moment of epiphany had come while conceiving the shape of a commission that he and his long-term collaborator Hans Matsch had received from the University of Vienna. In 1894 they were contracted to paint the ceiling of the university's great hall with the triumph of light over darkness, and personifications of the four principal faculties of study – Theology, Jurisprudence, Medicine and Philosophy. The university wanted safe personifications of these themes, according to norms first established during the Renaissance. Everything from Klimt's career to date, such as his beautiful but traditional paintings on the staircase of the Kunsthistorisches Museum and the sketches he produced while competing for the university project, would have led them to believe that's what they would receive.

Klimt's Faculty Paintings – as they became known – were among the most shocking of the early twentieth century. They are allegorical, but utterly unconventional. They are dystopian, and by the standards of the time, dangerously erotic and alluring. Their overall message is that there is a shortfall between ideal and reality, that brutish human nature can never be wholly overcome by education or society, and that sexual attraction has a power we ignore at our peril. *Jurisprudence*, described by the Hungarian art critic (and Klimt's friend) Ludwig Hevesi as a 'luxury hell', shows an old man on trial by 'three avenging goddesses of terrifyingly beautiful form' (again in Hevesi's words) with inscrutable and frighteningly beautiful bodies, representing the Furies of Greek mythology who hold humans to account for their apparent failings. *Philosophy* is a mystical sphinx, apparently dissolving before our eyes, because it is impossible ever to understand the world, or to be truly wise.

Medicine, first exhibited in 1901, was the most scandalous. Hygieia, the Greek goddess of medicine, is appropriately allegorical, clothed in mystical organic shapes and colours. But above her is a sinuous mass of naked imperfect humans, representing the people helped by medicine, including babies, the poor, the elderly, a skeleton and – most sensationally – a heavily pregnant woman. Conservative politicians rebuked the Ministry of Education for awarding the commission to Klimt. The university rejected the paintings, and Klimt, angered at the suggestion they become part of the new Museum of Modern Art, was prepared to buy them back and renounce the project (two were bought by his friend Moser; one by August Lederer, who together with his family was one of Klimt's greatest patrons). Tragically, they were destroyed in 1945.

Like the Pre-Raphaelites, the original Secession members, including Klimt, its first president (who was to leave the organisation in 1905, perturbed by its ties with commerce), saw themselves as a regenerative force, who would replenish art at the 'Ver Sacrum' or sacred spring. To do this, they could not step back from confronting the most difficult and primeval elements of life. As art was an expression of humanity, it had to be in tune with mankind's base instincts, the lows as well as the highs. Art was, as the writer Hugo von Hofmannsthal, Richard Strauss's librettist, described, 'the only reality, everything else is just a reflection in the mirror'.

Building freedom

In 1898 the Secession opened their headquarters on the Karlplatz, already the site of several important public institutions, including the Kunstlerhaus, the Musikverein, the Technical University, and Vienna's grandest Baroque church, the Karlskirche, built for the Emperor Karl in the 1730s. The architect, Joseph Maria Olbrich – himself a member of the Secession – had trained in the academic tradition, but was also familiar with the stylistic language of the ancient Greek, Babylonian and Egyptian temples which were all being excavated and brought to greater public attention in the early twentieth century. His express desire was 'to erect a temple of art, which would offer the art lover a quiet, elegant place of refuge'. According to the critic Hermann Bahr, spokesperson of the avant-garde literary group Young Vienna, the building was so striking that it stopped ordinary men and women in their tracks on their way to work. It was so unlike anything else around it that they could not take their eyes off it. More unflatteringly, it was lampooned as 'the golden cabbage head', the 'Assyrian inconvenience' or 'Mahdi's tomb' (after an Islamic leader in Sudan, whose mausoleum had recently been destroyed).

Perhaps we should take Bahr's words with a pinch of salt, because it's so in tune with the intention of the architect and commissioners that the Secession building should look like the headquarters of some arcane sect, but at the same time attractive to the everyman. Appropriately, this is a building that is both radical and timeless. It evokes and critiques the architectural forms developed in the West for Christian buildings, derived from Roman and Byzantine structures. Like the Karlskirche and so many of the best Habsburg Baroque churches, the Secession Building's façade is crowned with a great dome. This is where the similarities end. The Secession dome is a fluid and organic sphere of golden laurel leaves attached to a practically invisible iron structure. It seems to float in the sky rather than being attached to the building. The three thousand leaves were intended to evoke the laurel wreaths sacred to Apollo, the Greek god of the arts, and conventionally used to crown great poets and artists. They also recall the stunning pre-Greek and Roman gold filigree jewellery that had been discovered by the archaeologist Heinrich Schliemann at Hissarlik, the site of ancient Troy, in 1873, and which had made a sensation in Western Europe.

The Secession Building, painstakingly rebuilt at the end of the Second World War, is the epitome of the group's ideals: bright white, pristine, well designed, practical and beautiful. It is a simple architectural structure, formed of two bays with a recessed door at the centre, reached by a small flight of stairs. Built on a Greek cross plan, of brick with iron reinforcements, its flat walls of painted white plaster recall the plain lines of Assyrian and archaic Greek architecture, at least as they were understood in the late nineteenth century. The architectural ornamentation as well as the building materials are unadorned. There are none of the columns, pillars or architectural orders that were such a feature of Western European structures from the days of the ancient Greek city-states. And, most strikingly, there are no windows on the main façade.

Stylised laurel trees, with leaves, some picked out in gold, above the main door and at the corners draw your eye to the edges and centre of the building, and especially to the dome above. Three Greek gorgons, with terrifying masks, representing the connected arts of painting, architecture and sculpture, are above this door, indicating that it is a temple of the arts. Above the archway, underneath the dome, an inscription by Hevesi makes emphatic the purpose of the Secession, to produce art as artists wished, and in keeping with their time in the world: 'To each age its art, to art its freedom.' Inside the building visual artists were encouraged to dwell on the syncretic links between the visual and other art forms.

The vestibule was intended to be cleansing and solemn, to enable visitors to put off sordid and temporal life and prepare themselves for communion with the eternal. The building inside is a box-like structure, containing display spaces of different sizes, lit by natural light through the pitched glass roof. Light moves through it, rather than amplifying it, so that the spaces felt like 'the quiet cloisters of the soul', as Bahr put it. The display areas are entirely functional. All the internal walls could be moved, depending on the needs of the particular work being exhibited. From today's perspective this moveable white cube is how we expect a contemporary art gallery to feel. However, it is completely different from the ornamented palaces to art familiar to late nineteenth- and early twentieth-century visitors, such as Gottfried Semper's Kunsthistorisches Museum and Natural History Museum, or the Academy of Fine Arts and the Imperial Royal Austrian Museum of Art and Industry, all a short walk away along the Ringstrasse, where the works of historic and contemporary artists were exhibited. In these grandiose structures, in the highly decorated Renaissance style that the nineteenth-century establishment venerated, art had to fit into the spaces that someone else had made for it. The innovation of Olbrich's design was that the requirements of the living artist, and their vision for their work, took centre stage.

The Secessionists tried to support the purchase of contemporary works, – including Rodin's *Rochefort*, Segantini's *Wicked Mothers* and Van Gogh's *Wheatfields of Auvers* – in order to create a public gallery of modern art, but this dream never came to fruition. Their main achievement was in holding regular temporary exhibitions, showing the most radical and innovative art that was being produced across the Western world. They believed that their purpose was to educate the public and present a clear picture of modern art, so that public taste and aesthetic judgement would improve, and the commitment to showing contemporary art was intense. Twenty-three exhibitions took place at the Secession Building between 1898 and 1905 alone. Perhaps the most extraordinary exhibition was the fourteenth, held in 1902. This was devoted to Beethoven, who lived more than half his life in Vienna. Conceived as a celebration of the great composer's genius, twenty-one artists under the direction of Josef Hoffmann laboured to produce a 'total artwork' (*Gesamtkunstwerk*) that united various art forms – music, painting, sculpture, architecture. The work of art would emerge, in the artists' minds, from this interaction and interplay.

Central to this was Max Klinger's life-size polychromed marble statue of Beethoven. The composer was presented like a god, bare-chested, frowning as he thinks and creates, seated on a richly decorated throne that includes the temptation of Adam by Eve on its reverse. An eagle, symbol of Jupiter, king of the gods in the Roman pantheon, is at his feet. On the walls was Klimt's Beethoven Frieze, inspired by the composer Wagner's interpretation of Beethoven's 9th Symphony, celebrating the human soul's struggle for joy, encapsulated in the unity of all the arts. Suffering Humanity, beleaguered by 'Hostile Forces', including Sickness and Death, Lust, Intemperance and Wantonness, is driven by Compassion and Ambition to achieve pure happiness in Poetry and the other Arts, accompanied by a choir of angels from Paradise. As the 1902 exhibition catalogue put it, 'The Arts lead us into the ideal kingdom, which is the only place we can find pure joy, pure happiness and pure love.'

The Wiener Werkstätte

The Beethoven exhibition, in its complexity and variety, looked towards the happenings and performances of the twentieth century. Its makers and other members of the Secession saw a role for art far beyond museums and galleries. Many of the group's leaders wanted to change life by bringing the optimum standards of beauty and skill into the most prosaic of objects. To this end, Josef Hoffmann and Koloman Moser had founded the Wiener Werkstätte in 1903. The workshop was radical and obsessive in its commitment to the highest levels of artistic skill, and of innovation, because this would improve the quality of human life, and add to the happiness of mankind. A publicity leaflet of 1905 lambasts the 'limitless harm' done in the arts and crafts by low-quality mass production and slavish adherence to old forms, despite their limited relevance to modern life. Stating that 'it would be madness to swim against this tide. Nevertheless we have founded this workshop', Hoffmann and Moser shared a messianic commitment to the best quality design. This is demonstrated in the Werkstätte letterhead and visual identity. All the fancy serifs and swirls that ornament italic type have been removed, for a firm, stern and clean line. The interlocking Ws demonstrate the connection that the workshop's founders saw between all forms of art and life.

They also underline that every object made for the workshops shared the same source from the Sacred Way, signposted on the façade of the Secession Building. There was no distinction between 'fine' and 'applied' art. And a client, if they so desired, could have a 'total artwork', where every part of a building and its contents, from the roof down to the cellar, was designed by the workshop. In practice, however, this was only possible for the super-rich, such as the Belgian banking and railway magnate Adolphe Stoclet, who gave the Werkstätte free rein to design every element of his mansion, the Palais Stoclet, in Brussels, or (at a slightly less opulent level) rich Viennese families like the Gallias. The Werkstätte hoped – sometimes against hope – like similar initiatives across Europe such as London's Omega Workshop, Dublin's Dun Emer Guild or the German Bauhaus – that their clientele would diversify, and they would spread good design to the masses. In practice, they were only able to survive with financial support from family and friends. Cutlery, fabric, clothing, buildings, chairs, beds, paintings, glass, tableware, jewellery and sculpture all formed part of the multifarious and varied production of the workshop. In one significant element they differed from similar groups of artists active all over Europe and America in the years between 1848 and the First World War, and that was in their overriding commitment to quality rather than universalism.

A tea service by Hoffmann demonstrates this well. Since the eighteenth century, drinking tea, coffee or chocolate had become one of the key elements of civilised European life. Tea, imported from India and China, was the subject of a ritual, which if not as precise and measured as those of the Japanese, gave pleasure and solace to millions. Charles Rennie Mackintosh and his wife Margaret Macdonald, friends and associates of the Werkstätte artists who exhibited at the Secession, had designed and constructed several tea rooms for Miss Kate Cranston in central Glasgow. Tea houses, like Viennese cafés, were open to everyone, women as well as men. At home, taking tea was an important domestic ceremony, presided over by the woman of the household.

Specialised equipment was manufactured and sold for what had by now become everyday drinks. Tea and coffee services were among the most successful and commercial items produced by ceramic factories and metal workers. But Hoffmann's tea service takes a step back from mainstream production. This set is one of the earliest productions of the workshop, made in the year of its foundation. It consists of a small tea pot, a slightly larger samovar (heated on a spirit stove) to keep extra water hot, a jug for milk or cream, and a lidded sugar bowl. The service is highly utilitarian, made of metal, so the pot would stay warm for longer, and a little lid over the spout of the samovar enabled you to keep the water boiling at any time. Yet it is also made of the best quality materials.

Silver has been beaten into shape, using a hammer wielded by hand rather than a production-line technique, emphasising the materiality and the man-made aspect of the vessels. Red cabochon gemstones, shaped and polished to retain their natural forms rather than faceted, have been applied in exquisite finishes to the edges of the stove and the lids of the samovar, tea pot and sugar bowl, so that these can easily be lifted up with one finger. They make a strong visual contrast with the beaten silver surface, and the black ebony that tops the gems and covers the handle of the samovar. Each object is decorated with the initials of the commissioner – AB – applied in silver wire on top of the beaten metal. The elegant angular forms of the lettering match the cubes and squares of the vessels – and indeed of the Secession Building itself.

There is nothing complicated or worrying about Hoffmann's motivation for the Werkstätte. If, in practice, the workshop's products were restricted to those who were sufficiently wealthy to pay for them, there was nothing to stop them being made out of less pricey materials so that a wider demographic to own and use them. These were functional, beautiful objects, and no disquiet could be attached to them.

The Kiss

The Kiss, by Klimt, is by far the most popular work in Vienna's Belvedere Gallery. It may even be the most famous single piece of art in Vienna. Like many teenagers of my generation, I loved *The Kiss*. I had a crumpled postcard stuck to my wall with Blu Tack. I took it with me to university, where I discovered many of my female peers were attracted by the same image. We never discussed it – it seemed too personal – but I expect that, like me, they found it sensual and exciting. The kiss itself was idealised, made into a ritual, highly stylised and very separate from reality. More than this, I was drawn to the face of the woman, inexplicably frozen in ecstasy. This was as much for the colours and the textures as what the picture represented.

In *The Kiss*, a man and a woman are entwined together, in a pose that is as uncomfortable as it is erotic, in front of a golden form composed of swirling circles. This resembles the halo or aureole that often surrounds sacred figures in Christian and Buddhist art. The woman is kneeling on what appears to be a grassy field covered with purple, blue and yellow spring flowers. Her feet curl uncomfortably around the edge of the meadow, jutting into a background (is it a sky?) in gold paint and leaf. There is nothing naturalistic here. The flowers of the meadow are blobs of paint, resembling the details of a medieval millefiori tapestry, cloisonné enamel work or the individual tesserae of a mosaic. Together they form a beautiful, organic decorative pattern.

The couple's bodies are covered, but their clothing, if that is what it is, is very unusual. The man is swathed in a shapeless, mainly golden garment that covers all but his neck, head and hands, and which is criss-crossed with differently sized rectangles of grey, black, white, brown and gold, together with swirling circular forms that are commonly found across *Jugundstil* ('youthful style') or art nouveau art. He reaches around to clasp and to protect the woman. Her body is lithe and slim. She too wears a golden robe adorned with splashes of colour, which on closer inspection are flowers. They are more stylised than the white and blue petals, with roughly painted green leaves, that adorn her reddish-gold hair. While the man's clothing is shapeless, hers carefully follows the contours of her body. Her shoulders are bare. One hand clasps the man's, slipping under the folds of his robe, as it if is the coverlet they are sleeping under together. Her other hand is elegantly stretched around his neck.

The Kiss is a moment of ecstasy and metamorphosis. It takes the couple – who may be Klimt and his long-term lover, the fashion designer Emilie Flöge – out of their earthly existence into a dream-like world. Klimt presents them as gods. A European looking at this picture might think of the myth of Danaë, who although locked in a tower by her father was able to make love with Zeus, transformed into a shower of gold. Yet there is something unsettling in this dream-world. The tiny, vulnerable woman could be being protected by the man. But it could also be read as control. His body is hidden, while hers is on show. She would find it difficult to break out of his arms. For all the beauty of the work, it is often more than a little disturbing. Accusations of pornography were made against Klimt from the earliest days of the Secession. Whatever the truth of these – and there is probably no way of ever completely knowing – it isn't impossible to deny the erotic motivation of much of his work. Sexual subjects, like *The Kiss*, encouraged him to produce some of his very finest paintings and drawings.

Egon Schiele

A different approach to the erotic, more shocking for contemporaries, can be found in Egon Schiele's work. Schiele's career was exceptionally short. He died at the age of twenty-eight, in October 1918, three days after his pregnant wife, Edith Harms. They were victims of influenza, in the worst month of the last pandemic before Covid-19. Spanish flu particularly targeted the young and healthy. Many, like Egon and Edith, died suddenly, with little warning.

The myth of Schiele the tortured, neurotic, stigmatised artist is exacerbated by his early death. His was an exceptional talent, his work far rawer and more shocking than the refined and decorative *Jugendstil* of the Wiener Werkstätte, and even of Klimt. Schiele's brilliance as a draughtsman led to his acceptance, despite his modest background (his father was a stationmaster), by the Academy of Fine Arts in Vienna. Like Klimt, he found the conventional atmosphere stultifying and constraining, and in 1909, when he was nineteen years old, left the academy to form a radical group which proclaimed self-determination for every individual artist, the *Neukunstgruppe* (New Art Group).

Like many young artists, Schiele had no money to pay a model. Schiele's gaunt pictures and drawings often feature the exaggerated features of the artist himself. His sitters included his lovers, members of his wife's family, and prostitutes, as well as his patrons, wealthy industrialists including the Lederer family, who were such fervent champions of Gustav Klimt. But Schiele's angular portraits can be brutally and medically sexual. They are not always easy to look at. He shows naked men and women as they were, without an airbrush. Every spot and wrinkle, every abnormality is captured. Only sixty years after John Ruskin had been unable to consummate his marriage with Effie Gray because he was horrified by her pubic hair, it is not surprising that Schiele's drawings and paintings of naked, bony men and women in contorted poses, showing their genitalia and exposing their body hair, were considered both scandalous and unappealing.

In his early twenties, Schiele had moved to his mother's hometown of Český Krumlov in Bohemia with his teenage lover Wally. The town expelled him, troubled by his lifestyle, and by the example of corrupt behaviour his art and his studio practices could suggest to adolescents. In April 1912 he spent twenty-four days in prison, accused of molesting an underage girl. The charge was unproven, but he was convicted for giving children access to 'immoral' drawings, and endured the shock of seeing one of his drawings burnt in court. Thanks to the trauma of his prison experience, Schiele felt persecuted by society, going so far as to portray himself as the early Christian martyr St Sebastian, who although shot with countless arrows, survived. For Schiele these were truly the barbs of outrageous fortune.

Schiele's art was intended to shock, not so much for its sexual content, but for its realism. While Klimt's paintings take you into dreams and reverie, as unnerving as it may be, Schiele's art is of our world: gritty, frank, always questioning. It is frighteningly intimate, whatever the subject, and takes you into the private musings of the artist, and of his sitter. If you were painted or drawn by Schiele, you did not expect to be flattered. Sometimes this was cruel, but at its best it was unreserved, uncompromising and undeniably truthful.

These qualities are to the fore in Schiele's tender and loving drawing of his sister-in-law Adèle in her underwear. Although her outfit looks like modern gym clothes, this would have been wholly inappropriate clothing in any public environment in the

1910s. Adèle is wearing items that she would never have shown to anyone but her nearest and dearest, and indeed her sister Edith, Egon's wife, was not entirely happy about Adèle sitting for her husband. There's something endearingly intimate and attractive about this woman in a very private moment. Her messy hair is tumbled together on top of her head in a loose ponytail, and she looks at ease, but tired. She isn't in her best lingerie, but in garments that are comfortable and functional and ugly – a sleeveless green undershirt like a vest, black stockings and baggy white drawers pulled up to the top of her thighs. Adèle hugs her left leg in a moment of introspection and reverie, and looks at someone, presumably Schiele himself.

Unlike the Empress Sisi, or Klimt's woman kissing, there's nothing coy or hidden about her position. From a distance of a hundred years, there is something incredibly normal and modern about Adèle. She is a woman in control of her body, and the impact it has on others. She is also, it appears, choosing what is shown of her, and is able to show her body unrestrained by tight corsetry. It's worth remembering that one of the greatest innovations of the early twentieth century, so blissfully remembered by women who grew up at this time, was the liberty bodice, which had no boning and allowed children and young girls to develop without constricting their waist. We have come a long way from the Empress Sisi, her body controlled by firm corsets – even if that was her choice. In Schiele's work, all aspects of identity, including sexuality and desire, appear uncompromising and real.

***

Not everyone, by any means, felt comfortable with this viewpoint. While Schiele was studying at the Academy of Fine Art, another child of a minor Austrian state official was making the first of several failed attempts to be admitted to this gilded circle. This man sat the entrance exams in 1907 and again in 1908. He passed the first section, but reportedly failed to progress because his portfolio of works included too few heads. One of the assessors, taking pity on the youth, is reported to have suggested he try his hand at architecture.

The young man was Adolf Hitler, who remained embittered and disillusioned by his rejection by the Academy – and as he perceived it, by the city and culture of pre-war Vienna – until the end of his life. He drifted until the outbreak of the First World War, earning a poor living in Vienna as a jobbing artist, colouring postcards for sale, working as a house painter, occasionally living in a dosshouse. Hitler felt affronted and disgusted by the work of Schiele and Kokoschka, which was preferred to his more traditional offerings. Kokoschka was included in the Exhibition of Degenerate Art (Entartete Kunst) staged in Munich in 1937. Having escaped from Germany to Prague in 1934, the artist fled to London in 1938 to avoid Nazi persecution.

The topsy-turvy society running off the rails because of too much liberty, represented by Expressionist styles and subject matter, was anathema to Hitler and many others. In order to step back from the edge of the anarchy he perceived in the avant-garde of Vienna and Berlin, and the dissolute social order they represented, it would be necessary to go back to basics, to reintroduce control and subject society to a sudden shock. This was as true of society as a whole as it would be for art. The results would almost be fatal for Europe and for the world. It is tempting to speculate what might have been if the young Hitler had not been so out of tune with the intoxicating but frightening freedoms available in Vienna in the early twentieth century.

Louise Bourgeois, *Maman*

13

NEW YORK: REBELLION

1929–1970

From the middle years of the nineteenth century, millions of Europeans, from Ireland to Russia, left the Old World to escape (as they hoped) grinding poverty, discrimination and persecution. Landing at Ellis Island on Manhattan, they looked forward to a new land of opportunity. Here the new arrivals hoped to live the 'American dream' and its promise of 'Life, Liberty and the pursuit of Happiness', as the Founding Fathers of the American Republic had put it a century before. Some things about the United States were true. In the north, at least, there was the opportunity to follow the religion or profession one wished, and to live one's life in a bewildering variety of ways.

It *was* possible – and there were enough examples of success to make this credible – to arrive in America with nothing and die in a mansion. It was rarely clarified, however, that freedom included the full gamut of possibilities, rags as well as riches, and that many opportunities were only open to those who were white and male. The truth was that very few immigrants were able to translate their aspirations for prosperity and independence into reality. Most of the European poor who arrived in sight of the Statue of Liberty abandoned their hopes in the factories and sweatshops of Manhattan. They lived hard lives, sending money back to their families in Europe, often dreaming nostalgically of returning 'home' one day themselves.

Americans, too, still saw themselves in the light of Europe. You only need to read the novels of Henry James, Edith Wharton or Louisa May Alcott to see how American culture was in thrall to the idea that European civilisation – whether art, music or literature – was superior to anything home-grown. It was really in response to the US's involvement in the First World War that this began to change significantly. Americans had always developed their own cultural forms, but now they exported them to Europe and beyond. During the 1930s, North American cinema and popular music, from Fred Astaire, Ginger Rogers and Shirley Temple to Scott Joplin, Billie Holiday and Rodgers and Hammerstein, spread all over the world (Anne Frank, hiding from Nazi persecution in Amsterdam, stuck photos of Hollywood movie stars to her bedroom wall, like millions of other adolescent girls).

The 1930s, 40s and early 50s were a period of profound change for most Americans. The prosperity and hedonism of the 1920s ended in the stock market crash of 1929. And although the impact of the Great Depression was felt across the world's industrialised economies, it was undeniably cata-strophic for Americans, because there was no social safety net. A quarter of the working population were unemployed – and more in some areas. Men who had fought in the First World War found themselves and their families on the street, or having to move across the country to find work. In the south, the Great Migration intensified; in the south-west, more than 3.5 million left the Great Plains because of the prolonged drought known as the Dust Bowl. And then came the Second World War. The United States, pulled by the Japanese attack on their fleet at Pearl Harbor into the conflict they had hoped to avoid, threw resources and people into theatres of war in Europe, Asia and the Pacific. Bruised and battered, the postwar settlement in these areas was based on the two pillars of the American dream, a free-market economy and a democratically elected government, financially and militarily supported by the United States. American forces were stationed to keep the peace in central Europe and in east Asia. The armed truce was also maintained by the threat of nuclear war. The mushroom clouds that rose above Hiroshima and Nagasaki in 1945, and the numerous test detonations by the US, the USSR and their allies, maintained a sense of fear across the world, despite the bright optimism of most American propaganda in the 1940s and 50s.

By 1945 the United States was an empire in all but name, and the dominant power of the non-communist world. America's military and naval superiority was matched by its cultural dominance. Young people in the 1960s and 70s, wherever they grew up, wore blue jeans, listened to American music, watched American movies and craved milkshakes, French fries and hamburgers. The symbols of prosperous, progressive America, including Hollywood, Disneyland, the Cadillac and skyscrapers, were familiar, and mostly envied, all over the world.

Just as familiar and just as archetypically American were another set of values: dissent and rebellion. The very persona of being a teenager, and rejecting the norms of adulthood, was a highly successful export. The term (first used in 1913) had been properly introduced to consumers in the United States in 1944, as a marketing tool to monetise the spending power of adolescents, and to heighten their sense of difference from their elders – and their anger at them. This potent combination of capitalism and rebellion made it a heady and sometimes dangerous mixture. The 1960s and 70s were celebrated for mass protest movements, from flower children and hippies to those rebelling against military intervention in Vietnam and protesting against nuclear weapons. The model of America encouraged these teenagers (a generation known as the Baby Boomers) to live well, but also – like the posters of James Dean whose moody image covered many a teenage bedroom – to be a rebel, with or without a cause.

The Big Apple

Most non-Americans see the country through the mirror of New York, and it houses most iconic images of America, including the Statue of Liberty, the Chrysler Building and skyscrapers. However, New York is something of an outlier in American terms. In the late eighteenth century it was briefly the capital of its state, and (more briefly) the national capital. But from the 1940s until the early twenty-first century, New York was the single most important city in the world. Most influential ideas, music, literature, culture, fashion and social attitudes hailed from the Big Apple. Nowhere was this truer than in the visual arts. A succession of rebellions and departures from the status quo transformed how artists thought and practised across the globe.

Some of the explanation lies in the topography of New York. Unlike most American metropolises, this is not a homogenous planned city built on a grid, but a collection of islands. The particular shape of Manhattan Island, and the rocks it is built on (still very evident in Central Park), has shaped the city. So has its evolution over centuries. Broadway, one of New York's most familiar streets, meanders through the city like the hunting trail it was for hundreds of years, before giving its name to the world's premier musical theatre district. Visiting New York is an enervating experience. You can feel the energy of the city in the air, from the incessant din, diminishing but never ceasing, even in the middle of night. Walking the streets, or even travelling underground on the subway, you sense the differences as you move between districts.

Partly it is the draw of New York itself, a city that like medieval London was believed to have streets paved with gold. Even today, in the age of mass air transportation, it remains the largest port on the eastern seaboard of the United States. Since the nineteenth century, it has attracted successive waves of refugees, fleeing economic or political difficulties in every part of the world. One reason, indeed, for the worldwide dominance of the New York art scene from the 1950s to the 1980s was the galvanising arrival of European refugees in the 1930s and 40s, including Arshile Gorky, Piet Mondrian and Hans Hofmann. Its reputation for openness, as well as the ability to hide and be anonymous in its packed streets and tenements, have encouraged many to make their homes here. Others have migrated for more positive reasons. For most of the later twentieth century New York was the city that almost everyone dreamed of visiting or settling in.

With people of every religion and identity, New York became a city of enormous ethnic and social divisions, symbolised by the white Jets and Puerto Rican Sharks of Leonard Bernstein's *West Side Story* (1957), a modern adaptation of Shakespeare's *Romeo and Juliet*, and of even greater disparity of wealth. In the 1950s the elegant penthouses and townhouses of the Upper East Side, where well-heeled plutocrats formed collections of the best art money could buy made a strong contrast with the warring migrant communities of the Upper West Side, the post-industrial wasteland of Lower Manhattan, the sweat-shops of the Garment District and the crowded slums of Hell's Kitchen and Chinatown. Harlem, north of Central Park, was home to the city's Black communities, migrants from the American South.

Downtown, the part of the city that the residents of the Upper East Side would avoid (except on their journey to work in the Financial District), became a series of centres of counterculture. Greenwich Village was where the Beat generation hung out, a loose group of writers including Jack Kerouac and his friends Gregory Corso and Allen Ginsberg. The name was coined by Kerouac, for those who were 'down and out' or 'bea-tific', favouring spirituality over consumerism, out of tune with the prevalent mood of optimism, imperialism and progress. Beatniks became familiar across the English-speaking world as those who rejected mainstream culture, and who considered themselves (often happily) outcasts from conventional society.

If you walk south-east towards Washington Square, and then down to Houston Steet, you reach the area known as SoHo (South of Houston), which became home to many artists seeking an affordable place to live and work. But artists also inhabited whatever part of the old industrial city was cheap, squatting in disused factories and commercial or office spaces that were down on their luck, from Chelsea in the west to Kips Bay in the east, and down to the docks of Lower Manhattan. Here the light was good, and there was enough room to develop their paintings, sculptures, installations or 'happenings'. New York artists pioneered loft living, now the preserve of monied professionals, as a pragmatic solution to their housing needs. Many of these areas, but most of all SoHo and the Village, are now commercialised and somewhat tawdry. It can be hard to sense the radicalism and creativity concentrated in these streets only sixty years ago.

Art as pop culture

Andy Warhol was an unlikely rebel, a lover of commerce, money, the rich and famous who was also a serial disruptor and agitator. The young Andrew Warhola grew up in the industrial city of Pittsburgh in north-western Pennsylvania. His parents were emigrants from Slovakia, and he was the first of his family to go to university. Warhol – he soon dropped the a – studied at the Carnegie Institute of Technology, and moved to New York to begin working as a commercial artist and illustrator. He was a talented, prolific draughtsman. It's hard to understand the transition from his light and frothy drawings – mainly of elegant shoes – of the 1950s to his trademark paintings based on newspaper ads and clippings, international celebrities like Elvis, Marilyn Monroe and Mao Zedong, and acts of terror such as execution in an electric chair, car accidents or plane crashes. These images are extremely famous. You might not know the artist, but you will recognise Warhol's images, almost forty years after his death.

Warhol's transition from an illustrator into a globally recognised artist was extraordinary. Partly it was the result of his admiration of his contemporaries Jasper Johns and Robert Rauschenberg. They made art based on everyday objects and concepts, from flags and targets to discarded furniture and ephemera, even rubbish. It was ingenious, and greatly admired – in 1964 Rauschenberg won the Grand Prize for Painting at the Venice Biennale. The success would have appealed to Warhol, who was always interested in recognition, as well as money. Warhol was unashamedly capitalist. He loved stuff, and delighted in enjoying the fruits of his labour, endlessly partying and travelling, and assembling an extensive collection of jewellery, decorative arts and folk art.

Primarily, Warhol's artistic shift and success were the result of his exceptional talent. He had an innate ability to innovate, and to evolve ways of expressing himself which were intelligent and easy to understand, using traditional art forms as well as film. He was a brilliant but complicated man who surrounded himself with entourages and cliques, his studio assistants and hangers-on, whom he dropped when they were of no interest or use to him, as well as the rich and famous. The clever and cruel 'fifteen minutes of fame' tag attributed to Warhol remains central to contemporary celebrity culture.

Warhol was the king of Pop Art. Pop rejected the individuality of art by reducing the role of the artist's hand. His studio, which moved through various locations in the rougher and cheaper parts of Manhattan, was called the Factory, with all the connotations of the production line, a place where art was made in multiples, and by many. You didn't need any art skill to work in the Factory. The Welsh musician John Cale, co-founder of the Velvet Underground, who Warhol supported in their early days, and who was one of the many creatives and social-ites who hung around the space, recalled there was always someone making a screen test, or a screen print, the Warholian medium par excellence. His 'paintings' are principally screen prints – a photographic image printed onto a canvas that had already been painted, either in a single colour or in blocks of colour which approximate to the main contours of the printed image. The idea was to remove the process of making as far as possible from the finished artwork, while still enabling it to be marketed as art, with greater financial value than a simple reproduction.

Campbell's Soup Cans, made in 1962, proclaims Warhol's desire to celebrate ordinary culture, to cock a snook at the 'established' subjects of art, and to make money. Campbell's Soup was a staple of the American post-war diet, in a culture of plenty that promoted ready-made food. Everyone could fill their bellies quickly and with minimal effort. It was the basic comfort food of post-war America, consumed by everyone, either straight up like Warhol himself, who had a can for lunch most days for about twenty years, or in increasingly synthetic confections like chicken crispy tray bake, created by 'labor-saving' housewives from the convenience foods of tinned soup and frozen meat and vegetables, topped with potato crisps.

Warhol's picture subverted painting as a medium of invention and individualism. The thirty-two canvases of the finished artwork refer to the '32 varieties' of Campbell's Soup that were on sale in 1962, from the pretentious asparagus and chicken gumbo to the basic vegetable and tomato (they were originally exhibited on thirty-two separate shelves so that they resembled the cans themselves). Warhol consciously wanted the work to look machine-made, as smooth and seamless as a print, so the pictures were created with a combination of reproductive techniques, including projecting, tracing and printing, as well as painting. He was working in an established tradition of twentieth-century avant-garde artists, starting with Marcel Duchamp, who in 1917 had elevated a factory-produced ceramic urinal to the level of art, submitting it to a New York exhibition signed as the work of 'R. Mutt'. Warhol signed the soup cans that served as his models, and sold them too.

Pop Art was unashamedly popular. Warhol and other 'pop stars' like Claes Oldenburg or Richard Hamilton took consumer objects from ordinary life – Coke cans, vacuum cleaners – and made their art in forms which shouted their everyday nature, and which everyone could identify with. Take the Coke can: as Warhol wrote, the same can was in the reach of everyone, from the homeless person on the street to movie stars, and even the president. By making such objects into art, you democratised art, and placed it in the reach of everyone. Whatever you think of Warhol and his methods, moving art away from the process of making to message, from the art school to the factory or the street, was a highly successful form of rebellion.

Abstract expressionism, action and colour field painting

For all the optimism of the post-war period in the United States, as exemplified in Warhol's celebration of consumerism, it was also a time of coming to terms with a changed status quo. From the late 1920s to the early 1950s, the country had undergone immense social and economic change. In the 1940s and 50s, progressive Americans were deeply worried by the threat of nuclear war, as well as the legacy of the Holocaust and the 'total war' of the Second World War. How could one continue to blindly uphold the values of 'human civilisation' when humans were capable of such abhorrent brutality and cruelty?

In such a world, it isn't surprising that a number of artists questioned how it was possible to continue to make art that was made with thought and rational principles, that reflected ideas and narratives, as well as the appearance of the human world, and which had a sense of public purpose. The loosely based group of New York artists known as the Abstract Expressionists – including Mark Rothko, Barnett Newman,

Helen Frankenthaler, Willem de Kooning, Lee Krasner and Jackson Pollock – were united primarily in their sense of moral purpose, their anger with and alienation from mainstream American society, and their conviction that abstract forms could convey strong emotional or expressive meaning. They rejected straightforward representation in favour of forms that everyone could understand, because they were abstract and not bound by convention or culture.

These artists knew each other, and sometimes they worked in close artistic and personal relationships. Almost unanimously, they rejected shared labels, preferring to see themselves as artists with common concerns and questions about how to make art rather than part of a movement. Nevertheless, abstract expressionism, promoted by the critics Clement Greenberg and Harold Rosenberg, was exported across the world. It was undeniably the most influential artistic style of the late twentieth century. Abstraction was embraced by Greenberg because it was the logical progression of modernism. There is more than some irony that an approach to making art which sprung from a revulsion with mainstream American culture became used as a positive expression of American identity.

Jackson Pollock is the most famous of these artists. This is partly because he became an unexpected media star, an updated version of the troubled genius that has been so popular since the days of Michelangelo and Caravaggio. Photos and film footage captured by Hans Namuth in 1950 show Pollock painting on the floor in his studio and on a sheet of glass outdoors, moving balletically around the surface he was painting. His arms and legs become as much part of the painting process as the implements he chose to use. A cigarette hangs out of his mouth as he concentrates. It helps that Pollock, as he appears in these images, was charismatic, intensely masculine and highly driven. But Pollock hated how he had been portrayed, feeling that it had misrepresented him and his technique. Namuth's attempt to turn Pollock into a personality contributed to the artist's spiralling descent into alcoholism and bodily abuse, culminating in a fatal gin-fuelled car crash in August 1956.

Pollock was not an easy man, nor had he had an easy life. His childhood, in Wyoming, California and Arizona, had been disturbed by movement and poverty. For all his talent and energy, he battled with a sense of identity and purpose. In the 1940s, inspired by the theories of the unconscious developed by Freud and Jung, as well as his own experience of psycho-therapy, and interested in the automatic drawing practised by European Surrealists, Pollock began to see painting as an expression of the human mind, of a moment in time. Around this time another painter, the native New Yorker Lee Krasner, came into his life. Unlike Pollock, she was at the centre of the city's art world, and she embedded him in this scene.

In 1947, Pollock developed a new technique which went against his art school training – he had studied at the Arts Student League in New York – and the way he had worked as a mural painter for the government-funded Federal Art Project in the 1930s. For centuries, painters had tended to work on can-vases that had been primed, or prepared with a ground layer of gesso or rabbit glue on which it was easier to paint. From the late 1940s Pollock chose to paint on rough unprepared canvas, laid on the ground rather than placed horizontally on an easel. He didn't use normal artist's paint, but enamel, the sort used for radiators or cars, sometimes thinned with turpentine, some-times sticky and viscous. Pools of paint contrast with swirled lines, like liquid icing, or other areas where the paint has been blurred or spread with the artist's hand. Pollock thought care-fully about how paint behaves, and the artistic possibilities this brought. Rather than using a brush, he poured or dripped the paint directly on to the canvas, sometime using sticks, a palette knife or his fingers to move it around. Sand, cigarette butts, nails and fragments of wood all found their way into Pollock's working materials.

This was an interactive process. The artist didn't necessarily know at the start where or how the work would end. Patterns of drips in one colour provided the basis for the painting, a structure or form on which the artist could riff. From 1947, Pollock numbered rather than named his works. This was to depersonalise the pictures, and to make clear his commitment to abstraction. A painting was like a piece of music. But, as he worked, it became evident that abstraction could be connected to something from the human world, as well as emotions or feeling. Take *Painting No. 30*, also known as *Autumn Rhythm*, painted in 1950. The colours of the work – muted tones of yellow, grey and black, on a raw off-white canvas – recall the end of the year. And the rhythm of the picture is natural, like a dance of leaves skittering in the wind, the colours of the deep night sky, or the flux and change of the weather. The swirls and organic forms, clearly made by a hand, contribute to the sense that Pollock's work is in harmony with the unconscious world. As he moved around his canvas, paint pot in hand, he reacted and adapted to the paint he'd already thrown or spattered on it. He made instinctive decisions about what to do next. Sometimes it's said we shouldn't be looking at Pollock's work on the wall, but although much of his painting was done on the floor, he always intended his art to be hung upright, in a house or gallery.

Pollock wasn't the only painter to be making material and medium the message of their work. The other transformative advance was made by Helen Frankenthaler, despite the

concerted bias that existed against women artists of this generation. Frankenthaler's own reputation was undermined by her
relationship with Clement Greenberg, and her thirteen-year
marriage to the Abstract Expressionist Robert Motherwell. Her
experience was not untypical. Lee Krasner, for all her brilliance,
was generally known as Pollock's muse and wife. And Anni
Albers, who with her husband Josef ran the hugely influential
art education programme at Black Mountain College in the
Blue Ridge Mountains, where many New York artists trained
or taught, had little public profile, unlike her (devoted) spouse.

Aged only twenty-three, Frankenthaler experimented with
letting paint soak into an canvas laid flat on the floor of her
studio. Inspired by Pollock – she swore an oath never to abandon his example – and watercolour technique, she thinned
her oil paint with turpentine so that it was absorbed by the
untreated canvas, leaving stains on the surface. She manipulated these by tilting her canvas and manoeuvring brushes,
sponges and rollers so that these naturally created shapes took
the form she wanted. This was the start of what became known
as colour field painting or post-painterly abstraction, where
colour, hue and tonality literally become part of a painting's
structure and materiality. Later in life, Frankenthaler wrote
that this had evolved, on 26 October 1952 to be precise, from a
'combination of impatience, laziness, and innovation'. But this
is unfair. She was ambitious, experimental and a risk-taker.

This breakthrough work, *Mountains and Sea*, is nine feet
wide and seven feet tall, and very loosely figurative. Charcoal
was used to draw the contours of areas of washy paint in blue,
pink and green. These represent the wild rocks, hills and water
of the Cape Breton coastline of Nova Scotia in Canada, which
Frankenthaler had recently visited. The painting records her
impressions of this landscape in a very lively and bodily way.

Frankenthaler recalled that as she worked, moving around the canvas and approaching it from every side, it felt like the landscapes 'were in my arms as I did it'. The result, with its floating fields of translucent and subtly blended colours, unashamedly celebrates beauty and also powerfully attracts the eye. There is something of the unplanned messy side of life that Frankenthaler had loved from childhood, once recalling that she had liked to pour her mother's red nail polish into the washbasin to see the patterns and colours it made. Like Pollock, her work developed as the outcome of long-held thoughts and musings, the marriage of her mind and her body, a personal interaction with the world far removed from bombastic and nationalistic politics. Frankenthaler could paint in the way she did because no one else had her wrist, determining how she held a brush or for how long, and no one else thought exactly as she did. 'I didn't know what it was until it was manifest,' she wrote of what she had done on the floor of her studio in October 1952. 'The only rule is that there are no rules.'

It was other – male – artists who capitalised on Frankenthaler's innovation. They were looking for an alternative to Pollock and de Kooning's more physical approach to paint. In early 1953, the painters Morris Louis and Kenneth Noland visited Frankenthaler's studio with Clement Greenberg, to see *Mountains and Sea*. This was the moment they had been waiting for. They went back to Washington DC and developed more abstract, austere compositions based on the optical effects of colour and tone in paint. In the 1960s, it was Louis and Nolan – not Frankenthaler – who were lauded as the leaders of colour field painting, which under the sponsorship of Greenberg (no longer involved with Frankenthaler) became the apex of painterly production.

For all the excitement that Frankenthaler's work had

generated, she was criticised for a 'wishy-washy style', and for her apparent lack of objectivity, in contrast to the perceived rigour of male artists. Her 1953 New York show, which included *Mountains and Sea*, was summarised by the *New York Times* as 'sweet but unambitious'. Frankenthaler's love of colour, pattern and decoration was belittled as a 'feminine' tendency, suitable for apartments, but not for museums. These sexist comments came from critics like Harold Rosenberg, who saw painting as a battleground between artist and medium, or indeed Greenberg's followers, who argued for more detached and objective art. Although Frankenthaler was the only woman of her generation to enjoy success throughout her career, she was, as the New York art dealer André Emmerich commented, always viewed 'as a woman painter and therefore not quite in the same league as the male heavy hitters of her generation'.

Despite this, Pollock and Frankenthaler's paintings are examples of a sea change in Western art. The performative act of making became as important an artwork as the final object. This approach could be applied to every type of artistic expression. Art moved away from its traditional forms of painting and sculpture, made as the culmination of an idea expressed and refined following extensive preparation, to much freer and wide-ranging concepts of what art was. If it was just flinging paint, what was the skill in it? Surely anyone could do it. It is true that we can all pour or soak paint onto a canvas, but only an exceptionally talented practitioner can do it well, and produce something as compelling as it is beautiful. The drip and stain paintings work because of the years of education, training and practice that had gone before them, by artists who understood the possibilities of paint and how to exploit them. The drips and stains aren't left to happen, but are shaped and manipulated by the artist. It's analogous in many ways to playing jazz. A talented and well-trained musician, able to modulate and vary the noises they make on their instrument, produces a performance which is never the same, no matter how many times they repeat it. In the same way, the paintings of Pollock, Frankenthaler and their contemporaries are never identical. There should be something depressing and dystopian about them because of their rejection of narrative and storytelling. And yet they are exuberant, full of movement, and often joyful.

Happenings and Fluxus

Inspired by these painters, younger New York artists sought to create a new type of artwork made from commonplace materials. But these weren't even radiator paint and sand, but chairs, food, electric lights, old socks, smoke, water. In the words of the artist Allan Kaprow, Pollock had left art 'at the point where we must become preoccupied with and even dazzled by the space and objects of our everyday life'. From the late 1950s to the 1960s, the avant-garde moved on, making Pollock's work on paper and canvas seemed old-fashioned. The art of this new generation was more than a rather insular and self-centred reaction to an individual's emotions; it aimed to become part of life. For these artists, art wasn't an activity that took place in the studio. It included events and performances that happened in the streets, in public spaces and in homes, and these could be as natural and normative as eating or sleeping. The audience were active participants, experiencing and shaping what went on, rather than passively observing. Kaprow, for instance, made a piece called *Eat*, which took place in a series of caves of the former Ebling brewery in the Bronx in late January 1964.

Participants entered through an old door, where they were startled by a man saying repeatedly 'Get 'em', and walked to a platform where they were offered red or white wine, fruit or freshly fried banana fritters. They climbed a ladder to a smaller cave where someone cut, salted and handed out boiled potatoes. They could also visit a small log cabin where they could pull slices of bread and jam from between the logs. All the time, their activities were accompanied by the persistent tick of a metronome, set at the rate of a human heartbeat.

Kaprow was connected to an international group called Fluxus, founded by the Lithuanian American artist George Maciunas. Fluxus is hard to define because it was in flux – the name means a flowing outwards – and it had members who operated across the world, but particularly in New York, Germany and Japan. Maciunas himself wanted Fluxus to 'promote a revolutionary flood and tide in art, promote living art, anti-art'. He was erratic and autocratic, expelling artists from the group when he took against them. But in essence these artists, whether they were in or out of Fluxus, rejected the 'mummification' of art galleries, concert halls and theatres in favour of streets, homes and railway stations. They were anti-establishment and anti-institution. Their art was closely related to music and performance. Many Fluxus associates, including the time-based media artist Nam June Paik and Allan Kaprow himself, were drawn to the electronic musician and composer John Cage, and his idea that you should start an artwork without knowing how it would end. Art began to be seen as an emanation of life. Everything was art, and Fluxus was involved in all aspects of an artist's existence. In New York, Maciunas took over deserted industrial buildings in the seedy downtown area of SoHo, establishing the (sometimes chaotic) Fluxhouse Cooperatives that managed work-life spaces for artists. Another group set up FOOD, a co-operative restaurant for creatives described as 'an artistic intervention in an urban setting'.

Perhaps the ultimate irony came when a long-term member of the New York avant-garde became increasingly close to one of the most popular musicians in the world. In 1966 John Lennon of the Beatles met Yoko Ono at the Indica Gallery in London, where she was about to open an exhibition. Ono, born in Japan but living in New York since the early 1950s, had been part of the Fluxus group for years, making works like *Painting to be stepped upon* (1961), which invited people to walk on a piece of canvas on the floor, or *Cut piece* (1964), a performance, first made at Carnegie Hall, where audience members could cut away sections of her clothing.

Lennon was reportedly nonplussed by much of the work on show at the Indica. It included a piece called *Add Colour Painting*. This consisted of wood panels with cut-out Perspex covering, brushes and paints, and was an open invitation for the viewer to have a go themselves. Ono commented on this work: 'It is very important to have art which is living and changing. Every phase of life is beautiful; so is every phase of a painting.' But there was an unstoppable attraction between them. Less than a year later, Lennon sponsored Ono's one-woman show at the Lisson Gallery in London. When she phoned his home, he explained to his wife Cynthia – whom he'd met at Liverpool Art College – that he was being pursued by a crazy artist. Nine months later they were lovers, and embarked on a succession of jointly conceived artistic creations. In May 1968 poor Cynthia returned early from holiday in Greece to find them in the family's Arts and Crafts mansion in Surrey, drinking tea together on the sofa. Yoko Ono was wearing Cynthia's dressing gown, and her slippers were outside the bedroom Cynthia shared with her husband. Within six months the couple were divorced.

In March 1969, Yoko Ono and John Lennon marked their recent marriage with a series of 'Bed-ins for Peace' in Amsterdam. They took a suite in the Hilton, on the edge of the old city centre, and invited the world's press into their bedroom between 9 a.m. and 9 p.m. daily for a week. The bed-ins were a protest at the Vietnam War – at the same time, marches and protests were taking place all over the Western world – and Ono and Lennon wanted to make an artwork which would draw public attention to the cause. In true Fluxus style, the couple, and Ono's five-year-old daughter Kyoko, made art, which was stuck on the walls of the bedroom, from paper, pencils and whatever materials were to hand. They also made music, and local celebrities and friends came to jam with them. The journalists, expecting something more interesting (the cover of their 1968 experimental album, *Two Virgins*, had, after all, shown the pair naked), were surprised to find the couple, sometimes joined by Kyoko, sitting or lying in the bed, modestly dressed in white nightclothes – 'like a pair of angels', in Lennon's words. There was something uncannily low key and quiet about this particular happening, created by the most high-profile couple in the world.

Internal rebellion

Artistic rebellion could be just as powerful and effective if it was internalised, without a blaze of publicity. One of the less celebrated twentieth-century artistic migrants to New York (at least for most of her life) was a young French woman who arrived in the city in 1938, newly married to her handsome and supportive American art historian husband. Louise Bourgeois, or Mrs Robert Goldwater, became the person that everyone knew – but the artist known to almost no one. Until well into the 1960s, thirty years into her artistic career, she was primarily considered a glamourous, charming appendage to her professor husband, raising their three sons and dabbling in art, like so many academic spouses. But Louise Bourgeois was no dabbler. Over seventy years she determinedly made a body of work that confronts difficult questions about her – and our – identity.

In many ways Bourgeois's whole life and art was a series of rebellions. Born in Paris in 1911, her family ran a tapestry restoration business. Louise was devoted to her mother, who never recovered from Spanish flu – one of the many victims of the pandemic of 1919 – and spent portions of her young adult life caring for her. In contrast, she and her father had a stormy relationship. She adored him, but abhorred his succession of affairs, including with the family's English au pair. In turn he raged at Louise for leaving Paris and the gallery she'd established with her father's financial backing.

But rather than being consumed by wild fury, Bourgeois channelled it into her drawings and sculpture. Her art is finely crafted and controlled, sometimes angry, other times malevolent, very personal, always stimulating, highlighting confinement, power, the unconscious and sexual desire. A picture of Louise aged seventy by the photographer Robert Mapplethorpe shows her with a laughing smile, as she strokes the top of her sculpture *Fillette* (Little Girl), a gigantic phallus with a rough head and over-sized testicles. The photo was commissioned for the cover of the catalogue for her 1982 retrospective at MoMA, but as Bourgeois recounted, the sculpture was cropped out because 'the museum was so prudish'.

Louise's marriage to Goldwater had been a means of escape from Paris and a family structure that was dangerously close.

In New York, ostensibly leading a conventional life as wife and mother, she found herself as an artist, drawing on her childhood and her own troubling experience of motherhood, when the mother is supposed to subjugate herself to her babies, which leaves little for herself. Like the Abstract Expressionists (with whom she exhibited in the 1940s and 50s), she was deeply interested in ideas of the unconscious and psychoanalysis, but her art developed along a different trajectory. Phallic, vaginal and breast-like shapes spring out of her art, sometimes in hidden ways. Bourgeois is a hard artist to straitjacket, and although her life and work intersected with feminism, she did not want to be described as a feminist artist. Her preoccupations – jealousy, anger, rejection – were shared by all humans, even if her means of expressing them was often tied to her gender.

The spider became a creature inseparable from Bourgeois's work and her identity. Like the artist, it is full of contradictions. In twentieth-century popular culture, it could be both friendly, as in E. B. White's children's classic *Charlotte's Web* (first published in 1952), or a chimera to excite and to terrify, as in the black widow, which eats her mate and poisons her enemies. Bourgeois's view was typically idiosyncratic. On the one side, she connected spiders, and their weaving, with her own artistic practice. Of course, many artists in the Western tradition, including Velázquez and Rubens, had done this before her. For anyone with a classical education, such as Bourgeois herself, the spider immediately recalled Arachne, the weaver extraordinaire who had the temerity not only to challenge the goddess Athena to a weaving competition, but to win. In the Roman poet Ovid's compelling poetic retelling in his *Metamorphoses*, Athena flew into a rage and destroyed Arachne's handiwork. When Arachne hanged herself in shame, the goddess finally took pity and turned her into a spider. For Bourgeois, having grown up in a tapestry workshop, where she learned to draw and make art, the myth had even more particular resonance.

The connection to the family business meant that Bourgeois saw spiders as comforting, maternal figures. Specifically she compared them to her own mother, whom she characterised as 'my best friend', writing in *Ode à Ma Mère* that she was 'deliberate, clever, patient, soothing, reasonable, dainty, subtle, indispensable, neat, and as useful as a spider'. But as a mother herself, she knew the downsides of maternity. Much of her work is concerned with articulating these irreconcilable conflicts and differences, the interchange between making children and feeling unmade – physically, emotionally and intellectually – by the process.

These inner conflicts are articulated in the almost ten-metre-tall sculpture *Maman*, which was part of the inaugural commission for the Turbine Hall at Tate Modern in May 2000. This huge steel spider, on pendulous legs with sharp talons, dominated the vast industrial space, making visitors feel tiny, insignificant and powerless. Despite her size, scale and solid metal, she is surprisingly fragile, with a delicate ribcage that looks as if it could be snapped, and teetering legs that hardly support her bulbous body. Standing under *Maman* and looking up, you see a wire sac of smooth, exquisitely carved marble eggs, seventeen in total, in white and grey. The eggs, and a series of breast-like bulges in the mesh, both singly and clustered, make it evident that this is a female, fecund spider, who both weaves and gives birth.

Yet this mother is eyeless and headless, perhaps implying her lack of interest in the world around her, including her children. She is beautiful, productive and orderly, but also potentially frightening, a creator of life with the power to maim and destroy. Bourgeois's *Maman* articulates the artist's struggles – familiar to every mother, particularly of young children – with maternity, the demands it imposes, and the feeling of anger it can bring, along with the very human desire even as a mature woman to still have a nurturing, comforting mother oneself. This powerful and disquieting work, made by someone who only had a respected voice at the end of her life, is emblematic of one of the most important but incomplete rebellions of mid-twentieth-century America, waged by women against a conservative and patriarchal society.

Social rebellion and commentary

The other incomplete social change, in a city housing the world's diaspora, was that of race equality. For all the twentieth century, New York was a multicultural city, on the one hand vibrant, but also full of inevitable tensions and inequalities, as migrants – Black, Irish, Italian, Polish, Puerto Rican – tended to live in separate communities. The interfaces between these areas were often troubled. The difficulties experienced by incomers to New York, particularly by African Americans, finds one of its most powerful expressions in Jacob Lawrence's *Migration Series*, a group of sixty small painted panels made in the early 1940s. Although paintings from this work were the first objects by a Black American artist to enter MoMA's collection, it was only in the 2000s that they became a regular part of the MoMA gallery experience.

The Great Migration had been a mass act of rebellion, of refusing to put up with a situation that was untenable. More than six million Black Americans, the descendants of enslaved peoples, left the southern states to which their ancestors had been forcibly transported, for the Midwest and the north-east between 1910 and 1970. The north was not perfect. *Migration Series* documents race riots, discrimination and segregation, the poor housing of the migrants, their unsanitary conditions, the dangerous factories, railways and laundries where many of them worked, and their vulnerability to tuberculosis and other serious illnesses. But it also shows voting, education, better food and the spiritual and cultural sustenance provided by churches.

Lawrence drew extensively on his experiences as a child in the northern cities to animate his series. As he recalled in the 1990s, 'My family was part of that migration.' His mother Rosa, a domestic worker from Virginia, and father Jacob, a railway cook from South Carolina, had moved to Atlantic City in New Jersey, where their son Jacob was born in 1917. When his parents separated, Jacob and his siblings stayed with their mother, moving first to Philadelphia, where Lawrence lived in a foster home when his mother needed to leave the city to find work, and latterly to Harlem in the north of Manhattan Island. Harlem had been developed in the late nineteenth century as an exclusive suburb of elegant brownstone town-houses set along wide avenues for wealthy New Yorkers. When they moved further out of the city to the peace and space of the suburbs, migrant communities moved in. By the 1910s the neighbourhood was home to tens of thousands of Black Americans.

Lawrence's family integrated into Harlem life by that most traditional of routes, the church. Attending community work-shops at the Utopia Children's House, an urban settlement intended to serve the needs of Black working women, Lawrence came to the attention of the visionary painter Charles Alston. Under Alston's wing, he developed as an artist at the Harlem Art Workshop and in a corner of Alston's studio. Inspired by a lecture by the self-taught historian Charles Seifert at the Harlem YMCA on African history, Lawrence, still only twenty years old, and hired as a painter (like Jackson Pollock) for President Roosevelt's Federal Art Project, decided to focus his attention on history painting, traditionally one of the most respected genres of Western art.

Lawrence tackled the biographies of key figures of African American history in the Caribbean and the United States – Haitian revolutionary Toussaint Louverture, abolitionist Frederick Douglass and Harriet Tubman, leader of the Underground Railroad – in small groups of paintings. In 1940, with a grant from the Julius Rosenwald Fund that supported Black creatives, he turned his attention to an even more ambitious theme, the 'Migration of the Negro', that had shaped his life, and those of so many of his contemporaries. Thanks to the grant he was able to rent a studio space large enough to work concurrently on the sixty paintings he had envisaged.

Lawrence's vision was to create a group of works which together told a compelling story of the Great Migration. Each of the individual paintings is tiny, but together they have a cinematic quality. Lawrence worked on the captions, identifying the theme for each work before turning to paint. The paintings, first exhibited at the Edith Halpert Gallery in 1942, made a sensation. Twenty-six were published as a portfolio in *Fortune* magazine – unprecedented exposure for a Black American artist. And in that year the entire series was purchased by two prestigious public galleries, the Museum of Modern Art in New York and the Phillips Collection, Washington DC.

The pictures chart the reasons why African Americans left the South – the needs of northern industry and the persuasive powers of labour agents, crop failure, lynchings, discrimination, lack of educational opportunities, as well as love and wishing to do the best possible for one's family. Although New York was better than what the migrants had left behind, Lawrence does not shy away from the difficult conditions in their new homes. Interviewed late in life, he remembered his sources had been varied. Books from the library, for sure, but more importantly, the street orators and the newspapers of his Harlem youth. As Lawrence remembered it, they had been full of tales of brutality against Black Americans. Another source, more potent and powerful, were his own memories. He recalled that in childhood there was always a new family who had recently arrived from the South, and efforts were made to help them, finding clothes for the much colder north, and coal for the furnace.

Lawrence's small paintings are very powerful. They are pared down and ostensibly simple, remarkable for their narrative focus, clear outlines and strong contrasting colours. Repeated visual tropes return. The first and final pictures show a crowded railway platform. As Lawrence's caption to the final painting in the series states, 'And the migrants kept coming'. Everything, yet nothing, had changed. For at least another thirty years after the series was first exhibited, millions of Black Americans chose to leave their homes in the southern states for the northern industrial centres. In 1900, only 8 per cent lived above the Mason–Dixon Line. Seventy years later, nearly 50 per cent lived in the north.

The people of 'And the migrants kept coming' could be anywhere. There is no sense of a particular place. The implication, of course, is that this is impersonal because this was happening everywhere, simultaneously, across the American South. Small children, even babies, and large suitcases line the platform edge. Behind stand serried ranks of men and women, smartly clothed. The outline, almost abstract colours give a sense of uniformity to the migrants; green and black are punctuated with occasional accents of red, yellow and turquoise, with even more infrequent white. These strong blocks of colour, contrasting with the washy brown-grey lines of the platform, rails and station, emphasise the vitality and dynamism of the migrants. Their faces are blank, as in all of Lawrence's series, accentuating our sense of the huge numbers who felt they had no choice but to leave their homes.

***

New York's legacy of challenging every norm means that we will never have a consistent view of its period of greatest artistic change and revolution. As the innovations of the Abstract Expressionist, Pop and Fluxus artists gained in fame and success, the styles and conventions of their most celebrated practitioners were exported around the globe. The American cultural domination of the West ensured that art students across Europe, Asia and the Americas produced local versions of the fashionable art of twentieth-century New York. Yet its art scene was neither homogeneous nor full of commercially successful artists. Lawrence and Bourgeois – one because of their race, the other because of their child-bearing – really only became names to conjure with later in their lives. Lawrence is still a painter far less known than he should be. Gender, race and privilege remain significant barriers to understanding and appreciating the artistic legacy of late twentieth-century New York, as they are for the city's living artists. Rage and rebellion, channelled through conviction and self-belief, continue to give New York's artistic community a particular dynamism and purpose.

Aerial view of the city of Brasília and Lake Paranoa

14

BRASÍLIA: LOVE

1956–1980

In almost every part of the world, the 1950s were perceived as a decade of progress. After the horrors of the Second World War, individuals, regions and nations proclaimed their desire to build a better world. This was as true of dictatorships as democracies. From the English Midlands to Taiwan, from the Punjab to the Russian steppes, new urban plans and cities were envisaged. A love for the modern was often combined with contempt for the old. Across the industrial cities of Europe, terraced housing, considered unhygienic, dirty and cramped, was razed to the ground and replaced with new purpose-built estates of flats, connected by walkways, lifts and landscaped grounds, intended to give families the means of living both as nuclear units and within a wider community. Many were on previously undeveloped greenfield sites, creating neighbourhoods from scratch. Their creators believed that with bricks and mortar (or, more accurately, concrete), they would bind individuals, families and communities together, radiating fellow-feeling and love. From a distance of seventy years, the optimism of these utopian plans is palpable, wherever their location, whatever their ideology, and however they failed.

Building Utopia

Many of these cities were inspired by the theories and construction methods of the Swiss urban visionary Le Corbusier. Born into a family of watchmakers in French-speaking Switzerland, his canonisation as the principal architectural thinker of the mid- and late twentieth century was almost universal. The hallmark of Le Corbusier's approach was to provide the best quality architecture with the optimum materials to benefit the individual and the wider community. His ideas had such a large impact because of his leading role in the International Congresses of Modern Architecture, organised by zealous and influential progressive architects from 1928 to 1959. Each conference addressed a principle of the modern movement, and the most significant, in Athens in 1933, was devoted to the 'Functional City'. The Athens Charter, as it became known, aspired to banish the 'chaos' brought by the machine age, by recognising that cities shared four basic functions – transportation, work, dwelling and recreation – but that each city was different, by virtue of its particular geographic, environmental, political, social and economic circumstances. It was one of the most influential documents of the twentieth century, having an impact on people's lives that could only be rivalled by war and revolution.

Through zoning, cities would become more efficient and pleasurable places for living, because each function would take place in clearly defined but inter-related areas. As the charter put it: 'The city should assure both individual liberty and the benefits of collective action on the spiritual and material planes.' Particular care was devoted to controlling the spread of industrial zones, and to prioritising housing in the best, or most congenial, parts of the city. This meant those areas sheltered from the wind and protected from flooding, with ready access to green spaces, good light and good views, separated from polluted arterial roads. The dwelling quarters should be near permanent and protected areas for recreation, making the best of whatever natural features the location had to offer, providing defined spaces that benefited the community, such as youth clubs, playgrounds, community centres and schools, and enabling everyone to spend 'week-end free time in accessible and favourable places', such as public parks, stadiums, forests and beaches.

Given that most of the architects involved were European, it is surprising that the most ambitious and complete 'Functional City' ever built was not in Europe, Russia or North America, but in Brazil – the largest, most populous, diverse and tumultuous country in the New World. This city, Brasília, aimed not merely to re-energise a neighbourhood but to transform the state itself.

Why Brazil?

Post-war Brazil was not the most obvious place to build Utopia. It was troubled, its political system uncertain and its population growing rapidly. The country was simultaneously home to traditional ways of life that had survived for millennia, rapid industrial development and the beginnings of agro-industrial decline, and its people included some of the very richest and some of the very poorest in the world. The complex character of modern Brazil can be traced to its conquest by a group of Portuguese adventurers in 1500. A fleet under the command of Pedro Álvares Cabral, sailing around the west coast of Africa towards the Spice Islands in the South China Sea, found itself (probably by accident) on the opposite side of the Atlantic. The territory, christened the 'True Cross' by its new conquerors, was shortly renamed Brazil, because of brazilwood, a tree found in the coastal regions that yielded a lucrative red dye. The new name tells you everything you need to know about how these Europeans saw Brazil. The land and its peoples were to be mercilessly and systematically exploited. Their only purpose was to produce goods and raw materials for use by the territory's new masters.

The local population was too small to serve the colonists' objectives, so millions of Africans were forcibly transported across the Atlantic to work on the plantations of Brazil. The country became a striking mixture of enslaved Africans, indigenous peoples and white Europeans. While the whites amassed enormous fortunes from the worldwide export of Brazilian sugar and coffee, their workers lived in dire conditions, deprived of liberty, health and even sufficient food. Because Brazil was a slave society for more than 350 years, when slavery was finally abolished in 1888 the lives of the indigenous and African Brazilian populations scarcely changed.

By the 1950s, seventy years after abolition, to be a Black Brazilian was still to be a third-class citizen. Although the capital Rio de Janeiro, São Paulo and the other cities of the south-eastern seaboard were increasingly rich and prosperous, they were also filled with economic migrants from the Brazilian interior and southern Europe who had come seeking a better life. The Black Brazilian migrants lived on the streets or in the *favelas*, slums of ramshackle shelters made from recycled materials, with no sewage systems, roads, schooling or medical care, while wealthy white people enjoyed standards of living hardly bettered anywhere in the world. The stunning natural setting of Rio, with Sugarloaf Mountain and the white sands of Copacabana Beach, threw this contrast into even starker relief.

This is perhaps most striking in Nelson Pereira dos Santos's groundbreaking 1955 film *Rio, 40 Graus* (*Rio, 40 Degrees*). Shot in grainy black and white, dos Santos's masterpiece moves between the slums and the tourist and business areas of the city. It is beautiful, prosaic and tragic in equal measure. Inspired by Italian post-war films like Vittorio De Sica's *Bicycle Thieves* (1948), and like them using non-professional actors, *Rio, 40 Graus* follows the lives of five young peanut-sellers from the *favelas*. All are Black or mixed race. It is pitiful: all these boys want is to earn a living for their families, and to own a football so that they can play together. Kind Jorge, who wishes to buy medicine for his sick mother, is hit by a car as he runs from a rival gang of boys. The film ends with a group of proud multi-racial Brazilians dancing samba, the syncopated dance style that has become a symbol of national identity, to music celebrating the abolition of slavery. It cuts to Jorge's mother, a descendant of slaves, alone at her window, and pans over the magical lights, hills and coast of the city at night. *Rio, 40 Graus* is fiction, but it highlights the best and the worst of twentieth-century Brazil: the joy, creativity and diversity exemplified by samba, and the crushing poverty and inequality endured by many of the country's inhabitants.

Into this mix came a politician with a clear and compelling vision of Brazil's future – Juscelino Kubitschek, who was elected president in 1955. Kubitschek came from a poor family in the prosperous south-eastern state of Minas Gerais. Through hard work and doggedness (his forceful mother Julia, part-Czech and part-Roma, taught him that 'a job begun must be a job concluded'), as well as good fortune, he became a doctor, and earned enough to make property investments that provided economic security for him and his family. From the early 1930s JK (as he was generally known) was involved in politics, firstly as a local deputy, then mayor of the state's capital city, Belo Horizonte, and subsequently as governor of Minais Gerais. Like many mid-twentieth-century statesmen, democrats and dictators alike, he wished to improve infrastructure, based on the belief that power generation and the combustion engine led to industrialisation, full employment and the improvement of agriculture and education. What distinguished Kubitschek from his peers was his confidence, optimism and missionary zeal, combined with human decency. He was a brilliant communicator, with a talent for a catching and convincing marketing slogan. Even his principal political opponent, Carlos Lacerda, admitted that JK was 'the nicest person in the world'.

In 1955, following the suicide of the former dictator, then president, Getúlio Vargas, JK won the country's presidency – although with only just over a third of the vote – on a utopian and nationalist platform. His 'Targets Plan' (Plano de Metas) was the basis of his electoral success. It set out thirty-one goals in the priority areas of transportation, energy, heavy industry and food, under the slogan 'Fifty years in Five'. It was not dissimilar to Stalin's successive Five-Year Plans, or Mao Zedong's Great Leap Forward. The intention was a Brazilian 'levelling up', linking the prosperous coastal cities with the isolated and impoverished interior. Progress was unexpectedly fast. First, the road network more than doubled; although ten thousand kilometres isn't much in a country of Brazil's size, it was a start. And, by 1958, the first vehicles with more than half their parts manufactured in Brazil had appeared on the roads.

Even more impressively, by the end of Kubitschek's presidency in 1961, industrial productivity had increased by an estimated 80 per cent. The average Brazilian's standard of living had never been higher. JK's motivation was to get labour-saving goods – from cars to fridges and washing machines – in the hands of the Brazilian people, and to provide jobs making these items for Brazilians, because he saw this as essential for the country's future. Industrial development would bring Brazil up the pecking order in the community of nations and make the country more than an exporter of raw materials. It would also begin to reduce the enormous disparities of wealth, living standards and social status that were the legacy of a colonial system underpinned by slavery.

In Kubitschek's view this was so important that it didn't matter if this was made possible by international capital. In the words of his economic advisor Roberto Campos, JK valued 'where the factory was', not 'where the shareholder lived'. Love him or loath him – and he remains a divisive figure in Brazilian politics – Kubitschek was effective, at least in the short term. But for his critics – from the Communist Party and trade unions to farm workers and intellectuals – opening up the Brazilian economy to multinational ownership was a disastrous move. He saddled the country with massive debt. His successor as president, Jânio Quadros, complained that borrowing had doubled from $1.5 to $3 billion (JK countered that he would have borrowed as much as $20 billion if it had got things done). Inflation rose by almost 50 per cent and the cost of living tripled during the five years of Kubitschek's presidency. And corruption was almost inevitable in order to achieve such impressive results in so short a time period. JK himself was accused of embezzling money while in office.

Brasília – an 'impossible Utopia'

Central to Kubitschek's vision of Brazil, where opportunities were open to everyone, was a new capital city. This wasn't a fresh idea. The concept and even the name Brasília had first surfaced in the 1820s, when Brazil declared independence from Portugal. And although the Second Brazilian Constitution of 1891 had committed to moving the capital from the south-east to a location closer to the middle of the country, nothing had happened, nor did it look likely to, in spite of the references in the 1934 and 1946 constitutions to the construction of a new capital. But Kubitschek was determined. On 20 September 1956 the Urbanising Company of the New Capital of Brazil – Companhia Urbanizadora da Nova Capital do Brasil, or Novacap – came into legal existence. The city was to be built on the Central High Plateau, in a location specified in the legislation as along the 15th parallel, between 47 and 48 degrees longitude. The site was settled because it was the centre of Brazilian territory, and could therefore connect the inner reaches of Amazonia with the rest of the country. This was literally in the middle of nowhere on a vast and scarcely inhabited plain – a semi-arid zone with scrubby vegetation and more jaguars than people. The political opposition decided not to oppose the legislation bringing Novacap into being because they thought the location would make Brasília undeliverable. How wrong they were. The city was built within three years. On 21 April 1960 (the date was chosen so that Brasília would share a foundation date with ancient Rome), Kubitschek inaugurated the capital that had seemed for many the height of madness.

Kubitschek had wanted to entrust the design of the entire city to the architect he most admired and trusted, Oscar

Niemeyer, and the engineer Israel Pinheiro. Both had worked with JK since his Belo Horizonte days. Novacap was led by Pinheiro, but Niemeyer convinced Kubitschek to run an open competition to choose the urban plan. This was judged by a panel which included internationally recognised planners, as well as Niemeyer himself. It was possibly also at Niemeyer's instigation that Le Corbusier wrote in 1955 to the Brazilian government, informing them of his willingness to create a 'Pilot Plan' for the new capital, as he had done for Bogotá in Colombia. Although this offer was not accepted, the nomenclature stuck. The subsequent architectural competition was called the National Competition for the Pilot Plan for the New Capital of Brazil (today the Pilot Plan is what the city's inhabitants call the original buildings of Brasília). The task for the competing architects was deceptively simple. They were requested to provide a basic layout of Brasília, indicating how they would arrange the principal elements of the city, the location of these sectors and how they would interconnect, and the distribution of open spaces and lines of communication, to the scale of 1:25,000, together with a supporting report.

With one dissenting voice (another Brazilian), the panel agreed to award the competition to Niemeyer's mentor and long-standing friend Lúcio Costa. Born in France to Brazilian parents, Costa had returned to South America in adolescence. In 1930, he was appointed head of the Art Academy in Rio, where he introduced modernist architecture, including the ideas of Le Corbusier, to the curriculum. Although his tenure was short, his students included a young Oscar Niemeyer. From the late 1930s, Costa headed up Brazil's nascent heritage architectural service, concerned to preserve indigenous and vernacular buildings. He argued that the globalisation of the 1920s, especially the spread of Hollywood cinema, had produced superficial structures in 'pseudo' styles – the castle, the hacienda – that were destroying Brazilian vernacular architecture. He valued architecture, however modest – like the verandas at the front of most houses – rooted in everyday life, adapted to the local climate and incorporating Brazilian traditions, whether Portuguese colonialist or indigenous. Local building styles were, in Costa's eyes, more aligned to the modern architecture that he admired than the pretentious 'fake' structures.

We can see this combination of local tradition and modernity in the Ministry of Education and Health in Rio, built between 1937 and 1943. Costa assembled a young team, including Niemeyer, with Le Corbusier as consultant, to design and build a major public building that was to be both Brazilian and very modern. In some ways it is a classic Corbusian highrise, elevated on piles (*pilotis*), built of concrete and glass, with sun shades (*brises-soleils*) and strong sculptural elements, such as the curved blue structures that hide the water tanks and lift machinery on the roof. But it has been successfully adapted to meet local needs and to reflect local traditions. The sun shades, for instance, are adjustable, and built in as architectural features on every north-facing window, to deal with the strength of the tropical sun. Traditional Portuguese Brazilian blue and white tiles (*azulejos*) were used for the abstract wall murals, and local Rio grey granite – in contrast to the imported stone used for many of the city's public buildings – faces the sides.

The Ministry of Education and Health and the Pilot Plan for Brasília express Costa's conviction that good buildings and urban design are engines of positive moral and social change. The town planner 'must be imbued with a certain dignity and nobility of purpose'. From this integrity will spring a sense of 'order, fitness and proportion' that confers 'real monumentality' upon the city and its architecture. Costa's plan for Brasília was both practical and aesthetic. Considerations of drainage, transportation, power distribution and sewage were paramount. Fundamentally, however, it reflected a belief that beauty and aesthetics, if in tune with the spirit of a place, shape and improve the lives of the people who live and work there. Consequently, the design of Costa's Pilot Plan consciously melded Brazilian history with modernity. Brazil, 'Land of the True Cross', was in the 1950s an overwhelmingly Catholic country. The axes that cross at right angles at the centre of the Pilot Plan were explicitly compared by Costa to the cross on which Christ was crucified, as well as 'the initial gesture of someone designating a place and taking possession of it'. But as a whole, Brasília was conceived in the shape of an aeroplane, a powerful, optimistic symbol of the future and of progress. The new city would be 'capital of the highways and skyways' – transporting the nation in the right direction.

The wings, along the horizontal axis, were to be the residential quarters. The cockpit and fuselage – those elements that hold the living spaces together – are what Costa called the 'monumental radial artery'. Here would be placed the civic and administrative centre of the new capital, the government offices, the military barracks, the railway station and the cultural buildings, as well as 'lungs' provided by botanical and zoological gardens. With good government, exercised in good buildings, Brasília would literally take flight, leading the country 'on a route to an impossible Utopia'. Using words and ideas that would have been familiar to Romans of the first century BCE, Costa argued that the new city had to be more than a 'mere organic identity' (*urbs*) but a community of citizens (*civitas*), with 'the virtues and attributes appropriate to a true capital city'. To function, this capital must be no technocratic machine, but a place 'of vitality and charm, conducive to reverie and intellectual speculation', a beacon of culture, positively shaping a nation. A few years after its inauguration, the city was described by Lúcio Costa as the interaction of four different scales: the monumental scale, the residential, the gregarious and the bucolic.

Building Brasília

In his memoirs, Niemeyer recalled flying over the chosen site with the new president:

> It was a huge and dismal patch of wilderness in the remote central interior plain. But, to my surprise, my doubts crumbled away in the face of his optimism. Everything about him was so clear and transparent, his vision and determination were so contagious, that I was soon persuaded that in a couple of years our country's new capital would rise up from this place at the farthest reaches of the earth.

The division of the urban fabric between residential and monumental areas was practical as well as ideological. It made it possible to build what were essentially two cities with incredible speed. The most important was the centre of government, intended to embody the idea of an egalitarian society. It was planned along a fourteen-kilometre motorway, a twentieth-century interpretation of the great boulevard leading into major new cities, as in Constantinople, St Petersburg or Washington DC. The major governmental buildings stretch along five kilometres of this avenue, what Costa called the Monumental Axis. The form and disposition of these structures were part of

Costa's plan. He did not believe in God, but there is something spiritual about his conception of the new capital city as the 'arch-secular dream of a Patriarch'.

The triangular Place of the Three Powers, a piazza at the heart of the city, was to exemplify the separation of powers on the classic eighteenth-century democratic model, between justice, the executive and the legislature, and their equality – and connectedness – as the principal organs of democratic government. Costa describes the triangle as 'an elemental form' connected to architecture 'of the most remote antiquity'. It is revealing of his ideas of democratic and regularised government – surely shared by JK – that the Supreme Court and the Presidential Palace are at the base of the triangle, and the National Congress, its members elected in Brazil by universal suffrage since the 1930s, at its apex. From the beginning, the Congress was intended to face onto a mall where parades and processions were to take place, and where space was also left for a cathedral.

The palatial seats of the three powers were inspired by traditional Brazilian architecture: the *fazendas*, low houses with their verandas, open to the world and with the excellent light that Costa had extolled in his paean to traditional architecture. The official buildings and structures of Brazil were intended to be open and accessible to all. In Brasília, the exercise of power takes place in buildings with huge windows and glass walls, surrounded by monumental columns and pillars that taper at the top, enabling viewers to see inside. No railings separate the public from these state palaces or from their activity.

The National Congress, both modernist and Brazilian, is in the central parkland of the great square of the three powers, beside a large reflecting pool. It brings Costa's urban plan and

Niemeyer's architecture together, as it stands in the middle of the two six-lane motorways that are the principal avenues of the city. The building's central plinth extends to the edges of these roads, seeming to touch them, making manifest the elected representatives' connection to the people they represent. The plinth holds two structures in white concrete that look as if they have landed from outer space, or have been enlarged from the sculptures of Brancusi or Barbara Hepworth. The shallow dome of the Senate and the inverted dome of the Chamber of Deputies flank two twenty-seven-storey towers, joined by a bridge, that house the administrative offices. A long ramp leads from the driveway to the National Congress, one part going to the entrance of the building, the other leading to the marble-clad roof. This was intended by Niemeyer to function as a public plaza, giving the people a role, not just their representatives. Security concerns, and a change of government, meant that this was closed off in the 2010s. Since then, Brazilians have taken to the roof and to the green plaza to protest, reclaiming the public space exactly as Niemeyer had intended.

The glass box of the Presidential Palace (Planalto) is surrounded by ingenious marble-clad piers that hold up the roof, but expand and contract organically, seeming to disappear as they reach the top. The palace floats like a spaceship just above the ground, with a ramp leading from the highway to the entrance. This is a building of ideology, expressed through its openness, placing the president's decisions in the pure light of the world so that they are transparent to all. Across the square is the smaller, more elegant Supreme Court. It is built on the same principles, growing out of a large plaza, itself supported by a glass structure, that rises from the ground. The façade colonnade supports the roof that shades the glass surface, reducing the entry of sunlight – sensible in this sun-baked region – but also making the building seem less fantastical, and more grounded in the realities of the world.

All of these public buildings were designed by Oscar Niemeyer. They have a pure, soaring form, like drawings translated into three dimensions. Because the site was designed to work over a long distance, from afar the structures look more like free-standing artworks than functional buildings. Niemeyer wanted central Brasília to feel as if it came from another planet, and certainly visiting the site is an experience that shocks and surprises. None of the buildings seem capable of support, they float in the air like feathers, or as if by magic, with ample space and light. They recall Baroque cathedrals, but even more consciously they are built on natural forms, inspired by sensual curves that Niemeyer admired in both the human form and the Brazilian landscape. If you think Niemeyer's architecture is otherworldly, you have to remember the astonishing variety of Brazil, including his native city of Rio with its constant changes of level and form. Bossa nova music, with its anarchic, unconventional beat, is the perfect soundtrack to Niemeyer's buildings.

Concrete was the material that made these fantastic and wild shapes possible. It was perfect for the circumstances in which Niemeyer was working. In Europe and North America, steel structures were the carapace around which concrete was added, producing rigid, angular buildings which can feel like mathematical equations rather than an organic form. Steel was rare and expensive in 1950s Brazil, but there were large numbers of labourers available to mix, pour and shape concrete. Niemeyer thus embraced the possibilities of a material that you poured, because it enabled the architect to suggest 'the curve, the free and different space'. Architecture had to be functional, but for Niemeyer it also needed to be grounded in its locality as well as in its purpose.

These ideas are perhaps most apparent in Brasília's cathedral, designed in 1958, and already partially complete by 1960. It doesn't seem possible that this building, with each pier like the poles of a tent, could be created from the gravity-defying monumentality of concrete. Sixteen white piers rise spectacularly from a drum. They are parabolic, and discombobulate because they grow thinner as they grow taller, culminating in a circle, the ribs radiating out in points, with thorns radiating from the top. Is it a crown of thorns, or a pair of praying hands? The genius of Niemeyer's cathedral is that both remain a possibility.

Niemeyer was an atheist, but his cathedral is a moving and spiritual space, dominated by the power of colour and light. You enter the cathedral from below, through a dark crypt which takes you from a tunnel underneath the square into the light. As you look up, around the building, your gaze is drawn circularly and gradually up to the apex. The deep blue sky, with clouds scudding across the high plain, emerges from behind the sixteen structural ribs. Even within the impressive context of central Brasília, this building stands out, although it is not particularly tall. It is on a plain square, alone except for four daunting and dominating bronze statues of the Four Evangelists and a simple white bell tower. An ovoid shape to the side is the baptistry. Niemeyer often took inspiration from fine art in his buildings, and it is hard not to think here of the strange forms of Surrealist artists, especially Joan Miró.

Separate from the monumental centre, Costa had envisioned

areas where work and life came together at the intersection of the city's two main arteries. In his mind, these were the perfect places for the offices of the 'liberal' professions: banks, commerce, shops and markets, as well as what is rather drily called the 'entertainment centre', for sport and leisure, with 'something in it of Piccadilly Circus, Times Square and the Champs Élysées'. There is a real mid-twentieth-century flavour to his surmise that the façades of the theatres, cinemas, bars and cafés along this strip would provide an ideal site for 'illuminated advertisements'. Hidden from this is the transportation hub – a clear point of Costa's scheme is that 'man and motor' must be kept apart. However, the city, as built, and as he recognised in his plan, depends on their co-existence. The car was so central to Costa's conception of Brasília that he called it 'a family member'.

One of the oddities of central Brasília, particularly for Brazilians, is that 'there is only the house and work'. There aren't beaches, streets or corners – all those spaces that Brazilians elsewhere in the country, particularly in the eastern cities, tend to congregate in. As the French writer Simone de Beauvoir perceptively commented as early as 1961, the public life of the city is lacking. 'What possible interest could there be in wandering about? The street, that meeting ground of … passers-by, of stores and houses, of vehicles and pedestrians … does not exist in Brasília and never will.' In response to this, the citizens have made the bus station – intended by its designer to be a service area not a destination – into one of the true centres of the city. It's crowded, lively, anarchic, full of small shops, takeaway joints and street vendors. It's one of the few parts of the capital that feels like the rest of Brazil.

A machine for living?

The Athens Charter had identified dwelling as the 'prime centre of urban planning', and the residential 'wings' of Brasília, divided by the massive roads that led to the Monumental Axis, contained all the functional requirements of life – housing, commerce, education, healthcare. Each wing was divided into nine bands, numbered 100 to 900. Bands 100 to 400 were the superquadratas, or residential neighbourhoods, on two strips on either side of the main city boulevard. Band 500 is a commercial zone, also including communal facilities such as doctors' surgeries and libraries. Bands 600 and 900 contain more specialist community services, such as senior schools that children from all the residential areas attend. Band 700 has terraced houses, mixed with blocks of flats on the northern side. Block 800, on the edge of the city, remains underdeveloped. On the model familiar from early Soviet Russia's dom-kommuna or Le Corbusier's Unité d'Habitation in Marseilles, some functions, such as childcare, were intended to take place communally within the blocks, rather than in each individual family unit.

Each superquadrata was conceived of four blocks of mid-rise flats, designed on a friendly, human and communal scale. None was more than six storeys tall, and because they were placed at right angles, in single or double rows, connected by groups of trees (Costa envisaged that each of these 'green lungs' would consist of one tree species), people would feel like they were living in a 'haze of greenery'. A typical block contained thirty-six flats, grouped in three sets of apartments around separate entrances. The neighbourhoods were self-sufficient but connected, in what Costa called 'a linked series'. Each was meant to have its own services, including shops, schools for children, a community club, libraries, churches, swimming pools, playgrounds and doctors' surgeries, a petrol station and a police and first aid station, and to be linked by pedestrian paths and walkways to the neighbouring group of blocks. They were owned by the government, and rented to its employees.

Block 308 Sul, the 'show superquadrata', was built for employees of the Bank of Brazil, by architects hired directly by the bank. Constructed according to Costa's specifications and to Niemeyer's plan, it is a vision of a modernist paradise. Like the other blocks, it is made of concrete slabs. The public areas of the buildings have pure and simple lines, with black reflective floors and white walls, some covered in tiles, and it's easy to move from inside to outdoors. Despite the heat of the Brazilian high plain, the spaces feel cool and refreshing. The buildings are well ventilated, and the bright light is filtered out. On one side, windows in black frames are built directly into the wall. The other side of the building has open lattices of concrete, called *cobogos*, allowing for controlled ventilation. The *pilotos* at ground level mean that everyone could walk from block to block, and enjoy the communal gardens landscaped in sculptural shapes by Roberto Burle Marx, a long-time collaborator of Costa and Niemeyer, who had worked with them long ago on the Ministry of Education and Health in Rio. A pond with a tiled base reflects the green of the trees, and the glass fronts of the flats.

A paradise for the few

These apartments and their environments are beautiful, calm and communal spaces. It's no surprise that they are still much sought-after residences. But from the start, they never housed the variety of people they were intended for. Many of the flats, not just Block 308 Sul, were designed for middle-class families who moved to Brasília to maintain their government or public-sector jobs. Like most Brazilians of this class they were privileged, and as a matter of course employed live-in servants. These maids were crammed into tiny spaces next to the kitchens, while their employers and their children enjoyed comfortable living and sleeping areas. Other domestic workers were relegated to the periphery of the city. From the beginning, it was clear that Brasília was more equal for some than for others. The optimistic vision of its founders was never deliverable. One of Costa's greatest regrets was Brasília's satellite towns – which would be required once the city's population grew above seven hundred thousand – had not been architecturally designed or rationally planned.

Why was this case? First, the speed of the build meant that corners had to be cut and ideologies curtailed. No time was lost in the construction of the city, as it had to be functional before JK's term of office was over. Building work started even before ink was dry on a design. Once the foundations were drafted, work would start. This was efficient, but it meant that decisions about structures, let alone details, were decided on the fly. And the pressure to build meant that the safest and most responsible procedures were not often followed. We will never know how many workers may have died in the haste to speed up construction, and whether – as has been said – some lie buried under the buildings made with their hands, or others were beaten and abused by draconian taskmasters.

The workers, called *candangos*, were conscripted from all over the nation to work on Brasília. They were praised as heroes, and were justifiably proud of what they had achieved. But the elegance of the superquadratas was not for them. Even while Brasília was being built, its outskirts included a stretch known as Cidade Livre, the free city, or the capital's Wild West. Niemeyer remembered 'a long mud-covered road packed with jeeps, horses and carts, lined with low brick buildings housing stores, bars, restaurants, clubs and the local prostitutes'. This was where the builders lived in dusty cities of tents, some way from the accommodation that was provided for the president, architects and lead engineers. The scandal continued once Brasília was open for habitation. The manual workers were either sent home or condemned to live in segregated campsites, not dissimilar to the *favelas*, on the outskirts of the new city.

Niemeyer felt strongly that his vision of Brasília as a utopian city had not been realised. In his memoirs, he nostalgically recalled the building of the city, when the workers, engineers and architects had been equal partners. They weren't building 'a backward provincial city' but one that was modern and of the moment, an expression of Brazil's importance on the world stage, and of the country's commitment to equity. To Niemeyer's dismay, this positive spirit did not endure. He wrote: 'On the inauguration day, with the President of the Republic, the generals in their full-dress uniforms, the deputies dressed to the nines, all state officials and their high-society ladies in their finest jewellery, everything changed. The magic was shattered in a single blow.'

Epilogue

Brasília, in the words of the journalist Otto Lara Resende, was the product of four men – JK, Israel Pinheiro, Oscar Niemeyer and Lúcio Costa – and 'of a rare conjunction of four types of madness: Juscelino's, Israel's, Niemeyer's and Lúcio Costa's.

Perhaps the city's oddity is best evoked by Clarice Lispector, one of the most brilliant short-story writers of the mid-twentieth century. Ukrainian-born, Recife- and Rio-raised, Lispector was simultaneously beguiled and appalled by Brasília, which she first visited in 1962. She creates a fantasia of a city that was actually the remnant of a past civilisation, inhabited in the fourth century BCE by blond giants and giantesses, excavated in 1960 like Sleeping Beauty's castle, emerging perfect and pristine from the earth. Lispector – presciently, as it would turn out – equated Brasília with the buildings of a totalitarian state.

Twelve years later, a decade after military dictatorship had been imposed, she returned to the city, and reflected again on the nation's new capital in the short story 'Brasília'. The place excited and terrified her in equal measure. It is stunning, first class. Everything is perfection. But, as Lispector writes, we don't always want the world to be excellent. We're happy and content with second best. Like Simone de Beauvoir, she found the city's perfection unnerving and anti-human. There is no room for failure, or for ordinariness, like local coffee bars. The everyday does not exist. She concludes: 'Brasília is splendour. I am utterly afraid.'

By this point, Niemeyer had long fled the country. For Zaha Hadid, one of the architects who most admired his work – and who had grown up in Iraq, another country with a complex and difficult present – Brasília was just a place with space for armies to drive through. In the 1980s, when democracy returned to Brazil, there were attempts to move the seat of government closer to the major population centres of Rio and São Paulo.

Niemeyer and Costa had wanted to build 'a city that helps others'. Sadly, Brasília can feel impersonal and remote, like a massive office block, buffeted by the seasonal winds that sweep across the country's central plain. It continues to be the city of the car: in the 2020s, at least half a million people commute into Brasília daily, to service the lives of those living in the superquadratas or in huge luxury gated complexes like Lago Sul around the city's artificial lake. A more common Brasílian experience is to be found in Santa Luzia, one of the country's newest *favelas*. Masses of houses, constructed from reused materials and corrugated iron, set along unpaved tracks, welcome about ten new families daily. These people come from the north-east, historically the centre of the slave trade and the agricultural estates. They live in extreme poverty, reliant on handouts from charities, and from private donations. Animals roam the streets; rubbish, sewage and water run everywhere. A vast rubbish dump, Lixão da Estrutural, provides income for two thousand families, but its towers of rubbish, ten metres high, threaten the water supply of millions of people.

The communal and equal life that Niemeyer and Costa hoped for is not always there. And in this 'perfect' 1960s paradise, preservation has been prioritised over people. Brasília's UNESCO listing in 1997 pushed more workers out of the city. Brasília was planned for a population of half a million, but today more than three million live in its metropolitan area. (It is estimated that by 2030 it will house 5.5 million people.) Brasília is far from perfect, but nonetheless it represents an ideal of love, respect and care for everyone in a nation, regardless of their colour, wealth or creed. It is telling that in January 2023, when supporters of former president Jair Bolsonaro attempted to overthrow Brazil's democratically elected government, they launched their attacks at Niemeyer's National Congress, Supreme Court and Presidential Palace on Costa's Place of the Three Powers. For all its many problems, Brasília still embodies the hopes, dreams and love of the idealistic men who founded and built it.

High-angle view of Kim Il-Sung Square and the Juche Tower

15

PYONGYANG: CONTROL

1953–2000

'It was a bright cold day in April, and the clocks were striking thirteen.'

With this bleak sentence, at once familiar and dissonant, George Orwell begins his celebrated novel of life in a totalitarian state. I first read *Nineteen Eighty-Four* in the autumn of 1989. At the time, I was studying the beginnings of the French Revolution at school. At home, I was glued to the TV screen, watching every evening on the news the collapse of the Berlin Wall and the Warsaw Pact. In 1989 it felt like the world was on the cusp of a great change – a moment as significant as 1789 when, as the poet William Wordsworth wrote of his experiences in Revolutionary Paris, 'Bliss was it in that dawn to be alive, / But to be young was very heaven!'

In 1989 it felt strangely comforting to be reading Orwell – his dystopian vision was one that, at least to my naive adolescent mind, had been decisively repudiated by recent events. But Orwell had written *Nineteen Eighty-Four* because in 1948 he could see that in spite of the fall of fascism, totalitarianism was here to stay. And he was right. As the first quarter of the twenty-first century draws to a close it's sobering to realise how many people across the world today live in countries where every aspect of life, public and private, is under state control. Added to which, new technology has made possible the surveillance of whole populations in a way that echoes the portrait of society Orwell envisaged in his novel.

The true *Nineteen Eighty-Four*?

No real place, however, is as close to Orwell's fictional account of London, the principal city of Airstrip One, as Pyongyang, capital of the Democratic People's Republic of Korea. It is the centre of an isolated state, ruled by a dynasty with almost complete authority over most aspects of life, from dawn to dusk. Pyongyang's inhabitants are woken daily at 7 a.m. by an alarm call that penetrates every dwelling in the city (on Sundays, their day off, the alarm is somewhat muted). Life at work and home includes compulsory political learning sessions; participation in 'spontaneous' processions and demonstrations is also the norm. The streets of Pyongyang are clean, empty, and carefully ordered. It is as if the people are subordinate to the urban plan and the architecture.

Everything, from how you dispose of your rubbish to how you spend your free time is regimented. Most leisure activities take place in groups controlled by residents' committees. Televisions and radios are sold locked to state channels. Mobile phone and Wi-Fi access, for locals, is restricted to a state network separate from the global internet. Clothing, hairstyles and make-up are checked by the officials in each block of flats or district. Many women wear smart outfits with modest skirts below the knee, like those of a 1960s Western office worker, or Korean national dress. Men wear workers' suits, familiar from 1940s and 50s images of Soviet Russia, with caps or relics of uniform from their years in the army.

There is some, but very limited, private enterprise and banking. People live in accommodation provided by the state and they do not (at least in theory) own property. Car ownership is still relatively rare, and people walk, cycle or use the trams, buses or metro line. Even internal travel, without proper documentation, is impossible.

Life and work in Pyongyang, the show city of North Korea, is dedicated to the maintenance of the regime established by the Kim dynasty. Devotion to the Great Leader, Kim Il-Sung, his son the Eternal Leader Kim Jong-il and grandson Kim Jong-un, the Supreme Leader, is an essential part of life. In fact, it has become the state religion. Education, in school, university and in later life, is focused around the god-like activities of the Kims, and in particular those of the Great Leader. No North Korean adult can leave the house without a Kim Il-Sung badge attached to their lapel. Time in North Korea, as measured by the Juche (Self-Reliance) Calendar, begins at the moment of his birth, and the Day of the Sun – his birthday – is the most important state holiday. On this day, you will see North Koreans, in their best clothes, processing to the nearest statue of the Great Leader. Only having paid him reverence, with an offering of flowers (ideally the Kim Sungia violet orchid, or the Kim Jungia red begonia), can their day of rest begin.

History

The Kim family's rise to power was surprising but absolute. In September 1945 a portly Korean communist in his early thirties returned to the land of his birth, wearing the uniform of a Russian army captain. Several weeks earlier the Soviet authorities had assumed full military control of northern Korea from the Japanese, who had annexed the whole peninsula in 1910. Under Japanese rule, Korea had become the second most industrialised nation in Asia. The Russians were looking for a Korean to head the puppet regime they wished to establish in this new territory, valuable for its strategic location between China, Russia and Japan, and its industrial wealth, which was mostly (at this time) concentrated in the north. This army captain, named Kim Il-Sung, was not the most likely candidate to become its leader.

Born on the outskirts of Pyongyang in 1912, on the day the *Titanic* sank, Kim had left Korea as a child. He had spent most of the 1930s fighting as a communist guerrilla in north-eastern China, and the 1940s as a battalion commander in the 88th Brigade of the Soviet Army. His written Korean was poor, and his personal appearance was un-statesmanlike (a dismissive contemporary compared him to a 'fat delivery boy from a neighbourhood Chinese food stall'). But his reasonable command of Russian, his North Korean origins and his undeniable military exploits meant that within six months he was the territory's ostensible leader. It was the Russians, however, who were pulling the strings. Every decision had to approved either by the Soviet embassy in Pyongyang, or the Politburo in Moscow.

Like the Americans, their former Second World War allies, the Russians were determined to establish their influence in the Korean Peninsula. A provisional line of demarcation between the Russian and American zones had been drawn as early as August 1945 along the 38th parallel. In 1948, two states were established – the Republic of Korea (ROK) in Seoul and the Democratic People's Republic of Korea (DPRK) in Pyongyang. Each state claimed to be the legitimate ruler of the peninsula, and although reunification seemed the answer, how was it to be achieved? Initially neither the Russians nor the Americans had any appetite for further conflict. But in late 1949, everything changed. The Soviet Union had successfully tested its first nuclear device, and its largest neighbour, China, was now communist. Stalin felt more secure. It felt less of a risk to allow the bellicose Kim Il-Sung to invade South Korea and 'liberate' its people from their American handlers. The gamble, however, was to go horrifically wrong.

The war began in late June 1950; by early August President Kim's optimism seemed justified, as the North Korean forces controlled almost all of the Korean Peninsula. The tables were swiftly turned, however, when a United Nations force, led by the Americans, repelled the North Koreans and their leadership fled to China. A massive Chinese military invasion of North Korea pushed the UN armies back to the 38th parallel. Trench warfare, and the indiscriminate killing of civilians by both sides, led to the death of perhaps as many as two million Koreans, mainly in the DPRK. Incendiary bombing razed towns, cities and villages of North Korea to the ground. In August 1951, the Hungarian war correspondent Tibor Meráy reported his impression of 'travelling on the moon because there was only devastation' and wrote that there were 'no more cities in North Korea'. In 1953, an armistice treaty was signed, establishing the Demilitarized Zone on the front line. This zone, which intersects with the 38th parallel, remains the border between South and North Korea to this day.

The result of the Korean War was to greatly strengthen

Kim Il-Sung's authority. He was no longer one of a number of Soviet-supported leaders, but the individual who had personally taken North Korea through the 'Great Patriotic War'. A wave of nationalism – ably exploited by Kim and his many propagandists – discredited his opponents, most of whom were either ethnic Koreans from the USSR, from South Korea or recent returnees from China. The Workers' Party of Korea was formed in 1949 from the merger of the two Korean communist parties, and led by Kim Il-Sung. In 1953, after the death of Stalin, President Kim declared himself Supreme Leader of the Democratic People's Republic of Korea. He began to purge the Workers' Party of those opposed to his personal rule.

Juche, the North Korean value system devised by Kim Il-Sung and strengthened by successive regimes, is based on national autonomy. It was explained by Kim Il-Sung in 1972: 'In a nutshell, the idea of Juche means that the masters of the revolution and the work of construction are the masses of the people.' It is people-centred socialism, emphasising independence and self-sufficiency. However, it was in that very year that the dominance of one person, not the people, in North Korea was confirmed. Kim's birthday – 15 April – became the country's main public holiday. From this time, statues of the Great Leader began to appear all over North Korea. Juche has become a state-sponsored religion, and the three Kim leaders are worshipped as its gods.

Hagiography

For over fifty years North Koreans have been taught to idolise and worship the President and Great Leader Kim Il-Sung,

Franz Xaver Winterhalter, *Empress Elisabeth of Austria*, 1865 CE

Gustav Klimt, *Portrait of Hermine Gallia*, 1904 CE

Egon Schiele, *Seated Woman with Bent Knees*, 1917 CE

View of the Maria-Theresien-Platz, with the Kunsthistorisches Museum, off the Ringstrasse, 1860–75 CE

Max Klinger, *Beethoven*, 1893–1902 CE

Josef Hoffmann, tea service, MAK, 1904 CE

Gustav Klimt, *The Kiss*, 1907–8 CE

Helen Frankenthaler, *Mountains and Sea*, 1952 CE

The Manhattan
skyline, New York

Andy Warhol, *Campbell's Soup Cans*, 1962 CE

Jacob Lawrence,
*And the migrants
kept coming,*
1940–1 CE

Jackson Pollock,
*Painting No. 30
(Autumn Rhythm),*
1950 CE

John Lennon
and Yoko Ono at
the Hilton Hotel,
Amsterdam,
25 March 1969

The National Congress, Brasília, 1956–8 CE

The Presidential Palace (Planalto), Brasília, 1958 CE

Cathedral of Brasília, designed 1958 CE

Housing building
of a superquadrata

Square of the Three Powers, looking towards
the Supreme Federal Court, Brasília

Soldiers paying respect to the two statues of the Dear Leaders
on the Grand Monument on Mansu Hill, Pyongyang, 2012 CE

Interior of a subway station,
Pyongyang, 2010 CE

A mass dance performance on
Kwangbok Street, 2010 CE

The Arch of Reunification, Tongil (Reunification) Highway, 2001 CE

Dancers in front of the rising sun over Mount Paektu during the Arirang Mass Games, 2012 CE

and the Great General his son, Kim Jong-il, who have made their country the strongest in the world. The Great Leader's whole life has been mythologised, from birth to death. He is often shown on horseback, in a pose that recalls Jacques-Louis David's painting of Napoleon crossing the Alps, riding on a white charger above the clouds. (In 2022, film clips of Kim Jong-un were released, showing him on a creamy horse, looking resolutely out to sea, trying to emulate his grandfather's mythic pose.) Kim Il-Sung's past was altered so that it became one with the revolutionary struggle. In a version of his autobiography, allegedly written in the 1950s, he recalls that, aged six, he took part in the infamous 1 March 1919 demonstration against the Japanese, 'the day when I witnessed Korean blood being spilled for the first time'. He also remembers being told stories of the October Revolution, and of Stalin and Lenin, at his father's knee. He is said to have punctured the bicycle tyres of Japanese officials, and torn up official Japanese textbooks. All this seems possible, if a little implausible. It is hard to know what the truth is, as reportedly the stories of the Great Leader are regularly revised, so that they attune with the current concerns of the party.

This is nothing to the god-like heroism imputed to Kim Jong-il. Mount Paektu, on the border of China and Korea, and the highest mountain on the Korean Peninsula, is said to have been where Kim Jong-il was born – according to some accounts, in a cave in the midst of the revolutionary struggle against the Japanese. Paektu is the sacred mountain central to national identity, particularly since the 1920s, when it became a Korean counterpoint to the Japanese Mount Fuji. Kim Jong-il's hagiography is Christ-like. The women and soldiers present at his birth instantaneously hailed him as 'the bright star of Mount Paektu', and news is said to have spread through the country and beyond of this wonderful portent, even reaching as far as Tokyo where Japanese officials apparently recorded a belief that this 'heaven-sent boy' would bring independence to Korea. Given that Kim was born in 1941 or 1942, when Japanese control of Korea was still strong, and eleven years before the conclusion of the Great Patriotic War in 1953, this seems surprisingly prescient. By the age of six, he is said to have been so brilliant that his mother followed his lead. By ten, he was with his father at the Supreme Headquarters, giving him advice on the progress of the war. His father is reported to have been so impressed that he gave him his pistol, symbolic of the ultimate transfer of power.

The little village outside Pyongyang which the family supposedly came from has become a shrine, where people bring offerings, queue dutifully to see the family's house and drink water from the well, even taking it away in bottles. Symbols of the Kim dynasty and representations of their cult are everywhere. Even on buses you will find handwritten notices with the Great Leader's statements. All over the country, images in the social realist style pioneered in the Soviet Union during the 1940s and 50s present the Kims as benevolent father figures. A golden statue at Kaeson (Triumph) metro station in Pyongyang, showing Kim Il-Sung addressing the people with elevating rhetoric, sets the tone. Sometimes the Kims are military generals, heroically enabling the North Korean people to achieve their independence; farmers, benignly supervising agricultural activity; or inspiring orators, bringing joy and prosperity to the lives of workers. On other occasions they are kindly, seated in parks, surrounded by flowers and by hordes of beaming, well-behaved and well-fed children.

The city as state

The personality cult of the Kim family has increasingly been woven into the fabric of Pyongyang. This city on the wide Taedong River is the capital of two of the most ancient Korean kingdoms, over two thousand, perhaps three thousand, years old. Its founding father is claimed as Dangun, the legendary god king of Korea, 'grandson of heaven' and 'son of a bear', who is reputed to have built the walled city of Asadal, near the site of modern Pyongyang (in 1993, North Korean archaeologists claimed that Dangun was a real person, and that they had discovered his tomb on Mount Taebaek, on the outskirts of Pyongyang). The only 'ancient' building in the city, the sixth-century Potong Gate, once the western entrance to Pyongyang and rebuilt at least three times, is deliberately used as the axis of a vista which leads to the futuristic Ryugyong Hotel, a sci-fi rocket-like concrete structure, incomplete but fully glazed, which seems to pierce the sky. The contrast between the bright future offered by the Ryugyong Hotel and the small, encircled and unimpressive Potong Gate is brilliantly deliberate. Here, as all over Pyongyang, buildings are used to proclaim the irrelevance of previous history, when contrasted with the progress and bright future offered by Juche and the Kims.

Many of the city's half a million inhabitants had been left homeless and an estimated 75 per cent of the built environment destroyed by bombing during the Korean War. For the new regime this catastrophe presented an opportunity. The old city was swept away, and Pyongyang re-imagined as a paradise on a planned grid, on the model of Soviet metropolises. The rebuilding was led initially by the Moscow Architectural Institute, making it clear who was really in charge, although Kim Jung-Hee, a founder of the Korean Architects Alliance, drew up the city's master plan. There was no issue with resolving who owned land, since everything was in the possession of the state, and the planners could do anything they wanted.

As a result, parts of Pyongyang feel more like the new conurbations in the former Soviet republics than an east Asian city. The winding alleys and organically shaped streets you see on maps and photographs from the early twentieth century were replaced with grand boulevards, straight lines and angular intersections (although the practicalities imposed by the river and geology, as well as the existing rail network, meant that some small vestiges of the former city remained). Most accommodation was provided by concrete housing blocks on the Le Corbusier model, but far taller. Each housing area was arranged into groups of about five thousand people, with shared facilities, such as shops, nurseries, schools and chemists. The inspiration is not very different from the superquadratas in Costa and Niemeyer's Brasília.

Pyongyang was rebuilt as a living – and changing – expression of state ideology. From the beginning, the street plan was organised in conjunction with the sites for major monuments, which dominate the city's vistas. The city is packed with monuments, squares and public buildings, axially linked and interlinked, so that you look, for instance, from the Grand Monument to the Kims on Mansu Hill on the west side of the river to the Workers' Party Foundation Monument on the east. Another axis takes you from Kim Il-Sung Square on the west of the Taedong to the Juche Tower, directly opposite on the east side. The connection is strong, and more powerful than if there was a bridge between them. Standing on parts of Kim Il-Sung Square, you are meant to feel as if the Juche Tower is part of the same structure, and the powerful and otherwise omnipresent river is invisible, subordinate to the power of the state.

The main boulevard, Sungri (Victory) Street, runs from the Triumphal Arch in the north, past the Mansu Hill monument to Kim Il-Sung Square at the ceremonial heart of Pyongyang. This is the largest space in the city, the site of parades and rallies, and capable of holding up to a hundred thousand people. Looking towards the river, at the top of the square is the Grand People's Study House, built using a neoclassical plan in a traditional Korean style, but on a grandiose scale, with thirty-four green-tiled saddle roofs. Study, while working, is a cornerstone of Juche ideology, and the Study House, completed to celebrate Kim Il-Sung's seventieth birthday in 1982, dominates the square. The pavements and roads are marked out, so that everyone knows where to stand on parade days. Kim Il-Sung Square reaches down to the Taedong River, looking directly over to the Juche Tower. Built from granite (there is allegedly a block for every day of Kim Il-Sung's life) and also completed in 1982, it stands 170 metres tall, a memorial to the power and ideology of the first Kim leader. At the bottom, three bronze figures hold the hammer, sickle and brush – the symbols of the Workers' Party of Korea.

Ideology and architecture are combined in North Korea. Kim Jong-il is even credited with writing a treatise, *On the Art of Architecture* (1991). Some of the text is standard Marxist-Leninist thinking: architects must reject bourgeois ideas, and their buildings must remain revolutionary. Other parts are equally hackneyed, reflecting what most modern architecture students would have been taught anywhere in the world; namely, that architecture is closely related to social history, and architecture must combine national sensitivities with modernism. The most interesting parts of the book explore Kim Jong-il's views on monumental space, as this is the template on which Pyongyang has been laid out. Space needs to have a focus point – for instance a portrait, or sculpture – which the surrounding area must not dominate. Behind this, there should be a backdrop that blocks off the surrounding building or landscape, further framed by a number of symmetrical elements, which achieve the essential balance of respect and dignity. This serves to concentrate attention on the focus point. The space must have one side open, enabling it to project out and dominate its environs, and to let people in, symbolising the future.

You can see this approach in the construction of many of the city's architectural set pieces, such as the Mansu Hill Grand Monument. Here, the focus has evolved from one enormous bronze statue of Kim Il-Sung, sculpted to mark his sixtieth birthday in the red-letter year of 1972, to two. A companion bronze of Kim Jong-il was erected in 2012, the year after his death. They are vast. Standing sixty-six feet high, they make not just ordinary people, but even the figures in the accompanying sculptural friezes (themselves over fifteen feet tall) seem minuscule. Both are shown as active, open leaders. The elder Kim is speaking, gesturing with his right hand, pointing 'the way ahead' and receiving the adulation of the people, while he looks directly at the Monument to Party Founding, a stone sculpture of three vast hands clutching the hammer, sickle and brush, on the other side of the river. Kim Jong-il smiles warmly, as if listening appreciatively to his father's wise words.

Father and son stand in front of a giant mosaic of Mount Paektu, the birthplace of Korean socialism, which itself falls away into insignificance before their superhuman powers. At the sides, two appropriately symmetrical and dynamic sculptural groups, representing Liberation from Japan, and the Achievements of Socialism, show the North Korean people moving to glory under the Kims' leadership. The vast square in front of the monument is normally populated by North

Koreans making their ritual bows. Visitors are obliged to buy a bouquet of plastic flowers and lay it before the statues, before kowtowing reverently to them. (Prudently, the flowers are recycled and resold.)

In the middle distance, sometimes hard to see in the city's haze, appears the Monument to Party Founding, flanked by two groups of residential buildings that echo the flags held aloft by the sculptural groups on Mansu Hill. This is imposing and striking, architecture as totalitarian theatre, intended to make the ordinary person feel small and insignificant except when part of an organised group.

Probably the most complete set of images is entwined in the fabric of Pyongyang's metro system, in its totality an underground monument to the glories of the Kims, the achievements of the DPRK and the natural beauties of North Korea. The murals and mosaics which decorate hallways and platforms emphasise the message that the underground was built 'with our own technique, our own materials and our own efforts'. It is a physical manifestation of Juche, although the model is of course not North Korean but the Moscow metro of the 1930s and 40s. The metro was constructed from high-quality materials, and is carefully maintained. The platforms are vaulted halls held up by columns decorated in traditional architectural form; beautiful multi-coloured glass chandeliers, reminiscent of the work of the North American glass artist Dale Chihuly, are suspended from the ceilings. It is said to be the cheapest system to travel on in the world.

Many of the decorations show the Kims giving guidance to the people and workers. In one, at Tongil station, Kim Il-Sung, shown in a golden aureole because he is the sun itself, watches happy North and South Koreans embrace each other in unity, under the North Korean flag. The hall at Hwanggumbol includes a painting of Kim Il-Sung beaming, his hands on his hips, in bright sunlight in the middle of a vast field at harvest time, which stretches out to the city and the mountains in the far distance. (He looks surprisingly like his grandson Kim Jong-un.) Two respectful workers, appropriately smaller (but still well fed), approach the Great Leader with a harvest offering.

At Yonggwang station, there is an enormous mural of Kim Jong-il in a 1970s parka, open-necked shirt and slacks, standing on an outcrop of land carefully chosen so that he doesn't just loom over the trees in the valley below him, but over the mountain range in the middle distance. Framed by the backdrop of the vast snow-covered peak of Mount Paektu, he is both friendly, smiling as he takes his leisure in the great outdoors, and approachable (dressed not in uniform or a suit but in casual clothing), although monumental. People, travelling to work or home on the underground, only go up to his knees. His superiority is evident. This is the benevolent autocrat and dictator.

These monuments are meant to look as if they have always been there. But they have evolved, in keeping with new times and preoccupations. For instance, the statue of Kim Il-Sung at Mansu Hill originally wore a Chairman Mao suit, but by 2012 he was in a more Western suit with tie. Kim Jong-il's overcoat became a parka, more in keeping with his reputation for being a man of the people, tirelessly giving on-the-spot advice to his countrymen for even the most trivial of matters. This is typical of how Pyongyang itself has changed, moving from a classic Soviet plan to one with more idiosyncratic elements that reflect the Kim dynasty's particular brand of authoritarian socialism as well as regional approaches to art and architecture.

North Korean architects have long been fascinated by

other architectural styles. The state architectural school, the Paektusan Academy of Architecture, has a large and excellent collection of photographs and plans of great buildings across the world. And to see Pyongyang, whether in reality or through the medium of Google Maps, is to witness bigger and brighter interpretations of the architectural styles found in cities across the world, from London and New York to Dubai and Nur-Sultan. The Triumphal Arch of 1982 is, for example, specifically over thirty feet taller than the Arc de Triomphe in Paris. There are few places where size would matter more.

Since the 1980s, the regime has concentrated on 'iconic' buildings and monuments, which can be seen across the city and are known even outside North Korea. They give focus and visual identity to the city. Often these are in materials and shapes which seem to defy gravity, such as the Pyongyang Ice Rink, built in the shape of a skater's helmet, the space-age double towers of the Koryo Hotel and the May Day Stadium, formed from sixteen parabolic arches in the form of the mountain magnolia, the national flower, floating on a river. Take the Arch of Reunification, which spans the main motorway approaching Pyongyang from the south. It is at the northern end of Tongil (Reunification) Highway, which – if Korea were to unite – would run from Pyongyang to Seoul. The arch consists of two Korean women, carved from huge blocks of white granite, their hands joining in the middle of the road to hold aloft a plaque adorned with a bronze map of the Korean Peninsula. They loom almost one hundred feet above travellers as they drive along the mostly empty motorway. It is hard not to be impressed by the technical ingenuity required to build human figures as architecture on such a scale.

North Korea's architects have shown ever more ambition and originality over the last decade. Under the rule of Kim Jong-un and his 'Strong and Prosperous Nation' policy, the country has both embraced a hard-line approach to nuclear armament and rebuilt its capital as a showcase for increasingly flamboyant architectural set pieces. The Supreme Leader's 2016 architectural manifesto, *For Building a Thriving Nation*, wishes architects not just to combine tradition with modernity, as his father had done, but to build monumental structures that will surpass global standards and remain immaculate, even long into the future.

Changjion Street, on the west bank of the Taedong between Kim Il-Sung Square and the Mansu Hill Grand Monument, is a collection of strange towers that look as if they are made of striped Lego, framing the Okryu Bridge. These glossy structures, colourfully lit at night, unlike most of Pyongyang, were built at breakneck speed in less than a year during 2012, to house workers. They are now a high-class area where a cup of coffee costs about four times the city's norm. Mirae Scientists Street, constructed three years later and intended to house the intellectual elite along the banks of the river, is an ensemble of high-rise flats in pastel turquoise and salmon pink, recalling the colours of national dress and the smooth sheen of traditional ceramics. Their curved, playful shapes are apparently based on the calligraphy brush with which Koreans traditionally write. More surprising, given its vast scale, is the turquoise and white Galaxy Tower at the end of the boulevard shaped (according to your taste) to resemble either a stretched atom or a modernist pagoda. Sunrise (Ryomyong) Street, is full of buildings that resemble a giant toytown, from shops that take the form of giant petals to multi-coloured towers patterned with geometrical shapes in contrasting colours.

Collectively, these streets and buildings express a sense of whimsy and playfulness which seems distinctive to this isolated country, separated by choice from most of the world.

New Pyongyang is a shining new urban vision, complete with pleasure domes, including a theme park, a dolphinarium and a water park. It is like a combination of Disney and Willy Wonka, mediated through a North Korean version of K-pop, bright, cheerful, repetitive and catchy. In order to fit into this brave new world, many of the city's existing tower blocks have been painted in pastel colours. From the air, the impression is of a child's rainbow city (although without the unicorns), a socialist paradise where pleasure is as important as duty. Perhaps the most Day-glo – appropriately enough – is the Mangyongdae Children's Palace, first constructed in 1989, in the west of the city near the birthplace of Kim Il-Sung. Run by the Youth Corps of North Korea, this is one of a number of centres where Young Pioneers, aged between eight and fourteen, are trained in dance, music, gymnastics, arts and crafts. The Mangyongdae Palace, which forms part of many foreigners' tours of the country, is a complex that has been resourced and decorated to give a particular picture of North Korea to the outside world, with brilliant prodigy children performing complex feats of dance, music and song. Its imposing brutalist façade transforms into a cosy, welcoming interior, with bright colours, organically shaped soft furnishings, pastel lighting, a 3D map of Korea and a vision of the galaxy on the ceiling which looks like a bigger version of the glow-in-the-dark stars found on Western children's walls. Yet this is a children's centre with a difference – an enormous rocket, the dominant feature in the foyer, is a potent reminder of the country's nuclear and space ambitions.

For all the fun, joy and perhaps some subversion, the ultimate purpose of everything in North Korea remains control. We can admire as well as fear the architectural and spatial ingenuity that goes into not just building unbelievable structures but in marshalling living souls together to create a living work of art – the extraordinary Mass Games. Group dancing is a common activity. Out on the streets and in the parks, women of all ages regularly gather to perform traditional dances, in long-sleeved and full-skirted Korean costume. The Mass Games developed from this tradition, combined with the Soviet Spartakiads, international sports events established in opposition to the 'capitalist' Olympics. These gymnastic, dance and music spectaculars have run almost annually in Pyongyang since 1946, celebrating Korean identity and the North Korean state.

The Mass Games are seen as key to the development of Juche because they depend on many thousands of people working to one end. In 1987, Kim Jong-il went as far as to state that 'Through mass gymnastic performances, the Party members and other working people are firmly equipped with our Party's Juche idea, and the validity and great vitality of our Party's lines and policies, the embodiment of the idea, are demonstrated far and wide at home and abroad.' As a means to foster national pride and unity, the Mass Games artistically tell the story of North Korea, from its inception as former colony to, in the regime's words, the 'almost Utopian ascent' into an 'industrialised power standing on its own sovereign feet'.

Since 2002, they have been known as the Arirang Games, taking their name from a much-loved Korean song, beloved on both sides of the Demilitarized Zone, with which the performance begins. A lone female singer takes the stage. She is gradually joined by more musicians and singers, in vast numbers, and the song ends with a marvellous choreographed sequence, dancers in bronze robes with golden fans singing and dancing as the sun rises behind them. As it is a story of separation between a man and a woman, it is also used to symbolise the separation of the two Koreas, and the desire for their ultimate reunion.

By any account Arirang is an amazing feat, and the Mass Games are justly famed. They bring together almost a hundred thousand people, synchronising their bodies to create moving images. Perhaps the most astonishing sequence uses tens of thousands of school children. Dancing, waving, jumping and singing performers hold up a succession of coloured cards to form striking large-scale live pictures: the triumphant struggle of the North Koreans, led by the Kims, against the Japanese; the self-sufficiency of the North Korean people's state; the two deified leaders, whose saintly images are encircled with gold; and concluding with the hoped-for unity of the Korean Peninsula, with one government, two systems. But the wider and less benign purpose of the event is to promote discipline, collectivism, physical fitness and, above all, loyalty to the state.

The arts, and particularly the built environment, are of central importance to the regime because they beautify and give meaning to its mechanisms of control, making people 'feel' and 'believe' rather than think analytically. This is a government which will do almost anything to retain its power and to maintain its ideology, even subjecting its people to food shortages and famine to preserve the illusion of self-sufficiency. Architecture is valued in North Korea for its ability to coerce and control. But even in this crooked and corrupt state there is some beauty. The Socialist Paradise of Pyongyang is only for the lucky few, a *Truman Show* version of the West, serving to keep the elite loyal to the Kim family. Yet there are things to learn – and even some to admire, in spite of everything – from this city that values architecture, urban planning and community.

CONCLUSION

Humans have always made art. They have always thought about what art is, and what art means. And they have used art to express ideas about themselves and the society they live in, as well as to leave a legacy for the future.

In this book I have given a structure to the range and ingenuity of human visual creativity that has been made by millions of lives within urban communities across the world. As I've looked, thought and written, I've been struck by connections and continuity far more than by difference. Fundamentally, humans don't change. Art continues to be made for purposes that would still seem familiar to the peoples of Babylon, Jerusalem and Rome. Principally, this is to fulfil our needs for shelter, sustenance, spirituality, pleasure, order and community. Yet art is by no means an unequivocal power for good. It can create envy and anger, greed and arrogance. And there is no more effective way of controlling people, influencing what they believe, organising them, and even the mechanics of how they live.

I planned and wrote much of this book during lockdown, when it was hard to travel or to interact with anyone outside my immediate family. Although limited to my locality, through art I could roam freely across the world and across time, encountering a variety of people and their ideas. That's because works of art have the power – whether we come across them in person or through images – to take our minds to new places, away from the quotidian and to connect us with a vast range of human possibilities. Great art opens up experiences that are beyond our ken. It can make us happy, or it can make us cry. It can remind us of loved ones or reanimate memories. Furthermore, it can calm and soothe us. Both during the pandemic, and the uncertainty that continues, art has often reassured me of the endurance of the human spirit. In a strange sense, there's something particularly comforting in reflecting on art made during moments of far greater adversity and difficulty. It's well worth remembering that inspiration and beauty can come out of conflict, trial and injustice.

Although their makers may be gone, artworks are not mute. They tell many stories, about their creators and original owners, and those who have encountered them. Art is a connector, linking us to people or experiences that have vanished. The Benin Bronzes remain evocative testimonies of a rich culture plundered but not annihilated. And walking around the ruins of Roman Pompeii you still sense the combination of prosperity and confidence of a civilisation that never believed it would become a ruin.

It's undeniable that much art has been made or collected by elites. There is no shortage of information about the rulers of Babylon who stamped their names and titles on the walls and foundations of the city, the Ming Emperors whose regnal mark appeared on every pot or dish fired during their reign, or the North Korean Supreme Leaders whose images are everywhere in modern Pyongyang. There is far less known about women, both as makers and as consumers of art, than about men. We are unlikely to be able to fully plug this gap, because women are found less than men in the documentary record that underpins the writing of history, even today. Yet more than almost any historical source, art can emotionally connect us to the nameless of previous ages. The fragments of wall paintings and ceramics discovered on the floor of the Dar al-Khilafa palace in Samarra evoke the lives and experiences of people who are completely lost to us – the enslaved men and women who lived for the pleasure of the Abbasid caliphs. The weathered marble floors of Constantinople's Hagia Sophia make you think of the millions of people who have visited it for worship or for wonder. Who used and cherished a finely crafted object like the Japanese lacquered wooden box covered with silver and gold cartwheels? Looking at it, admiring its shining complexity, we imagine it used to store valued possessions, perhaps make-up, or paper and ink. This one object brings to life the combination of ordinariness and transcendent beauty which is one of the essential elements of human existence.

Every object tells many stories, and I have only scratched the surface. There is much more to muse on and discover. Writing this book, I have become so much more appreciative of the things that are near at hand, from the coffee cup I use every day to the pictures on my wall, and what they tell us about ourselves and about others. But there is something very special about what I unapologetically call great art. Having something beautiful in your life is undoubtedly transformative. Using it or seeing it is a continual pleasure. You don't need to own it personally; you just have to be able to consider it as yours. This could be a building you pass every day, a sculpture in a public gallery, a bowl or plate you cherish, an image you save or a film you watch. Next time you do so, share the experience with someone else. Find out what excites them, and what makes them happy. In our lives, whatever we do, and however we think, we can all contribute to the story of art, even if only by loving it.

LIST OF ILLUSTRATIONS

Burgerzall, 1648–65 CE, Amsterdam, The Netherlands. ©
John Goodall

262 Johann Melchior Dinglinger, Georg Friedrich Dinglinger, Georg
Christoph Dinglinger, Johann Benjamin Thomae and assistants,
The Throne of Grand Mogul Aurengzeb, 1701–8 CE, wood, gold,
silver, partly gilded, enamel, precious stones, pearls, lacquer painting, 58 x 142 x 114cm. Dresden, Staatliche Kunstsammlungen,
Green Vault, inv.: VIII 204. Photo Scala, Florence/bpk, Bildagentur
für Kunst, Kultur und Geschichte, Berlin

290 Trafalgar Square from the south, with Nelson's Column, the
National Gallery and St Martin-in-the-Fields, London, United
Kingdom. © John Goodall

320 Joseph Maria Olbrich, The Secession Building, Karlsplatz, 1898
CE, Vienna, Austria. © John Goodall

348 Louise Bourgeois's *Maman* sculpture on display during the
Unilever Series: *Louise Bourgeois, I Do, I Undo and I Redo*,
May–December 2000, Turbine Hall, Tate Modern, London, 1999
CE, steel and marble, 927.1 × 891.5 × 1023.6 cm. © The Easton
Foundation

378 Brasília from the air: aerial view of the city and Lake Paranoa,
1983 CE. Luisa Ricciarini/Bridgeman Images

402 High-angle view of Kim Il-Sung Square and the Juche Tower,
Pyongyang, North Korea, 2010 CE. © Eric Lafforgue. All rights
reserved 2023/Bridgeman Images

Section 1

Babylon

Pieter Bruegel the Elder, *The Tower of Babel*, around 1560 CE, oil on
panel, 74.6 x 59.9 cm. Museum Boijmans Van Beuningen, Rotterdam.
Acquired with the collection of: D.G. van Beuningen 1958, 2443 (OK)

Probably from Uruk, Proto-Cuneiform tablet with seal impressions,
c. 3100–2900 BCE, clay, 5.4 × 6 × 4.1 cm. Metropolitan Museum of
Art, New York. Purchase, Raymond and Beverly Sackler Gift, 1988,
1988.433.1

Babylonian, Cyrus Cylinder, after 539 BCE, fired clay, 21.9 x 22.8 cm
(length). British Museum, London, 1880 1880,0617.1941. © The
Trustees of the British Museum

Babylon, 1930s reconstruction of the Ishtar Gate completed using

Jerusalem

Rome

Roman, view of the exterior of the Ara Pacis Augustae, 13–9 BCE, marble, Rome, Italy. Bridgeman Images

Roman, view of the exterior of the Ara Pacis Augustae, Rome (detail), decorative floral friezes, 13–9 BCE, marble, Rome, Italy. G. Dagli Orti/© NPL – DeA Picture Library/Bridgeman Images

Roman, short wall of Boscoreale cubiculum (bedroom), Room M of the Villa of Publius Fannius Synstor, c. 50–40 BCE, fresco, 265.4 × 334 × 583.9 cm, Boscoreale, Pompeii, Rome. Metropolitan Museum of Art, New York, Rogers Fund, 1903, 03.14.13a–g

Roman, view of the Forum, Pompeii, with Vesuvius in the background, first century CE. Pompeii, Italy. Bridgeman Images

Roman, caldarium in the Forum Baths, Pompeii, c. 64 CE, Pompeii, Italy. L Romano/© NPL – DeA Picture Library/Bridgeman Images

Roman British, Corbridge, Hadrian's Wall, c. 160–300 CE, Northumbria, England, UK. © John Goodall

Roman, internal view of the Pantheon, 118–125 CE, concrete, brick and marble, Rome, Italy. © John Goodall

Baghdad

Abbasid, probably southern Iraq, bowl with Kufic inscription, 'Made by Abu al-Taqi', ninth century CE, ceramic, earthenware, painted in cobalt blue on an opaque white glaze, 6.4 x 21.9 cm. Brooklyn Museum, Gift of the Ernest Erickson Foundation Inc., 86.227.14

Abbasid, Samarra, haram wall painting fragments, ninth century CE, painting on plaster, 11 x 10 x 1.5 cm. Excavated by Ernst Herzfeld, Samarra, Iraq. British Museum, London, OA+.10620. © The Trustees of the British Museum

Spanish (probably Almería), Almoravid, fragment with wrestling lions and harpies, early twelfth century CE, silk lampas with supplementary discontinuous metal-wrapped patterning wefts, 50 x 43 cm. Museum of Fine Arts, Boston, Ellen Page Hall Fund, 33.371

Khafif, apprentice of Àli ibn 'Isá, astrolabe, ninth century CE, brass. Presented by J. A. Billmeir, 1957. Museum of the History of Science, Oxford, inv. 47632

Residence of the Caliph Mu'tasim, ninth century CE, Samarra. © NPL – DeA Picture Library/C. Sappa/Bridgeman Images

Abassid, probably from Samarra, pair of doors carved in the 'bevelled style', ninth century CE, carved teak, 221 x 51.4 x 104.8 cm. Metropolitan Museum, New York, Fletcher Fund, 31.119.1

Yahya ibn Mahmoud ibn Yahya ibn Aboul-Hasan ibn Kouvarriha al-Wasiti, scholars in the Library of the 'House of Wisdom', in the *Maqamat al-Hariri*, 1236–7 CE, 37 x 28 cm. Paris, Bibliothèque Nationale de France, MS Parisinus Arabus 5847, fol. 5v. © Archives Charmet/Bridgeman Images

Section 2

Kyoto

Minamoto Toshifusa (?), *Lotus Sutra*, chapter on 'Expedient Means' (*Chikubushima Sutra*), eleventh century CE, ink on paper scroll, 29.6 x 528.5. Tokyo, National Museum, B-2401. ColBase: Integrated Collections Database of the National Institutes for Cultural Heritage, Japan

Fujiwara no Yorimichi (commissioner), Phoenix Hall/Hōōdō, Byōdō-in, Uji, Japan, 1050–3 CE. © Michel Guillemot. All rights reserved 2023/ Bridgeman Images

Heian Japan, page from the *Collection of Poems* by Lady Ise (Ise shū), early twelfth century CE, decorated paper, mounted as a hanging scroll, 138 × 42.5 cm. Metropolitan Museum of Art, New York, Mary Griggs Burke Collection, Gift of the Mary and Jackson Burke Foundation, 2015, 2015.300.231

Heian Japan, landscape screen, probably eleventh century CE, pigment on silk, six-fold screen, each 146.4 x 42.7 cm. Kyoto, National Museum, A甲227. ColBase: Integrated Collections Database of the National Institutes for Cultural Heritage, Japan

Heian Japan, *The Tale of Genji*, 'The Eastern Cottage' (Azumaya I), early twelfth century CE, colours and ink on decorated paper. Tokugawa Art Museum. The Picture Art Collection/Alamy Stock Photo

Heian Japan, toiletry case with cart wheels in a stream, twelfth century CE, lacquered wood, 22.4 x 30.6 x 13.5 cm. Tokyo National Museum, H-4282. ColBase: Integrated Collections Database of the National Institutes for Cultural Heritage, Japan

Beijing

Chinese, the Yongle Emperor in the Dragon Chair, probably fifteenth century CE, ink and colours on silk (hanging scroll), 220 x

150 cm. National Palace Museum, Taipei. Pictures from History/ Bridgeman Images

Chinese (formerly attributed to Shen Du), tribute giraffe with attendant, sixteenth century CE, ink and colour on silk (mounted as a hanging scroll), 171.5 x 53.3 cm. Philadelphia Museum of Art, Philadelphia, Gift of John T. Dorrance, 1977, 1977-42-1

Chinese, portrait of an official in front of the Forbidden City, Beijing, fifteenth century CE, painting on silk, approx. 200 x 115 cm. National Museum of China, Beijing. Pictures from History/Bridgeman Images

Persian, royal reception in a landscape, left folio from the double frontispiece of a *Shahnama* (Book of Kings) of Firdausi, 1444 CE, opaque watercolour, ink, gold and silver on paper, 32.7 x 22. Cleveland Museum of Art, Cleveland, John L. Severance Fund 1956.10

Chinese, stem porcelain cup, 1426–35 CE, porcelain, underglaze blue and red with incised dragons in red against blue waves, and anhua dragons painted in slip on the interior, 15.2 x 10.5 cm. British Museum, London, PDF, A.626. Courtesy of the Trustees of the Sir Percival David Foundation; © The Trustees of the British Museum

Chinese, blue and white porcelain jug in the shape of a tankard, early fifteenth century CE, glazed and unglazed porcelain, 14 x 14.2 cm. London, British Museum, donated by EB Havell, 1950,0403.1. © The Trustees of the British Museum

Chinese, red-glazed porcelain wine cup, 1403–25 CE, glazed porcelain, 10.5 x 15.5 cm. London, Victoria and Albert Museum, given by Mr. W. G. Gulland, accessioned in 1905, 168-1905. London, Victoria and Albert Museum

Florence

Michelozzo di Bartolomeo, Palazzo Medici, 1444–60 CE, Florence, Italy. © John Goodall

Benedetto da Maiano, Giuliano da Sangallo and Cronaca, Palazzo Strozzi, begun 1489 CE, completed 1548, Florence, Italy. © John Goodall

Donatello, *David*, c. 1440 CE, bronze, 158 cm high. Museo Nazionale del Bargello, Florence. Photo © Raffaello Bencini/Bridgeman Images

Sandro Botticelli, *Primavera*, c. 1480 CE, tempera on panel, 202 x 314 cm. Gallerie degli Uffizi, Florence, 1890 n.8360. Photo © Raffaello Bencini/Bridgeman Images

Raphael (Raffaello Sanzio), *The Madonna of the Pinks* ('La Madonna dei Garofani'), c. 1506–7 CE, oil on yew, 27.9 x 22.4 cm. Bought with the assistance of the Heritage Lottery Fund, the Art Fund (with a contribution from the Wolfson Foundation), the American Friends of the National Gallery, London, the George Beaumont Group, Sir Christopher Ondaatje and through public appeal, 2004, NG6596. © Trustees of the National Gallery, London

Masaccio, *The Holy Trinity, with the Virgin, St John and donors*, 1427–8 CE, fresco, 667 x 317 cm. Santa Maria Novella, Florence. Photo © Nicolò Orsi Battaglini/Bridgeman Images

Leonardo da Vinci, A rearing horse and heads of horses, a lion and a man: *Study for the Battle of Anghiari*, c. 1503 CE, pen and ink, wash, a little red chalk on paper, 19.6 x 30 cm. Royal Collection Trust, RCIN 912326. Royal Collection Trust/© His Majesty King Charles III 2023

Section 3

Benin

Edo peoples, Benin, memorial head of a queen mother (iyoba), early sixteenth century CE, brass, 51 x 16 x 18 cm. Formerly Ethnologisches Museum, Staatliche Museen zu Berlin, inv. no. III C12507, ownership transferred to Nigeria, 2022. Photo © Dirk Bakker/Bridgeman Images

Edo peoples, Benin, ivory mask of Queen Idia, sixteenth century CE, ivory, iron and copper alloy, 24.5 x 12.5 x 6 cm. British Museum, London, Af1910, 0513.1. © The Trustees of the British Museum

Edo peoples, Benin, plaque with four page figures in front of the palace compound, sixteenth–seventeenth century CE, brass, 55 x 39 x 6.5 cm. British Museum, London, Af1898, 0115.46. © The Trustees of the British Museum

Olfert Dapper, view of the city of Benin with the royal palace, Nigeria (detail), engraving from *Naukeurige Beschrijvinge Der Afrikaensche Gewesten . . .* ('A Description of Africa'), by Olfert Dapper, first published Amsterdam, 1668. © A. Dagli Orti/© NPL – DeA Picture Library/Bridgeman Images

Unidentified British photographer, members of the British expedition to Benin City with objects from the Royal Palace, 1897, gelatin silver print, 16.5 x 12 cm. British Museum, London, Af, A79.13. © The Trustees of the British Museum

Edo peoples, Benin, salt cellar with European figures, 1525–1600 CE, ivory, 29.3 x 11 cm. British Museum, London, Af1878,1101.48.a-c © The Trustees of the British Museum

Amsterdam

Rembrandt van Rijn, *The Sampling Officials of the Amsterdam Drapers' Guild*, 1662 CE, oil on canvas, 191.5 × 279 cm. Rijksmuseum, Amsterdam, on loan from the city of Amsterdam, SK-C-6

Nicolas Maes, *Interior with a Sleeping Maid and her Mistress* ('The Idle Servant'), 1665 CE, oil on oak, 70 × 53.3 cm. National Gallery, London, bequeathed by Richard Simmons, 1847, NG207. © Trustees of the National Gallery, London

Johannes Vermeer, *View of Houses in Delft*, known as 'The Little Street', c. 1658 CE, oil on canvas, 54.3 x 44 cm. Amsterdam, Rijksmuseum, gift of H. W. A. Deterding, London, SK-A-2860

Jan Steen, *The Merry Family*, 1668 CE, oil on canvas, 110.5 x 141 cm. Rijksmuseum, Amsterdam, on loan from the city of Amsterdam (A. van der Hoop Bequest), SK-C-229

Pieter Claesz, *Still Life with a Turkey Pie*, 1627 CE, oil on panel, 76.5 x 135 cm. Amsterdam, Rijksmuseum, purchased with the support of the Vereniging Rembrandt and the Stichting tot Bevordering van de Belangen van het Rijksmuseum, 1974, SK-A-4646

Anonymous, dolls house of Petronella Oortman, after 1686–1710 CE, wood, tin, glass, marble, paper, copper, velvet, yarn and embroidery, 255 × 190 × 78 cm × 28 cm. Amsterdam, Rijksmuseum, transferred 1875, BK-NM-1010

Frans Post, *Brazilian Landscape*, 1660s CE, oil on panel, 48.3 x 62.2 cm. National Gallery of Ireland, presented by Captain R. Langton Douglas, 1923, NGI.847. © National Gallery of Ireland

Delhi

Mughal craftsman, Shah Jahan's lotus wine cup, 1657 CE, white nephrite jade, 18.7 x 14cm. Victoria and Albert Museum, London, purchased with Art Fund support, and the assistance of the Wolfson Foundation, Messrs Spink and Son, and an anonymous benefactor, IS.12-1962. © Victoria and Albert Museum, London

Nanha (painter) and Mir 'Ali Haravi (calligrapher), The Emperor Shah Jahan with his Son Dara Shikoh, Folio from the Shah Jahan Album, c. 1620 CE (painting), ink, opaque watercolour, and gold on paper, 38.9 x 26.2 cm. Metropolitan Museum of Art, New York, purchase, Rogers Fund and the Kevorkian Foundation Gift, 1955, 55.121.10.36

Taj Mahal, 1631–48 CE, Agra, India. Pictures from History/David Henley/Bridgeman Images

Interior dome of the Taj Mahal, 1631–48 CE, Agra, India. © Ann & Bury Peerless Archive/Bridgeman Images

Interior view of the Taj Mahal, 1631–48 CE, Agra, India, looking down on the screen, and ceremonial tombs of Mumtaz Mahal and Shah Jahans. © Ann & Bury Peerless Archive/Bridgeman Images

The Marble Throne, Public Audience Chamber, Red Fort, 1639–48 CE, Delhi, India. © Ann & Bury Peerless Archive/Bridgeman Images

The Private Audience Chamber, Red Fort, 1639–48 CE, Delhi, India. © Ann & Bury Peerless Archive/Bridgeman Images

London

John Everett Millais, *Ophelia*, 1851–2 CE, oil on canvas, 76.2 x 111.8 cm. Presented by Sir Henry Tate, 1894, N01506. © Tate

Jan van Eyck, *Portrait of Giovanni(?) Arnolfini and his Wife*, 1434 CE, oil on oak, 82.2 × 60 cm. National Gallery, London, bought, 1842, NG186. © Trustees of the National Gallery, London

William Holman Hunt, *The Light of the World*, 1900–4 CE, oil on canvas, 304.8 x 193 cm. St Paul's Cathedral, London, given by the Right Hon Charles Booth. © John Goodall

Sir George Gilbert Scott, Midland Grand Hotel, 1865–76 CE, from the south, London, United Kingdom. © John Goodall

William Barlow, the railway shed, St Pancras station, 1864–68 CE, London, United Kingdom. © John Goodall

Sir George Gilbert Scott, the Albert Memorial, opened 1872 CE, Kensington Gardens, London, United Kingdom. © John Goodall

Gustave Doré, *Over London, By Rail*, 1869–72 CE, engraving, 19.8 x 24.8 cm. Bridgeman Images

Section 4

Vienna

Franz Xaver Winterhalter, *Empress Elisabeth of Austria*, 1865 CE, oil on canvas, 255 x 133 cm, Hofburg, Vienna. Bridgeman Images

Gustav Klimt, *Portrait of Hermine Gallia*, 1904 CE, oil on canvas, 170.5 × 96.5 cm. National Gallery, London, acquired 1976, NG6434. © Trustees of the National Gallery, London

Egon Schiele, *Seated Woman with Bent Knees*, 1917 CE, gouache, watercolour and black crayon on paper, 46 cm × 30.5 cm, The National Gallery, Prague. Bridgeman Images

View of the Maria Theresia Platz, off the Ringstrasse, 1860–75 CE, Vienna, Austria. © John Goodall

Josef Hoffmann, tea service, 1904 CE, silver, coral and wood. MAK, Vienna. © NPL – DeA Picture Library/G. Nimatallah/ Bridgeman Images

Max Klinger, *Beethoven*, 1893–1902 CE, bronze, marble, amber and tiles, height 310 cm. Museum der Bildenden Künste, Leipzig. © Martin Allen. All rights reserved 2023/Bridgeman Images

Gustav Klimt, *The Kiss*, 1907–8 CE, oil on canvas, 180 x 180 cm. Belvedere Gallery, Vienna. Bridgeman Images

New York

Helen Frankenthaler, *Mountains and Sea*, 1952 CE, oil and charcoal on unsized, unprimed canvas, 219.4 x 297.8 cm. Helen Frankenthaler Foundation, New York, on extended loan to the National Gallery of Art, Washington, DC

The Manhattan skyline, New York, USA. © Laurence Dutton. All rights reserved 2023/Bridgeman Images

Andy Warhol, *Campbell's Soup Cans*, 1962 CE, acrylic with metallic enamel paint on canvas, 32 panels, each canvas, 50.8 x 40.6 cm. MOMA, New York, partial gift of Irving Blum Additional funding provided by Nelson A. Rockefeller Bequest, gift of Mr and Mrs William A. M. Burden, Abby Aldrich Rockefeller Fund, gift of Nina and Gordon Bunshaft, acquired through the Lillie P. Bliss Bequest, Philip Johnson Fund, Frances R. Keech Bequest, gift of Mrs Bliss Parkinson, and Florence B. Wesley Bequest (all by exchange), 476.1996.1-32. © 2023 Andy Warhol Foundation/ARS, NY/TM. Licensed by Campbell's Soup Co. All rights reserved

Jacob Lawrence, *And the migrants kept coming*, 1940–1 CE, casein tempera on hardboard, 30.5 x 45.7 cm. MOMA, New York, Gift of Mrs David M. Levy, 28.1942.30. © 2023 Jacob Lawrence/Artists Rights Society (ARS), New York

Jackson Pollock, *Painting No. 30* (*Autumn Rhythm*), 1950 CE, enamel on canvas, 266.7 × 525.8 cm. Metropolitan Museum, New York, George A. Hearn Fund, 1957, 57.92. © 2023 Artists Rights Society (ARS), New York

John Lennon and Yoko Ono at the Hilton Hotel in Amsterdam, 25 March 1969 (b/w photo). Bridgeman Images

Brasilia

Oscar Niemeyer, the National Congress, Brasília, Brazil, 1956–8 CE. ©
NPL – DeA Picture Library/Bridgeman Images
Oscar Niemeyer, the Presidential Palace (Planalto), Brasília, Brazil, 1958
CE. Photo © Collection Artedia/Bridgeman Images
Oscar Niemeyer, Cathedral, Brasília, Brazil, designed 1958 CE. Lou
Avers. Picture Alliance/DPA/Bridgeman Images
Housing building of a superquadra, Brasília, Brazil. Photo © Collection
Artedia/Bridgeman Images
Square of the Three Powers, looking towards the Supreme Federal
Court, Brasília, Brazil. © SZ Photo/Ingrid Kassebeer-Voss/
Bridgeman Image

Pyongyang

Soldiers paying respect to the two statues of the Dear Leaders on
the Grand Monument on Mansu Hill, Pyongyang, 2012 CE. © Eric
Lafforgue. All rights reserved 2023/Bridgeman Images
North Korean people reading the official state newspaper in a subway
station, Pyongyang, 2010 CE. © Eric Lafforgue. All rights reserved
2023/Bridgeman Images
North Korean young adults during a mass dance performance in front
of buildings on Kwangbok Street on Military Foundation Day,
Pyongyang, 2010 CE. © Eric Lafforgue. All rights reserved 2023/
Bridgeman Images
Arch of Reunification, Tongil (Reunification) Highway, 2001 CE. © Eric
Lafforgue. All rights reserved 2023/Bridgeman Images
North Korean dancers in front of the rising sun over Mount Paektu
made by children holding up
boards during Arirang Mass Games in May Day Stadium, Pyongyang,
2012 CE. © Eric Lafforgue. All rights reserved 2023/Bridgeman Images

ACKNOWLEDGEMENTS

I set out to write the sort of book which took a grand narrative, but which was also immersed in detail, that drew connections across countries and millennia, but was grounded in the particular, and a love of objects. The sort of book I wanted to read, but could not exactly find about art. I have been inspired by historians and art historians, including Fernand Braudel, Ernst Gombrich, Simon Schama, Mary Beard, Tom Holland, William Dalrymple and Peter Frankopan, who are able to approach the past in a broad, inclusive way. My approach has inevitably been influenced by my upbringing in Belfast during the Troubles, in a conflicted society where images were used to define and separate two tribes. Art is often a way of articulating difference, and division. But we should not forget that it can connect us to people in times or places that seem remote, so that their experiences talk to our own.

I owe a great debt to my parents, Jennifer and Norman Campbell, and my siblings, Lucy and Alastair, who immersed me in conversation, books and culture from a young age. At school and university, I was fortunate to be taught by broad-minded and rigorous scholars in Belfast and later at Oxford and in London. I thank Stephen Doherty (†) and Jim Grew (†), Alexander Murray, Leslie Mitchell, Hartmut Pogge von Strandmann, Jennifer Fletcher and Patricia Rubin for all that I have learnt from you, and for looking and thinking with the benefit of your minds and eyes.

I have been fortunate to live most of my life in four cities, Belfast, Oxford, London and Dublin, with fine public art collections and buildings that are freely and generously available to their inhabitants, and to be of an age to have benefited from the opportunities of the internet and of cheap travel. Furthermore, I'm indebted to the many generous mentors and good examples I have been fortunate enough to encounter in my museum career – including S. B. Kennedy (†), Anne Stewart, Kim Mawhinney, Eileen Black, John Murdoch, Christopher Brown, Jon Whiteley (†), Timothy Wilson, Catherine Whistler, Kate Eustace, Colin Harrison, Neil MacGregor, Charles Saumarez-Smith, Luke Syson, Carol Plazzotta, Dillian Gordon, Martin Wyld, Ashok Roy, Kathy Adler, Mary Hersov, Xa Sturgis, Axel Rüger, Dora Thornton, Carl Strehlke, Joanna Cannon, Debby Swallow, Ernst Vegelin, Aviva Burnstock, Frances Morris, Roly Keating, Nicholas Penny, Anne Hawley, Evelyn Welch, Colin Bailey, Elizabeth Easton and Gabriele Finaldi.

I owe a particular debt to Gabriele, who extremely generously let me take some time away from the National Gallery, during an exceptionally busy period, to work on this book, and to John Booth, Chair of the National Gallery Board. I thank all my former National Gallery colleagues for their support, in many different ways. I am especially grateful to Christine Riding and Julie Firth for their kindness and forbearance, and to Tracy Jones for her invaluable advice. My thanks are also due to Mary Keane, Chair of the National Gallery of Ireland, and the whole team at the NGI, especially Jacinta Benetti, Gillian DeMarco, Patricia Golden, Andrew Hetherington,

Gemma McArdle and Kim Smit. The staff of many libraries, particularly the National Gallery, Courtauld Institute, Warburg Institute, London Library, British Library, the Durning Library, Kennington, the National Art Library and the National Gallery of Ireland have been unstintingly kind and helpful, over many years. The wider Campbell and Goodall families and my friends have been ever supportive, in offering me childcare, space and even places in which to think and write.

I have learnt so much from colleagues, including those mentioned above, and Paul Ackroyd, Sébastien Allard, Jeremy Ashbee, Susanna Avery-Quash, Graeme Barraclough, Tim Barringer, Andrea Bayer, Rachel Billinge, Polly Blakesley, Thomas Bohl, David Bomford, Alixe Bovey, Xavier Bray, Stephanie Buck, Jill Burke, Emma Capron, Stefano Carboni, Alan Chong, Martin Clayton, Donal Cooper, Anna Contadini, Bart Cornelis, Alan Crookham, Barbara Dawson, Vincent Delieuvin, Jill Dunkerton, Anna Eavis, David Ekserdjian, Miguel Falomir, Susan Foister, Cecilia Frosinini, Michael Gallagher, Alexandra Gerstein, Michael Hall, Gill Hart, Katrin Henkel, Tom Henry, Sarah Herring, Daniel Herrmann, Frederick Ilchman, Nancy Ireson, Larry Keith, Dagmar Korbacher, Sally Korman, Jane Knowles, Tim Knox, Amanda Lillie, Laura Llewellyn, María López-Fanjul y Díez del Corral, Rebecca Lyons, Thomas Marks, Priyesh Mistry, Minna Moore Ede, Rachel Moss, Jacqueline Musacchio, Scott Nethersole, Fabrizio Nevola, Britta New, Aimee Ng, Michelle O'Malley, Richard Plant, Elizabeth Prettejohn, Ben Quash, Sean Rainbird, Chris Riopelle, Anne Robbins, Jason Rosenfeld, Hannah Rothschild, Neville Rowley, Xavier Salomon, Peter Schade, Jenny Scott, Desmond Shawe-Taylor, Rupert Shepherd, Bill Sherman, Jennifer Sliwka, Marika Spring, Cecilia Treves, Letizia Treves, Sarah Vowles, Betsy Wieseman, Colin Wiggins,

Lucy Whitaker, Alison Wright and Stephan Wolohojian. Our conversations and collaborations, over many years, have impacted on this book. I would also like to thank my former students, particularly Alasdair Flint, Imogen Tedbury, Amanda Hilliam and Anna McGee, and the members of the National Gallery's George Beaumont Group and the George Beaumont Circle, who have tolerated me testing out many of these ideas, over more than a decade, in our special trips to museums, collections and places all over the world. Any errors, however, are my own.

I am enormously grateful to my editor, Holly Harley, and my agent, Jonathan Conway, for having belief in me and in this project, and for all their work to make this book as good as possible. At Bridge Street I would also like to thank Sameer Rahim, and everyone who has worked on my book, particularly Zoe Gullen for her expert copy-editing and for seeing the book through to press, Linda Silverman for all her help with images and the book's look and feel, Lucy Martin for her work on publicity and marketing, and Richard Collins for his proof-reading.

There are three people without whom this book could never have happened. Isobel and Eddie, thank you for tolerating, and sometimes enjoying, your mother's enthusiasms and interests. This book is for you, and for John, who brightens my life and makes everything possible.

SELECTED BIBLIOGRAPHY

I have included a selected bibliography for each chapter. At the outset I should like to particularly thank the many authors who have contributed to the *Grove Dictionary of Art* and Grove Art Online, the Smarthistory platform founded by Beth Harris and Steve Zucker, and the Metropolitan Museum of Art's Heilbrunn Timeline of History and Art History. These are invaluable introductory sources for the history of art, written accessibly for a general audience.

The collections pages of the British Museum, the Victoria and Albert Museum, the National Gallery, London, the National Gallery of Art, Washington DC, the J. Paul Getty Museum, the Metropolitan Museum of Art, the Cleveland Museum of Art, the Rijksmuseum and many others have also been exceptionally useful. I wish to acknowledge the many art historians and curators whose scholarly work is made freely available to a wide public through these inestimable resources.

I have also found the following art historical and historical works very valuable, across a number of chapters: M. T. Ansary, *Destiny Disrupted: A History of the World through Islamic Eyes*, New York, 2009; M. Beard, *The Roman Triumph*, Cambridge, MA, 2007; M. Beard, *Confronting the Classics: Traditions, Adventures and Innovations*, London, 2013; M. Beard and J. Henderson, *Classical Art: From Greece to Rome*, Oxford, 2001; F. Braudel, *The Mediterranean and the Mediterranean World in the Age of Philip II*, 2 vols, trans. S. Reynolds, 2nd revised edn, Berkeley, 1972–3; C. Dell (ed.), *What Makes a Masterpiece? Encounters with Great Works of Art*, London, 2010; J. Fox, *The World According to Colour: A Cultural History*, London, 2021; P. Frankopan, *The Silk Roads: A New History of the World*, London, 2015; E. H. Gombrich, *The Story of Art*, 16th edn, London, 2007; O. Grabar, R. Ettinghausen and M. Jenkins-Madina, *The Art and Architecture of Islam 650–1250*, New Haven and London, 2001; J. Hall, *The Artist's Studio: A*

Cultural History, London, 2022; T. Holland, *Persian Fire: The First World Empire and the Battle for the West*, London, 2005; T. Holland, *Dynasty: The Rise and Fall of the House of Caesar*, London, 2015; K. Hessel, *The Story of Art without Men*, London, 2022; N. MacGregor, *A History of the World in 100 Objects*, London, 2010; J. Marozzi, *Islamic Empires: Fifteen Cities that Define a Civilization*, London, 2019; L. Nochlin (ed. C. Grant), *Why Have There Been No Great Women Artists? 50th Anniversary Edition*, London, 2021; R. Parker and G. Pollock, *Old Mistresses; Women, Art and Ideology*, London, 1981; J. Ramirez, *Femina: A New History of the Middle Ages, Through the Women Written Out of It*, London, 2022; S. Schama, *Landscape and Memory*, London, 1995; S. Schama, *Simon Schama's Power of Art*, London, 2006; J. P. Stonard, *Creation: Art Since the Beginning*, London, 2021.

Introduction

For Michelangelo's letter to his brother Buonarotto from Pietrasanta (18 April 1518), see *Le lettere di Michelangelo Buonarotti*, ed. G. Milanesi, Florence, 1875, pp. 137–8; for the menu, G. Riley, *The Oxford Companion to Italian Food*, Oxford, 2007, pp. 325–6. The menu is on the back of a letter in the Casa Buonarotti, Florence, dated 18 March 1518. Milanesi's edition of Michelangelo's correspondence gives a good sense of the everyday quality of much of his life. For Manet, Titian and Velázquez, see D. Rosand, 'So-and-So Reclining on her Couch', in R. Goffen (ed.), *Titian's Venus of Urbino*, Cambridge, 1997, pp. 37–62; G. Tinterow and G. Lacambre, *Manet/Velázquez: The French Taste for Spanish Painting*, New York, 2003. For the criticism levelled at Olympia, see T. J. Clark, 'Olympia's Choice' in T. J. Clark, *The Painting of Modern Life*, Princeton, 1984, pp. 80–146; C. Bernheimer, 'Manet's Olympia: The Figuration of Scandal', *Poetics Today* 10:2 (1989), pp. 255–77, S. Levine, 'Manet's Olympia', *Art Journal* 52:4 (1993), pp. 87–91. A thoughtful analysis of the issues that images can present to the historian is summarised in A. Pegler-Gordon, 'Seeing Images in History', *Perspectives on History: The Magazine of the American Historical Association* 44:2 (February 2006). The journal *Text and Image: Essential Problems in Art History*, established at the Taras Shevchenko National University, Kyiv, in 2016, is devoted to developing communication between researchers who use images in a variety of disciplines. On cities, as an introduction, see J. Jacobs, *The Death and Life of Great American Cities*, New York, 1961; R. J. Holton, *Cities, Capitalism and Civilization*, London, 1986; C. Hibbert, *Cities and Civilisation*, New York, 1986; P. Hall, *Cities in Civilization*, London, 1998.

Babylon

For the biblical Tower of Babel, see Genesis, 11:1–9; for Bablyon in Revelation, 17:3–18 and 18:14. Pieter Bruegel's two Towers of Babel are in the collections, respectively, of the Kunsthistorisches Museum, Vienna and the Museum Boijmans Van Beuningen, Rotterdam.

For Herodotus, I have used Herodotus, *The Histories*, ed. A. D. Godley, Book 1, 178–216, Cambridge, MA, 1920. For the Code of Hammurabi, see 'The Code of Hammurabi', trans. L. W King, hosted at 'The Avalon Project: Documents in Law, History and Diplomacy', https://avalon.law. yale.edu/ancient/hamframe.asp. For a translation of the Cyrus Cylinder, see the Livius digital resource, https://www.livius.org/sources/content/ cyrus-cylinder/cyrus-cylinder-translation/. For Nebuchadnezzar's description of the outer walls of Babylon, see I. Spar and Mi. Jursa, *Cuneiform Texts in the Metropolitan Museum of Art, Volume IV,* New York, 2014, no. 166, pp. 282–4, pl. 133.

For clear introductions to Babylon and to the Babylonian world, see D. D. Oates and J. Oates, *The Rise of Civilization*, Oxford, 1976, and the entries in the *Grove Dictionary of Art* on the Ancient Near East, Babylon, Babylonian and Mesopotamia. See also D. Collon et al. (2003), 'Ancient Near East', Grove Art Online.; D. Collon et al. (2003), 'Mesopotamia', Grove Art Online; (2003), 'Babylon', Grove Art Online; J. Oates (2003), 'Babylonian', Grove Art Online; M. Seymour (2016), 'Babylon', Heilbrunn Timeline of Art History.

For Sumerian and Babylonian religion and texts, see T. Jacobsen, *The Treasures of Darkness: A History of Mesopotamian Religion*, New Haven, 1976; J. A. Black, G. Cunningham, E. Flückiger-Hawker, E. Robson and G. Zólyomi (trans.), *The Electronic Text Corpus of Sumerian Literature,* Oxford, 1998–2006, at https://etcsl.orinst.ox.ac.uk/; B. R. Foster (trans. and ed.), *The Epic of Gilgamesh,* New York, 2001; I. Spar (2009), 'Mesopotamian Creation Myths', Heilbrunn Timeline of Art History; I. Spar (2009), 'Flood Stories', Heilbrunn Timeline of Art History; L. M. Pryke, *Gilgamesh*, London, 2019.

For writing, see D. Charpin, *Reading and Writing in Babylon*, trans. J. M. Todd, Cambridge MA, 2010; I. Finkel, *The Cyrus Cylinder: The Great Persian Edict from Babylon*, London, 2021.

For the city and its civilisation, see J. Oates, *Babylon*, 2nd edn, London, 1986; H. Schmidt, *Der Tempelturm: Etemananki in Babylon*, Mainz, 1995; M. Van De Mieroop, *King Hammurabi of Babylon: A Biography*, Oxford, 2005; A. Gill, *Gateway of the Gods: The Rise and Fall of Babylon*, London, 2008; G. Leick, *The Babylonian World*, London and New York, 2009; P. Kriwaczek, *Babylon: Mesopotamia and the Birth of Civilization*, London, 2010; K. Radner, *A Short History of Babylon*, London, 2020; S. Dalley, *The City of Babylon: A History, c. 2000 bc–ad 116*, Cambridge, 2021.

For the reception of Babylon, see I. Finkel, M. J. Seymour and J. Curtis,

Babylon: Myth and Reality, London, 2008, and M. J. Seymour, *Babylon: Legend, History and the Ancient City*, London, 2014.

For the city's excavation, see A. H. Layard, *Discoveries in the Ruins of Nineveh and Babylon, With Travels in Armenia, Kurdistan and the Desert: Being the Result of a Second Expedition Undertaken for the Trustees of the British Museum*, London, 1853; R. Koldeway and A. S. Johns, *The Excavations at Babylon*, London, 1914; 'The Archaeological Revival of Babylon Project', whole issue, *Sumer* 35 (1979); for the Lion of Babylon, see 'The Lion of Babylon', Google Arts & Culture.

Jerusalem

The fundamental texts in the Hebrew, Christian and Islamic traditions come from the first Book of Kings and Surahs 17, 53 and 81 of the Quran. See also Psalm 137 and Ezra, 1–6. E. A. Seibert, A. Mein and C. V. Camp, *Subversive Scribes and the Solomonic Narrative: A Rereading of 1 Kings 1–11*, New York and London, 2006, looks at texts that undermine the legitimacy of Solomon. For accounts of the Mi'rāj and Isrā', see *Encyclopaedia Britannica*. For how the Mi'rāj developed see B. O. Vuckovic, *Heavenly Journeys, Earthly Concerns: The Legacy of the Mi'raj in the Formation of Islam*, New York and Abingdon, 2005. For early Islam, see G. W. Bowersock, *The Crucible of Islam*, Cambridge, MA, 2017; S. Yalman, based on original work by L. Komaroff (2001), 'The Birth of Islam', Heilbrunn Timeline of Art History; and more generally K. Armstrong, *A Short History of Islam*, New York, 2001, and T. Ansary, *Destiny Disrupted: A History of the World Through Islamic Eyes*, New York, 2010.

On Jerusalem in general, see S. Blair, J. Bloom, J. Murphy O'Connor and M. Turner (2022), 'Jerusalem', Grove Art Online; S. Sebag Montefiore, *Jerusalem: the Biography*, London, 2011, and V. Lemire (ed.), Jerusalem: History of a Global City, trans. J. Froggatt, Oakland, 2022. D. J. Lasker, 'The Date of the Death of Jesus: Further Reflections', *Journal of the American Oriental Society* 124:1 (2004), pp. 95–9, summarises the arguments concerning the historical date of Jesus' death. On Josephus and the Jewish War, see M. Goodman, *Josephus's The Jewish War: A Biography*, Princeton, 2019, For the Temple, see A. Parrot, *The Temple of Jerusalem*, London, 1957; H. Rosenau, *Vision of the Temple: The Image of the Temple of Jerusalem in Judaism and Christianity*, London, 1979; S. Goldhill, *The Temple of Jerusalem*, London, 2004; R. Griffith-Jones and E. Fernie (eds), *Tomb and Temple: Re-Imagining the Sacred Buildings of Jerusalem*, Woodbridge, 2018. A curious nineteenth-century re-imagining is found in 'Architectural model of the temple of King Solomon in Jerusalem', Metropolitan Museum of Art, metmuseum.org. On the Holy Sepulchre, V. Clark, *Holy Fire: The*

Battle for Christ's Tomb, London, 2005, and A. Borg (2003), 'Church of the Holy Sepulchre (Jerusalem)', Grove Art Online. On the Temple Mount, Y. E. Eliav, *God's Mountain: The Temple Mount in Time, Place, and Memory*, Baltimore, 2005, and R. Hillenbrand and L. Ritmeyer (2003), 'Temple Mount (Jerusalem)', Grove Art Online. For the Dome of the Rock, see K. A. C. Creswell, *Early Muslim Architecture*, 1, Oxford, 1969, pp. 65–129, 215–322; M. Rosen-Ayalon, *The Early Islamic Monuments of al-Ḥaram al-Sharīf: An Iconographic Study*, Jerusalem, 1989; G. Neciğoğlu, 'The Dome of the Rock as Palimpsest: 'Abd al-Malik's Grand Narrative and Sultan Sülemayn's Glosses', *Muqarnas* 25:1 (2008), pp. 17–105; O. Grabar, 'Ḳubbat al-Ṣakhra', in *Encyclopaedia of Islam*, 2nd edn, Leiden, 2009; O. Grabar, *The Dome of the Rock*, Cambridge, MA, 2006; M. Levy-Rubin, 'Why was the Dome of the Rock Built? A New Perspective on a Long-Discussed Question', *Bulletin of the School of Oriental and African Studies* 80:3 (2017), pp. 441–64. On the Aqsā Mosque, see K. A. C. Creswell 1969, op. cit., pp. 32–5, 373–80, and H. F. Al-Ratrout, *The Architectural Development of al-Aqsa Mosque in Islamic Jerusalem in the Early Islamic Period: Sacred Architecture in the Shape of the 'Holy'*, Monograph on Islamic Jerusalem Studies, 4, Dundee, 2004. For the early Islamic period in Jerusalem more generally, see O. Grabar, *The Shape of the Holy: Early Islamic Jerusalem*, Princeton, 1996. For Muqadisi's text in English see G. Le Strange, *Palestine under the Moslems*, London, 1890, pp. 123–4. For Mujir al-Din, see D. P. Little, 'Mujīr al-Dīn al-'Ulaymīɔs Vision of Jerusalem in the Ninth/Fifteenth Century', *Journal of the American Oriental Society* 115:2 (1995), pp. 237–47. His comment regarding the banana is cited by S. Goldhill, *Jerusalem, City of Longing*, Cambridge, MA, 2008, p. 112.

For Ezekiel's vision, see the Book of Ezekiel, 40–3. For Istanbul, a good introduction is A. Cutler, W. Denny and P. Magdalino (2022), 'Istanbul', Grove Art Online. For Justinian and Solomon, see G. Dagron, *Emperor and Priest*, Cambridge, 2003, pp. 109–10. For Vladimir of Kyiv's embassy, see *The Russian Primary Chronicle. Laurentian Text*, trans. S. H. Cross and O. P. Sherbowitz-Wetzor, Cambridge, MA, 1953, p. 111. On the Hagia Sophia, concise introductions are found in R. Cormack (2003), 'Hagia Sophia', Grove Art Online; W. Allen, 'Hagia Sophia, Istanbul', Smarthistory; E. Wegner (2004), 'Hagia Sophia, 532–37', Heilbrunn Timeline of Art History; and in the reference works by R. Krautheimer, *Early Christian and Byzantine Architecture*, 4th edn, Harmondsworth, 1986, and L. Rodley, *Byzantine Art and Architecture: An Introduction*, Cambridge, 1994. A contemporary account of the construction is found in Prokopios, *On Buildings*, trans. H. B. Dewing and G. Downey, Cambridge, MA, 1940. More detailed studies include R. L. Van Nice, *St Sophia in Istanbul: An Architectural Survey*, 2 vols, Washington DC, 1965–86; R. J. Mainstone, *Hagia Sophia: Architecture,*

Structure and Liturgy of Justinian's Great Church, London, 1988; R. Cormack, *The Byzantine Eye*, London, 1989; S. Yerasimos, *La fondation de Constantinople et de Sainte-Sophie dans les traditions turques: légendes d'Empire*, Istanbul and Paris, 1990; G. Necipoğlu, 'The Life of an Imperial Monument: Hagia Sophia after Byzantium', in R. Mark and A. Çakmak (eds), *Hagia Sophia: From the Age of Justinian to the Present*, Cambridge, 1992, pp. 195–225; and M. Ahunbay and Z. Ahunbay, 'Structural Influence of Hagia Sophia on Ottoman Mosque Architecture', in ibid., pp. 179–94. On Süleyman and the Süleymaniye Mosque, see S. Yalman (based on original work by L. Komaroff) (2002), 'The Age of Süleyman "the Magnificent" (r. 1520–1566)', Heilbrunn Timeline of Art History; J. M. Rogers, 'The State and the Arts in Ottoman Turkey. Part 1. The Stones of Süleymaniye', *International Journal of Middle East Studies* 14:1 (1982), pp. 71–86; G. Necipoğlu, 'The Süleymaniye Complex in Istanbul: An Interpretation', *Muqarnas* 3 (1985), pp. 92–117; G. Necipoğlu, *The Age of Sinan: Architectural Culture in the Ottoman Empire*, London, 2005; R. Milstein, 'King Solomon or Sultan Süleyman?', in E. Ginio and E. Podeh (eds), *The Ottoman Middle East: Studies in Honor of Amnon Cohen*, Leiden, 2013, pp. 13–24; Sinan, *Sinan's Autobiographies: Five Sixteenth-Century Texts*, trans. H. Crane et al., Leiden, 2014; C. Grenier, 'Solomon, his Temple, and Ottoman Imperial Anxieties', *Bulletin of the School of Oriental and African Studies* 85:1 (2022), pp. 21–46. For Raphael and the tapestries, see, most recently, T. P. Campbell, in D. Ekserdjian, T. Henry and M. Wivel (eds), *Raphael*, London, 2022. For the miracle of the healing of the lame man, see Acts, 3. On St Peter's, Bernini and Solomonic columns, see R. Preimesberger & M. Mezzatesta (2003), 'Bernini, Gianlorenzo', Grove Art Online; F. Baldinucci, *Vita del cavaliere ... Bernino* (MS. 1682), ed. S. Samek Ludovici, Milan, 1948, English trans., University Park, PA, 1966; J. B. Ward Perkins, 'The Shrine of St Peter and its Twelve Spiral Columns', *Journal of Roman Studies* 42 (1952), pp. 21–33; R. Wittkower, *Art and Architecture in Italy, 1600–1750*, Harmondsworth, revised 3rd edn, 1973; J. Montagu, *Roman Baroque Sculpture: The Industry of Art*, New Haven and London, 1989; R. Wittkower, *Gian Lorenzo Bernini: The Sculptor of the Roman Baroque*, revised 3rd edn, Ithaca, 1981; I. Lavin, 'Bernini's Baldachin: Considering a Reconsideration', *Römisches Jahrbuch für Kunstgeschichte* 21 (1984), pp. 405–14; R. Taylor, 'Solomonic Columns in England: The Origins and Influence of the Porch of St Mary the Virgin, Oxford', *Georgian Group Journal* 24 (2000), pp. 1–12; J. D. Stewart, 'Rome, Venice, Mantua, London: Form and Meaning in the "Solomonic" Column, from Veronese to George Vertue', *British Art Journal* 8:3 (2007), pp 15–23; L. Roberts, 'Bees in the frame: Part 1 – the Barberini bee', theframeblog.com (22 August 2017).

Rome

The key texts I have used include Cicero, *The Orations of Marcus Tullius Cicero*, trans. C. D. Yonge, London, 1856; Martial, *Epigrammaton libri*, ed. W. Heraeus and J. Borovskij, Leipzig, 1925, 1.23, 1.62, 2.14, 2.52, 3.51, 3.68, 3.72, 4.8, 5.20, 5.44, 6.42, 6.93, 7.35, 7.76, 9.33, 9.75, 11.51, 12.19, 12.70, 12.82; Ovid, *Fasti*, ed. and trans. J. G. Frazer, Cambridge and London, 1931; Pliny the Elder, *The Natural History*, ed. and trans. J. Bostock and H. T. Riley, London, 1855, Books 35–7; Plutarch, 'Life of Caesar', in *Lives*, trans. B. Perrin, Cambridge and London, 1919; Seneca, *Ad Lucilium Epistulae Morales*, ed. R. M. Gummere, 3 vols, Cambridge and London, 1917–25, Letter 56; Suetonius, *The Lives of the Caesars*, ed. and trans. A. Thomson, Philadelphia, 1889; Virgil, *Aeneid*, trans. T. C. Williams, Boston, 1910; Vitruvius, *The Ten Books on Architecture*, ed. M. H. Morgan, Cambridge and London, 1914. I have accessed these through the Perseus online platform maintained by Tufts University, Boston.

The Oxford Classical Dictionary, S. Hornblower and A. Spawford, eds., Oxford and New York, 2003, 3rd ed.; K. Galinksy, *Augustan Culture: An Interpretive Introduction*, Princeton, 1996; and K. Galinksy (ed.), *The Cambridge Companion to the Age of Augustus*, Cambridge, 2005, have been invaluable. For Rome in general, see S. B. Platner and T. Ashby, *A Topographical Dictionary of Ancient Rome*, London, 1929; E. Nash, *Pictorial Dictionary of Ancient Rome*, 2 vols, 2nd edn, London, 1968; C. Hibbert, *Rome: The Biography of a City*, Harmondsworth, 1985; T. Holland, *Rubicon: The Triumph and Tragedy of the Roman Republic*, London, 2003; M. Goodman, *Rome and Jerusalem: The Clash of Ancient Civilizations*, London, 2007; M. Beard, *SPQR: A History of Ancient Rome*, London, 2015; M. Beard, *Twelve Caesars: Images of Power from the Ancient World to the Modern*, Princeton, 2021.

For Pompeii, see J. Ward-Perkins and A. Claridge, *Pompeii ad 79*, Boston, 1978; L. Richardson Jr, *Pompeii: An Architectural History*, Baltimore, 1988; A. Wallace-Hadrill, *Houses and Society in Pompeii and Herculaneum*, Princeton, 1994; E. De Carolis, *Gods and Heroes in Pompeii*, Los Angeles, 2001; P. M. Allison, *Pompeian Households: An Analysis of the Material Culture*, Los Angeles, 2004; J. Harris, *Pompeii Awakened: A Story of Rediscovery*, London, 2006; J. J. Dobbins and P. W. Foss (eds), *The World of Pompeii*, London, 2007; M. Beard, *Pompeii: The Life of a Roman Town*, London, 2008; J. Berry, *The Complete Pompeii*, London, 2013. For a visual and textual resource of the Via della Abbondanza, see J. Stephens and A. Stephens (eds), Pompeii Perspectives (http://www.pompeiiperspectives.org) and on the Pompeii Forum, see http://pompeii.virginia.edu, directed by J. J. Dobbin.

For Roman painting and sculpture, see M. L. Anderson, 'Pompeiian

Frescoes in The Metropolitan Museum of Art', special issue of the *Metropolitan Museum of Art Bulletin* 45 (1987); P. Zanker, *The Power of Images in the Age of Augustus*, trans. D. Schneider, Ann Arbor, 1987; R. Ling, *Roman Painting*, Cambridge, 1991; D. E. E. Kleiner, *Roman Sculpture*, New Haven and London, 1994; F. Pesando, M. Bussagli and G. Mori, *Pompei: La pittura*, Florence, 2003; D. Mazzoleni, U. Pappalardo and L. Romano, *Domus: Wall Painting in the Roman House*, Los Angeles, 2004; and for the impact of Roman sculpture in post-medieval Europe, see F. Haskell and N. Penny, *Taste and the Antique: The Lure of Classical Sculpture, 1500–1900*, London and New Haven, 1981.

For the Ara Pacis, see Ara pacis (Rome), R. Stupperich, revised by T. Opper (2015). 'Ara Pacis (Rome)', Grove Art Online; S. Settis, 'Die Ara Pacis', *Kaiser Augustus und die verlorene Republik*, exhibition catalogue, Berlin, 1988, pp. 400–27; P. J. Holliday, 'Time, History, and Ritual on the Ara Pacis Augustae', *Art Bulletin* 72:4 (1990), pp. 542–57; J. Elsner, 'Cult and Sculpture: Sacrifice in the Ara Pacis Augustae', *Journal of Roman Studies* 81 (1991), pp. 50–61; D. Castriota, *The Ara Pacis Augustae and the Imagery of Abundance in Later Greek and Early Roman Imperial Art*, Princeton, 1995; D. A. Conlin, *The Artists of the Ara Pacis: The Process of Hellenization in Roman Relief Sculpture*, Chapel Hill, 1997; P. Rehak, 'Aeneas or Numa? Rethinking the Meaning of the Ara Pacis Augustae', *Art Bulletin* 83:2 (2001), pp. 190–208; M. J. Strazzulla, 'War and Peace: Housing the Ara Pacis in the Eternal City', *American Journal of Archaeology* 113:2 (2009), pp. 1–10; P. Jacobs and D. Conlin, *Campus Martius: The Field of Mars in the Life of Ancient Rome*, Cambridge, 2015. The online resource Ara Pacis (https://www.reed.edu/ara-pacis/contents.php), established and maintained by Charles Rhyne and Reed College, is most helpful.

For Roman Imperial construction more generally, see W. L. MacDonald, *The Architecture of the Roman Empire*, 2 vols, New Haven, 1965–86, vol. 1, rev. 2nd edn, 1982; J. B. Ward-Perkins, *Roman Imperial Architecture*, Harmondsworth, 1981; J.-P. Adam, *Roman Building: Materials and Techniques*, London, 1994; A. T. Hodge, *Roman Aqueducts and Water Supply*, 2nd edn, London, 2002.

For baths and bathing, G. G. Fagan, *Bathing in Public in the Roman World*, Ann Arbor, 1999; R. Taylor, *Public Needs and Private Pleasures: Water Distribution, the Tiber River, and the Urban Development of Ancient Rome*, Rome, 2000; K. W. Rinne, *The Waters of Rome: Aqueducts, Fountains, and the Birth of the Baroque City*, New Haven, 2010 (in terms of posterity); A. Hrychuk Kontokosta, 'Building the Thermae Agrippae: Private Life, Public Space, and the Politics of Bathing in Early Imperial Rome', *American Journal of Archaeology* 123:1 (2019), pp. 45–77.

Baghdad

Mansūr's celebrated remark is cited in A. Hourani, *A History of the Arab Peoples*, London, 1991, p. 33. For the comment about the Tigris related by al-Tabari, see H. Kennedy and ويهيدنك. 'The Feeding of the Five Hundred Thousand: Cities and Agriculture in Early Islamic Mesopotamia', *Iraq* 73 (2011), p. 189. For the city, see (2003), 'Baghdad', Grove Art Online; G. Le Strange, *Baghdad during the Abbasid Caliphate from Contemporary Arabic and Persian Sources*, Oxford, 1900; J. Marozzi, *Baghdad: City of Peace, City of Blood*, London, 2014. For the geography of the Abbasid period I have consulted W. C. Brice, *An Historical Atlas of Islam*, Leiden, 1981, and H. N. Kennedy, *An Historical Atlas of Islam/Atlas Historique de l'Islam*. 2nd revised edn, Leiden, 2002. For al-Jahiz, see Al-Jāḥiẓ, *Sobriety and Mirth: A Selection of the Shorter Writings of al-Jāhiz*, trans. J. Colville, London, 2002. For al-Tabari, see *The History of al-Tabari (Ta'rikh al-Rusul wa 'l-Muluk)*, vol. 27, *The 'Abbasid Revolution* [ad 743-750/ah 126–132] by J. A. Williams; vol. 35, *The Crisis of the 'Abbasid Caliphate* [The Caliphates of al-Musta'in and al-Mu'tazz ad 862–869/ah 248–255] by G. Saliba; vol. 38, *The Return of the Caliphate to Baghdad: The Caliphates of al-Mu'tadid, al-Muktafi and alMuqtadir* [ad 892–915/ah 279–302] by F. Rosenthal; vol. 18, *Between Civil Wars: The Caliphate of Mu'awiyah* [ad 661–680/ah 40–60] by M. G. Morony, vol. 18, 1985–. For al-Khatib al-Baghdadi, see Tarikh Baghdad, *Die Geschichte von Bagdad/The History of Baghdad*, Beirut, 1967; A. Rivera Medina, 'Al-Khatīb al-Baghdādī', in G. Dunphy and C. Bratu (eds), *Encyclopedia of the Medieval Chronicle*, http://dx.doi.org/10.1163/2213-2139_emc_SIM_00084.

For the Abbasid caliphs see M. A. Shaban, *The Abbasid Revolution*, Cambridge, 1970; M. M. Ahsan, *Social Life under the Abbasids*, London and New York, 1979; J. Lassner, *The Shaping of 'Abbāsid Rule*, Princeton, 1980; H. N. Kennedy, *The Early Abbasid Caliphate: A Political History*, London, 1981; H. N. Kennedy, *The Prophet and the Age of the Caliphates: The Islamic Near East from the Sixth to the Eleventh Centuries*, London, 1986; H. N. Kennedy, *The Armies of the Caliphs: Military and Society in the Early Islamic State*, New York, 2001; H. N. Kennedy, *The Court of the Caliphs*, London, 2004; H. N. Kennedy, *The Great Arab Conquests: How the Spread of Islam Changed the World We Live In*, London, 2007. For Harūn al-Rashīd and Charlemagne, see F. W. Buckler, *Harunu'l-Rashid and Charles the Great*, Cambridge, MA, 1931 (a new book, S. Ottewill-Soulsby, *The Emperor and the Elephant*, Princeton, 2023, is devoted to this subject). For the 'girl with the mole' cited on p. 104, see N. Abbott, *The Queens of Baghdad*, Chicago, 1946, pp. 144–5. For the two girls caught making love, also on p. 104, see al-Tabari, *Annales*, ed. M. J. de Goeje et al., Leiden 1879–1901, vol. 3, p. 590. For the slave girl who suffocated Caliph Hādi, see ibid., p. 571.

For an introduction to Abbasid art and architecture, see S. Yalman, based on original work by L. Komaroff (2001), 'The Art of the Abbasid Period (750–1258)', Heilbrunn Timeline of Art History; and G. Curatola: 'The Islamic Era', *The Art and Architecture of Mesopotamia*, New York, 2007, pp. 149–208.

For Baghdad and Samarra in the context of early Islamic architecture, see K. A. C. Creswell, *Early Muslim Architecture*, 2 vols, Oxford, 1932–40, revised edn of vol. 1 in 2 pts, Oxford, 1969; O. Grabar, *The Formation of Islamic Art*, New Haven and London, revised and enlarged, 1987; R. Ettinghausen and O. Grabar, *The Art and Architecture of Islam, 600–1250*, Harmondsworth, 1987; revised edition of the same, with M. Jenkins-Madina, *Islamic Art and Architecture, 600–1250*, New Haven and London, 2001; R. Hillenbrand, *Islamic Art and Architecture*, London, 1999; J. M. Bloom, *Early Islamic Art and Architecture*, Aldershot, 2002; V. Strika and J. Khalil, *The Islamic Architecture of Baghdad: The Results of a Joint Italian-Iraqi Survey*, Naples, 1987.

For Samarra, the fundamental topographical works are A. Northedge, *Samarra I: The Historical Topography of Samarra*, British Institute for the Study of Iraq, 2008; A. Northedge and D. Kennet, *Archaeological Atlas of Samarra: Samarra Studies*, British Institute for the Study of Iraq, 2015. For the UNESCO citation of Samarra, see https://whc.unesco.org/en/list/276/. The city has been on the 'at risk' register since 2007.

For the city more generally, see C. F. Robinson (ed.), *A Medieval Islamic City Reconsidered: An Interdisciplinary Approach to Samarra*, Oxford, 2001; J. Oates, A. Northedge, S. S. Blair and J. M. Bloom (2003), 'Samarra', Grove Art Online; A. Northedge: 'Remarks on Samarra and the Archaeology of Large Cities', *Antiquity* 79 (2005), pp. 119–29; M. Saba (2022), 'Samarra, a palatial city', Smarthistory.

For painting and stucco in Samarra, see E. Herzfeld, *Die Malereien von Samarra*, 1927, vol. 3 of *Die Ausgrabungen von Samarra*, Berlin and Hamburg, 1923–48; E. Hoffman, 'Between East and West: The Wall Paintings of Samarra and the Construction of Abbasid Princely Culture', *Muqarnas* 25 (2008), pp. 107–32; L. Burgio, R. J. H. Clark and M. Rosser-Owen, 'Raman Analysis of Ninth-Century Iraqi Stuccoes from Samarra', *Journal of Archaeological Science* 34 (2007), pp. 756–62; for palaces including those of Samarra, see G. Necipoğlu (ed.), *Ars Orientalis* 23 (1993), A Special Issue on Pre-Modern Islamic Palaces. For al-Shabushti's account of the throne room at Samarra, see H. N. Kennedy, *The Court of the Caliphs*, London, 2004, pp. 147–8.

For Ernst Herzfeld, see R. Ettinghausen, 'Ernst Herzfeld (1879–1948)', *Ars Islamica* 15–16 (1951), pp. 261–71; R. M. Lindsay., 'Introducing the Ernst Herzfeld Papers in the Metropolitan Museum, Department of Islamic

Art', samarrafindsproject.blogspot.com; R. M. Lindsey (2016), 'Ernst Emil Herzfeld (1879–1948) in Samarra', Heilbrunn Timeline of Art History.

On ceramics, https://islamicceramics.ashmolean.org/Abbasid/pottery.htm is a good introduction to the issues. Also see F. Sarre, *Die Keramik von Samarra*, 1925, vol. 2 of *Die Ausgrabungen von Samarra*, Berlin, 1923–48; A. Lane, *Early Islamic Pottery*, London, 1954; D. Whitehouse, 'Islamic Glazed Pottery in Iraq and the Persian Gulf: The Ninth and Tenth Centuries', *Annali: AION*, n.s.:29 (1979), pp. 44–61; H. Philon, *Early Islamic Ceramics: Ninth to Late Twelfth Centuries*, London, 1980; O. Watson, 'Ceramics', in T. Falk (ed.), *Treasures of Islam*, Geneva, 1985, pp. 206–9; A. Caiger-Smith, *Lustre Pottery: Technique, Tradition and Innovation in Islam and the Western World*, London, 1985; O. Watson, *Ceramics from Islamic Lands*, London, 2004.

For innovation, translation and science, see D. Gutas, *Greek Thought, Arabic Culture: the Graeco-Arabic Translation Movement in Baghdad and Early 'Abbāsid Society (2nd–4th/8th–10th Centuries)*, Abingdon, 1998; J. Freely, *Aladdin's Lamp: How Greek Science Came to Europe through the Islamic World*, New York, 2009; H. Belting, *Florence and Baghdad: Renaissance Art and Arab Science*, Cambridge, MA, 2011; F. S. Starr, *Lost Enlightenment: Central Asia's Golden Age from the Arab Conquest to Tamerlane*, Princeton, 2013.

For early Islamic glass, see S. Carboni and D. Whitehouse, *Glass of the Sultans*, New York, 2002; S. Carboni and Q. Adamjee (2002), 'Mosaic Glass from Islamic Lands', Heilbrunn Timeline of Art History; M. Saba 'Fragmentary but Fascinating: Architectural Glass from Samarra', Metmuseum.org.

For textiles, see E. Kühnel and L. Bellinger, *Catalogue of Dated Tiraz Fabrics*, Washington DC, 1952; E. Kühnel, 'Abbasid Silks of the Ninth Century', *Ars Orientalis* 2 (1957), pp. 367–71; M. Lombard, *Les Textiles dans le monde musulman*, Paris, 1978; A. Wardwell (2003), 'Islamic Art: Textiles' and 'Iraq and the Eastern Islamic Lands', Grove Art Online; E. Dospěl Williams, 'A Taste for Textiles: Designing Umayyad and 'Abbāsid Interiors', in G. Bühl and E. Dospěl Williams (eds), *Catalogue of the Textiles in the Dumbarton Oaks Byzantine Collection*, Washington DC, 2019; C. Mühlemann, 'Made in the City of Baghdad? Medieval Textile Production and Pattern Notation Systems of Early Lampas Woven Silks', *Muqarnas* 39 (2022), pp. 1–22. The quotations on p. 90 concerning the use of textiles come from al-Tabari, *Annales*, op. cit., vol. 3, p. 415 (for Mansūr), pp. 510–13 (for Mahdi).

On astrolabes, D. A King, 'A Catalogue of Medieval Astronomical Instruments to ca. 1500', www.davidking.org; D. A King, 'The Renaissance of Astronomy in Baghdad in the Ninth and Tenth Centuries: A List of

Publications, Mainly from the last 50 Years', www.davidking.org; 'Astrolabe Catalogue Home Page, Museum of the History of Science, Oxford', https:// www.mhs.ox.ac.uk/astrolabe/catalogue/; W. Greenwood, 'Seeing Stars: Astrolabes and the Islamic World', British Museum blog (January 2018), https://www.britishmuseum.org/blog/seeing-stars-astrolabes-and-islami c-world; W. Greenwood, 'How to Use an Astrolabe I Curator's Corner S3 Ep1', https://www.youtube.com/watch?v=N8oWGwcdFmA.

Kyoto

For introductions to Heian art and Heian Kyoto, see B. Abiko (2003), 'Heian Period', Grove Art Online; Department of Asian Art (2002), 'Heian Period (794–1185)', Heilbrunn Timeline of Art History; S. Coman (2021), 'Heian Period, An Introduction', Smarthistory; B. Coats, R. Wilson, H. Sørensen and G. Nakahashi (2003), 'Kyoto', Grove Art Online. For a historical overview, see R. Bowring and P. Kornicki, *The Cambridge Encyclopedia of Japan*, New York, 1993; J. W. Hall et al., *The Cambridge History of Japan. Volume 2: Heian Japan*, ed. D. H. Shively and W. H. McCullough, Cambridge and New York, 1999; For the history of Kyoto see R. A. Ponsonby-Fane, *Kyoto: The Old Capital of Japan*, Kyoto, 1956; for the court, see I. Morris, *The World of the Shining Prince: Court Life in Ancient Japan*, New York, 1964.

For studies of Japanese art of the Heian period, see R. T. Paine and A. Soper, *The Art and Architecture of Japan*, Harmondsworth, 1955, rev. 3rd edn, 1981, pp. 357, 362–3, 446–7; J. Rosenfield, *Japanese Arts of the Heian Period, 794–1185*, New York, 1967; T. Akiyama, *Japanese Painting*, New York, 1977; B. B. Ford and O. R. Impey, *Japanese Art from the Gerry Collection in The Metropolitan Museum of Art*, New York, 1989; P. Mason, *A History of Japanese Art*, Upper Saddle River, 2004; A. Willmann (2003, revised 2013), 'Yamato-e Painting', Heilbrunn Timeline of Art History. An important Japanese state website giving digital access to objects designated in Japan as national treasures and important cultural properties can be accessed at https://emuseum.nich.go.jp. The screen I discuss from the Kyoto National Museum can be found at https://colbase.nich. go.jp/collection_items/kyohaku/A%E7%94%B2227?locale=en.

For Jōchō and Byōdōin, see T. Fukuyama, 'Byōdōin to Chūsonji', *Nihon no bijutsu* [Arts of Japan] 9 (1964), trans. by R. K. Jones as *Heian Temples: Byodo-in and Chuson-ji*, Heibonsha Survey of Japanese Art, 9, New York and Tokyo, 1976; T. Akiyama, 'The Door Paintings in the Phoenix Hall of the Byōdōin as Yamatoe, *Artibus Asiae* 53:1/2 (1993), pp. 144–67; M. Hall Yiengpruksawan, 'The Phoenix Hall at Uji and the Symmetries of Replication', *Art Bulletin* 77:4 (1995), pp. 647–72; S.

Morse (2003), 'Jōchō', Grove Art Online; M. Hall Yiengpruksawan and S. Jung (2023), 'Byōdōin'. Grove Art Online.

For gardens, see L. Kuck, *The World of the Japanese Garden: From Chinese Origins to Modern Landscape Art*, revised edn, New York, 1968, rev. 1980, and S. Walker, *The Japanese Garden*, London, 2017.

For literary and textual sources, see A. Shepley Omori et al., *Diaries of Court Ladies of Old Japan*, trans. A. Shepley Omori and K. Doi, Tokyo, 1935; Murasaki Shikibu, *Genji Monogatari* (11th century), trans. by A. Waley and E. Seidensticker as *The Tale of Genji*, New York, 1976; Sei Shōnagon and I. Morris, *The Pillow-Book of Sei Shonagon*, London, 1979; Sugawara no Takasue no Musume, S. Arntzen and I. Moriyuki, *The Sarashina Diary: A Woman's Life in Eleventh-Century Japan*, New York, 2018; Murasaki Shikibu and D. C. Washburn, *The Tale of Genji*, trans. D. C. Washburn, New York, 2015; G. E. Ivanova, *Unbinding The Pillow Book: the Many Lives of a Japanese Classic*, New York, 2018. For Shōnagon's encounter with Nobutsune, see *The Pillow-Book*, op. cit., section 69 'Once during a long spell of rainy weather; for the garden after the rain', section 84 'I remember a clear morning'; for 'hateful things', section 14. For the Sarashina diarist's meeting with Minamoto no Sukemichi, see Sugawara no Takasue no Musume et al. 2018, op. cit., pp. 45–8, 48–9. For the relevant parts of the 'The Eastern Cottage', Chapter 50 of the *Tale of Genji*, see the Waley and Seidensticker edition, pp. 1033-39. Some scholars have suggested that Chapters 42 to 54 were not written by Murasaki Shikubi; however, the Sarashina diarist (writing in 1021) expresses her joy to have a complete version of the *Tale* in her hands, specifically mentioning the work extends to more than fifty chapters.

Beijing

For Beijing an introduction is H. Sørensen (2003), 'Beijing', Grove Art Online. The best introduction to art in China is C. Clunas, *Art in China*, 2nd edn, Oxford, 2009; J. Harrison-Hall, *China: A History in Objects*, London, 2017, is also good, through the specifics of particular items. For the Ming dynasty, introductory essays are Department of Asian Art (2003), 'Ming Dynasty (1368–1644)', Heilbrunn Timeline of Art History; C. Michaelson (2003), 'Ming Dynasty', Grove Art Online.

For the Ming emperors and society, see W. T. De Bary (ed.), *Self and Society in Ming Thought*, New York, 1970; E. L. Farmer, *Early Ming Government*, Cambridge, MA, 1976; C. O. Hucker, *The Ming Dynasty: Its Origins and Evolving Institutions*, Michigan Papers in Chinese Studies, 34, Ann Arbor, 1978; C. Clunas, *Empire of Great Brightness: Visual and Material Cultures of Ming China, 1368-1644*, London, 2007; C. Clunas,

Screen of Kings: Royal Art and Power in Ming China, London, 2013; and for a foreigner's take on China, see J. Spence, *The Memory Palace of Matteo Ricci*, London, 1985. For Oliver Goldsmith's reference to the 'Emperor Yonglo' in a work satirising manners in eighteenth-century London, see O. Goldsmith, *A Citizen of the World, or, Letters from a Chinese Philosopher, Residing in London, to his friends in the East*, Dublin, 1762, Letter 60, p. 6.

C. Clunas, and J. Harrison-Hall, *Ming: 50 Years That Changed China*, London, 2014, is a beautifully illustrated and informative summation of thinking about the early Ming dynasty and their cultural production. Also see the published proceedings of the conference that accompanied the exhibition, C. Clunas, J. Harrison-Hall and Y.-P. Luk (eds), *Ming: Courts and Contacts 1400–1600*, London, 2016, for a global perspective on the early Ming period, using a diverse array of historical sources. Zheng He's inscription in Fujian Province is recorded in English translation in T. Filesi, *China and Africa in the Middle Ages*, trans. D. Morison, London, 1972, doc. 6–65. For Ghiyath al-Din's visit, see 'Report to Mirza Baysunghur on the Timurid Legation to the Ming Court at Peking', in *A Century of Princes: Sources on Timurid History and Art*, selected and trans. W. M. Thackston, Cambridge, 1989. For Louis Le Comte's 1680s account of China, including the pagoda at Nanjing, see L. Le Comte, *Nouveaux memoires sur l'état de la Chine*, 1696, repr. in F. Touboul-Bouyere (ed.), *Un Jesuite á Pekin: Nouveaux memoires sur l'état present de la Chine, 1687–1692*, Paris, 1990.

For Ming painting, see J. Cahill, *Parting at the Shore: Chinese Painting of the Early and Middle Ming Dynasty, 1368–1580*, New York, 1978, and C. Clunas, *Chinese Painting and Its Audiences*, Princeton, 2017. For lacquer ware, see R. Krahl and B. Morgan, *From Innovation to Conformity: Chinese Lacquer from the 13th to 16th Centuries*, London, 1989. For the architectural commissions of the Ming emperors, see O. Sirén, *The Walls and Gates of Peking*, London, 1924; O. Sirén, *The Imperial Palaces of Peking*, 3 vols, Paris, 1926; N. Shatzman Steinhardt, *Chinese Imperial City Planning*, Honolulu, 1990; A. Paludan, *The Ming Tombs*, Hong Kong, Oxford and New York, 1991. For the Imperial Palace and its contents, see Y. Boda and W. Wango, *The Palace Museum: Peking*, New York, 1982; Y. Chongnian, *Beijing: The Treasures of an Ancient Capital*, Beijing, 1987.

For Ming porcelain generally, see P. David, *Illustrated Catalogue of [ceramics] … in the Percival David Foundation of Chinese Art*, London, 1973; D. Lion-Goldschmidt, *Ming Porcelain*, London, 1978; S. J. Vainker, *Chinese Pottery and Porcelain*, London, 1991; R. Krahl and J. Harrison-Hall, *Ancient Chinese Trade Ceramics*, Taipei, 1994; J. Harrison-Hall, *Catalogue of Late Yuan and Ming Ceramics in the British Museum*, London, 2001; R. Kerr, L. E. Mengoni and M. Wilson,

Chinese Export Ceramics, London, 2011; E. Ströber, *Ming: Porcelain for a Globalised Trade*, Stuttgart, 2013; J. Ayers, *Chinese and Japanese Works of Art in the Collection of Her Majesty The Queen*, London, 2016.

For the kilns at Jingdezhen see G. R. Sayer, *Ching-Te-Chen T'ao Lu or The Potteries of China*, London, 1951; M. Medley, *The Chinese Potter*, revised edn, Oxford, 1980; R. Tichane, *Ching-te-Chen: Views of a Porcelain City*, New York, 1983; *Imperial Porcelain of the Yongle and Xuande Periods Excavated from the Site of the Ming Imperial Factory at Jingdezhen*, Hong Kong, 1989; R. Scott, *Elegant Form and Harmonious Decoration: Four Dynasties of Jingdezhen Porcelain*, London, 1992; R. Scott (ed.), *The Porcelains of Jingdezhen*, Percival David Foundations Colloquies on Art and Archaeology, 16, London, 1993; R. Krahl, 'By Appointment to the Emperor: Imperial Porcelains from Jingdezhen and their Various Destinations', *Oriental Art* 48:5 (2002–3), pp. 27–32; R. Krahl (2003), 'Jingdezhen', Grove Art Online; M. Medley, *The Chinese Potter: A Practical History of Chinese Ceramics*, revised edn, London, 2006; M. B. Gillette, *China's Porcelain Capital: The Rise, Fall and Reinvention of Ceramics in Jingdezhen*, London, 2016; A. Gerritsen, *The City of Blue and White: Chinese Porcelain and the Early Modern World*, Cambridge, 2020.

For the trade in porcelain outside China, see B. S. McElney and L. Jian'an, *Chinese Ceramics and the Maritime Trade Pre-1700: Being the Catalogue of an Exhibition of Chinese Export Wares of Pre-1700 Date*, Bath, 2006; A. Gerritsen, 'Fragments of a Global Past: Ceramics Manufacture in Song-Yuan-Ming Jingdezhen', *Journal of the Economic and Social History of the Orient* 52:1 (2009), pp. 117–52; A. Gerritsen and S. McDowall, 'Material Culture and the Other: European Encounters with Chinese Porcelain, ca. 1650–1800', *Journal of World History* 23:1 (2012), pp. 87–113; E. Ströber, *Ming: Porcelain for a Globalised Trade*, Stuttgart, 2013; J. Hwang Degenhardt, 'Cracking the Mysteries of "China": China(ware) in the Early Modern Imagination', *Studies in Philology* 110:1 (2013), pp. 132–67.

Florence

For an introduction see C. Adelson et al., 'Florence', Grove Art Online. E. Welch, *Art and Society in Italy 1350–1500*, Oxford, 1997, remains a good entrée to Italian fifteenth-century art. F. Ames-Lewis (ed.), *Florence*, Cambridge, 2012, is a collection of essays by leading specialists in the field of Florentine patronage and art. S. Nethersole, *Art of Renaissance Florence: A City and Its Legacy*, London, 2019 is a good recent introductory text. P. L. Rubin, A. Wright and N. Penny, *Renaissance Florence: The Art of the 1470s*, London, 1999, is an excellent exhibition catalogue on the art of the later fifteenth century in Florence. For Italian altarpieces, see D. Ekserdjian, *The Italian Renaissance Altarpiece: Between Art and Narrative*, New Haven and London, 2021.

The key text, both for its extent and for the impact it had, remains Vasari's *Lives of the Artists*. I have used G. Vasari, *Le opere di Giorgio Vasari*, with annotations and commentary by G. Milanesi (1878–1885), 9 vols, reprinted Florence, 1973 (and vol. 3, p. 309, for his comment that Lorenzo de' Medici's day was 'truly a golden age for men of talent'). In English translation, see G. Vasari, *Lives of the Painters, Sculptors and Architects*, trans. G. du C. de Vere, with an introduction by D. Ekserdjian, London and New York, 1996 (which I have used); also the abridged Penguin Classics version, G. Vasari, *Lives of the Artists*, trans. G. Bull with notes by P. Murray, 2 vols, London, 2004. P. L. Rubin, *Giorgio Vasari: Art and History*, New Haven, 1995, is excellent on Vasari's contexts. I. Rowland and N. Charney, *The Collector of Lives: Giorgio Vasari and the Invention of Art*, New York, 2017, is a biographical study. M. W. Gahtan (ed.), *Giorgio Vasari and the Birth of the Museum*, Farnham, 2014, looks at Vasari and sixteenth-century collecting. Another key text is L. B. Alberti, De pictura (MS.; 1435) – see R. Sinisgalli (ed.), *Leon Battista Alberti, On Painting: A New Translation and Critical Edition*, Cambridge, 2011 (*On Painting*, trans. C. Grayson, ed. M. Kemp, Harmondsworth, 1991, is also readily available).

For biographical studies of the Medici family, see M. Hollingsworth, *The Medici*, London, 2017; C. Hibbert, *The Rise and the Fall of the House of Medici*, London, 1974, remains a very accessible read. For Lorenzo de' Medici, see F.W. Kent and C. James (eds), *Princely Citizen: Lorenzo de' Medici and Renaissance Florence*, Turnhout, 2013 (and p. 271 for Benedetto Dei's characterisation of Lorenzo as the 'master of the workshop'). For the family's women, see N. Thomas, *The Medici Women: Gender and Power in Renaissance Florence*, Aldershot, 2003; V. Conticelli and B. Edelstein (eds), *Eleonora di Toledo and the Invention of the Medici Court in Florence*, Livorno, 2023. N. Rubinstein, *The Palazzo Vecchio, 1290–1532: Government, Architecture and Imagery in the Civic Palace of the Florentine Republic*, Oxford, 1995, is a seminal study of the interaction between the exercise of power and imagery in the Florentine Republic. See also M. Trachtenberg, *Dominion of the Eye: Urbanism, Art and Power in Early Modern Florence*, Cambridge and New York, 1997. L. Sebregondi and T. Parks, *Money and Beauty: Bankers, Botticelli and the Bonfires of Vanities*, Florence, 2011, is a lively take on the millennial fervour of late fifteenth-century Florence, in the context of the city's exceptional wealth. R. C. Trexler, *Public Life in Renaissance Florence*, New York, 1980, is a key work on public life and spectacle. For Giovanni Rucellai, see G. Rucellai, *Giovanni Rucellai ed il suo Zibaldone*, ed. A. Perosa and F. W. Kent, 2 vols, London, 1981 (for Rucellai's comments on patronage, and its importance for the city, God and himself, see vol. 1, pp. 121–2). For the underside of magnificence, see S. Nethersole, *Art and Violence in Early Renaissance Florence*, New Haven, 2018. For Machiavelli and *The Prince*, see N. Machiavelli, *The Prince*, ed. and trans. Q. Skinner and R. Price, Cambridge, 2019.

On palaces and their contents, see R. Goldthwaite, *The Buildings of Renaissance Florence*, Baltimore, 1981; A. Goldthwaite, *Wealth and the Demand for Art in Italy*, London, 1993; R. A. Goldthwaite, *Banks, Palaces and Entrepreneurs in Renaissance Florence*, Aldershot, 1995; G. Clarke, *Roman House–Renaissance Palaces: Inventing Antiquity in Fifteenth-Century Italy*, Cambridge, 2003; J. R. Lindow, *The Renaissance Palace in Florence: Magnificence and Splendour in Fifteenth-Century Italy*, Aldershot, 2007; M. Ajmar-Wollheim and F. Dennis (eds), *At Home in Renaissance Italy*, London, 2006; C. Campbell, *Love and Marriage in Renaissance Florence: The Courtauld Wedding Chests*, London, 2009. For the Medici 1492 inventory, see *Lorenzo de' Medici at Home: The Inventory of the Palazzo Medici in 1492*, ed. and trans. R. Stapleford, University Park, PA, 2013. For the Strozzi family and their palace, see D. Lamberini (ed.), *Palazzo Strozzi metà millennio, 1489–1989*, Rome, 1991, and A. Lillie (2003), 'Strozzi Family', Grove Art Online. For Taine on Palazzo Pitti, see H. Taine, *Italy: Florence and Venice*, Philadelphia, 1869, p. 151.

On patronage networks, see P. Burke, *The Italian Renaissance: Culture and Society in Italy*, Princeton, 1986; F. W. Kent and P. Simons (eds), *Patronage, Art and Society in Renaissance Italy*, Oxford, 1987; C. C. Frick, *Dressing Renaissance Florence: Families, Fortunes, and Fine Clothing*, Baltimore, 2002; J. Burke, *Changing Patrons: Social Identity and the Visual Arts in Renaissance Florence*, University Park, PA, 2004; P. L. Rubin, *Images and Identity in Fifteenth-Century Florence*, New Haven, 2007; J. M. Musacchio, *Art, Marriage and Family in the Florence Renaissance*, New Haven, 2008.

For the making of art, see M. O'Malley, *The Business of Art: Contracts and the Commissioning Process in Renaissance Italy*, New Haven and London, 2005. A key work for how people perceived art remains M. Baxandall, *Painting and Experience in Fifteenth-Century Italy: A Primer in the Social History of Pictorial Style*, Oxford, 1972. E. Borsook, *The Mural Painters of Tuscany: From Cimabue to Andrea Del Sarto*, 2nd edn, revised and enlarged, Oxford, 1980, is excellent on painting commissions in chapels and churches.

For introductions to particular artists, see R. King, *Brunelleschi's Dome: The Story of the Great Cathedral in Florence*, London, 2000; J. Cadogan, *Domenico Ghirlandaio: Artist and Artisan*, New Haven and London, 2000; F. Caglioti (ed.), *Donatello, Il Rinascimento*, Venice, 2022 (also in English), and P. Motture (ed.), *Donatello: Sculpting the Renaissance*, London, 2023; J. Spike, *Masaccio*, New York, 1995; C. Elam and A. Debenedetti, *Botticelli Past and Present*, London, 2019; A. Cecchi, *Botticelli*, Milan, 2005. E. H. Gombrich, 'Botticelli's Mythologies: A Study in the Neoplatonic Symbolism of his Circle', *Journal of the Warburg and Courtauld Institutes* 8 (1945), pp. 7–60, reprinted in E. H. Gombrich, *Symbolic Images*, London, 1972, and C. Dempsey, *The Portrayal of Love: Botticelli's Primavera and Humanist Culture at the Time of Lorenzo the Magnificent*, Princeton, 1992, remain classic studies of the *Primavera*. Henry Fuseli's derogatory comments on the pre-Michelangelo Sistine Chapel are found at H. Fuseli, *The Life and Writings of Henry Fuseli*, London, 1831, vol. 3, pp. 182–3. The bibliography on Michelangelo is vast; good places to start are H. Chapman, *Michelangelo*, New Haven and London, 2006, and W. Wallace, *Michelangelo: The Artist, the Man and his Times*, Cambridge and New York, 2009. I have used the *Complete Poems and Selected Letters of Michelangelo*, trans. C. Gilbert, ed. R. Linscott, Princeton, 1980, and *The Poetry of Michelangelo*, an annotated translation by J. M. Saslow, New Haven, 1993. C. C. Bambach, *Leonardo da Vinci Rediscovered*, 3 vols, New York, 2019, is a key modern study. For Raphael, see most recently D. Ekserdjian, T. Henry and M. Wivel (eds), *Raphael*, London, 2022. For an engaging account of the conflict between Michelangelo and Leonardo, see J. Jones, *The Lost Battles: Leonardo, Michelangelo and the Artistic Duel that Defined the Renaissance*, London, 2010. For Mantegna and Bellini, see C. Campbell, D. Korbacher, N. Rowley and S. Vowles (eds), *Mantegna and Bellini*, London, 2018. For the impact of northern European paintings on Florentine artists, see P. Nuttall, *From Flanders to Florence: The Impact of Netherlandish Painting, 1400–1500*, New Haven, 2004. For the Renaissance nude, a wide-ranging recent study is J. Burke et al., The Italian Renaissance Nude, New Haven and London, 2021. On Bertoldo di Giovanni, his medal of Mehmed II (and those of other Italian artists) see C. Campbell and A. Chong, *Bellini and the East*, London, 2005, pp. 74–7, and A. Ng, A. Noelle and X. Salomon, *Bertoldo di Giovanni*, New York, 2019, cat. 15 a and b (and for images, https://www.britishmuseum.org/collection/object/C_1919-1001-1 and https://collections.vam.ac.uk/item/O134080/mehmed-ii-medal-di-giovanni-bertoldo/).

Benin

There is much current writing and discussion on the arts of the kingdom of Benin, including in the press. A good place to start for the art of Benin is P. Ben-Amos, 'Benin, Kingdom of', Grove Art Online. J. U. Egharevba, *A Short History of Benin*, Ibadan, 1934 (reprinted 1968) is a rare early history from a non-European author; ones from a European perspective are R. E. Bradbury, *The Benin Kingdom and the Edo-speaking Peoples of South-Western Nigeria*, London, 1957, and R. E. Bradbury and P. Morton-Williams, *Benin Studies*, London, 1973. P. Ben-Amos Girshick and J. Thornton, 'Civil War in the Kingdom of Benin, 1689–1721: Continuity or Political Change?', *Journal of African History*, 42:3 (2001), pp. 353–76, addresses a period of later political history.

W. Fagg, *Sculpture of Africa*, London, 1958, *Nigerian Images*, London, 1963, and *Divine Kingship in Africa*, London, 1978, are influential works by the long-term Keeper of Ethnology at the British Museum, who devised a chronology of Benin art that has been used by many scholars. J. Egharevba, *Descriptive Catalogue of Benin Arts*, Benin City, 1969, is by one of the earlier Nigerian historians of the art of Benin. P. Ben-Amos, *The Art of Benin*, London, 1980; K. Ezra, *Royal Art of Benin: The Perls Collection*, New York, 1992; B. Plankensteiner, 'Benin: Kings and Rituals: Court Arts from Nigeria', *African Arts* 40:4 (2007), pp. 74–87; B. Plankensteiner et al., *Benin Kings and Rituals: Court Arts from Nigeria*, Vienna, 2007; and B. Plankensteiner, *Benin*, Milan, 2010, are accessible academic accounts of the arts of Benin. See also P. M. Peek, *The Lower Niger Bronzes: Beyond Igbo-Ukwu, Ife, and Benin*, New York, 2020. P. Ben-Amos and A. Rubin (eds), *The Art of Power, the Power of Art: Studies in Benin Iconography*, Los Angeles, 1983, is a longer collection of separate studies. J. Nevadomsky, N. Lawson and K. Hazlett, 'An Ethnographic and Space Syntax Analysis of Benin Kingdom Nobility Architecture', *African Archaeological Review* 31:1 (2014), pp. 59–85, looks at the architecture of the Benin elite.

On the making and composition of the bronzes, see F. von Luschan, *Die Altertümer von Benin*, 3 vols, Berlin, 1919 (the celebrated comparison that von Luschan makes between the Benin bronzes and Benvenuto Cellini is in vol. 1, p. 15, the translation is by K. Wysocki Gunsch, p. 28 of her 2013 article cited below); P. J. C. Dark, *An Introduction to Benin Art and Technology*, Oxford, 1973; F. Willett, B. Torsney and M. Ritchie, 'Composition and Style: An Examination of the Benin "Bronze" Heads', *African Arts* 27:3 (1994), pp. 60–102; J. Nevadomsky, 'Art and Science in Benin Bronzes', *African Arts* 37:1 (2004), pp. 1–96; 'Benin Metal Traced to Germany', *Science* 380:6640 (2023), pp. 14–15. For an analysis of the bronzes as a sixteenth-century imperial ensemble, see K. Wysocki Gunsch, *The Benin Plaques: A 16th Century Imperial Monument*, London, 2017. For the ivory production of Benin, see W. Fagg, *Afro-Portuguese Ivories*, London, 1959; E. Bassani and W. Fagg, *Africa in the Renaissance: Art in Ivory*, New York, 1988; S. Preston Blier, 'Imaging Otherness in Ivory: African Portrayals of the Portuguese ca. 1492', *Art Bulletin* 75:3 (1993), pp. 375–96. For the queen mother, see F. E. S. Kaplan, 'Images of the Queen Mother in Benin Court Art', *African Arts* 26:3 (1993), pp. 54–63, 86–88; F.

E. S. Kaplan, 'Iyoba, the Queen Mother of Benin: Images and Ambiguity in Gender and Sex Roles in Court Arts', *Art History* 16:3 (1993), pp. 386–407.

For Europeans in early modern West Africa, see R. Hakluyt, *Hakluyt's Collection of the Early Voyages, Travels and Discoveries of the English Nation*, London, 1801 (R. Eden's account of the Wyndham Expedition of 1553 is on pp. 466–9); J. Adams, *Remarks on the Country Extending from Cape Palmas to the River Congo*, London, 1823 (p. 111 for the oba's divinity); R. Hakluyt, 'A voyage to Benin beyond the countrey of Guinea made by Master James Welsh, who set foorth in the yeere 1588', in *The Principal Navigations Voyages Traffiques and Discoveries of the English Nation*, Cambridge, 2014, vol. 6, pp. 450–458; O. Dapper, 'Benin', in *Naukeurige beschrijvinge der Afrikaensche gewesten*, Amsterdam, 1676, ed. and transcribed by A. Jones, Madison, 1998; J. D. Graham, 'The Slave Trade, Depopulation and Human Sacrifice in Benin History: The General Approach', *Cahiers d'Études Africaines* 5:18 (1965), pp. 317–34; A. F. C. Ryder, *Benin and the Europeans, 1485–1897*, Harlow, 1969; T. Hodgkin (ed.), *Nigerian Perspectives*, London, 1975; R. Law, *The Slave Coast of West Africa, 1550–1750: The Impact of the Atlantic Slave Trade on an African Society*, Oxford, 1991; M. D. D. Newitt, *The Portuguese in West Africa, 1415–1670: A Documentary History*, Cambridge, 2010. D.R. (presumably Dierick Ruiters) is cited in Hodgkin, op. cit., p. 156; for David van Nyendael's visit to Benin in 1700, see H. L. Roth, *Great Benin: Its Customs, Art and Horrors*, Halifax, 1903, p. 162, and T. Astley, *Astley's Voyages*, vol. 3, book 2, *Voyages and Travels to Benin*, London, 1746, p. 100. For a short account of the Benin ambassadors to Portugal in the late fifteenth and early sixteenth centuries, see B. Phillips, Loot: *Britain and the Benin Bronzes*, London, 2021, pp. 17–19.

On the British Punitive Expedition of 1897 and its aftermath, see R. K. Home, *City of Blood Revisited: A New Look at the Benin Expedition of 1897*, London, 1982; D. Hicks, *The Brutish Museum: The Benin Bronzes, Colonial Violence and Cultural Restitution*, London, 2020; Phillips 2021 (op. cit.); P. Docherty, *Blood and Bronze: The British Empire and the Sack of Benin*, London, 2021. O. B. Osadolor and L. E. Otoide, 'The Benin Kingdom in British Imperial Historiography', *History in Africa* 35 (2008), pp. 401–18, is interesting on British Imperial attitudes to Benin. For the early twentieth-century Western perception of the art of Benin, see J. Coote, 'General Pitt-Rivers and the Art of Benin', *African Arts*, 48:2 (2015), pp. 8–9; K. Wysocki Gunsch, 'Art and/or Ethnographica? The Reception of Benin Works from 1897–1935', *African Arts* 46:4 (2013), pp. 22–31. For Dr Roth's diary, see H. L. Roth, *Great Benin: Its Customs, Art and Horrors*, Halifax, 1903, app. 2, p. x.

For issues of restitution see, as a beginning, Hicks and Phillips's books cited above; T. Jenkins, 'From Objects of Enlightenment to Objects of Apology: Why You Can't Make Amends for the Past by Plundering the Present', in J. Pellew and L. Goldman (eds), *Dethroning Historical Reputations: Universities, Museums and the Commemoration of Benefactors*, London, 2018, pp. 81–92; B. Savoy, *Africa's Struggle for its Art: Story of a Postcolonial Defeat*, Princeton, 2022; J. Beurden, *Inconvenient Heritage: Colonial Collections and Restitution in the Netherlands and Belgium*, Amsterdam, 2022.

At the time of writing, many Western collections are engaged in the process of restituting objects from Benin to their place of origin, or considering their return. The Edo Museum of West African Art (EMOWAA), a new museum designed by David Adjaye, under the auspices of the EMOWAA Trust, is underway in Benin City, to support West African heritage and culture, including contemporary initiatives. A major international initiative, Digital Benin, is led by K. Agbontaen-Eghafona, F. Bodenstein, B. Plankensteiner, J. Fine, A. Luther et al, https://digitalbenin. org, hosted by MAARK, Museum am Rothenbaum, 2020. Digital Benin 'aims to bring an Edo-centric focus to the embeddedness of knowledges, traditions and histories of the objects', and will be ultimately transferred to a main host in Nigeria, to facilitate research by Nigerian scholars and a Nigerian public. The platform, which launched online in November 2022, is a comprehensive resource for accessing and studying Benin artefacts. The websites of the Boston Museum of Fine Arts (https://www.mfa.org/ collections/art-of-the-benin-kingdom), the British Museum, London (https://www.britishmuseum.org/collection/search?keyword=benin) and the Metropolitan Museum of Art, New York (https://www. metmuseum.org/art/collection/search?q=benin+city) remain excellent resources for the study of art works from Benin.

Amsterdam

For historical and cultural works on the Dutch Republic, see S. Schama, *The Embarrassment of Riches: An Interpretation of Dutch Culture in the Golden Age*, New York, 1987; G. Parker, *The Dutch Revolt*, revised edn, London, 1990; B. J. Kaplan, *Calvinists and Libertines: Confession and Community in Utrecht 1578-1620*, Oxford, 1995; A. van der Woude and J. de Vries, *The First Modern Economy: Success, Failure, and Perseverance of the Dutch Economy, 1500-1815*, Cambridge, 1997; J. Israel, The Dutch Republic: Its Rise, Greatness and Fall, 1477–1806 (Oxford History of Early Modern Europe), Oxford, 1998; M. Praak, *The Dutch Republic in the Seventeenth Century*, trans. D. Webb, 2nd revised edn, Cambridge, 2023; A. van der Lem, *Revolt in the Netherlands: The Eighty Years War, 1568-1648*, London,

2019. For Jacob Cats's influential emblem books, see J. Cats, *Moral Emblems, with Aphorisms, Adages, and Proverbs, of all Ages and Nations, from J. Cats and R. Farlie, with Illustrations Freely Rendered, from Designs found in their Works, by J. Leighton, F S A*, trans. and ed. R. Pigot, London, 1860; J. Becker (2003), 'Cats, Jacob (i)', Grove Art Online. For Descartes in the Netherlands, see *Encylopaedia Britannica*. For the original text of Descartes' letter of 5 May 1631 to J.-L. Guez de Balzac, co-founder of the Académie française, see http://www.homme-moderne.org/textes/classics/dekart/balzac.html; for an English translation, by J. Bennett, see https://www.earlymoderntexts.com/assets/pdfs/descartes1619_1.pdf, p. 22.

For Holland and globalisation, see K. Zandvliet (ed.), *The Dutch Encounter with Asia, 1600–1950*, Zwolle 2004; T. Brook, *Vermeer's Hat: The Seventeenth Century and the Dawn of the Global World*, London, 2009; K. Corrigan, J. van Campen and F. Diercks (eds), *Asia in Amsterdam: The Culture of Luxury in the Golden Age*, Salem and Amsterdam, 2015; B. Schmidt, *Inventing Exoticism: Geography, Globalism, and Europe's Early Modern World*, Philadelphia, 2015; C. Swan, *Rarities of these Lands: Art, Trade and Diplomacy in the Dutch Republic*, Princeton, 2021. On the Dutch Empire and colonialism, see J. Israels, *Dutch Primacy in World Trade*, Oxford, 1990; B. Schmidt, *Innocence Abroad: The Dutch Imagination and the New World, 1570–1670*, Cambridge and New York, 2001; J. Israels and S. B. Schwartz (eds), *The Expansion of Tolerance: Religion in Dutch Brazil (1624–1654)*, Amsterdam, 2007; B. Schmidt, *Going Dutch: The Dutch Presence in America 1609–2009*, Leiden and Boston, 2008; J. V. Roitman and G. Oostindee (eds), *Dutch Atlantic Connections, 1680–1800: Linking Empires, Bridging Borders*, Leiden, 2014; M. Groesen, *The Legacy of Dutch Brazil*, New York, 2014; S. Broomhall and J. Van Gent, *Dynastic Colonialism: Gender, Materiality and the Early Modern House of Orange-Nassau*, London, 2016; W. Klooster, *The Dutch Moment: War, Trade, and Settlement in the Seventeenth-Century Atlantic World*, Ithaca, 2016; P. C. Emmer and J. J. L. Gommans, *The Dutch Overseas Empire, 1600–1800*, Cambridge, 2020. On Black people in the Dutch Republic and more widely in early modern Europe, see E. Kolfin and E. Runia, *Black in Rembrandt's Time*, Amsterdam, 2020, and O. Otele, *African Europeans: An Untold History*, London, 2020. On slavery and its impact, see P. Emmer, *The Dutch Slave Trade, 1500–1850*, London and New York, 2005; E. Sint Nicolaas and V. Smeulders (eds), *Slavery: An Exhibition of Many Voices*, Amsterdam and Uitgeverij, 2021. To watch the Rijksmuseum 2021 International Symposium on Slavery, see https://www.rijksmuseum.nl/nl/stories/tentoonstellingen/slavernij/story/international-symposium-sources-on-slavery-and-slave-trade. For an internet encyclopedia of shipwrecks maintained by the Dutch Cultural Heritage Agency, see Maritime Stepping Stones (MaSS), a database of stories about wrecks and sites underwater and their cargoes, with a concentration on those involving Dutch vessels or in Dutch waters, at https://mass.cultureelerfgoed.nl/.

On art in Amsterdam and Delft, see J. Rosenberg, S. Slive and E. H. Ter Kuile, *Dutch Art and Architecture*, revised edn, Harmondsworth, 1977; J. M. Montias, *Artists and Artisans in Delft: A Socio-Economic Study of the Seventeenth Century*, Princeton, 1982; S. Alpers, *The Art of Describing: Dutch Art in the Seventeenth Century*, Chicago, 1983; B. Haak, *The Golden Age: Dutch Painters of the Seventeenth Century*, Amsterdam, 1984; P. C. Sutton, *Masters of Seventeenth-Century Dutch Genre Painting*, Philadelphia, Berlin and London, 1984; J. M. Montias, *Vermeer and his Milieu: A Web of Social History*, Princeton, 1989; S. Alpers, *Rembrandt's Enterprise: The Studio and the Market*, new edn, Chicago, 1990; S. Slive, *Dutch Painting, 1600–1800*, New Haven, 1995; W. E. Franits (ed.), *Looking at Seventeenth-Century Dutch Art: Realism Reconsidered*, Cambridge, 1997; H. Vlieghe, *Flemish Art and Architecture, 1585–1700*, New Haven, 1998; W. E. Liedtke et al., *Vermeer and the Delft School*, New York and London, 2001; J. M. Montias, *Art at Auction in 17th Century Amsterdam*, Amsterdam, 2002; W. E. Franits, *Dutch Seventeenth-Century Genre Painting: Its Stylistic and Thematic Evolution*, New Haven and London, 2004; R. E. O. Ekkart, Q. Buvelot and M. de Winkel, *Dutch Portraits: The Age of Rembrandt and Frans Hals*, The Hague and London, 2007; R. B. Yeazell, *Art of the Everyday: Dutch Painting and the Realist Novel*, Princeton, 2009; J. Moerman et al. (eds), *Pieter de Hooch in Delft: From the Shadow of Vermeer*, Delft, 2019. Peter Mundy's account of art collections in Amsterdam is recorded in P. Mundy, *The Travels of Peter Mundy*, London, 1907–36, vol. 4, *Travels in Europe*, 1925, pp. 70–1.

On Amsterdam's Town Hall, see K. Fremantle, *The Baroque Town Hall of Amsterdam*, Utrecht, 1959; W. Kuyper, *Dutch Classicist Architecture*, Delft, 1980; H. Zantkuijl (2003), 'Amsterdam Royal Palace', Grove Art Online.

On Petronella Oortman's dolls' house, see J. R. ter Molen, 'Een bezichtiging van het poppenhuis van Petronella Brandt-Oortman in de zomer van 1718', *Bulletin van het Rijksmuseum* 42:2 (1994), pp. 120–36; S. Broomhall, 'Imagined Domesticities in Early Modern Dutch Dollhouses', *Parergon* 24:2 (2007), pp. 47–68; S. Broomhall, 'Hidden Women of History: Petronella Oortman and her Giant Dolls' House', The Conversation, January 2019. Jessie Burton's *The Miniaturist*, London, 2014, is an enchanting novel partly inspired by Petronella Oortman's dolls' house.

On still-life painting, see P. Taylor, *Dutch Flower Painting, 1600–1720*, New Haven and London, 1995; M. Doty, *Still Life with Oysters and Lemon: On Objects and Intimacy*, Boston, 2002; H. Grootenboer, *The Rhetoric of*

Perspective: Realism and Illusionism in Seventeenth-Century Dutch Still-Life Painting, Chicago, 2005; J. Berger Hochstrasser, *Still Life and Trade in the Dutch Golden Age*, New Haven and London, 2007; A. Tummers and M. Bouffard-Veilleux, *Celebrating in the Golden Age*, Haarlem, 2011; Q. Buvelot and Y. Bleyerveld, *Slow Food: Dutch and Flemish Meal Still Lifes, 1600–1640*, The Hague, 2017. On the Dutch diet, and the source of the allegation that servants begged not to eat salmon more than twice weekly, see Schama 1987, op. cit., pp. 167–77, especially p. 169.

On Frans Hals: S. Slive, *Frans Hals*, London, 2014; S. M. Nadler, *The Portraitist: Frans Hals and His World*, Chicago, 2022. On Frans Post: P. Corrêa do Lago and B. Corrêa do Lago, *Frans Post, 1612–1680: Catalogue Raisonné*, Milan, 2007; K. Schmidt-Loske and K. Wettengl, 'Framing the Frame: Frans Post's View of Olinda, Brazil (1662)', *Rijksmuseum Bulletin* 68:2 (2020), pp. 101–25. On Rembrandt, C. White, *Rembrandt as an Etcher: A Study of the Artist at Work*, 2 vols, London, 1969; G. Schwartz, *Rembrandt: All the Etchings Reproduced in True Size*, Maarssen and London, 1977; W. Strauss and M. van der Meulen, *The Rembrandt Documents*, New York, 1979; D. Bomford, C. Brown and A. Roy, *Art in the Making: Rembrandt*, London, 1988; S. Schama, *Rembrandt's Eyes*, London, 1999; M. Westermann, *Rembrandt*, London, 2000; P. Crenshaw, *Rembrandt's Bankruptcy: The Artist, his Patrons and the Art Market in Seventeenth-Century Netherlands*, Cambridge, 2006; G. Schwartz, *Rembrandt's Universe: His Art, His Life, His World*, London, 2014; B. Wieseman, J. Bikker and G. Weber (eds), *Rembrandt: The Late Works*, London, 2014; S. Schrader et al (eds), *Rembrandt and the Inspiration of India*, Los Angeles, 2018; S. Buck and J. Müller (eds), *Rembrandt's Mark*, London, 2019; B. Brinkmann et al. (eds), *Rembrandt's Orient: West meets East in Dutch Art of the 17th Century*, Munich 2021. On Vermeer, L. Gowing, *Vermeer*, revised edn, London, 1997; the Essential Vermeer website, http://www.essentialvermeer.com, maintained by J. Janson; P. Roelofs and G. Weber (eds), *Vermeer*, Amsterdam, 2023; G. Weber, *Johannes Vermeer: Faith, Reflection, Light*, Amsterdam, 2022.

On the porcelain trade, see T. Volker, *Porcelain and the Dutch East India Company: As Recorded in the Dagh-registers of Batavia Castle, those of Hrado and Deshima and Other Contemporary Papers; 1602–1682*, Leiden, 1954; C. Viallé, 'The Documents of the VOC Concerning the Trade in Chinese and Japanese Porcelain between 1634 and 1661', *Asian Art* 22:3 (1992), pp. 6–34; J. Zhu, H. Ma, N. Li, J. Henderson and M. Glascock (2016), 'The Provenance of Export Porcelain from the Nan'ao One Shipwreck in the South China Sea', *Antiquity* 90:351 (2016), pp. 798–808. C. Jörg, 'The Porcelain Trade of the VOC in the 17th and 18th centuries', *Aziatische Keramiek* (March 2023), . This latter article is hosted on the website of Cooperation Asian Ceramics Netherlands, a free scholarly resource, https://www.aziatischekeramiek.nl.

Delhi

On the Mughal emperors, see B. Gascoigne, *The Great Moghuls*, revised edn, London, 1987; J. F. Richards, *The Mughal Empire*, Cambridge, 1993; M. Alam and S. Subrahmanyan (eds), *The Mughal State 1526–1750*, Delhi, 1998; S. Dale, *The Garden of the Eight Paradises: Babur and the Culture of Empire in Central Asia, Afghanistan and India (1483–1530)*, Leiden, 2004; Nur al-Din Muhammad Jahangir, *Tūzuk-ī Jahāngīrī* (c. 1624), ed., trans. and annotated by W. M. Thackston as *The Jahangirnama: Memoirs of Jahangir, Emperor of India*, Washington DC, 1999.

For foreign travellers at the Mughal Court, see F. W. Foster, *The Embassy of Sir Thomas Roe to the Great Mughal*, 1615–19, 2 vols, London, 1899 (for the drinking on the emperor's birthday in 1616, see vol. 1, p. 256); C. P. Mitchell, *Sir Thomas Roe and the Mughal Empire*, Karachi, 2001; J. B. Tavernier, *Travels in India*, trans V. Ball (first published 1889), 2 vols, Cambridge, 2012; L. Al-Azami, '400 Years of India and Britain: The Memoirs of Sir Thomas Roe', British Library blog (2019), available at https://blogs.bl.uk/untoldlives/2019/10/400-years-of-india-and-britain-the-memoirs-of-sir-thomas-roe.html; N. Das, *Courting India Seventeenth-Century England, Mughal India, and the Origins of Empire*, London 2023. For the rise of the East India Company, see W. Dalrymple, *The Anarchy: The Relentless Rise of the East India Company*, London, 2019; A. Mackillop, *Human Capital and Empire: Scotland, Ireland, Wales and British Imperialism in Asia, c.1690–c.1820*, Manchester, 2021; D. Howarth, *Adventurers: The Improbable Rise of the East India Company: 1550–1650*, New Haven and London, 2023. For Johann Melchior Dinglinger's Birthday of the Great Mughal, see J. Menzhausen and K. G. Beyer, *At the Court of the Great Mogul: The Court at Delhi on the Birthday of the Great Mogul Aureng-Zeb: Museum Piece by Johann Melchior Dinglinger, Court Jeweller of the Elector of Saxony and King of Poland, August II, Called August the Strong*, Leipzig, 1966, and D. Syndram, *Der Thron des Grossmoguls: Johann Melchior Dinglinger goldener Traum vom Fernen Osten*, Leipzig, 1996. For European courts, and the wider context of 'marvellous' and 'exotic' objects, a good introduction is W. Koeppe (ed.), *Making Marvels: Science and Splendor at the Courts of Europe*, New Haven 2019.

On Mughal art and patronage in general, see R. Skelton et al., *The Indian Heritage: Court Life and Arts under Mughal Rule*, London, 1982; J. Guy and D. Swallow, *Arts of India 1550–1900*, London, 1990; C. Asher, *Architecture of Mughal India*, Cambridge, 1992; S. Blair and J. M.

Bloom, *The Art and Architecture of Islam 1250–1800*, New Haven and London, 1992; S. Swarup, *Mughal Art: A Study in Handicrafts*, Delhi, 1996; D. Walker, *Flowers Underfoot: Indian Carpets of the Mughal Era*, New York, 1997; R. Nath, *Mughal Sculpture: Study of Stone Sculptures of Birds, Beasts, Mythical Animals, Human Beings, and Deities in Mughal Architecture*, Delhi, 1997; M. Alam, 'State Building under the Mughals: Religion, Culture and Politics', *Cahier d'Asie Centrale* 3–4 (1997), pp. 105–28; S. P. Verma, *Flora and Fauna in Mughal Art*, Bombay, 1999; J. Seyller, 'A Mughal Code of Connoisseurship', *Muqarnas* 17 (2000), pp. 176–202; E. Koch, *Mughal Art and Imperial Ideology: Collected Essays*, New Delhi, 2001; R. Crill, S. Stronge and A. Topsfield (eds), *Arts of Mughal India: Studies in Honour of Robert Skelton*, London, 2004; P. Moura Carvalho, *Gems and Jewels of Mughal India*, 2007, vol. 18 of *The Nasser D. Khalili Collection of Islamic Art*, ed. J. Raby, London, 1992–; S. Blair, J. Bloom, & R. Nath (2011), 'Mughal Family', Grove Art Online; W. Dalrymple and A. Anand, *Koh-i-Noor: The History of the World's Most Famous Diamond*, London, 2017. For Jahangir's nephrite cup in the British Museum, see https://www.britishmuseum.org/collection/object/W_1945-1017-257; for the object in the Victoria and Albert Museum, see https://collections.vam.ac.uk/item/O18896/jahangir s-jade-wine-cup-wine-cup-saida-ye-gilani/. For Shah Jahan's white nephrite cup, see https://collections.vam.ac.uk/item/O73769/wine-cu p-of-shah-jahan-wine-cup-unknown/. We do not know for sure what wine Shah Jahan would have drunk in this cup, although the Mughal emperors were known to enjoy red wine from Shiraz. For Samuel Pepys' diary and chintz, see https://www.pepysdiary.com/diary/1663/09/05/.

On Mughal painting, see S. C. Welch, *Imperial Mughal Painting*, New York, 1978; A. K. Das, *Mughal Painting during Jahangir's Time*, Calcutta, 1978; M. C. Beach, *The Imperial Image: Paintings for the Mughal Court*, Washington DC, 1981; T. Falk and M. Archer, *Indian Miniatures in the India Office Library*, London, 1981; P. L. Losty, *The Art of the Book in India*, London, 1982; A. K. Das, *Splendours of Mughal Painting*, Bombay, 1986; M. C. Beach, *Early Mughal Painting*, Cambridge, MA, 1987; S. C. Welch, A. Schimmel, M. L. Swietochowski and W. M. Thackston, *The Emperors' Album: Images of Mughal India*, New York, 1987; M. Beach, *Mughal and Rajput Painting*, Cambridge, 1992; S. P. Verma, *Mughal Painters and their Work: A Biographical Survey and Catalogue*, Delhi, 1994; M. Beach, A. Das, J. Losty, J. Seyller and M. Willis (2003), 'Indian Subcontinent: Mughal Painting and Sub-imperial Styles, 16th–19th Centuries', Grove Art Online; E. Wright, S. Stronge and W. M. Thackston, *Muraqqa' Imperial Mughal Albums from the Chester Beatty Library, Dublin*, Alexandria, VA, 2008; P. Kuhlmann-Hodick (ed.), *Indian Paintings: The Collection of the Dresden*

Kupferstich-Kabinett, Dresden, 2018. For the painting by Bichitr that removes Jahangir from the succession, see Chester Beatty Library, Dublin, In 07A.19, https://viewer.cbl.ie/viewer/image/In_07A_19/1/LOG_0000/. For the manuscript of Mir 'Ali Shir Nava'i's *Khamsa* owned by Jahanghir and Shah Jahan, see Royal Collection Trust, RCIN 1005032032, https://www.rct.uk/collection/1005032/khamsah-yi-navai-khmsh-nwyy-the-quintet-of-navai.

For Mughal architecture, see G. Hambly, *Cities of Mughal India: Delhi, Agra and Fatehpur Sikri*, London, 1968; S. Crowe, S. Hayward, S. Jellicoe and G. Patterson, *The Gardens of Mughal India*, London, 1972; E. Moynihan, *Paradise as a Garden in Persia and Mughal India*, London, 1979; W. E. Begley, 'The Symbolic Role of Calligraphy on Three Imperial Mosques of Shah Jahan', in J. Williams (ed.), *Kaladarsana: American Studies in the Art of India*, New Delhi, 1981, pp. 7–18; R. Nath, *History of Mughal Architecture*, vol. 1, New Delhi, 1982; S. Blake, *Shahjahanabad: The Sovereign City in Mughal India, 1639–1739*, Cambridge, 1991; E. Koch, *Mughal Architecture*, New York, 1991; C. Asher, *Architecture of Mughal India (The New Cambridge History of India)*, Cambridge, 1995; E. Koch, 'Mughal Palace Gardens from Babur to Shah Jahan (1526–1648)', *Muqarnas* 14 (1997), pp. 143–65; B. M. Alfieri, *Islamic Architecture of the Indian Subcontinent*, London, 2000; P. K. Sharma, *Mughal Architecture of Delhi: A Study of Mosques and Tombs (1556–1627 ad)*, Delhi, 2000; V. S. Pramar, *A Social History of Indian Architecture*, 2005. For William Finch's account of the gardens at Lahore during his 1608–11 travels in India, see W. Finch, in W. Foster, *Early Travels in India, 1583–1619*, London, 1921, pp. 165–6.

On the Red Fort, see R. Nath, 'The Moti Masjid of the Red Fort Delhi', in R. Nath, *Some Aspects of Mughal Architecture*, New Delhi, 1976; E. Koch, *Shah Jahan and Orpheus: The Pietre Dure Decoration and the Programme of the Throne in the Hall of Public Audiences at the Red Fort of Delhi*, Graz, 1988; E. Koch, 'Diwan-i 'Amm and Chihil Sutun: The Audience Halls of Shah Jahan', *Muqarnas* 11 (1994), pp. 143–65; R. Nath (2003), 'Lal Qil'a', Grove Art Online.

On the Taj Mahal, see R. Nath, *The Immortal Taj Mahal*, Bombay, 1972; W. Begley, 'Amanat Khan and the Calligraphy on the Taj Mahal', *Kunst des Orients* 12:1/2 (1978–9), pp. 5–39, 40–60; W. Begley, 'The Myth of the Taj Mahal and a New Theory of its Symbolic Meaning', *Art Bulletin*, 61:1 (1979), pp. 7–37; R. Nath, *The Taj and its Incarnation*, Jaipur, 1985; W. E. Begley and Z. A. Desai, *Taj Mahal, The Illumined Tomb: An Anthology of Seventeenth Century Mughal and European Documentary Sources*, Cambridge, MA, 1989; E. Koch, *The Complete Taj Mahal and the Riverfront Gardens of Agra*, London, 2006. For the words that Muhammed is said to have uttered at his ascension, see Begley

1979, op. cit., p. 25, n. 70 (E. Cerulli, *Il 'Libro della Scala' e la questione delle fonti arabo-spagnole della Divina Commedia*, Vatican City, 1949).

On Shah Jahan see W. E. Begley (ed.), *Shah Jahan Nama of Inayat Khan: An Abridged History of the Mughal Emperor Shah Jahan*, New Delhi, 1990; M. Nanda, *European Travel Accounts During the Reigns of Shahjahan and Aurangzeb*, Kurukshetra, 1994; M. C. Beach and E. Koch, *King of the World, The Padishahnama: An Imperial Mughal Manuscript from the Royal Library, Windsor Castle*, New Delhi and London, 1997–8; F. Nicoll, *Shah Jahan: The Rise and Fall of the Mughal Emperor*, London, 2009

On Aurangzeb, see K. S. Srivastava, *Two Great Mughals: Akbar and Aurangzeb*, Varanesi, 1998; A. Truschke, *Aurangzeb: The Life and Legacy of India's Most Controversial King*, Redwood City, 2017

London

The most comprehensive studies of the architecture of London are the *Survey of London* (London, 1900–), a detailed account of London, district by district, in over forty volumes to date, and Pevsner's volumes in London from the Buildings of England series. I have used the volumes for St Martin's in the Fields (I), vol. 16, ed. G. H. Gater and E. P. Wheeler, London, 1935; St Martin's in the Fields (II), vol. 18, ed. G. H. Gater and E. P. Wheeler, London, 1937; St Martin's in the Fields (III), vol. 20, ed. G. H. Gater and F. R. Hiorns, London, 1940; Lambeth: South Bank and Vauxhall, vol. 23, ed. H. Roberts and W. H. Godfrey, London, 1951; St James's Westminster I, vols 29 and 30, ed. F. H. W. Sheppard, London, 1960; St James' Westminster II, vols 31 and 32, ed. F. H. W. Sheppard, London, 1963; South Kensington Museums Area, vol. 38, ed. F. H. W. Sheppard, London, 1975. For the Pevsner series, I have consulted extensively B. Cherry and N. Pevsner, *The Buildings of England, London 2: South*, London, 1983; B. Cherry and N. Pevsner, *The Buildings of England, London 4: North*, London, 1998; S. Bradley and N. Pevsner, *The Buildings of England, London 6: Westminster*, London, 2003. I have also used P. Glanville, *London in Maps*, London, 1972, and C. Hibbert, *London: The Biography of a City*, London, 1977. For Cobbett and London as the 'wen', see W. Cobbett, *Rural Rides*, London, 1935 (first published 1830) p. 150. For Chateaubriand, and his 1822 return to London as ambassador, see *Mémoires d'Outre-Tombe, Book VI, To America 1791*, 'Prologue', trans. A. S. Kline, 2005, available at https://www.poetryintranslation.com/PITBR/Chateaubriand/ChateaubriandMemoirsBookVI.php#anchor_Toc115603116. On George IV, see C. Hibbert, *George IV*, London, 1976 (and pp. 782–3 for the infamous obituary in *The Times*).

For the Victorian architecture of London, I have also used A. Briggs,

Victorian Cities, London, 1963; J. Simmons, *St Pancras Station*, London, 1968; J. Summerson, *Victorian Architecture: Four Studies in Evaluation*, New York, 1970; F. Sheppard, *London, 1808–1870: The Infernal Wen*, London, 1971; J. Summerson, *The Architecture of Victorian London*, Charlottesville, 1976; G. Stamp, 'Sir Gilbert Scott's Recollections', *Architectural History* 19 (1976), pp. 54–73; A. S. Wohl, *The Eternal Slum: Housing and Social Policy in Victorian London*, London, 1977; R. Dixon and S. Muthesius, *Victorian Architecture: With a Short Dictionary of Architects*, London, 1978; D. Cole, *The Work of Sir Gilbert Scott*, London, 1980; F. M. L. Thompson (ed.), *The Rise of Suburbia*, Leicester, 1982; G. Stamp and C. Amery, *Victorian Buildings of London*, London, 1980; C. Fox, *London, World City, 1800–1840*, Essen, 1993; T. Hunt, *Building Jerusalem: The Rise and Fall of the Victorian City*, London, 2004; T. Hunt, *Ten Cities that Made an Empire*, London, 2014.

For the Pre-Raphaelites, see L. Parris, *The Pre-Raphaelites*, London, 1984 (reprinted 1994); T. Hilton, *John Ruskin*, 2 vols, New Haven and London, 1985–2000; T. Barringer, *Reading the Pre-Raphaelites*, New Haven, 1999; E. Prettejohn, *Art of the Pre-Raphaelites*, Princeton, 2000; A. Smith and R. Upstone, *Exposed: The Victorian Nude*, London, 2001; F. Moyle, *Desperate Romantics: The Private Lives of the Pre-Raphaelites*, London, 2009; D. Roe, *The Pre-Raphaelites: From Rossetti to Ruskin*, London, 2010; T. Barringer, J. Rosenfeld and A. Smith, *Pre-Raphaelites: Victorian Avant-Garde*, London, 2012; E. Prettejohn (ed.), *The Cambridge Companion to the Pre-Raphaelites*, Cambridge, 2012; A. Smith et al., *Reflections: van Eyck and the Pre-Raphaelites*, London, 2017; J. Holmes, *The Pre-Raphaelites and Science*, New Haven and London, 2018; M. E. Buron, S. Avery-Quash and R. Asleson, *Truth & Beauty: The Pre-Raphaelites and the Old Masters*, San Francisco, 2018; J. Marsh et al., *Pre-Raphaelite Sisters*, London, 2019; J. Holmes, *Temple of Science: The Pre-Raphaelites and Oxford University Museum of Natural History*, Oxford, 2020. On Millais, see J. Rosenfeld and A. Smith, *Millais*, London, 2007; J. Rosenfeld, *John Everett Millais*, London, 2012. For the Rossettis, see D. Roe, *The Rossettis in Wonderland: A Victorian Family History*, London, 2011; C. Jacobi and J. Finch, *The Rossettis*, London, 2023. For Elizabeth Siddal, see L. Hawksley, *Lizzie Siddal: The Tragedy of a Pre-Raphaelite Supermodel*, London, 2004; J. Marsh, *Elizabeth Siddal: Her Story*, London, 2023. For Holman Hunt, see J. Maas, *Holman Hunt and The Light of the World*, London, 1984; J. Bronkhurst, *William Holman Hunt: A Catalogue Raisonné*, London, 2006; C. Jacobi, *William Holman Hunt: Painter, Painting, Paint*, Manchester, 2006; C. Jacobi and K. Lochnan, *Holman Hunt and the Pre-Raphaelite Vision*, Toronto, 2008. For the artist's account of the making of *Ophelia*, see J. G. Millais, *The Life and Letters of Sir John Everett Millais*, London, 1899, pp. 59–79; for Elizabeth Siddal's travails as the model for *Ophelia*, see pp. 78–9.

For art and empire, see T. Barringer, G. Quilley and D. Fordham, *Art and the British Empire*, Manchester, 2006; A. Smith, D. Blayney Brown and C. Jacobi (eds), *Artist and Empire: Facing Britain's Imperial Past*, London, 2015.

For exhibitions, display and reproductive prints in Victorian London, see J. Maas, *Gambart: Prince of the Victorian Art World*, London, 1975; G. Waterfield (ed.), *Palaces of Art: Art Galleries in Britain, 1790–1990*, London, 1991; J. R. Davis, *The Great Exhibition*, Stroud, 1999; H. Hobhouse, *The Crystal Palace and the Great Exhibition: Art, Science, and Productive Industry, A History of the Royal Commission for the Exhibition of 1851*, New York, 2002; G. Waterfield, *The People's Galleries: Art Museums and Exhibitions in Victorian Britain*, London and New Haven, 2015; M. Tedeschi, '"Where the Picture Cannot Go, the Engravings Penetrate": Prints and the Victorian Art Market', *Museum Studies* 31:1 (2005), pp. 9–90; J. Conlin, *The Nation's Mantelpiece: A History of the National Gallery*, London, 2006; J. Meyer, *Great Exhibitions: London, New York, Paris, Philadelphia, 1851–1900*, Woodbridge, 2006; D. Esposito, 'Nineteenth-Century Reproductive Prints', *Print Quarterly* 25:2 (2008), pp. 222–3; C. Saumarez Smith, *The National Gallery: A Short History*, London, 2009; D. Eposito, 'Millais in Reproduction', *Print Quarterly* 27:2 (2010), pp. 207–11; S. Avery-Quash and J. Sheldon, *Art for the Nation: The Eastlakes and the Victorian Art World*, London, 2011; E. A. Pergam, *The Manchester Art Treasures Exhibition of 1857: Entrepreneurs, Connoisseurs and the Public*, Farnham, 2011; G. N. Cantor (ed.), *The Great Exhibition: A Documentary History*, London, 2013; T. Ghosh, 'Gifting Pain: The Pleasures of Liberal Guilt in London, a Pilgrimage, and Street Life in London', *Victorian Literature and Culture* 41:1 (2013), pp. 91–123; W. Hauptman, 'Hanging the Pre-Raphaelites and Others: The Royal Academy Exhibition of 1851', *British Art Journal* 19:1 (2018), pp. 4–28. For Victorian sculpture, see B. Read, *Victorian Sculpture*, New Haven and London, 1982; M. Droth et al. (eds), *Sculpture Victorious: Art in an Age of Invention, 1837–1901*, New Haven and London, 2014.

For Victoria and Albert's patronage and arts activity, and the Albert Memorial, see S. Bayley, *The Albert Memorial: The Monument in its Social and Architectural Context*, London, 1981; C. Brooks, *The Albert Memorial: The Prince Consort National Memorial: Its History, Contexts, and Conservation*, New Haven and London, 2000; C. Wainwright and C. Gere, 'The Making of the South Kensington Museum I', *Journal of the History of Collections* 14:1 (2002), pp. 3–23; J. Marsden (ed.), *Victoria & Albert: Art & Love*, London, 2010; J. Bryant, *Designing the V&A: The Museum as a Work of Art (1857–1909)*, London, 2017; A. N. Wilson, *Prince Albert: The Man Who Saved the Monarchy*, London, 2019.

The key literary and contemporary reportage texts that I have used are B. Jerrold and G. Doré, *London, A Pilgrimage*, London, 1872, and also available in a reprint edited by P. Ackroyd, London, 2005; several of Charles Dickens's 'London' novels, including *Oliver Twist*, 1838, *David Copperfield*, 1850, *Bleak House*, 1853, *Little Dorrit*, 1857, *Our Mutual Friend*, 1865; for *Vanity Fair*, see W. M. Thackeray, *Vanity Fair*, London, 1848; H. Mayhew, *London Labour and the London Poor; a Cyclopædia of the condition and earnings of those that will work, those that cannot work, and those that will not work*, London, 1853. The archive of Charles Booth's Inquiry into the Life and Labour of the People in London (1886–1903) is kept at the London School of Economics. His and his researchers' notebooks are accessible and searchable at https://booth.lse.ac.uk/notebooks. The formerly named 'Bird Place' appears in G. H. Duckworth's 'Notebook of 1899 Police District 32 [Trinity Newington and St Mary Bermondsey], District 33 [St James Bermondsey and Rotherhithe], District 34 [Lambeth and Kennington],District 35 [Kennington (2nd) and Brixton], District 41 [St Peter Walworth and St Mary Newington], District 42 [St George Camberwell], District 45 [Deptford]', p. 17.

Vienna

For the Austro-Hungarian Empire, including Emperor Frans Josef, see N. Stone, *Europe Transformed, 1878–1919*, 2nd edn, Cambridge, MA, 1999; A. Palmer, *Twilight of the Habsburgs: The Life and Times of Emperor Francis Joseph*, London, 1994; S. Beller, *A Concise History of Austria*, Cambridge, 2007; J. Boyer, *Political Radicalism in Late Imperial Vienna: Origins of the Christian Social Movement, 1848–1897*, Chicago, 2010; J. Kwan, *Liberalism and the Habsburg Monarchy, 1861–1895*, Basingstoke, 2013; P. M. Judson, *The Habsburg Empire: A New History*, Cambridge MA, 2018; M. Rady, *The Habsburgs: The Rise and Fall of a World Power*, London, 2020; J. Boyer, *Austria 1867–1955*, Oxford, 2022.

For Elisabeth of Austria and Hungary, see J. Haslip, *The Lonely Empress: Elizabeth of Austria*, London, 1987; A. Sinclair, *Death by Fame: A Life of Elisabeth, Empress of Austria*, London, 1998; O. Gruber Florek, '"I am a Slave to my Hair": Empress Elisabeth of Austria, Fetishism, and Nineteenth-Century Austrian Sexuality', *Modern Austrian Literature* 42:2 (2009), pp. 1–15; B. Hamann and R. Hein, *The Reluctant Empress*, trans. R. Hein, 14th edition, Berlin, 2018; M. E. Hametz and H. M. Schlipphacke (eds), *Sissi's World: The Empress Elisabeth in Memory and Myth*, New York, 2020.

On Freud, see E. Jones, *Sigmund Freud: Life and Work*, 3 vols, London, 1953–7; R. Wollheim, *Freud*, London, 1971; M. Gardiner (ed.), *The Wolf-Man by the Wolf-Man*, London, 1971 (for Sergei Pankejeff's account of Freud's comparison of psychoanalysis to archaeology, see p. 139); R. Wollheim, 'Freud and the Understanding of Art', *On Art and the Mind*, London, 1973, pp. 202–19; P. Gay, *Freud: A Life of our Time*, New York, 1987; E. H. Gombrich, 'Freud's Aesthetics', *Reflections on the History of Art*, London, 1987, pp. 221–39; L. Gamwell and R. Wells (eds), *Sigmund Freud and Art: His Personal Collection of Antiquities*, New York and London, 1989. For Freud's psychological works, see J. Strachey (ed.), *Standard Edition of the Complete Psychological Works of Sigmund Freud*, trans. J. Strachey and A. Freud, 24 vols, London, 1953–74. More generally, see E. J. Kandel, *The Age of Insight: The Quest to Understand the Unconscious in Art, Mind, and Brain, from Vienna 1900 to the Present*, New York, 2012. On psychiatry, mental illness and art, see G. Blackshaw and L. Topp (eds), *Madness and Modernity: Mental Illness and the Visual Arts, Vienna, 1900*, London, 2009; L. Topp, *Freedom and the Cage: Modern Architecture and Psychiatry in Central Europe, 1890–1914*, University Park, PA, 2017.

As an introduction to the arts and culture of Vienna, see M. Pippal, *A Short History of Art in Vienna*, Stuttgart, 2002; P. Hornsby et al., 'Vienna', Grove Art Online; A. Robertson, *The Crossroads of Civilisation*, Cambridge, 2022.

On Biedermeier, see G. Egger, *Vienna in the Age of Schubert: The Biedermeier Interior 1815–1848*, London, 1979; R. Waissenberger and H. Bisanz, *Vienna in the Biedermeier Era, 1815–1848*, New York, 1986; A Wilkie, *Biedermeier*, London, 1987; *Bürgersinn und Aufbegehren: Biedermeier und Vormärz in Wien, 1815–1848*, Vienna, 1987; K. A. Schröder, *Ferdinand Georg Waldmüller*, Munich, 1990; I. Brugger et al., *Wiener Biedermeier: Malerei Zwischen Wiener Kongress und Revolution*, Munich, 1992; S. Sangl, B. Stoeltie and R. Stoeltie, *Biedermeier to Bauhaus*, London, 2000; M. Morton (2003), 'Biedermeier', Grove Art Online; R. Bisanz (2003), 'Waldmüller, Ferdinand Georg', Grove Art Online; L. Winters et al., *Biedermeier: The Invention of Simplicity*, Milwaukee, 2006; A. Husslein-Arco and S. Grabner, *Ferdinand Georg Waldmüller 1793–1865*, Vienna, 2009. A. Husslein-Arco and S. Grabner (eds), *Is that Biedermeier?: Amerling, Waldmüller and More*, Munich, 2016.

For Viennese art and culture c. 1900, see S. Zweig, *The World of Yesterday*, New York, 1943 (first English edition); for his discussion of cafes as a 'democratic club, see pp. 61–2; F. Novotny, *Painting and Sculpture in Europe, 1780–1880*, Harmondsworth, 1970; R. Wagner-Rieger (ed.), *Wiens Architektur im 19. Jahrhundert*, Vienna, 1970; C. E. Schorske, *Fin-de-siècle Vienna*, New York, 1980; A. Janik and S. Toulmin, *Wittgensteins Wien*, Munich and Vienna, 1984; M. Marchetti, *Wien um 1900: Kunst und Kultur*, Vienna, 1985; K. Varnedoe (ed.), *Vienna, 1900: Art, Architecture and Design*, New York, 1986; H. Prigent, *Klimt, Schiele, Moser, Kokoschka: Vienne*

1900, Paris, 2005; A. Waugh, *The House of Wittgenstein*, London, 2008; G. Blackshaw (ed.), *Facing the Modern: The Portrait in Vienna*, London, 2013; P. Vergo, *Art in Vienna, 1898-1918: Klimt, Kokoschka, Schiele and their Contemporaries*, 4th edn, London, 2015; C. Brandstätter, R. Metzger and D. Gregori, *Vienna 1900 Complete*, London, 2018; C. Hug and H. Eipeldauer (eds), *Oskar Kokoschka: Expressionist, Migrant, European: A Retrospective*, Berlin, 2018; C. Brandstätter, A. J. Hirsch and H.-M. Koetzle, *Vienna, Portrait of a City*, Frankfurt, 2019; S. Fellner and S. Rollig, *City of Women: Female Artists in Vienna, 1900-1938*, Munich, 2019; A. Thacker, *Modernism, Space and the City: Outsiders and Affect in Paris, Vienna, Berlin and London*, Edinburgh, 2019; H.-P. Wipplinger (ed.), *Vienna 1900, Birth of Modernism: The Leopold Museum's Collection*, Cologne, 2019; J. Nentwig, *Vienna 1900/Wien*, Cologne, 2020. A much broader study, in which Vienna plays a part, is C. Magris, *Danube: A Journey through the Landscape, History and Culture of Central Europe*, New York, 2008 (reprint).

For Klimt, I have consulted M. E. Warlick, 'Mythic Rebirth in Gustav Klimt's Stoclet Frieze: New Considerations of Its Egyptianizing Form and Content', *Art Bulletin* 74:1 (1992), pp. 115-34; F. Whitford, *Gustav Klimt*, London, 1995; T. Marlowe-Storkovich, '"Medicine" by Gustav Klimt', *Artibus et historiae* 24:47 (2003), pp. 231-52; S. Koja, *Gustav Klimt: The Beethoven Frieze and the Controversy over the Freedom of Art*, Munich, 2006; R. Price, *Gustav Klimt: The Ronald S. Lauder and Serge Sabarsky Collections*, New York, 2007; K. C. Karnes, 'Wagner, Klimt, and the Metaphysics of Creativity in Fin-de-Siècle Vienna', *Journal of the American Musicological Society* 62:3 (2009), pp. 647-97; S. Ayres, 'Staging the Female Look: A Viennese Context of Display for Klimt's "Danaë"', *Oxford Art Journal* 37:3 (2014), pp. 227-44; D. Manderson, 'Klimt's Jurisprudence – Sovereign Violence and the Rule of Law', *Oxford Journal of Legal Studies* 35:3 (2015), pp. 515-42; A. Husslein-Arco, J. Kallir and A. Weidinger (eds), *The Women of Klimt, Schiele, and Kokoschka*, Vienna, 2015; T. G. Natter, *Klimt and the Women of Vienna's Golden Age, 1900-1918*, Munich 2016; L. Morowitz, '"Heil the Hero Klimt!": Nazi Aesthetics in Vienna and the 1943 Gustav Klimt Retrospective', *Oxford Art Journal* 39:1 (2016), pp. 107-29; T. G. Natter (ed.), *Klimt and Antiquity: Erotic Encounters*, Munich, 2017; A. Klee, S. Rollig and S. Auer (eds), *Beyond Klimt: New Horizons in Central Europe*, Munich, 2018; T. G Natter, *Gustav Klimt, Complete Paintings*, Frankfurt, 2018; S. T. Kruglikov, 'Ornament and Content: The Subject and Meaning of *The Kiss* by Gustav Klimt', *Art & Culture Studies* 4 (2022), pp. 140-65.

On Schiele, see J. T. Ambrózy, C. Metzger K. A. Schröder and E. Werth, *Egon Schiele*, Munich, 2017; K. Jesse and S. Rollig (eds), *Egon Schiele: The Making of a Collection*, Munich, 2018; M. Bisanz-Prakken, *Klimt /*

Schiele: Drawings, London, 2018. For the Secession, see K. H. Carl, *The Viennese Secession*, New York, 2011; V. Terraroli (ed.), *Ver Sacrum: The Vienna Secession Art Magazine, 1898–1903: Gustav Klimt, Koloman Moser, Otto Wagner, Alfred Roller, Max Kurzweil, Joseph M. Olbrich, Josef Hoffmann*, Milan, 2018; M. Brandow-Faller, *The Female Secession: Art and the Decorative at the Viennese Women's Academy*, University Park, PA, 2020. On the Wiener Werkstätte, see P. Noever and V. Dufour, *Yearning for Beauty: The Wiener Werkstätte and the Stoclet House*, Ostfildern-Ruit, 2006; C. Witt-Dörring, *Vienna: Art & Design, Klimt, Schiele, Hoffmann, Loos*, Melbourne, 2011; C. Witt-Dörring and J. Staggs, *Wiener Werkstätte, 1903–1932: The Luxury of Beauty*, New York and Munich, 2017. For the Gallia family and their apartment, see T. Lane with A. Smith, *Vienna 1913: Josef Hoffmann's Gallia Apartment*, Melbourne, 1984; T. Bonyhady, *Good Living Street: The Fortunes of my Viennese Family*, Sydney, 2011, and the 'Hoffmann Gallia Apartment', https://www.ngv.vic.gov.au/vienna/decorative-arts/hoffmann-gala-apartment.html.

New York

For a highly selective introduction to twentieth-century American history, see H. F. May, *The End of American Innocence: A Study of the First Years of our Own Time, 1912–1917*, London, 1960; R. Wiebe, *The Search for Order*, New York, 1967; T. Roszak, *The Making of a Counter Culture: Reflections on the Technocratic Society and Its Youthful Opposition*, Berkeley, 1969; L. Chandler, *America's Greatest Depression*, New York, 1970; A. J. Matusow, *The Unraveling of America: A History of Liberalism in the 1960s*, New York, 1984; D. Hounshell, *From the American System to Mass Production, 1800–1932*, Baltimore, 1985; R. Daniels, *Coming to America: A History of Immigration and Ethnicity in American Life*, New York, 1991; J. T. Patterson, *Grand Expectations: The United States, 1945–1974*, Oxford and New York, 1996; D. M. Kennedy, *Freedom from Fear: The American People in Depression and War, 1929–1945*, Oxford and New York, 1999; L. Cohen, *A Consumer's Republic: The Politics of Mass Consumption in Postwar America*, New York, 2008; M. Dickstein, *Dancing in the Dark: A Cultural History of the Great Depression*, New York, 2009. On the history and culture of New York, see R. Caro, *The Power Broker: Robert Moses and the Fall of New York*, New York, 1974; D. Halle (ed.), *New York and Los Angeles*, Chicago, 2003; R. Shorto, *The Island at the Center of the World*, New York, 2004; G. G. Chauncey, *Gay New York: Gender, Urban Culture and the Making of a Gay World, 1890–1940*, updated edn, New York, 2008; E. Homberger, *New York: A Cultural History*, New York, 2008; K. Jackson, *Encyclopedia of New York*, 2nd edn, New Haven, 2010

On Abstract Expressionism, see C. Greenberg, *Art and Culture*, Boston, 1961; H. Rosenberg, *The Tradition of the New*, New York, 1961; W. Rubin, *Dada and Surrealist Art*, London, 1969; D. Ashton, *The Life and Times of the New York School*, Bath, 1972; J. Wechsler, *Surrealism and American Painting*, New Brunswick, 1977; A. Cox, *Art-as-politics: The Abstract Expressionist Avant-Garde and Society*, Ann Arbor, 1982; F. Frascina and C. Harrison, *Abstract Expressionism and Jackson Pollock*, Milton Keynes, 1983; G. S. Goldhammer, *How New York Stole the Idea of Modern Art: Abstract Expressionism, Freedom, and the Cold War*, Chicago, 1983; M. Auping, *Abstract Expressionism: The Critical Developments*, London, 1987; C. Ross (ed.), *Abstract Expressionism: Creators and Critics. An Anthology*, New York, 1990; D. Shapiro and C. Shapiro, *Abstract Expressionism: A Critical Record*, Cambridge, 1990; S. Polcari, *Abstract Expressionism and the Modern Experience*, Cambridge, 1991; D. Ashton, *The New York School: A Cultural Reckoning*, Berkeley, 1992; A. E. Gibson, *Abstract Expressionism: Other Politics*, New Haven and London, 1999; N. Jachec, *The Philosophy and Politics of Abstract Expressionism, 1940–1960*, Cambridge, 2000; D. Anfam, 'Abstract Expressionism', Grove Art Online. D. B. Balken, *Abstract Expressionism*, London, 2005; E. G. Landau (ed.), *Reading Abstract Expressionism: Context and Critique*, New Haven and London, 2005; J. M. Marter (ed.), *Abstract Expressionism: The international Context*, New Brunswick, 2007; I. Sandler, *Abstract Expressionism and the American Experience: A Re-evaluation*, Lenox, MA, 2009; C. Craft, *An Audience of Artists: Dada, Neo-Dada, and the Emergence of Abstract Expressionism*, Chicago, 2012; D. Anfam, *Abstract Expressionism (World of Art)*, 2nd edn, London, 2015; D. Anfam, *Abstract Expressionism*, London, 2016; J. M. Marter and G. F. Chanzit, *Women of Abstract Expressionism*, Denver, 2016; M. Leja, *Reframing Abstract Expressionism: Subjectivity and Painting in the 1940s*, New Haven and London, 2018; B. Franzen and B. Dodenhoff, *The Cool and the Cold: Painting from the USA and USSR 1960–1990*, Cologne, 2020; C. Darwent, *Surrealists in New York: Atelier 17 and the Birth of Abstract Expressionism*, London, 2023.

On Jackson Pollock, S. Rodman, *Conversations with Artists*, New York, 1957; A. Kaprow, 'The Legacy of Jackson Pollock, *Artnews* (October 1958); A. H. Barr and S. Hunter, *Jackson Pollock et la nouvelle peinture américaine*, Paris, 1959; F. V. O'Connor, *Jackson Pollock*, New York, 1967; W. Rubin, 'Jackson Pollock and the Modern Tradition', *Artforum* 5:2–5 (1967), no. 2 pp. 14–22, no. 3 pp. 28–37, no. 4 pp. 18–31, no. 5 pp. 28–33; F. V. O'Connor and E. V. Thaw (eds), *Jackson Pollock: A Catalogue Raisonné of Paintings, Drawings and Other Works*, 4 vols, New Haven, 1978, and Supplement No. 1, New Haven, 1995; J. Potter, *To a Violent Grave: An Oral Biography of Jackson Pollock*, New York, 1985; S. Naifeh and G. W. Smith, *Jackson*

Pollock: An American Saga, New York, 1989; K. Varnedoe, P. Karmel, E. Levine and A. Indych-López, *Jackson Pollock*, New York, 1998; P. Karmel (ed.), *Jackson Pollock: Interviews, Articles, and Reviews*, New York, 1999; Y. Szafran, *Jackson Pollock's Mural: The Transitional Moment*, Los Angeles, 2014; G. Delahunty et al., *Jackson Pollock: Blind Spots*, London, 2015; M. Schreyach, *Pollock's Modernism*, New Haven, 2017.

For Lee Krasner, B. H. Friedman, *Lee Krasner Paintings, Drawings and Collages*, London, 1965; B. Rose, *Krasner/Pollock: A Working Relationship*, East Hampton and New York, 1981; B. Rose, *Lee Krasner: A Retrospective*, Houston, 1983; E. G. Landau and J. D. Grove, *Lee Krasner: A Catalogue Raisonné*, New York, 1995; A. M. Wagner, *Three Artists (Three Women): Modernism and the Art of Hesse, Krasner, and O'Keeffe*, Berkeley, 1996; R. C. Hobbs, *Lee Krasner*, New York, 1999; E. Nairne (ed.), *Lee Krasner: Living Colour*, London, 2019; M. Gabriel, *Ninth Street Women: Lee Krasner, Elaine de Kooning, Grace Hartigan, Joan Mitchell, and Helen Frankenthaler. Five Painters and the Movement that Changed Modern Art*, New York, 2019.

On Helen Frankenthaler, see E. C. Goossen, *Helen Frankenthaler*, New York, 1969; B. Rose, *Helen Frankenthaler*, New York, 1971 (and pp. 54–61 for Frankenthaler on *Mountains and Sea*); J. Elderfield, *Helen Frankenthaler*, New York, 1987; E. A. Carmean, *Helen Frankenthaler: A Paintings Retrospective*, New York, 1989; A. Rowley, *Helen Frankenthaler: Painting History, Writing Painting*, London, 2007; A. Nemerov, *Fierce Poise: Helen Frankenthaler and 1950s New York*, New York, 2021.

For Mark Rothko, P. Selz, *Mark Rothko*, New York, 1961; D. Ashton, *About Rothko*, New York, 1983; J. E. B. Breslin, *Mark Rothko: A Biography*, Chicago, 1993; D. Anfam (ed.), *Mark Rothko: The Works on Canvas: Catalogue Raisonné*, New Haven, 1998; M. Rothko and M. López-Remiro, *Writings on Art*, New Haven and London, 2006; A. Borchardt-Hume and B. Fer, *Rothko*, London, 2008.

On Fluxus, H. Sohm and H. Szeeman, *Happening und Fluxus: Materialen*, Cologne, 1970; H. Ruhe, *Fluxus, the Most Radical and Experimental Art Movement of the Sixties*, Amsterdam, 1979; B. Moore, *Fluxus I: A History of the Edition*, New York, 1985; C. Phillpot and J. Hendricks, *Fluxus: Selections from the Gilbert and Lila Silverman Collection*, New York, 1988; J. Pijnappel, *Fluxus Today and Yesterday*, London, 1993; T. Kellein, *Fluxus*, London; 1995; A. Noel and E. Williams (eds), *Mr Fluxus: A Collective Portrait of George Maciunas, 1931–1978*, London, 1997; K. Friedman, *The Fluxus Reader*, Chichester, 1998; A. Dezeuze, *The 'Do-It-Yourself' Artwork: Participation from Fluxus to New Media*, Manchester, 2010; S. Fricke, A. Klar and S. Maske, *Fluxus at 50*, Bielefeld, 2012.

On Yoko Ono, Y. Ono, *Instruction Paintings*, New York, 1995; Y. Ono, *Grapefruit*, New York, 2000; Y. Ono, *Yoko at Indica: The Unfinished*

Paintings and Objects, London, 1966; C. Iles, *Yoko Ono: Have you Seen the Horizon Lately?*, Oxford, 1997; I. Pfeiffer and M. Hollein, *Yoko Ono: Half-a-wind Show: A Retrospective*, Frankfurt, 2013; and more generally, C. Wood, *Performance in Contemporary Art*, London, 2018; M. Yoshimoto, *Into Performance: Japanese Women Artists in New York*, New Brunswick, 2005. For an audio account of the Amsterdam 'Bed-in for Peace' see https://www.youtube.com/watch?v=Ai5cCxX0UBw; for Ono and Lennon's Montreal bed-in (directed by the two protagonists), see https://www.youtube.com/watch?v=mRjjiOV003Q.

For Allen Ginsberg, the Beat poets and their links to visual culture, see J. Clellon Holmes, 'This is the Beat Generation', *New York Times Magazine* (16 November 1952), pp. 10–22; K. Rexroth, 'Disengagement: The Art of the Beat Generation', *New World Writing* 11 (1957), pp. 28–41; A. Kaprow, 'The Legacy of Jackson Pollock', *ARTnews* (October 1958), pp. 24–6, 55–6; N. Chassman (ed.), *Poets of the Cities: New York and San Francisco, 1950–1965*, Dallas, 1974; L. Phillips, *Beat Culture and the New America, 1950–1965*, New York, 1995; D. Belgrad, *The Culture of Spontaneity: Improvisation and the Arts in Postwar America*, Chicago and London, 1998; P.-A. Michaud, *Beat Generation: New York, San Francisco, Paris*, Paris, 2016.

For Pop Art and Andy Warhol, see S. Stich, *Made in USA: An Americanization in Modern Art in the '50s and '60s*, Berkeley, 1987; M. Livingstone, *Pop Art: A Continuing History*, London, 1990; S. Madoff, ed., *Pop Art: A Critical History*, Berkeley, 1997; T. Crow, *The Rise of the Sixties: American and European Art in the Era of Dissent*, New Haven, 2005; J. Morgan, *The World Goes Pop*, London, 2015; A. Warhol with P. Hackett, *POPism: The Warhol '60s*, New York and London, 1980; P. Hackett (ed.), *The Andy Warhol Diaries*, New York and London, 1989; A. Warhol et al., *Andy Warhol*, Stockholm, 1968; S. Koch, *Stargazer: Andy Warhol's World and his Films*, revised edn, New York, 1985; C. Ratcliff, *Andy Warhol*, New York, 1983; V. Bockris, *Warhol*, London, 1989; K. McShine et al., *Andy Warhol: A Retrospective*, New York, 1989; A. R. Pratt (ed.), *The Critical Response to Andy Warhol*, Westport, 1997; G. Frei and N. Printz (eds), *The Andy Warhol Catalogue Raisonné*, London and New York, 2002; G. Muir and Y. Dziewior (eds), *Andy Warhol*, London, 2020; for John Cale's memories of the Factory, see 'My 15 Minutes', *Guardian* (12 February 2002). For Warhol on coke, see A. Warhol, *The Philosophy of Andy Warhol*, New York, 1975.

On Louise Bourgeois, see D. Wye (ed.), *Louise Bourgeois*, New York, 1982; M.-L. Bernadac, *Louise Bourgeois*, Paris and New York, 1996; M.-L. Bernadac and H.-U. Obrist (eds), *Destruction of the Father, Reconstruction of the Father: Writings and Interviews, 1923–1997*, Cambridge, MA and

London, 1998; R. Crone and P. Schaesberg, *Louise Bourgeois: The Secret of the Cells*, Munich, London and New York, 1998; M. Bal, *Louise Bourgeois' Spider: The Architecture of Art-Writing*, Chicago, 2001; R. Storr, *Louise Bourgeois*, London and New York, 2003; M. Nixon, *Fantastic Reality: Louise Bourgeois and a Story of Modern Art*, Cambridge, MA, 2005; M. Morris, P. Herkenhoff and M.-L. Bernadac, *Louise Bourgeois*, London, 2007; L. Bourgeois, P. Amsellem and A. Norrsell, *Louise Bourgeois: Maman*, Stockholm, 2007; R. Storr, *Intimate Geometries: The Life and Work of Louise Bourgeois*, London, 2016; R. Rugoff, J. Lorz, R. Cusk and L. Cooke, *Louise Bourgeois: The Woven Child*, London, 2022.

A key foundational anthology of the Harlem Renaissance is A. Locke (ed.), *The New Negro*, New York, 1925. On the Harlem Renaissance, see D. L. Lewis, *When Harlem Was in Vogue*, New York, 1981; D. C. Driskell, D. L. Lewis and D. Willis, *Harlem Renaissance: Art of Black America*, New York, 1987; G. Hutchinson, *The Harlem Renaissance in Black and White*, Cambridge, 1995; A. H. Kirschke, *Aaron Douglas: Art, Race, and the Harlem Renaissance*, Jackson, 1995; R. J. Powell et al., *Rhapsodies in Black: Art of the Harlem Renaissance*, London, 1997; P. Archer-Shaw, *Negrophilia: Avant-Garde Paris and Black Culture in the 1920s*, New York, 2000; G. Hutchinson (ed.), *The Cambridge Companion to the Harlem Renaissance*, Cambridge and New York, 2007; A. Kirschke, *Art in Crisis: W. E. B. DuBois and the Struggle for African American Identity and Memory*, Bloomington, 2007; D. L. Baldwin and M. Makalani, *Escape from New York: The New Negro Renaissance beyond Harlem*, Minneapolis, 2013; C. A. Wall, *The Harlem Renaissance: A Very Short Introduction*, New York and Oxford, 2016.

For Jacob Lawrence, see P. Hills and E. H. Wheat, *Jacob Lawrence: American Painter*, Seattle, 1986; R. J. Powell, *Jacob Lawrence*, New York, 1992; P. T. Nesbett and M. Dubois (eds), *Jacob Lawrence: Paintings, Drawings and Murals (1935–1999). A Catalogue Raisonné*, Seattle, 2000; P. T. Nesbett and M. Dubois (eds), *Over the Line: The Art and Life of Jacob Lawrence*, Seattle, 2000; P. Hills, '"In the Heart of the Black Belt": Jacob Lawrence's Commission from Fortune to Paint the South', *International Review of African American Art* 19:1 (2003), pp. 28–36; L. Dickerman, E. Smithgall, E. Alexander, *Jacob Lawrence: The Migration Series*, New York, 2015; E. H. Turner and A. B. Bailly (eds), *Jacob Lawrence: The American Struggle*, Salem, 2019.

Brasília

For a good filmed introduction to Brasília, see R. Williams, 'Building Brasília', https://heni.com/talks/building-brasilia. For the Athens

Charter of 1933, see the Getty Conservation Institute: Cultural Heritage Policy Documents (https://www.getty.edu/conservation/publications_ resources/research_resources/charters/charter04.html). To watch *Rio, 40 Graus,* see https://www.youtube.com/watch?v=V81QK2SNuIo.

On the architecture and planning of Brasília, see L. Costa, 'Relatório do plano pilôto de Brasília = Beschreibung des Orientierungs fuer Brasilia', *Módulo* 3:8 (1957), pp. 33–48, published in English as L. Costa, 'Prizewinning Report on Brasília', *Ekistics* 5:30 (1958), pp. 139–42; W. Holford, 'Brasília: The Federal Capital of Brazil', *Geographical Journal* 128:1 (1962), pp. 15–17; E. N. Bacon, *Design of Cities,* London, 1967, rev. 1975, pp. 237–41; N. Evenson, *Two Brazilian Capitals: Architecture and Urbanism in Rio de Janeiro and Brasília,* New Haven, 1973; L. Costa, 'L'urbanisme de Brasília', *La Nouvelle Revue des Deux Mondes* (1973), pp. 129–33; N. W. Sodré, *Oscar Niemeyer,* Rio de Janeiro, 1978; O. Niemeyer, *architetto: catalogo della mostra,* Venice, 1979; ICOMOS, World Heritage List, No. 445, Advisory Body Evaluation, Paris, 1986, http:// whc.unesco.org/en/list/445/documents/; H. Holston (ed.), *The Modernist City: An Anthropological Critique of Brasília,* Chicago, 1989; L. Costa, *Report of the Pilot Plan for Brasília,* Brasilia, 1991; D. K. Underwood, *Oscar Niemeyer and the Architecture of Brazil,* New York, 1994; J. Pessôa, *Lúcio Costa: Documentos de Trabalho,* Brasília, 1998; M. da Silva Pereira, 'L'Utopie et l'historie. Brasília: Entre la certitude de la forme et le doute de l'image', in *Art d'Amérique latine, 1911–1968,* Paris, 1992, pp. 462–71; P. Andreas and I. Flagge, *Oscar Niemeyer: eine Legende der Moderne/A Legend of Modernism,* Frankfurt, Basel and Boston, 2003; K. Frampton, 'Le Corbusier and Oscar Niemeyer: Influence and Counter Influence 1929–1965', in C. Brillembourg (ed.), *Latin American Architecture, 1929–1960: Contemporary Reflections,* New York, 2004, pp. 35–49; F. El-Dahdad (ed.), *CASE. Lúcio Costa. Brasília's Superquadra,* New York, 2005; M. Casciato and S. von Moos (eds), *Twilight of the Plan: Chandigarh and Brasília,* Mendrisio, 2007; Instituto do Patrimônio Histórico e Artístico Nacional (IPHAN), 'Plano Piloto 50 anos: cartilha de preservação – Brasília, Brasília, 2007', 'Brasília 1960–2010', *Docomomo Journal* 43 (2010), issue dedicated to Brazil; S. Ficher and A. Schlee, *Guia de obras de Oscar Niemeyer. Brasília 50 anos/Guide of the Works of Oscar Niemeyer, Brasília 50 Years,* Brasília, 2010; O. Niemeyer, *The Curves of Time: The Memoirs of Oscar Niemeyer,* London, 2000 (and for specifically on curves, Brasília and the Cidade Livre see Frontispiece, pp. 70–2); O. Niemeyer, *Minha Arquitetura: 1937–2005/My Architecture: 1937–2005,* Rio de Janeiro, 2005; R. J. Williams, *Brazil: Modern Architectures in History,* London, 2009; J. Tavares, 'The Competition for Brasilia's Pilot Plan: Territory and Infrastructure', *Docomomo* 43:2 (2010), pp. 8–13; M. E. Costa (ed.), *Lúcio Costa, Arquiteto,* Brasília, 2010; F. de Holanda, *Brasília – Cidade Moderna, Cidade Eternal,* Brasília, 2010; A. Xavier and J. Katinsky (eds), *Brasília.*

Antologia Crítica, São Paulo, 2012; P. Palazzo and L. Saboia, 'Capital in a Void: Modernist Myths of Brasília', *Traditional Dwellings and Settlements Review* 24:1 (2012), pp. 5–15; D. Matoso Macedo and S. Ficher, 'Brasília: Preservation of a Modernist City', *Conservation Perspectives: Conserving Modern Architecture* (Getty Conservation Institute), Los Angeles, 2013, https://www.getty.edu/conservation/publications_resources/newsletters/28_1/brasilia.html; M. Stierli, 'Building No Place: Oscar Niemeyer and the Utopias of Brasília', *Journal of Architectural Education* 67:1 (2013), pp. 8–16; P. Jodidio, *Oscar Niemeyer, 1907–2012: The Once and the Future Dawn*, Cologne, 2016; C. E. Comas, 'Brasília. Lúcio Costa', in *The Companions to the History of Architecture, Vol. IV, Twentieth-Century Architecture*, ed. D. Leatherbarrow and A. Eisenschmidt, Hoboken, 2017; C. Cabral (2019), 'Brasília', Grove Art Online; C. Cabral (2019), S. Ficher and A. Schlee (2020), 'Costa, Lúcio', Grove Art Online; J. Katinsky and A. Anagnost (2020), 'Niemeyer (Soares Filho), Oscar', Grove Art Online; for the UNESCO citation and listing, see https://whc.unesco.org/en/list/445/.

For broader historical context, I have used T. E. Skidmore, *Politics in Brazil*, Oxford, 1967; E. B. Burns, *A History of Brazil*, New York, 1993; R. Levine, *The History of Brazil*, New York, 2003; R. R. Ioris, *Transforming Brazil: A History of National Development in the Postwar Era*, London, 2014; L. M. Schwarcz and H. M. Starling, *Brazil: A Biography*, New York, 2018; H. S. Klein and F. Vidal Luna, *Modern Brazil: A Social History*, Cambridge, 2020; J. N. Green and T. E. Skidmore, *Brazil: Five Centuries of Change*, 3rd edn, Oxford, 2021; L. M. Schwarcz, *Brazilian Authoritarianism: Past and Present*, trans. E. M. B. Becker, Princeton, 2022.

For Clarice Lispector, see 'Brasília: Five Days' (1964) and 'Brasília' (1974), in C. Lispector, *The Complete Stories*, trans. K. Dodson, Cambridge, MA, 2015. For Simone de Beauvoir's visit to Brasília, see S. de Beauvoir, *La Force des Choses*, Paris, 1963, pp. 577–8; T. Martin (2020), 'Simone de Beauvoir's travel to Brazil', https://lirecrire.hypotheses.org/3017; For Zaha Hadid on Brasília, see I. Borden, 'A Tale of Three Cities, New York, Brasília, Moscow (Zaha Hadid on the Broader Possibilities of Urban Architecture)', *Architectural Design* 71:5 (2001), pp. 58–69.

Pyongyang

G. Orwell, *Nineteen Eighty-Four*, London, 1949. For two biographies of Orwell (they were famously banned in his will), see D. J. Taylor, *Orwell: The Life*, London, 2003, and G. Bowker, *George Orwell*, London, 2003. For a comprehensive account of Orwell's writing, see G. Orwell, *The Complete Works of George Orwell*, ed. P. Davison, 20 vols, London, 2000. For Wordsworth's reflections on his experiences in France, see 'The

French Revolution as it Appeared to Enthusiasts at its Commencement', in *The Prelude*, London, 1805.

For Korean and North Korean history, see C. K. Armstrong, *The North Korean Revolution, 1945–1950*, Ithaca, 2003; B. Cumings, *Korea's Place in the Sun: A Modern History*, New York, 2005; B. Szalontai, *Kim Il Sung in the Khrushchev Era: Soviet–DPRK Relations and the Roots of North Korean Despotism, 1953–1964*, Washington DC, 2005; B. Martin, *Under the Loving Care of the Fatherly Leader: North Korea and the Kim Dynasty*, New York, 2004; C. Springer and B. Szalontai, *North Korea Caught in Time: Images of War and Reconstruction*, Reading, 2010; J. Kim, *A History of Korea: From 'Land of the Morning Calm' to States in Conflict*, Bloomington, 2012; C. K. Armstrong, *Tyranny of the Weak: North Korea and the World, 1950–1992*, Ithaca, 2013; D. Oberdorfer and R. Carlin, *The Two Koreas: A Contemporary History*, New York, 2013; E. Park, *Korea: A History*, Redwood City, 2022; V. Cha and R. Pacheco Pardo, *Korea: A New History of South and North*, New Haven and London, 2023. For an overview of how socialist fraternal countries helped to rebuild Korea after the war, see Y. S. Hong, 'Through a Glass Darkly', in Y. S. Hong (ed.), *Cold War Germany, the Third World, and the Global Humanitarian Regime*, New York, 2015, pp. 51–82. For Kim Il-Sung's biography, and his account of participating in the demonstration of 1 March 1919, see *Kim Il-Sung, A Biography*, vol. 1, Beirut, 1973, p. 41.

For contemporary history and reportage, see M. Breen, *Kim Jong-Il: North Korea's Dear Leader*, Chichester, 2004; J. Becker, *Rogue Regime: Kim Jong Il and the Looming Threat of North Korea*, Oxford, 2005; G. Delisle, *Pyongyang: A Journey in North Korea*, London, 2006; A. N. Lankov, *North of the DMZ: Essays on Daily Life in North Korea*, Jefferson, 2007; B. Demick, *Nothing to Envy: Real Lives In North Korea*, London, 2010; D. McNeill, 'Pyongyang Unwrapped', *Index on Censorship* 40:1 (2011), pp. 125–31; T. Ali, 'In Pyongyang', *London Review of Books*, 34:2 (26 January 2014); V. D. Cha, *The Impossible State: North Korea, Past and Future*, London, 2012; J. Jin-Sung, *Dear Leader: North Korea's Senior Propagandist Exposes Shocking Truths Behind the Regime*, London, 2014; P. French, *North Korea: State of Paranoia*, London, 2014; A. Lankov, *The Real North Korea: Life and Politics in the Failed Stalinist Utopia*, New York and Oxford, 2015; A. Lowry, 'Pyongyang's Missing Millions', *London Review of Books*, 40:23 (6 December 2018); N. Bonner, *Printed in North Korea: The Art of Everyday Life in the DPRK*, London, 2019; A. Fifield, *The Great Successor: The Divinely Perfect Destiny of Brilliant Comrade Kim Jong Un*, London, 2019; M. Palin, *North Korea Journal*, London, 2019; R. Lloyd-Parry, 'Diary: In Pyongyang', *London Review of Books* 41:2 (24 January 2019); D. Tudor and J. Pearson, *North Korea Confidential: Private Markets, Fashion Trends, Prison Camps, Dissenters and Defectors*, North Clarendon, 2020; L. Miller,

North Korea. Like Nowhere Else: Two Years of Living in the World's Most Secretive State, Tewkesbury, 2021, O. Kongdan and R. Hassig, *North Korea in a Nutshell: A Contemporary Overview*, Lanham, 2021.

For North Koreans' narratives, see C.-H. Kang, P. Rigoulot and Y. Reiner, *The Aquariums of Pyongyang: Ten Years in the North Korean Gulag*, revised edn, London, 2006; B. Harden, *Escape from Camp 14: One Man's Remarkable Odyssey from North Korea to Freedom in the West*, London, 2013; S. Kim, *Without You, There Is No Us: My Secret Life Teaching the Sons of North Korea's Elite*, London, 2015; Y. Park, *In Order to Live: A North Korean Girl's Journey to Freedom*, London, 2016; H. Lee, *The Girl with Seven Names: Escape from North Korea*, London, 2016; M. Ishikawa, *A River in Darkness: One Man's Escape from North Korea*, London, 2018; J. Park and S.-L. Chai, *The Hard Road Out: One Woman's Escape From North Korea*, Manchester, 2022; M. Macias, *Black Girl from Pyongyang: In Search of My Identity*, London, 2023.

For architecture and urban planning, Kim Il Sung, 'On Mapping Out the Master Plan for the Postwar Reconstruction of Pyongyang', in *Works*, vol. 6, Pyongyang, 1981, p. 237; H. C. Gyu, F. Hoffmann and P. Noever, *Blumen für Kim Il Sung: Kunst und Architektur aus der Demokratischen Volksrepublik Korea/Flowers for Kim Il Sung: Art and Architecture from the Democratic People's Republic of Korea*, Vienna, 2010; J. Prokopljević, 'Hapkak and Curtain Wall: Imaginaries of Tradition and Technology in the Three Kims' North Korean Modern Architecture', *S/N Korean Humanities*, 5:2 (2019), pp. 59–86; C. Bianchi, K. Drapić and P. Iyer, *Model City Pyongyang*, London, 2019; C. H. Kim, 'Pyongyang Modern: Architecture of Multiplicity in Postwar North Korea', *Journal of Korean Studies*, 26:2 (2021), pp. 271–96; O. Wainwright, *Inside North Korea*, Cologne and London, 2022; D. Gabriel and A. Kácsor, 'Architecture in Anticipation: Building Socialist Friendship Between Hungary and North Korea in the 1950s', *Art History* 45:5 (2022), pp. 996–1015.

For Arirang and the Mass Games, E. T. Atkins, 'The Dual Career of "Arirang": The Korean Resistance Anthem That Became a Japanese Pop Hit', *Journal of Asian Studies* 66:3 (2007), pp. 645–87; L. Burnett, 'Let Morning Shine over Pyongyang: The Future-Oriented Nationalism of North Korea's "Arirang" Mass Games', *Asian Music* 44:1 (2013), pp. 3–32; Y.-S. Jeona, 'Arirang as the Cultural Code of the 21st Century North Korea', *South/North Korean Humanities* 2:1 (2016), pp. 45–75; B. R. Young, 'Cultural Diplomacy with North Korean Characteristics: Pyongyang's Exportation of the Mass Games to the Third World, 1972–1996', *International History Review* 42:3 (2020), pp. 543–55.

INDEX

claudd @ hotmail.
com